Accessing Kant

Accessing Kant
A Relaxed Introduction to the *Critique of Pure Reason*

Jay F. Rosenberg

CLARENDON PRESS · OXFORD

*This book has been printed digitally and produced in a standard specification
in order to ensure its continuing availability*

OXFORD
UNIVERSITY PRESS

Great Clarendon Street, Oxford OX2 6DP

Oxford University Press is a department of the University of Oxford.
It furthers the University's objective of excellence in research, scholarship,
and education by publishing worldwide in

Oxford New York

Auckland Cape Town Dar es Salaam Hong Kong Karachi
Kuala Lumpur Madrid Melbourne Mexico City Nairobi
New Delhi Shanghai Taipei Toronto
With offices in
Argentina Austria Brazil Chile Czech Republic France Greece
Guatemala Hungary Italy Japan South Korea Poland Portugal
Singapore Switzerland Thailand Turkey Ukraine Vietnam

Oxford is a registered trade mark of Oxford University Press
in the UK and in certain other countries

Published in the United States
by Oxford University Press Inc., New York

© Jay F. Rosenberg 2005

The moral rights of the author have been asserted

Database right Oxford University Press (maker)

Reprinted 2009

ISBN 978-0-19-927582-3

Preface

My custom over the past forty years has been to reward myself for completing the manuscript of a book by giving myself free rein in writing its preface. This book is no exception. Consequently, what immediately follows is a free-wheeling, overly mannered, and self-indulgent preface. Some readers find that sort of thing off-putting. If you do, then just skip over to the Introduction. Otherwise, start here.

Kant is hard to access. Understanding him requires a good bit of *context*, both historical and problematic, and mastery of a considerable amount of idiosyncratic *terminology*. Thus, although the classroom sessions during which, for the past thirty years, I've been introducing advanced philosophy students to Kant's *Critique of Pure Reason* have always nominally been meetings of a seminar, it has inevitably turned out that I've done most of the talking. In the course of three decades, I have consequently accumulated a thick collection of what are basically lecture notes.

When I began seriously to consider formally retiring from teaching, it occurred to me that, once I did so, advanced philosophy students would subsequently have to be introduced to Kant's *Critique of Pure Reason* by someone else. This was a sobering thought. I realized, of course, that even now *most* advanced philosophy students are introduced to Kant's work by someone else, but the thought of a future in which this unfortunate state of affairs would become absolutely universal filled me with anticipatory regret.

Perhaps, however, this dire consequence could be ameliorated. All need not be lost. There were, after all, all those lecture notes, and philosophers, I recalled, had been reading and profiting from Aristotle's lecture notes for over 2,000 years. This was a heartening thought. Of course, I am not worth mentioning in the same breath with *Aristotle*, but the thought that perhaps *some* advanced philosophy students might someday read and profit from my lecture notes nevertheless sufficed to replace my anticipatory regret with a faint embryonic hope.

Of course, *because* I am not worth mentioning in the same breath with Aristotle, I also realized that it was unrealistic to suppose that anyone would be interested in publishing my lecture notes as such. But, just as I was on the verge of lapsing into ultimate despair, it occurred to me that, during the past thirty-five years, I had written several *books* which actually *had* been published, and this was a liberating thought. I immediately resolved to transform my mass of lecture notes into an engaging and instructive book, one that could introduce future generations of advanced philosophy students to Kant's *Critique of Pure Reason my* way, the way I had been doing so for three decades. The work that you have in hand is that book.

My way of trying to help advanced students to access Kant is a direct descendant of Wilfrid Sellars's legendary introduction to Kant and the First Critique. Sellars was a gifted and inspiring teacher, and it was under his tutelage that I first began to understand and appreciate Kant's extraordinary philosophical accomplishments. In consequence, although it has been colored by almost forty years of subsequent ruminations, encounters with alternative interpretations, and interactions with bright doctoral students, what is offered here is a generally *Sellarsian* interpretation of Kant. (Among said bright doctoral students, three names especially stand out: C. Thomas Powell, Jim O'Shea, and Mary MacLeod. This is a good opportunity publicly to express my thanks for what they taught me about Kant.)

The practice of presenting substantial philosophical theses and insights with the aid of *pictures* derives from Sellars as well. "All philosophers think in pictures," he once said. "The only difference is that I put mine on the blackboard." Most of the illustrations in this book are more or less mutated descendants of pictures that he passionately sketched for us on assorted blackboards in Pittsburgh more than four decades ago. The discovery that the transcendental synthesis of the imagination and the transcendental unity of apperception were actually suitable motifs for pictorial representation was rather unexpected, but Sellars's sketches proved surprisingly instructive. Although the technique indeed has its limitations, it has subsequently proved helpful to many generations of students, and I have consequently enthusiastically resolved to perpetuate it here.

The operation of transforming my messy lecture notes into a first draft of this elegant book was completed during a year in Bielefeld, Germany, funded partly by my home institution, the University of North Carolina at Chapel Hill, as a Research and Study Leave, and partly by the remainder of a generous Alexander von Humboldt Research Award. I am grateful for both sources of support, but, since the euro gained 20 percent against a weak dollar during that year, especially for the second one.

The year brought many worthwhile experiences—conferences, lectures, and symposia in various parts of Germany and stimulating visits with colleagues in Ireland and Denmark—but none was more interesting and instructive than two semester-long seminars on substantial parts of Kant's *Critique of Pure Reason* conducted by Professor Michael Wolff in Bielefeld. Professor Wolff's approach to Kant's work is in the best German scholarly tradition, informed by a deep and wide-ranging historical knowledge and taking full advantage of all the subtle techniques of textual hermeneutics and classical philology. I had no idea how much fun it could be to spend an hour or two evaluating candidate antecedents for one of Kant's ambiguous pronouns—or how much one could learn in the process.

That research year also brought the war in Iraq, which, in one form or another, continues to provide an intrusively real and practical contrast to my purely theoretical intellectual pursuits. One can't help but be disturbed by such contrasts, but, absent channels of influence or even a forum for effective self-expression, one's options are rather severely limited. I take some comfort in the conviction that helping others to access Kant is an intrinsically worthwhile enterprise, whatever the transient political and military state of the world.

Meanwhile, after having given the first draft of the book a test run with another group of bright graduate students back in Chapel Hill, I am now *semi*-retired and back living in Old Europe for another six months. The process of converting that first draft into the improved final version that you now have in hand has been much assisted by the reactions of said group of bright graduate students—especially Matthew Chrisman, who provided many pages of useful written comments and questions—and two officially anonymous colleagues who reviewed the draft manuscript for the Oxford University Press. My thanks to all of them, and to Paul Guyer and Allen Wood, who generously approved my making extensive expository use of their outstanding translation of the First Critique.

Being semi-retired is enjoyable. One's administrative burdens evanesce; one's instructional obligations diminish; and there is finally enough time for lots of non-disciplinary reading. In contrast, being 62 years old is proving less enjoyable. Intimations of mortality proliferate, and the body increasingly rebels against what the spirit still regards as perfectly reasonable impositions. It's enough to make one wish that mind–body dualism were a coherent philosophical view. No such luck. Just another fragile organism, hanging in there and muddling through. Salut!

JAY F. ROSENBERG

November 2004

Contents

Contents

Introduction: Two Ways to Encounter Kant

The focus of this book is Immanuel Kant's *Critique of Pure Reason*. One might well wonder whether the world needs another book about Kant's *Critique of Pure Reason*. By now, surely, everything worth saying about Kant's *magnum opus* has already been said, probably more than once. There is a certain amount of truth in that. As Richard Rorty has observed, the work is a sort of watershed text of academic philosophy.

[Kant] simultaneously gave us a history of our subject, fixed its problematic, and professionalized it (if only by making it impossible to be taken seriously as a "philosopher" without having mastered the first *Critique*).[1]

There are consequently literally hundreds of books about Kant's *Critique of Pure Reason*, and one might indeed wonder whether the world needs yet another. So I embark upon this project with a good deal of trepidation. If there is to be any point to it, in other words, this will have to be more than *just another* book about the First Critique.

---

[1] Richard Rorty, *Philosophy and the Mirror of Nature* (Princeton: Princeton University Press, 1979), 149. Rorty, by the way, doesn't regard any of these Kantian accomplishments as a good thing. Parenthetically, the *Critique of Pure Reason* is also called the "first *Critique*"—or, as I'll henceforth write it, to avoid additional italics, the "First Critique"—because Kant subsequently published two more "Critiques"—the *Critique of Practical Reason* (the "Second Critique") and the *Critique of Judgment* (the "Third Critique").

Two styles of historical philosophizing

The work of a great historical figure like Kant can be approached in two quite different ways, one fairly austere and the other comparatively relaxed. Somewhat tongue in cheek, I call them 'Apollonian' and 'Dionysian'. The Apollonian approach is marked by an especially close reading of the text, philological attention to nuances of interpretation, a careful tracing of intellectual influences, and a continuous awareness of the broader historical, cultural, and socio-political setting within which the work developed and emerged. The figure who results is someone we might call "The Scholars' Kant". He is not infrequently represented as a *merely* historical figure, deeply conditioned by his times and consequently long since superseded and in most respects philosophically obsolete. The principal virtues of his Apollonian portrait are historical accuracy, sharpness of detail, and exegetical rigor. There are several excellent Apollonian books about Kant's *Critique of Pure Reason*.[2] Anyone who contemplates seriously engaging the work beyond the introductory level should become thoroughly acquainted with more than one of them—more than one, because even such Apollonian books are written by practicing philosophers who characteristically have their own substantial personal interpretive and intellectual agendas.

The Dionysian approach, in contrast, aims at depicting what we might call "The Living Kant", a practicing philosopher who is much smarter than most of us and consequently capable of teaching us a great number of interesting things. The working premise of this approach is that Kant is intelligently and creatively responding to a problem-space which transcends its historical setting. His insights, strategies, and at least some of his positive theses thus both can and should be preserved, adapted, and reformulated to shed light on those problems as they have reemerged within the contemporary philosophical dialectic. Philosophers who take the Dionysian approach tend not to write whole books about Kant's *Critique of Pure Reason*, but rather deploy discussions of aspects of Kant's work selectively, sometimes critically and sometimes constructively, as conceptual tools and expository media in the course of developing and

---

[2] Perhaps the two most important are Henry E. Allison, *Kant's Transcendental Idealism* (New Haven and London: Yale University Press, 1983) and Paul Guyer, *Kant and the Claims of Knowledge* (Cambridge and New York: Cambridge University Press, 1987). An elegant and accessible recent addition to the Apollonian literature is Sebastian Gardner's *Kant and the Critique of Pure Reason* (London and New York: Routledge, 1999).

2

arguing for their own positive philosophical views and theses. I've used Kant's First Critique in this way myself in a number of works,[3] and much of what I've had to say about it on such occasions has found its way, more or less evolved, into this volume.

The present work is thus rather unusual. It is a whole book about Kant's *Critique of Pure Reason* written from a *largely* Dionysian perspective. At the center of my attention, that is, will be a number of perennial philosophical puzzles and problems, and my main project will be to learn what Kant has to teach us about them—to get an articulate critical grasp of how he understands them, how he attempts to resolve them, and to what extent he succeeds. But since this project presupposes that we also have a reasonable grasp of what Kant in fact had to *say*—and since any introduction to Kant's First Critique, even a relaxed one, should also be an introduction to the *text* of the First Critique—from time to time it will prove both inevitable and appropriate to adopt a more Apollonian stance and to engage at least some selected stretches of text in a comparatively rigorous historical and exegetical frame of mind. The upshot will be that I will occasionally wind up discussing certain parts of the work as many as three times, from different perspectives—e.g., first strategically, as embodying a proposed solution to some particular philosophical problem; then tactically, as attempting to secure that solution by deploying particular conceptual and argumentative resources; and finally exegetically, confirming the claims made from the first two perspectives by finding them concretely represented in determinate bits of text.

The *canonical* text, of course, is Kant's *Kritik der reinen Vernunft*, originally published in two editions, 1781 (standardly designated 'A') and 1787 (standardly designated 'B').[4] In this book, however, I shall need to cite

---

[3] e.g., in *One World and Our Knowledge of It* (Dordrecht: D. Reidel Publishing Co., 1980); *The Thinking Self* (Philadelphia: Temple University Press, 1986); and *Thinking about Knowing* (Oxford and London: Oxford University Press, 2002).

[4] The best contemporary edition, including both A and B, is probably the "Philosophische Bibliothek" version published by the Felix Meiner Verlag (Hamburg, 1998). This is perhaps a good occasion to mention another especially relevant work by Kant, the *Prolegomena*, or, in full dress, *Prolegomena to any Future Metaphysics that will be able to present itself as a Science* (in German: *Prolegomena zu einer jeden kuenftigen Metaphysik, die als Wissenschaft wird auftreten koennen*). Kant published the *Prolegomena* in 1783, two years after the first edition of the *Critique of Pure Reason*, intending it as a "simplified" introduction to the main ideas and results of his new "critical philosophy". Several English translations are available, e.g., by J. Ellington (Indianapolis: Hackett Publishing Co., 1977). Some of the terminology of the *Prolegomena* has found its way into the ongoing Kant literature, but the work as a whole turns out not to be exceptionally helpful for understanding the First Critique, especially the difficult bits.

Kant's work in English, and that brings me to the topic of *translations*. At present, there are in print no fewer than five English translations of the *Kritik der reinen Vernunft*. Two have largely outlived their usefulness—one by J. M. D. Meiklejohn, originally published in 1855, and one by Max Mueller, first published in 1881. Most contemporary work during the past seven decades cites the translation by Norman Kemp-Smith, first published in 1929 and last revised in 1933.[5] Although interest in the First Critique was strikingly reinvigorated in the English-speaking world by the publication in the mid-1960s of new (relatively Apollonian) interpretive books by P. F. Strawson and Jonathan Bennett,[6] Kemp-Smith's translation remained canonical for another thirty years. Finally, a new "unified edition" of the *Critique of Pure Reason* translated by Werner Pluhar appeared in 1996, followed in 1998 by a version translated and edited by Paul Guyer and Allen Wood, informed by the best current Apollonian scholarship and issued in the prestigious Cambridge series of retranslations of Kant's principal works.[7] This will almost certainly become the new definitive English-language version of the First Critique. Since it is surely preferable to use the most accurate and informative version available, with the kind permission of Cambridge University Press and the translators, citations in this book will be taken from the Guyer–Wood translation.

---

[5] (London: Macmillan; New York: St Martin's Press, 1929, 1933, 1965).

[6] P. F. Strawson, *The Bounds of Sense* (London: Methuen, 1966); Jonathan Bennett, *Kant's Analytic* (Cambridge and London: Cambridge University Press, 1966).

[7] Pluhar (Indianapolis and Cambridge: Hackett Publishing Co., 1996). Guyer and Wood: (Cambridge: Cambridge University Press, 1998). While Kemp-Smith had corrected many of the deficiencies of his predecessors' translations, scholarly work during the subsequent seventy years revealed its not inconsiderable shortcomings and idiosyncrasies. Both current editions clearly improve on it. Despite a few troublesome idiosyncrasies of its own, the Pluhar edition is generally accurate, readable, and quite inexpensive, hence perhaps especially useful for teaching. The Guyer–Wood translation, however, is distinguished by its exceptional scholarship, reflected in fifty pages of "Editorial Notes", *inter alia* cross-referencing topics addressed in the First Critique to the balance of Kant's corpus, both pre- and post-critical. Unlike Pluhar's monstrous 186-page index, which is so comprehensive as to be entirely useless, the index offered in Guyer and Wood is helpful, although perhaps a bit too compact. For a while, in fact, the most effective way to find a particular passage may well be the searchable *electronic* version of the Kemp-Smith edition available on the Internet. Both Pluhar and Guyer–Wood supply German–English and English–German glossaries, and both provide generally helpful introductory essays—by Guyer and Wood for their translation and by Patricia Kitcher for Pluhar's. Pluhar also offers a copious Selected Bibliography of primary, secondary, and collateral sources.

This book's goals and strategies

Although this is a whole book about the *Critique of Pure Reason*, it is not a book about the whole *Critique of Pure Reason*. The famous nineteenth-century neo-Kantian Hans Vahinger is reputed always to have begun his course of lectures on the First Critique in the same way. The students would be seated in the grand lecture hall, pencils poised, and Vahinger would dictate: "*Gott*. Comma. *Freiheit*. Comma. Und *Unsterblichkeit*. Punkt."[8] God, freedom, and immortality are, in one sense, what the *Critique of Pure Reason* is about, but I'll be saying very little about immortality, still less about freedom, and hardly anything about God.

God, freedom, and immortality are the classical themes of *speculative* metaphysics, but unlike the concepts of a *metaphysics of nature*—paradigmatically space, time, substance, and causation—which, Kant was convinced, can be philosophically accommodated along "the secure course of a science" (Bvii), traditional attempts to bring such supersensible themes within the scope of theoretical reason, he observed, had yielded nothing but disagreement and paradox. One of Kant's leading theses in the First Critique is that this outcome was inevitable, for theoretical reason has no legitimate application outside the boundaries of possible experience. In particular, Kant concludes, our *moral* practices—exercises of *practical* reason—unavoidably rest on assumptions regarding God, freedom, and immortality that theoretical reason can neither confirm nor deny. They are, in that sense, a matter of faith—and that is what Kant means when he reports in the Preface to B that he "had to deny *knowledge* in order to make room for *faith*" (Bxxx). That is the work's critical outcome; i.e., that is why it is a *critique*.

Well over half of the First Critique, in fact, is devoted to what Kant calls "Transcendental Dialectic", a detailed critical exploration of various specific ways in which theoretical reason is inclined to overstep its proper limits. Since the culprit is *reason*, the offences in question characteristically take the form of *bad arguments*, i.e., bits of reason*ing* which purport to establish conclusions to which we are not in fact entitled. Kant looks especially at three families of arguments: a group of *Paralogisms*, fallacious arguments which purport to establish that the self is a soul as traditionally conceived, i.e., a single, temporally continuous, non-composite, and

---

[8] "*God*. Comma. *Freedom*. Comma. And *immortality*. Period."

hence imperishable and immortal subject of thoughts; a group of *Anti-nomies*—pairs of prima facie equally plausible arguments with opposing conclusions—which leave reason interminably oscillating between competing metaphysical views of freedom and the natural world; and the traditional empirical, cosmological, and ontological "proofs" of the existence of God, each of which, Kant concludes, ultimately rests on a "dialectical illusion". In this book, I will have something to say about the Paralogisms, and I shall offer a brief exploration of one of the Antinomies, but I will essentially ignore the topic of God.[9]

Most of this book, however, will be devoted to the *constructive* aspects of the *Critique of Pure Reason*, the positive account of our conceptions and cognitions that Kant offers in the first two main divisions of the work, the "Transcendental Aesthetic" and the "Transcendental Analytic". 'Transcendental', it should by now be obvious, labels one of Kant's main fundamental working notions. "I call all cognition *transcendental*," he writes (B25; cf. A11–12), "that is occupied not so much with objects but rather with our mode of cognition of objects insofar as this is to be possible *a priori*."

Now Kant's philosophical terminology is often both technical and idiosyncratic, so later we'll have to get around to talking specifically about 'cognition', 'objects', and '*a priori*'. For the time being, however, not to put too fine a point on it, we can think of *transcendental* inquiries as what we would nowadays call *epistemological* inquiries: that is, inquiries concerning the sorts of things we can know and our ways of knowing them. Very roughly, then, the Transcendental Aesthetic is concerned with our knowledge of space and time, and the Transcendental Analytic with our knowledge of the law-governed natural world of causally interacting material substances. And there is another sort of knowledge which figures centrally in the First Critique—both positively in the Transcendental Analytic and negatively in the Paralogisms of the Transcendental Dialectic—namely, our knowledge of ourselves. That all these sorts of knowledge in fact *hang together*—and how they do so—will turn out to be an important part of Kant's story.

In the first two chapters of this book, I will be basically engaged in attempting to secure and roughly situate, both historically and

---

[9] Although Kant's insightful criticisms of the traditional "proofs" of the existence of God are certainly worthy of attention, ignoring the topic of God remains a healthy practice which I heartily commend in general.

problematically, a general overview of that story. What this implies *inter alia* is that, for the most part, except in an anticipatory way, I won't be looking at or talking explicitly about the specific *text* of the *Critique of Pure Reason* at all. What is missing from most studies, especially Apollonian studies, of the First Critique is, so to speak, the Big Picture—a perspicuous presentation of the problematic aims and resolutive strategies of the constructive part of Kant's work as a coherent whole, bracketing as far as possible its technical vocabulary and suspending any discussion of its tactical details. To produce such a picture, what I need to do is, as it were, coordinate enough dimensions of philosophical choice to generate a conceptual space within which the general shape, the *Gestalt*, of Kant's constructive work can be discerned and then brought into sharper relief. Metaphorically speaking, I will locate myself *within* Kant's work, and take a Janus-faced look at the balance of philosophical history, *looking back* at the essentials of the dialectics that formed the setting for Kant's contribution—roughly, the problems as he found them—and *looking forward* at contemporary incarnations of those problems—roughly, constructing mappings from Kant's conceptual space to our own. Here, for example, is a problem that exercised the pre-Socratics, that is surprisingly easy to make our own, and that lies at the very center of Kant's concerns.

The Pythagorean puzzle

I can begin by reminding you of something your arithmetic teacher doubtless told you back in elementary school: You can't add apples and oranges. While one might think of clever ways of quarreling with that claim, it's not what I want to worry about. The chances are, however, that she went on to say that you *can* add apples and apples or oranges and oranges, and that is much more puzzling. For how does one add apples? I have a pretty good idea of how to *grow* apples. I know how to *slice* apples and how to *eat* apples. I don't know how to *juggle* apples, but I've seen it done. But just how does one *add* apples? If someone handed me two or three apples and asked me to slice them, or to eat them, or even to juggle them, I'd at least be able to set about complying with his request. But if he asked me to *add* them, I wouldn't know how to begin—and I wager that you wouldn't either.

The point of these whimsies, of course, is to remind us that the operation of addition is defined over *numbers*, not over apples. A claim such as "2 apples plus 3 apples equals 5 apples", then, must be a kind of shorthand for a story about *both* numbers *and* apples, and if we think about it for a moment, it's pretty clear, at least roughly, how that story goes.

Consider those physical operations that we might call "grouping together" operations. These *are* defined over apples; that is, apples are one sort of thing that we can group and regroup, in bowls or baskets, for instance, or just in heaps. Whenever we've got a group of apples, there's another operation we can perform that will result in associating a number with it. We can *count* the apples in the group. Now suppose we begin with two groups of apples. There are then two scenarios we might follow to figure out how many apples we have all together. We might first count the apples in each group and then add the two numbers we've arrived at. Or we might first combine the two groups by gathering all the apples together and then count the apples in the one larger group we've arrived at. What a claim such as "2 apples plus 3 apples equals 5 apples" tells us is that *it doesn't matter which scenario we follow.* If we do everything correctly, the number that results from first counting and then adding—Route A—is the same as the number that results from first grouping and then counting—Route B (see Fig. 0.1).

Now it needn't have turned out that way. If we had begun with globs of mercury, or quarts of liquid (some of which was water and some alcohol), or fertile rabbits (and counted slowly), the result of counting and adding might have been very different from the result of grouping together and counting. It's just a *fact* that grouping apples turns out to behave like adding numbers, that is, in more technical language, that the physical operation of grouping apples is *isomorphic* to the mathematical operation of adding numbers.

This sort of grouping, adding, and counting is the simplest example of *applied mathematics*. Counting is just the most fundamental form of

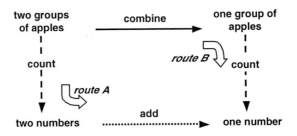

FIG. 0.1.   Applied arithmetic: adding apples

measurement, measurement of "how many", and grouping together is a particularly simple-minded example of a physical operation. But the pattern we have found is characteristic of the most sophisticated experimental confirmations of the most rarified theories in mathematical physics. Again and again, we discover that it doesn't seem to make any difference which scenario we follow to arrive at a description of the result of performing some physical operation. We can either *first* measure the values of specific input-parameters and *then* derive the desired description of the relevant outcome-parameters by theoretical computations—Route A—or we can *first* perform the physical operation on the inputs and *then* measure the value of the resultant outcome-parameters directly—Route B (see Fig. 0.2). Again and again, it turns out to be a fact that the world contains *physical* operations and magnitudes that are in this way "well behaved" with respect to specific *mathematical* operations and items (integers, complex numbers, differential equations, vectors, tensors, groups, etc.).

Now, even before Plato, philosophers found this fact utterly amazing. We live in a world that is *mathematically intelligible*. There *is* such a thing as applied mathematics or, equivalently, mathematical physics.[10] Why this should be so is the first puzzle. I'll call it the Pythagorean puzzle: Why is the world so cooperative? Why is applied mathematics or mathematical physics even *possible*? It is a puzzle that is absolutely central to Kant's project in the *Critique of Pure Reason*, although he, of course, formulated the question differently. One way he asked it (B19) was, "How are synthetic judgments *a priori* possible?" But we are getting ahead of our story. Before we can properly appreciate Kant's question, we will need to take a broad historical look at such notions as *intelligibility* and *cognition* in

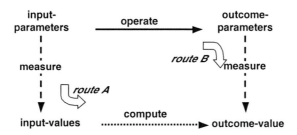

Fig. 0.2. Mathematical physics: testing a hypothesis

[10] Indeed, as chaos theory and fractal geometry have shown, even the randomness and irregularities in the world are, in their own way, mathematically intelligible.

general. My next immediate project, in consequence, is to take you on a thematically and problematically structured whirlwind tour of the history of philosophy from the pre-Socratics through Hume. What follows, in short, will be a paradigm of the Dionysian approach. At the end of this tour we will again meet Kant's question, but we will be better able to understand why he asked it and how he himself understood it—and we will have accumulated a toolbox of viewpoints, concepts, and distinctions that will subsequently help us understand how he proposed to answer it.

Intelligibility: From Direct Platonism to Concept Empiricism 1

Plato's chief metaphysical concern was to understand how reality can be intelligible *at all*. The Pythagorean puzzle which he had inherited from his predecessors is part of that problematic, but the fundamental issues lie deeper and are significantly broader. Together, they constitute the perennial theme of *unity and diversity*, of Ones and Manys.

Universals and modes of being

Here one is inclined to think first of the problem of universals: Many *individual items* that can be "called by the same name", e.g., belong to one *kind* or exemplify one *quality*. Plato is puzzled about how to explain the unity here, and, as is well known, he makes an initially intuitively appealing move. He *reifies* the Ones, *separates* them from the Manys, and sets the Manys in *relation* to them: Many particular individuals "participate in" one real separate Form.

The fundamental role of Platonic universals, the Forms, is thus to serve as *principles of intelligible unity* in explanations of sameness and change. Plato's is notoriously a two-world ontology. The realm of *per se* intelligible items—items which are fixed, eternal, and immutable—is not a human realm. We do not live among the Forms. But, to play any explanatory role, this realm nevertheless needs to be a humanly *knowable* realm, despite the fact that the place where we *do* live—the realm of transience, multiplicity, and change—is not ultimately real. Understanding the possibility of such knowledge thus crucially depends upon understanding the *relationship* between the two realms.

Plato tries out various characterizations of this relationship, in terms of resemblance or "participation" or "striving", but, as is also well known, each of these characterizations generates its own set of problems. The appeal to the notion of *resemblance*, for example, construes the Forms as passive, but any attempt to base our knowledge of them on our grasp of such relations of resemblance rapidly leads to the infinite regresses of the Third Man. If, on the other hand, the Forms themselves need to *act* on us in order for us to know them, the immediate question becomes how such timeless and unchanging items could possibly do so. Thus, as early as the *Phaedo*, Plato is led to distinguish the *transcendent* Forms, e.g., the Hot Itself, from *immanent* Forms, e.g., the Hot in the Hot Thing. Our knowledge of the ultimately real transcendent Forms is thus, at least to begin with, *indirect*, somehow mediated by the Forms immanent in the world that we inhabit. On this Socratic/Platonic picture, the object of philosophical inquiry is to get us from such indirect knowledge of the Forms to *direct acquaintance* with them.

The Platonic theme of intelligibility has a second dimension which can be captured in a question that also mightily exercised the pre-Socratics, namely: How is it possible to think what is *not*? Call this Parmenides' puzzle. If one is committed to a relational theory of thinking, structured, for instance, in terms of an analogy between *thinking of* and *seeing*—a plausible immediate consequence of acknowledging the characteristic "aboutness" of thought—the idea that one could think of something that was not *in any way* real obviously becomes untenable.[1] This is a second deep motive for introducing a notion of *modes of being*.

Descartes' distinction between objective reality—the sort that results from something's being thought—and formal reality—the sort that can make a thought true—is *inter alia* a response to Parmenides' puzzle. Objective reality is a sort of second-class existence conferred by the act of thinking. An *act* of thinking as such has formal reality. Its *content*, however, has as such only objective reality. The *esse* of content is *concipi*. A thought is *true* if what has objective reality in it *also* has formal reality independent of it—a relation of "metaphysical correspondence" analogous to the one supposed to obtain between Plato's immanent and transcendent Forms.

---

[1] For a clear and dramatic instance of this line of thought, see *Theaetetus*, 188e–189b.

The historical link between Plato's and Descartes' distinctions is the sort of *theological Platonism* that emerges in the work of, e.g., Augustine and Aquinas. Theological Platonism is itself a response to the puzzle of how permanent unalterable Forms could act on us to produce our knowledge of them. It is best understood as resulting from two moves. The first move is, so to speak, to *mentalize* the relationship of unity and diversity, transposing the picture of many individual particulars exemplifying one universal into that of many individual *instances* "falling under" one *concept*. The second move is then to identify the *esse* of intelligibles—paradigmatically universals, but, significantly, also laws of nature—with *concipi by God*. Plato's Forms become "archetypal ideas in the Divine mind". By acting on us, the agent-person *God*—rather than the universals themselves, i.e., God's ideas—brings it about that we can think the universal in the particular. The problem of how unalterable transcendent Forms can act on us thereby disappears, only to be replaced by the question of how a transcendent God, whose essence is also timeless and immutable, can act in the historical human world.

For notice that, on this picture, just as on Plato's, *we* are not in direct contact with the intelligibles *per se*. Our ideas are, at best, *representations* of God's archetypal ideas. And this opens the door to a *skepticism* about our knowledge of universals precisely parallel to traditional skepticism about our knowledge of individuals (about which more later). Where direct Platonism confronts us with an epistemic-ontological mystery—How could there be a *relation of acquaintance* between us and transcendent Forms?—theological Platonism rejects the possibility of such a relation at the price of making room for *skeptical doubts*—Why should we suppose that the intelligible structure that we ostensibly discern in the world corresponds to God's constitutive conception of it? Descartes' only answer, that "God is not a deceiver", is hardly reassuring, much less explanatory. Kant, to anticipate, takes this dilemma very seriously, and so rejects all forms of Platonism. On his view, the realm of intelligibles must be a *human* realm.

Structure in the realm of intelligibles

The realm of universals is a realm of *intelligibles* in part by virtue of having a multi-dimensional *structure*. Attributive universals, for example, are either monadic, qualities or kinds, or polyadic, relations. Such classical predicables, in turn, differ in their degree of *abstractness* or *generality*—ranging from the more generic, e.g., being an animal, to the more specific, e.g., being a dog—and in their degree of *complexity*—ranging from the simpler, e.g., being black or being white, to the more complex, e.g., being checkered. Two theses about this structure were traditionally taken for granted:

1. Where there are complex qualities, there must be simpler qualities; hence, there must be *absolutely* simple qualities.
2. Where there are more generic kinds, there must be more specific kinds; hence, there must be *most* specific kinds. (Plato's "indivisibles"; Aristotle's "infima species")

When these theses were combined with the Aristotelian picture of *specification by conjunction* (*per genus et differentia*), the result was the classical hierarchical "Tree of Porphyry" (Fig. 1.1). This picture may remind us of the otherwise curious medieval notions that God is absolutely simple and that what is absolutely specific is *infinitely* complex, about which we'll have more to say shortly.[2]

Theological Platonism is a form of *Conceptualism*, roughly, the view that only particulars have formal being. The *esse* of universals is *concipi*.[3] If, in turn, we also follow the tradition in regarding someone's possessing a concept as his having a *mental ability*, so that, for instance, possessing simple concepts is being able to think of simple qualities and relations, what show up at the bottom of the hierarchy of concepts are thoughts of

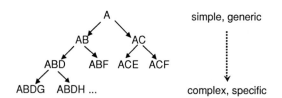

FIG. 1.1.   The Tree of Porphyry

---

[2] There is, in fact, yet a third dimension of structure, first properly noticed in the seventeenth and eighteenth centuries: viz. the relationships among *determinables* and *determinates*, e.g., colored → red → crimson → Harvard crimson. This can be combined with the conjunctive model of specification in various ways, but there is no straightforward way to reduce it to that model.

There's also an odd minority movement running from Plotinus through Spinoza to Hegel and Heidegger according to which the *summum genus* is *Being*. What gets conjoined to induce specificity must then of course be *Non-Being* (or, perhaps, Nothing).

[3] *Nominalism*, in contrast, is the view that only particulars have *any* sort of being (at all).

most specific items and hence, in some sense, the *most complex* thoughts. In Descartes' story, such thoughts are identified with *sensations* or *sense impressions*.

At the beginning of the Second Meditation, Descartes explicitly associates the senses with the body and groups sensing together with such plainly corporeal abilities as eating and walking:

Sense-perception? This surely does not occur without a body, and besides, when asleep I have appeared to perceive through the senses many things which I afterwards realized I did not perceive through the senses at all. (AT 27 = CS 18)[4]

But very soon thereafter, he is at pains to bracket the implicit commitment here to the formal existence both of bodily sense organs and of perceived material objects, and so to reduce sensing to a purely mental activity, a species of thinking:

Lastly, it is also the same 'I' who has sensory perceptions, or is aware of bodily things *as it were* through the senses. For example, I am now seeing light, hearing a noise, feeling heat. But [it is possible that] I am asleep, so [I can suppose] all this is false. Yet I certainly *seem* to see, to hear, and to be warmed. This cannot be false; what is called 'having a sensory perception' (*sentire*) is just this, and in this restricted sense of the term it is simply thinking. (AT 29 = CS 19; first emphasis mine)[5]

The distinction between formal and objective reality consequently gets applied directly to sense impressions. When, while proving a theorem of Euclidean geometry, for instance, I think of an isosceles triangle, although my thought somehow involves triangularity, it is obviously not itself triangular. On Descartes' account, triangularity has objective being in the thought. Since sense impressions *are* thoughts, they are also not triangular. Only an extended substance could *formally* instantiate triangularity. Triangularity thus gets into our sensory experience in exactly the same way as it gets into the abstract geometric thoughts of a mathematician, namely, objectively; it has objective being in our sense impressions.

Descartes thus draws a distinction between thinking of an instance of isosceles triangularity, which is finitely complex—amounting to thinking

---

[4] From the translation of *Meditations on First Philosophy* by John Cottingham, Robert Stoothoff, and Dugald Murdoch, in *The Philosophical Writings of Descartes*, (Cambridge and New York: Cambridge University Press, 1984). Citations by CS are to that version; by AT, to the page numbers of the canonical Adam and Tannery edition of the Latin text, given marginally by Cottingham *et al.*

[5] I offer an extensive and detailed analysis of Descartes' First *Meditation* in ch. 1 of *Thinking about Knowing* (Oxford: Oxford University Press, 2002).

of a three-sided plane figure, two of whose sides are equal in length—and sensing an individual isosceles triangle. Since Descartes identifies such sense impressions with thoughts of most-specific items, he regards them as "*infinitely* complex" and hence also as "confused". We can attain the sort of understanding that is captured in clear and distinct ideas only through an analytic process of definition that terminates, breaking down an initially conjunctively complex concept completely and exhaustively into its simple constituents—but that is just what cannot happen if we begin with an infinitely complex thought. Sensory experience thus cannot yield genuine knowledge of concrete individuals, since this would require us to think qualities as specified *ad infinitum*, which we cannot do.

Our ability to have thoughts of individuals is called *intuition*. In the Sixth *Meditation*, for instance, Descartes appeals to intuition to elucidate the difference between "pure intellection" and *imagination*.

So, for example, when I imagine a triangle, I not only understand that it is a figure bounded by three lines, but at the same time I also intuit [*intueor*] by my powers of discernment these three lines as present—this is what I call "imagining". (AT 72 = CS 50)

Descartes contrasts this example with the case of a chiliagon. He can understand that a chiliagon has a thousand sides as readily as he can understand that a triangle has three, but when he attempts to *imagine* a chiliagon, he does not "intuit them as present". Although our faculty of intuition presents individual items as subjects for singular judgments, in other words, it does not, even in imagination, present all of an item's qualities severally and as such—not even, as the example of the chiliagon shows, all of an item's *essential* qualities. Our intuitional faculty is thus through and through "confused". Descartes consequently regards it as dispensable.

Besides, I believe that this power of imagining that is in me ... is not a necessary element of my essence, that is, of the essence of my mind; for although I might lack this power, nonetheless I would undoubtedly remain the same person as I am now. (AT 73 = CS 51)

Kant, we shall see, fundamentally disagrees: "[The] representations of outer sense [i.e., of individual items determinately located in space] make up the proper material with which we occupy our mind. ..." (B67).

Although his working paradigms tended to be concepts of particular thinking subjects, e.g., of Julius Caesar, Leibniz also represented concepts of *individuals* as being absolutely specific and infinitely complex.

In particular, he thought of such individual concepts as *complete*, identifying an individual uniquely across all possible worlds, and he explicitly recognized that, on this account, there can be no *semantic* difference between general and singular judgments. Every judgment represents the same connection among concepts, viz., the *containment* of its predicate concept(s) in its subject concept. All true judgments are consequently "analytic", i.e., their truth can be established by an analysis of the concepts contained in them. True judgments about individuals are "infinitely analytic".

Leibniz essentially followed Descartes, however, in holding that knowledge requires something like a clear and distinct idea. A true judgment is *known* only if it is clearly and distinctly understood *as* analytic, i.e., if one has run through and completed an analysis of the subject and found it to contain the predicate. The act of grasping an *individual* concept in this way is another example of *intuition*.

Given the infinite complexity of individual concepts, only God could grasp one in such an act of intuition.[6] God commands a faculty of *intellectual* intuition. He gets cognitively in touch with an individual *by means of* its individual concept. On both Descartes' and Leibniz's accounts, however, *we* cannot get cognitively in touch with individuals at all. The best we can do is sensory experience, but such ideas are "confused" and cannot constitute genuine knowledge. In contrast, again to anticipate, Kant held that human perception is also a legitimate way of getting *cognitively* in touch with individuals, i.e., involves a legitimate, knowledge-yielding sort of intuition. This, however, can't be and isn't an intellectual intuition. *Our* mode of intuition is *sensory*, not conceptual— and so, *contra* Descartes, Kant concludes that sensing is *not* just a species of thinking. Thereby, we shall see, hangs a long and complicated tale.

The official Cartesian story about human perception evolved into a multi-level theory which distinguished among (a) a "material idea", a disturbance of the corporeal brain normally resulting from the action of an extended object on the sense organs; (b) a corresponding sense impression, the "confused" thought thereby evoked in the mind; (c) an

---

[6] Curiously, on Leibniz's view there is a way that we can *sort of* be aware of an infinite number of qualities, viz., through "petit perceptions". His model is hearing the ocean's roar. His official view is that such an awareness is itself complex, compounded of petit perceptions of the innumerable tiny sounds made by each of the innumerable tiny wavelets. These petit perceptions were supposed to be just like ordinary perceptions, only *not conscious*. We are aware of them, as it were, not distributively but only collectively. This view drove orthodox Cartesians crazy. They didn't know what to make of "non-conscious thoughts", i.e., mental goings-on of which one was not individually aware.

immediate spontaneous judgment, e.g., "There's a bent object over there"; and (d) a learned critical judgment, e.g., "It's really straight (since straight objects half-immersed in water look bent)". The relata of the correlative theory of truth, in turn, were the judgments and the object, not the sense impressions and the object, and this allowed for some maneuvering with respect to sense impressions.

A sense impression of a blue circle, for instance, was not itself blue and circular—for it would then have to be extended in space[7]—but rather a complex thought with blueness and circularity among its *contents*. In contrast, the cortical counterpart of such a sense impression, the "material idea" both could be and, on Descartes' official position, actually was *formally* circular, a disturbance of an extended circular region in the brain. Blueness, however, was not formally instantiated in the brain in the way that circularity was. The blue content of the sense impression was rather the counterpart of the *minute texture* or *quivering* of the relevant cortical region produced by the geometrical-vibrational fine-structure properties of its extended substantial cause. The cortical counterpart of the blue content of the sense impression was thus a "materially false idea". On Descartes' official view, in fact, *nothing* was literally, formally blue. The idea of blue was through and through a "confusion".[8]

Locke and Berkeley went along with Descartes in thinking of sense impressions as cognitive-epistemic items belonging to the same category as thoughts. Something circular or triangular could be "in the mind" only objectively. Both adopted a conceptualist stance with regard to universals, but with a difference. Locke was a *determinable* conceptualist. On his view, one could have an "abstract idea" of a "triangle in general" that was neither right, acute, or obtuse, neither equilateral, isosceles, or scalene. Berkeley was a *determinate* conceptualist. On his view, all occurrent thoughts must be of *absolutely specific* qualities. We cannot have Lockean *general* "abstract ideas". All our ideas are ideas of sense, and "abstractness" is a matter of the *use* we make of some of them in reasoning.

---

[7] Descartes himself was not always as clear about this as he should have been. Since, on his story, a circle existing objectively in a sense impression of a blue circle could be *identical* to a formally existing circle—one item; two modes of being—he sometimes thought of it as having all the characteristics of the formally existing circle. He didn't properly appreciate the deep problems with this view: How could something existing objectively in a mind—in an unextended and thinking substance—*literally* have a shape and answer to the axioms and postulates of a geometry?

[8] Recall, in this connection, Spinoza's identification of sensations with "confused" thoughts of brain states. The *abstract* ideas of blueness and circularity mobilized in the corresponding spontaneous and critical *judgments*, in contrast, had no cortical counterparts.

The distinction between Lockean realism and Berkeleian idealism, on the other hand, turned on disagreements regarding *formal* reality. What corresponded to the Cartesian line of thought regarding circularity and blueness that we have just surveyed is Locke's distinction between *primary* and *secondary* qualities. In Locke's idiom, *both* sorts of quality can exist formally in a material object, but are, so to speak, differently instantiated there. The *esse* of the contents of a sense impression of a blue circle—call them 'circularity$_S$' and 'blue$_S$'—is *percipi*, a species of *concipi*, i.e., objective reality. Locke's account of the correlative formal reality essentially parallels Descartes': Circularity as it is formally instantiated in matter (extended substance)—call it 'circularity$_1$'—both resembles and causes the circularity$_S$ objectively existing in our sense impressions. Blueness as it is formally instantiated in matter—call it 'blue$_2$'—however, exists, as it were, in the mode of potentiality, as a power or disposition to cause blue$_S$ sense contents in perceivers.

In Locke's terminology, circularity$_1$ and blue$_2$ are respectively primary and secondary qualities, and so both are formally real, although only the former is literally an occurrent *quality*. In Berkeley's terminology, however, the primary and secondary qualities are circularity$_S$ and blue$_S$, and Berkeley's usage was the one that stuck. In this idiom, the *esse* of both primary and secondary qualities is unproblematically *percipi*. What Berkeley then explicitly challenges is the coherence of the thesis—evidently espoused by both Descartes and Locke—that sense impressions could have a (formally real) material cause whose *occurrent* qualities all resembled only the primary qualities in sensory experience with respect to being, in essence, mathematical and structural, e.g., purely geometrical.

Concept Empiricism

Despite their many commonalities, Descartes and Leibniz, on the one hand, and Locke and Berkeley, on the other, are notoriously supposed to differ in that, whereas the former pair were *rationalists*, the latter pair were *empiricists*. What does this distinction amount to? As it turns out, Kant has his own story to tell here,[9] but we're still, as it were, in the process of preparing to meet Kant, and so I'll tell one of my own that doesn't explicitly mention his. Later we might ask how the two stories compare.

---

[9] See, e.g., his comparison of Locke and Leibniz at A271/B327.

Empiricism in general is captured by the formula: All *knowledge* is *derived* from *experience*. The three emphases mark what Wilfrid Sellars called "accordion words"—terms whose uses expand and contract and thereby produce a great deal of philosophical music. Now, on the model given by the Tree of Porphyry, it is clear enough that if we are equipped with sufficient *simple* concepts, we will be able to construct all sorts of complex ones; so one big question during the seventeenth and eighteenth centuries precisely concerned the source of our stock of simple concepts. How do we come to have the abilities to think of simple ideas or simple relations? Locke's official answer particularized the general formula of empiricism: All our *concepts* ("ideas") are *derived* from *sense impressions*— where "derivation" was understood on the model of a sort of "mental chemistry", including processes of "analysis" and "synthesis", through which complex ideas could be broken down into simpler constituents, and new complex ideas could be produced from simpler ones already at hand. This is the thesis of *Concept Empiricism*.

According to the operative paradigm of Concept Empiricism, from complex sense impressions of, for instance, red triangular figures, red circles, red squares, and so on, by exercising a basic mental ability, "abstraction", we come to be able to think of just *red*. Abstraction was thus regarded as fundamentally the activity of disjoining what is conjoined in sensory experience. Relations were handled in a parallel fashion. For example, from sense impressions of (schematically expressed) A next to B, C next to D, E next to F, and so on, by means of abstraction, we come to be able to think of *next-to-ness*, i.e., acquire the simple concept of spatial adjacency. But it was clear that many of our important concepts resisted this sort of treatment.

Such logical concepts as negation and disjunction, for example, proved difficult, as did our concepts of ideal mathematical objects, e.g., points and lines. In particular, however, Locke had trouble accounting for our concepts of *substance* (including both individual substances and material substratum) and *necessary connection* (including both causal and logical implication). The problematic of individual substances derived from the observation that a thing is distinct from a mere conjunction of its qualities. Socrates is wise, pale, snub-nosed, etc., but Socrates is not identical with his wisdom, paleness, snub-nosedness, etc. If we abstract from our complex concept of Socrates each of these qualities that he *has* or *exemplifies*— in search of the individual Socrates himself, as it were—it is not clear what, if anything, remains. This is the line of thought that leads to the

Lockean conception of *matter* as a *bare substratum*, "something, I know not what". Berkeley notoriously challenged the coherence of this conception—there is no difference between an idea of "something, I know not what" and no idea at all—and Hume notoriously abandoned it in favor of an account which identified individuals with "bundles" of qualities standing in determinate relationships to one another.

Locke's particular difficulties with respect to our concepts of logical and causal relationships stemmed from his general epistemological commitments. Both logical and causal necessitation were traditionally understood on the model of relationships of (logical or causal) *implication* obtaining between universals. An abstractionist account of our cognitive grasp of such relationships would perhaps in principle be available to a Direct Platonist whose paradigm for our epistemic access to such necessary connections *in re* was the sort of insistent authority of *seeing*. If we could, in essence, just *directly see* that (again put schematically) *A*s causally necessitate *B*s, *C*s causally necessitate *D*s, and so on, then we could arrive at a concept of causal necessitation by a process of abstraction entirely analogous to that by means of which we ostensibly arrive at a simple concept of *red*.

Locke, however, was fundamentally committed to a *representative* theory of seeing, and taking that as a paradigm for our epistemic access to relationships of implication among universals leads straightforwardly to the Conceptualist sort of *Representative Platonism* that we have already encountered in its theological variant. We "see" connections among the Forms, so to speak, only *as represented*, and this opens the door to skepticism about connections among the Forms *as they are*. We might, for instance, "see" that *every event must have a cause*, but there is no convincing way to argue that formal reality necessarily conforms in this respect to our representations of it. Hume was clearly influenced by this line of thought, and it constitutes an important part of Kant's problematic.

In Hume's philosophy, the basic commitments of Concept Empiricism are rigorously and consistently carried through to their inevitable conclusions. Fundamental to Hume's epistemology is an austere conception of sense impressions. When I am confronted, for instance, with a chunk of anthracite coal, it is tempting to characterize my corresponding sense impression as being of *a black thing*, an impression from which one could "abstract" not only the concept *black* but also the concept *thing*. Similarly, while I am watching a game of billiards, when the impact of the cue ball sends the red ball rolling across the felt, it is tempting to characterize my corresponding complex sense impression in part as being of *one thing hitting another and thereby causing it to move*, an impression from which one could presumably then "abstract" the concept *cause*. Hume, however, insists that neither *thing* nor *cause* gets into the sense impression. On his view, we need to "pare down" our descriptions of sense impressions to a minimalist level: roughly, descriptions framed entirely in terms that refer only to a basic core set of proper and common sensibles.[10]

As we recall, Descartes construed sense impressions as cognitive-epistemic items, i.e., as belonging in the same category as explicit thoughts that something is the case. On his official theory, it is *judgments* that are true or false, and judgment, in turn, is a complex activity involving both the understanding and the *will* (although Descartes offers us no proper theory of the will). The understanding presents contents for judgment; the will then assents to (or denies) those contents. Assent is not part of the content presented by the understanding, but is added by the will. On this account, my *belief* that there is a red triangle over there consists in general in my will's assenting to the thought or "idea" of a red triangle; my *perceptual* belief, in particular, in its assenting to the corresponding *sensory* thought or idea, i.e., to a sense impression of a red triangle. In such cases, I remain free to suspend judgment, i.e., to neither assent to nor deny the content presented by my understanding, but in the case of a "clear and distinct" idea, my assent is, so to speak, *constrained* or *compelled*. One *cannot but* assent to a clear and distinct idea. Such constrained or compelled assent is Descartes' model for our knowledge of *universal necessary* truths.

Does Hume also think of sense impressions as cognitive-epistemic items? It's hard to give a straightforward answer. On the one hand, he explicitly characterizes some *ideas*—the "lively" and "vivid" ones—as *beliefs* that something is the case, which is certainly epistemic—and impressions belong in the same category as ideas. So, if we attend to this aspect of Hume's account, sense impressions also appear to be cognitive-epistemic items: roughly, a collection of basic *convictions* from which other

---

[10] "Proper sensibles" are qualities and relations limited to and definitive for a single mode of sensing, e.g., colors for sight, sounds for hearing, flavors for taste, odors for smell, and felt warmth/coolness for touch. "Common sensibles" are qualities and relations available through more than one sensory faculty, e.g., shapes through both sight and touch. As we shall see, at least part of Hume's reason for excluding concepts like *thing* and *cause* from the potential contents of sense impressions is that such concepts have *logical* and *modal* aspects which cannot plausibly be aligned with any of our sensory faculties.

beliefs ultimately derive their epistemic "force" or "vivacity". But, on the other hand, from this perspective it's hard to see where to locate sensible qualities and relations within Hume's story. A conviction presumably can't itself *be*, e.g., red or triangular, so Hume *ought* to distinguish a perceptual belief from its sensory content. Yet Hume apparently doesn't draw any act–content or act–object distinction in the case of impressions.

There are structural features of his philosophy which inhibit his doing so. In particular, Hume explicitly espouses a *Separability Principle*: What is distinguishable is separable; what is separable can exist separately. If an impression *qua* conviction were distinguishable from its content, then, each would need to be capable of existing without the other—but what sense can we make of the notion of a conviction existing without a content?

Since awareness of a complex *as* a complex is possible only if its components are distinguishable, one obvious corollary of Hume's Separability Principle is what we might call his Combination Principle: The impression of a complex is a complex of impressions. Particular instantiations of this principle, however, confront us with a variety of puzzles, and the principle itself ultimately undermines any attempt to distinguish an impression *qua* act from its object or content.

One family of instantiations, for example, concerns relations: The impression of items in a relation is a relation of impressions of items. Schematically we might write: an impression of $(xRy) =$ (an impression of x) R^* (an impression of y), and that, of course, immediately raises the question of how we should understand the relations R and R^* here. Hume was inclined unreflectively to identify them, and for some relations, the resultant claims at least seem straightforward and unproblematic, e.g., that the impression of a succession is a succession of impressions (although that is a thesis that Kant will clearly and decisively reject). Other relations, however, clearly pose difficulties. An impression of (a next to b), for instance, could hardly be (an impression of a) next to (an impression of b) unless, as seems highly implausible, impressions themselves could be located in space. And, recalling our earlier discussion, although Socrates is distinguishable from his paleness, the impression of a pale man surely couldn't be a pale impression of a man. But that is what the Principle of Combination applied to monadic qualities—schematically: the impression of (an F item) $=$ an F^* (impression of an item)—evidently implies, at least if one unreflectively identifies F and F^*. In this way, the corrosive effects of the Principle of Combination would gradually eat away any distinction of act from content in the case of Humean impressions.

Essentially the same dynamic is at work in Hume's well-known critique of the concept of causation. Classically, causation was treated as a species of implication. Like logical implication, it comes with 'necessarily's and 'must's. Hume accepts the tradition's identification of causation with a relation of necessitation *in re*. There can be genuine causal relations in nature, that is, only if one event can have the power to necessitate another. But even Plato was already clear that *sensory* experience can, at best, tell us only what *in fact* happens, not what *must necessarily* happen.[11] Call this Plato's Insight. Hume resolutely draws the Concept Empiricist conclusion: We cannot have any legitimate idea of such *causal power* or *efficacy*.

> If we really have an idea of power, we may attribute power to an unknown quality: But as 'tis impossible, that the idea can be derived from such a quality, and as there is nothing in known qualities, which can produce it; it follows that we deceive ourselves, when we imagine we are possessed of any idea of this kind, after the manner we commonly understand it. All ideas are derived from, and represent impressions. We never have any impression, that contains any power or efficacy. We never therefore have any idea of power. (*THN* I. iii. 14; 161)[12]

As we have observed, Descartes located our epistemic access to the necessity requisite for causation in the *compelled assent* to an *experienced connection*. Hume's positive story at this point apes Descartes' account, but only in its superficial structure. For on Hume's view, we *experience* no relation of connection. Every impression of a relation dissolves into a relationship of constituent impressions. And for Hume our "assent" to what we do experience is not "compelled" but entirely *de facto*. Compulsion comes in only as a phenomenon of association, in the form of a *feeling* constantly conjoined with certain "expectations", themselves constantly conjoined in regular succession with certain impressions. It is simply a brute fact that, when one has been exposed to a suitable experiential regularity, one's subsequent impressions of the "cause" C—e.g., a flash

---

[11] Actually, Plato didn't think that sensory experience could get us even that far. Sensory experience can tell us only how things here and now *seem*, not how they actually *are*, much less how they always *must be*, nor, for that matter, to mention another central Platonic theme, how they *ought to be*.

[12] Citations in this form are to David Hume, *Treatise of Human Nature* by book, part, and section, followed by the page number in the canonical edition, edited by L.A. Selby-Bigge, (Oxford: Clarendon Press, 1888 and multiply reprinted). In the interest of readability, I have modernized Hume's orthography.

of lightning, an impact—come to be constantly conjoined with, i.e., associated with or followed by, expectations in the form of *ideas* of the "effect" E—e.g., a clap of thunder, a movement—which are themselves *accompanied by* an "impression of reflection" having the form of a feeling of "being compelled". Such expectations and their affective accompaniments, that is, manifest only a *meta*-regularity, instantiated by the lightning–thunder regularity, the impact–movement regularity, the fire–smoke regularity, and indefinitely many others. Such an account is plainly no help at all in accounting for beliefs in *general* truths about causal relationships.[13]

Hume's official view is thus that we *don't actually have* a concept of necessary connection at all, but rather "mistake" something else—associations of ideas arising from constant conjunctions of impressions and attended by feelings of compulsion—for the classical idea of causation. We don't have such a concept because, as we have seen, according to the leading principles of Concept Empiricism, we *can't* have such a concept. Analogously, Hume argued, the concept of a persisting (individual) substance is also one that we cannot have. We cannot have it, in essence, because we have no impression of persistence.[14] The contents of our sensory consciousness are in constant and rapid flux. "Our eyes cannot turn in their sockets without varying our perceptions" (*THN* I. iv. 6; 252). What does sometimes happen, he suggests, is that a stretch of experience contains a series of very *similar* impressions following closely upon one another, and, not registering the transitions, we *mistake* such a succession of contiguous resembling impressions for the experience of a persisting item. A good model for Hume's story is thus what in fact happens at the movies, where we mistake a rapid succession of transitory still pictures projected on the screen for persisting images in continuous motion.

Most dramatically, however, Hume saw that Concept Empiricism implied that we also can have no proper conception of *ourselves*, that is, of a single persisting subject of all those diverse experiences, the haver of all those myriad impressions.

If any impression gives rise to the idea of self, that impression must continue invariably the same, thro' the whole course of our lives; since self is supposed to

---

[13] More generally, Hume doesn't have a good story to tell about any thoughts of the form "Every A is B"; nor does he have anything useful to say about *logical* necessity. He doesn't seem to have left room for it.

[14] There's a complicated and fascinating conceptual struggle concealed behind this unadorned remark. We'll have occasion to look at it in detail when we come to Kant's positive account of our concept(s) of substance(s).

exist after that manner. But there is no impression constant and invariable. (*THN*. I. iv. 6; 251)

Thus when Hume goes looking for himself, so to speak, notoriously all that he finds are diverse ideas and impressions.

For my part, when I enter most intimately into what I call *myself*, I always stumble on some particular perception or other, of heat or cold, light or shade, love or hatred, pain or pleasure. I never can catch *myself* at any time without a perception, and never can observe any thing but the perception.... And were all my perceptions removed by death, and could I neither think, nor feel, nor see, nor love, nor hate after the dissolution of my body, I should be entirely annihilated, nor do I conceive what is farther requisite to make me a perfect non-entity. (*THN*. I. iv. 6; 252)

Descartes and Leibniz, of course, held that we do indeed possess coherent concepts of causal necessitation, individual substances, and ourselves as experiencing subjects, but neither had any useful, i.e., non-theological, story to tell about how we come to have them. The traditional Rationalist alternative to Concept Empiricism was bare *innatism*—"Concept Non-Empiricism", so to speak—according to which we simply possess innately, for instance, an ability to think distinct events as necessarily connected (although experiential regularities may well be needed to "trigger" exercises of that ability). And even canonical "Rationalists" tended toward a broadly empiricist account of concepts that *weren't* innate.[15]

Synthetic *a priori* judgments

When we look for a pattern common to the cases on which Concept Empiricism founders, one thing that we notice is that each involves judgments to the effect that in *every* instance where something is the case, something else *must* be the case—call these "every–must" judgments—and the concepts or ideas typically invoked in such judgments. These, as we have seen, include the concepts and judgments that lie at the center of traditional Rationalist metaphysics: "Through *every* change, substance *must* persist." "*Every* event *must* have a sufficient cause." "*Every* occurrence of a sufficient cause *must* be followed by an occurrence of its necessary effect." But they are also characteristic of mathematics:

---

[15] Thus Leibniz: "Nihil est in intellectu quod non prius feruit in sensu, nisi ipsi intellectus." ("Nothing is in the mind that does not first occur in the senses, except for the mind itself.")

e.g., "The sum of the interior angles of *every* triangle *must* be equal to two right angles", and—here we finally reestablish contact with the Pythagorean puzzle—they are indispensable elements of post-Galilean (and, especially saliently, of Newtonian) mathematical physics: e.g., "For *every* action there *must* be an equal and opposite reaction." Such every–must judgments are paradigms of what Kant called *synthetic a priori* judgments.

Kant's terminology rests on two different contrasts—one between *analytic* and *synthetic* judgments, and one between *a priori* and *a posteriori* judgments. The first of these is a relative both of Locke's distinction between "trifling" and "ampliative" truths and of Hume's contrast between "relations among ideas" and "matters of fact". Kant introduces it this way:

In all [affirmative] judgments in which the relation of a subject to the predicate is thought...this relation is possible in two different ways. Either the predicate *B* belongs to the subject *A* as something that is (covertly) contained in this concept *A*; or *B* lies entirely outside the concept *A*, though to be sure it stands in connection with it. In the first case, I call the judgment *analytic*, in the second *synthetic*. ... One could also call the former *judgments of clarification*, and the latter *judgments of amplification*, since through the predicate the former do not add anything to the concept of the subject, but only break it up by means of analysis into its component concepts, which were already thought in it (although confusedly); while the latter, on the contrary, add to the concept of the subject a predicate that...could not have been extracted from it through any analysis. (A6–7/B10–11)

During the last fifty years, a great deal of critical ink has been spilled over the question of whether there is a coherent and explainable distinction between analytic and synthetic judgments, but these disputes have fundamentally concerned a notion of "truth by virtue of meaning" that was substantially broader than Kant's own notion of "analytic truth", which in essence presupposed the traditional *conjunctive* model of conceptual content reflected in the Tree of Porphyry. The paradigm of a Kantian analytic truth has the form "All *AB* are *B*", and the closest he could come to the contemporary notion of a judgment "true by virtue of meaning" would be that of a judgment "true by (explicit) definition": e.g., given that '*D*' $=_{df}$ '*AB*', the judgment "All *D* is *B*".

Although we will later see that Kant's theory of concepts differs in significant ways from traditional accounts, he retains the idea that possessing a concept consists in having a mental ability that is exercised in occurrent thoughts. Consequently, the reasoning by which he undertakes to establish that this or that predicative judgment is analytic or synthetic literally takes the form of a *thought experiment*, i.e., considering whether in *thinking* the subject, one necessarily explicitly or implicitly *thinks* the predicate.[16] He concludes, for instance, that "All bodies are extended" is analytic, since "I need only to...become conscious of the manifold[17] that I always think in [the concept of a body] in order to encounter this predicate therein", whereas "All bodies are heavy", in contrast, is synthetic, since "the predicate is something entirely different from that which I think in the mere concept of a body in general" (A7/B11).

It is reasoning of this sort, for instance, that convinces Kant that all *mathematical* judgments are synthetic (A10/B14). Thus he argues that in thinking "$7 + 5$", we think only "the unification of both numbers in a single one", but not "what this single number is". The arithmetical judgment "$7 + 5 = 12$" is consequently synthetic, since "the concept of twelve is no means already thought merely by my thinking of that unification of seven and five" (B15). Analogously, since the concept of straightness "contains nothing of quantity, but only a quality" (B16), the geometrical judgment that a straight line is the shortest distance between two points comes out synthetic, and a similar line of reasoning also applies to the judgment that the sum of the interior angles of a triangle is equal to two right angles. It is important to be clear, however, that, although he does sharply distinguish it from the question of their analyticity, Kant by no means denies the *necessity* of such mathematical truths. "It must first be remarked that properly mathematical propositions are always *a priori* judgments and are never empirical, because they carry necessity with them, which cannot be derived from experience" (B14).

Necessity, that is, is a mark, not of analytic judgments, but of *cognitions a priori*. Kant calls a cognition *a priori* just in case it is "independent of all experience and even of all impressions of the senses", and contrasts such cognitions with "*empirical* ones, which have their sources *a posteriori*, namely in experience" (B2). The sort of "independence from experience"

---

[16] It is admittedly not entirely obvious what we are to make of "thinking the subject" and "thinking the predicate", much less of *covertly* or *implicitly* "thinking the predicate" *in* "thinking the subject". The best we can do, I think, is to take Kant's examples at face value and assume that they give us a grasp of the relevant distinctions that is at least clear enough to enable us usefully to proceed.

[17] Kant uses the noun 'manifold' (*das Mannigfaltige*) to refer to any plurality or multiplicity of (any sort of) items thought of as such, i.e., as a "many" in contrast to a "one". The idea operative here is that some (complex) concepts are constituted out of, and so implicitly contain, a manifold of other (simpler) concepts.

that Kant has in mind tracks with Plato's Insight: "Experience teaches us
...that something is constituted thus and so, but not that it could not be
otherwise" (B3).

Nowadays it is customary to think of such modal status in terms of
"possible worlds"; what is necessary is what holds in "all possible
worlds". Various species of necessity, in turn, correspond to restrictions
on the universe of "possible worlds". Logical necessities hold in all
logically possible worlds; natural necessities, in all *physically possible* worlds,
etc. On this model, the sort of necessity that concerns Kant might be
described as what holds in all *humanly possible* worlds, i.e., in any world
that *we* could encounter in experience. An account of just who *we* are will
consequently turn out to be a crucial part of his story.

In any event, what is at issue in *a priori* cognitions is the idea of a sort of
generality that is not "derived from experience" in the sense of being, so to
speak, an inductive projection of empirical regularities on the model: "All
observed cases are X; hence (probably) all cases are X". Kant calls it *strict
universality*.[18] "Necessity and strict universality are...secure indications
of an *a priori* cognition, and also belong together inseparably" (B4).

The every–must judgments that demarcate the limits of Concept Empiricism in particular manifest both such necessity and strict universality.
They are, consequently, *a priori* judgments. But they are also, Kant observes, *synthetic* judgments.

Take the proposition: "Everything that happens has its cause." In the concept of
something that happens, I think, to be sure, of an existence that was preceded by a
time, etc., and from that analytic judgments can be drawn. But the concept of a
cause lies entirely outside that concept, and indicates something different from the
concept of what happens in general, and is therefore not contained in the latter
representation at all. (A9/B13)

And this is perhaps even more evident in the case of the every–must
judgments that express fundamental principles of mathematical physics:
Consider, for example,

the proposition that in all alterations in the corporeal world the quantity of matter
remains unaltered, or that in all communication of motion effect and counter-effect
[i.e., action and reaction] must always be equal. In both of these not only the
necessity, thus their *a priori* origin, but also that they are synthetic propositions is
clear. For in the concept of matter I do not think persistence, but only its presence in

---

[18] "Experience never gives its judgments true or strict but only assumed and comparative
universality (through induction)...." (B3).

space through the filling of space. Thus I actually go beyond the concept of matter in order to add something to it *a priori* that I did not think *in it*. The proposition is thus not analytic, but synthetic, and nevertheless thought *a priori*, and likewise with the other propositions of the pure part of natural science. (B17–18)

As promised, then, we have again met the question that, Kant tells us, contains "the real problem of pure reason": namely, "How are synthetic judgments *a priori* possible?" (B19). One thing that we have discovered, however, is that the "real problem of pure reason" is in fact a complex of interrelated problems. I have here arrived at Kant's question by following a historical route primarily concerned with issues regarding our possession of certain concepts that prima facie cannot be "derived from experience"—we can now call them *a priori* concepts—and that is certainly one of its salient aspects in Kant's own thought. Although his leading question nominally concerns a particular family of judgments, he writes that we can see such an *a priori* origin "not merely in judgments . . . but even in concepts" (B5). We have already mentioned the concepts of substance and causation, and Kant provocatively adds others, for instance:

Gradually remove from your experiential concept of a *body* everything that is empirical in it—the color, the hardness or softness, the weight, even the impenetrability—there still remains the *space* that was occupied by the body (which has now entirely disappeared), and you cannot leave that out. (B5–6)

But there is also, of course, the problem of synthetic *a priori* judgments themselves. If the *only* provenance of such "every–must" judgments were classical metaphysics, then something like Hume's skeptical proposal that, since neither reason nor experience can establish their legitimacy, we so to speak "commit them to the flames" might perhaps prove sustainable.[19] But if such judgments are also indispensable for mathematical physics and, if Kant is right, even for mathematics *per se*, then the prima facie case surely favors the view that they must be both cognitively respectable and epistemically legitimate, and the issue of the ground and nature of this legitimacy becomes a real and pressing one. Can such every–must judgments have *for us* the sort of epistemic authority that entitles us to regard them as expressions of *knowledge*?

---

[19] "When we run over libraries, persuaded of these principles, what havoc must we make? If we take in our hand any volume; of divinity or school metaphysics, for instance; let us ask, *Does it contain any abstract reasoning concerning quantity or number?* No. *Does it contain any experimental reasoning concerning matter of fact and existence?* No. Commit it then to the flames: for it can contain nothing but sophistry and illusion" (*Enq.* xii. 3)..

The *leitmotif* of this chapter has been conceptual intelligibility, but through it we have inexorably been led to another, intimately related, central theme of the *Critique of Pure Reason, epistemic legitimacy*. In order to complete the Big Picture of Kant's work that I have promised to deliver, that theme must now become the central focus of my explorations. That, however, deserves a chapter of its own.

Epistemic Legitimacy: 2
Experiential Unity, First
Principles, and Strategy K

Hume's empiricist commitments, we have seen, deny us various epistemic entitlements. Since all knowledge must be derived from experience—in Hume's Concept Empiricist version, all ideas must be derivable from impressions—there are concepts which we take ourselves to have but actually cannot have, and, correlatively, there are "every–must" judgments that we in fact do make but cannot legitimately make.[1] We cannot derive these concepts and judgments from experience, because we do not encounter them in our sense impressions. It is important to recall here that Hume's account of "impressions" hovers ambiguously between being a story about conceptually basic *sensory contents* and being one about epistemically basic *empirical convictions*. Correlatively, the "derivation" of ideas from impressions is sometimes a matter of "abstracting" some contents from others, but it is also sometimes a matter of *justifying* some judgments (beliefs) by evidentially grounding them on others. On either reading, however, Hume treats "experience" as consisting merely in *having sense impressions*, and that is an assumption that Kant can and does reject.

---

[1] These fundamental empiricist commitments, we might notice, are themselves expressed in "every–must" judgments. Since they formulate *norms* or *standards* of epistemic legitimacy, however, what they express are presumably prescriptive 'ought's rather than descriptive 'is's, and so, Hume evidently supposes, they are not themselves rendered illegitimate by the empiricist strictures that they ostensibly articulate. There is arguably more than just an appearance of paradox here.

In contrast to Hume, Kant explicitly distinguishes sensory contents from cognitive judgments. As we shall later see in detail, the Kantian unit of "experience" is consequently not a mere sensation or sense impression but, in first approximation, an ostensible *perceptual encounter with an object* that includes a cognitive-epistemic episode of "taking something *as* something" or "taking something *to be the case*", the content of which is not just an "idea", but rather the sort of thing that can be expressed in a perceptual judgment. In Kant's story, in other words, our experience is, from the beginning, an experience of *objects in nature*, i.e., causally interacting individual substances in space and time. Acknowledging this circumstance and adopting a corresponding methodological perspective is an important part of the "Copernican revolution" that Kant proposes to carry through in philosophy (Bxvi–xxii).

If Kant agrees that *a priori* concepts and synthetic *a priori* judgments cannot be "derived from experience", then, it is not because, as Hume would have it, the *contents* of "experience" are limited to (spontaneous convictions regarding) a basic core set of proper and common sensible qualities and relations.[2] As Kant sees it, the real problem is not with "experience" but with "derived". The legitimacy of our employing certain concepts (*a priori* concepts) and making certain judgments (synthetic *a priori* judgments) cannot consist in their derivability from experience— that is, in the possibility of "abstracting" them from or justifying them by appeal to the *contents* of experience—because it is already presupposed by the *fact* of experience. It is a condition of the possibility of our *having* any experiences, properly so called, at all.

Hume, in essence, *posits* a standard of cognitive-epistemic legitimacy and then asks *whether*, given that standard, we can have all the concepts that we think we have and be entitled to all the judgments to which we think we are entitled. Kant's question, in contrast, is not *whether* but *how*: "How are synthetic judgments *a priori* possible?" He begins with the fact of a rich conceptually structured knowledge-yielding experience of objects in nature, and proceeds to inquire into the conditions which make possible its *presumptive* epistemic legitimacy. Thus, whereas Hume argues that there are certain concepts that we cannot have, since we lack the experiences (i.e., sense impressions) from which we could legitimately derive (i.e., abstract) them, Kant argues that we have *experiences* that we could not

---

[2] The parenthetical phrase is intended to remind us again of the ambiguous character of Humean "impressions".

have unless we *legitimately* possessed just those concepts. His notorious "transcendental deduction of the pure concepts of the understanding" is the centerpiece of that argument.

Empirical deductions and transcendental deductions

Kant borrowed the term 'deduction' from the legal jargon of his time. A deduction was an argument intended to supply an answer to a question of the form "*Quid juris?*" ("With what right?"). Suppose, for instance, that I notice you admiring a luxurious automobile parked by the curb and offer to sell it to you at a reasonable price. Your first reaction might very well be to raise the question of whether I am *entitled* to do so. Do I have the *right* to sell you that car? With what right do I offer to do so?

The usual answer is that it's *my* car, i.e., that I have a *legal right of ownership* in it. This, in turn, is something that I can normally establish ultimately by demonstrating that certain matter-of-factual states of affairs do obtain or have obtained—documents were signed, money changed hands, etc. Various legal codes and judicial rulings specify that by and in virtue of doing such things in particular conditions, I acquire specific rights to use and dispose of the automobile in question.

The rights that concern Hume and Kant, in contrast, are *epistemic* rights, that is, rights relating to our performance of various cognitive acts: specifically, our employing certain concepts (*a priori* concepts) and our endorsing certain judgments (synthetic *a priori* judgments). In Hume's story, an epistemic right is established in much the way that a legal right of ownership is ultimately established, i.e., by demonstrating that certain matter-of-factual states of affairs do obtain or have obtained—for instance, that all the constituents of the relevant ideas have an original source in sense impressions. Such a demonstration is what Kant calls an "empirical deduction", and he insists that it does not, by itself, establish any epistemic rights at all. It only "shows how a concept is acquired through experience and reflection on it, and therefore concerns, not the lawfulness [i.e., its epistemic legitimacy] but the fact from which the possession has arisen" (A85/B117).

Kant's point is that such a Humean "empirical deduction" could at best establish only a *derivative* or *conditional* epistemic right. The most that it could show is that an original epistemic legitimacy *presumed* to attach to particular sense impressions has been *transmitted* to certain "ideas" and judgments through the logical and mental operations—e.g., analysis (abstraction), synthesis (combination), and inference—by which those ideas or judgments have been "derived" from those impressions. The epistemic legitimacy of the impressions and operations themselves is simply taken for granted.

Analogously, my "empirical deduction" does the job of establishing the legitimacy of my claimed legal right of ownership in the automobile only if the authority or bindingness of the legal codes and judicial rulings that pertain to the states of affairs that I cite is taken for granted. In this sense, what I demonstrate is also only a derivative or conditional right. The authority of the codes and rulings is *here* simply posited, and my "deduction" at best establishes that I and others have performed specific acts through which presumptively legitimate original legal ownership rights regarding the automobile in question have been transmitted to me.

The point is brought into sharp relief when we recall Descartes' demonic skepticism. What would be wrong with thoughts whose immediate source or origin was a *genie malign*? One possibility, of course, is that such thoughts would be false, i.e., that what existed objectively in them did not also exist formally, independently of them. But there would still remain a problem even if all such thoughts happened to be true. The problem would be precisely that they only *happened* to be true. The will of such a malicious demon is arbitrary and capricious, and so the thoughts that it caused us to have, even if true, would themselves be entirely devoid of epistemic authority. There needn't be any *connection* between what has objective being in the thoughts that the demon causes us to affirm and what has formal being independently of those thoughts.

What is needed, in other words, is a way of establishing an *original* legitimacy for certain concepts and judgments, i.e., a *non-derivative* epistemic authority that can then be transmitted to others. What Kant is looking for, to put it differently, is a strategy for (somehow) justifying the epistemic *first* principles of experience.

For where would experience itself get its certainty if all rules in accordance with which it proceeds were themselves in turn always empirical, thus contingent?; hence one could hardly allow these to count as first principles. (B5)

Reasoning that secures such an original epistemic legitimacy is what Kant calls a "*transcendental deduction*". In my automotive analogy, for instance, a "transcendental deduction" would secure the original authority of the relevant legal codes and judicial rulings—that is, it would (somehow) legitimize our *practice* of vesting conventional rights of use and disposition regarding certain items in particular persons on the basis of certain, essentially arbitrary, interpersonal performances. Various strategies for carrying out such a "jurisprudential" transcendental deduction can be extracted from the history of social and political philosophy and the philosophy of law, but exploring them would take us too far afield from the specific themes of the First Critique.

What plays the role of such a transcendental deduction in Descartes' philosophy is his proof of the existence of God. That is what secures a non-derivative epistemic authority for certain thoughts, specifically, for our "clear and distinct ideas". It is what entitles Descartes to posit a connection between such a thought's being *ours* and that thought's being *true*. God differs essentially from a *genie malign* in that his perfect benevolence is manifested, *inter alia*, in his making a content's formal reality a *ground* for its objective existence in our clear and distinct ideas. This is a direct counterpart to Leibniz's view that God creates the best of all possible worlds. His moral perfection guarantees the "preestablished harmony" among all the infinitely many self-contained ("windowless") individual monads. Similarly, for Descartes, God's moral perfection guarantees a preestablished harmony between our clear and distinct ideas and formal reality. Only such a God, Descartes concludes, could underwrite the *epistemic authority* of clear and distinct ideas. Indeed, only by virtue of God's benevolence is the fact that we "clearly and distinctly perceive" something *any kind of reason at all* for us to believe it.

Our Big Picture will finally begin to come into focus, then, only when we have a grasp of Kant's strategy for producing *his* transcendental deduction. What we need to understand is how he proposes to establish an original epistemic authority for the *a priori* concepts and every–must judgments presupposed in our having the rich sorts of perceptual experiences that we do. *Merely* enriching the notion of "experience", however, does not suffice for an acceptable account of the possibility of epistemically legitimate synthetic *a priori* judgments. One useful way to see this is by exploring the modes and strategies of epistemic legitimization that would be posited by a contemporary successor to Hume's empiricism.

Neo-Humean empiricism: two sorts of epistemic authority

What sorts of epistemic authority could a belief have? What kinds of reasons for believing do we nowadays acknowledge? There are, of course, many possible answers, but one widely accepted picture is a sort of *neo-Humean empiricism*, as I shall call it. Echoing Hume's conviction that judgments based neither on "abstract reasoning concerning quantity or number" nor on "experimental reasoning concerning matter of fact and existence" are only "sophistry and illusions" (*Enq.* xii. 3), neo-Humean empiricism holds that the epistemic warrant for any legitimate belief must be either, broadly speaking, *logical* or *experiential*. Here 'logical' corresponds roughly to Kant's 'analytic', and 'experiential' to his '*a posteriori*'.

What replaces Hume's distinction between "impressions" and "ideas", in turn, is the distinction between experientially warranted beliefs that *record observations*, i.e., the contents of individual experiences, and those that are *based on evidence*, i.e., inferred from premises recording such observations. On this account *evidential* warrants rest on reliable correlations. The observed occurrence of some event E is *evidence* for the truth of a non-observational judgment J just in case the truth of J and the occurrence of E are *regularly or reliably correlated*, that is, just in case J is always or often true when E obtains.[3]

Beliefs that are *logically* warranted, in contrast, include not only logical truths narrowly conceived but also beliefs that can plausibly be regarded as Kantian "analytic truths", as "true by definition", or even as "true by virtue of meaning". Correlatively, an observation O provides a *logical* warrant for a non-observational judgment J just in case the fact that O (logically, conceptually, or semantically) *entails* that J is true, or equivalently, that it is inconsistent to affirm O and deny J. As I have already remarked, particular versions of this characterization have been vigorously criticized during the past fifty years, and the present version is hardly immune to such criticism. One traditional charge is that these notions cannot be made respectably precise and perspicuous; but for what we are after, a rough-and-ready intuitive characterization is actually preferable. Such a more relaxed take on Kant's own analytic–synthetic distinction, after all, should only make it easier to accommodate epistemically the sorts of judgments that he regarded as problematically synthetic *a priori*.

Now one thing that apparently follows from these general neo-Humean commitments is that the possibility of our having *any* evidential warrants for members of a particular family of non-observational beliefs or, equivalently, judgments presupposes that some beliefs belonging to that family can be

---

[3] More precisely, evidence for the truth of a specific *sort* of judgment is constituted by the regular co-occurrence of a specific *kind* of event, but, that said, in the interests of expository felicity, I'll retain the more casual mode of expression.

logically warranted. The argument is fairly straightforward. Let J be any non-observational judgment belonging to the family of beliefs in question. Then

(a) The occurrence of some event E counts as evidence for the truth of the non-observational judgment J if and only if J is often or always true when E occurs.

(b) Our belief that J on the basis of *ostensible* evidence E will be warranted only if we are warranted in judging that E is (actually) evidence for the truth of J.

(c) We are warranted in judging that E is (actually) evidence for the truth of J only if we are warranted in judging that J is often or always true when E occurs.

(d) We can warrantedly judge that J is often or always true when E occurs only if we can *discover* that the truth of J and the occurrence of E are regularly or reliably correlated.

(e) We can discover that the truth of J and the occurrence of E are regularly or reliably correlated only if we can, at least sometimes, know or at least warrantedly judge that E occurs and *independently* know or at least warrantedly judge that J is true.

(f) Hence no ostensible evidence E, however elaborate, could be our *sole* basis for a warranted judgment that J is true. There must be at least one other way of warranting a judgment that J is true on which to base a *warranted* belief that E is evidence for the truth of J.

(g) Hence, on pain of circularity or infinite regress, if we can ever be evidentially warranted in judging that J is true, there must be at least one *non-evidential* way of warranting a judgment that J is true.

(h) But the only form of non-observational and non-evidential warrant is *logical* warrant.

(i) Hence, we can have evidential warrant for members of a particular family of non-observational beliefs only if some beliefs belonging to that family can be *logically* warranted.

Just about everything in this argument is potentially controversial. Step (b), for instance, says, in essence, that something can function for us as evidence only if we can legitimately recognize that it *is* evidence, a view that contemporary "reliability theorists" and other "epistemic external-ists" would challenge.[4] Step (h), which here simply reproduces the basic

---

[4] In *Thinking about Knowing* (Oxford and London: Oxford University Press, 2002), I argue in detail that such epistemic externalism is ultimately unacceptable, but that is too long a story usefully to recapitulate here.

commitment of the neo-Humean empiricism whose consequences I am exploring, is itself obviously disputable. And other steps can certainly also be contested, although they are all, I think, both arguably plausible and traditionally accepted. Rather than considering the argument piecemeal, however, what I want to do is to explore the skeptical consequences of what I will call the *Sophistry and Illusion Corollary*:

> (SIC)   If particular non-observational beliefs of a given sort *cannot* be logically warranted, then no such beliefs can be warranted *at all*.

How should we interpret the notion of a *sort* or *family* of judgments or beliefs? The traditional answer appeals to their *subject matter*, i.e., what the beliefs or judgments are *about*. One recent application of (SIC), for instance, concerned our beliefs about *other people's pains*. Any specific version of neo-Humean empiricism must make some assumptions about what sorts of beliefs are observationally warranted or, equivalently, about what sorts of events or states of affairs are, so to speak, unproblematically experientially available to us to serve as possible evidence. Hume, as we have seen, had an austere conception of such epistemically fundamental experiences, but one important way in which neo-Humean empiricism is more relaxed and accommodating is precisely by allowing them a richer conceptual content. The discussion centered on other people's pains, for instance, took it for granted that other people's *behavior*—their movements and utterances—as well as damage to their bodies was "directly observable", but that beliefs about their *pains* stand in need of a different form of epistemic warrant.

The natural move is then obviously to hold that beliefs about other people's pains are *evidentially* warranted precisely by observations of their bodies and behavior. When another person's body is damaged, for instance, and she then winces, cries out or groans, and favors the damaged part, that is a reliable indication that she is in pain. But here it is possible to raise skeptical doubts. A regularity of this sort perhaps obtains in my own case—i.e., between *my* feeling pain and what I sometimes observe regarding my own body and behavior—but what epistemic assurance can I have that I am not in such respects unique? How could I discover that a correlation analogous to the one that holds for me also holds for other people, i.e., that what I sometimes observe about their bodies and behavior is regularly accompanied by—or, for that matter, *ever* accompanied by—*their* feeling pain? For I cannot, of course, observe or otherwise experience *someone else's* pain.

The Sophistry and Illusion Corollary identifies the sole remaining option: There must be some observations that could *logically* warrant my belief that another person is in pain. But that is just what observations cannot do, for there are no truths about a person's body or behavior that *entail* that she is in pain. Any behavior, however elaborate, could in principle be a case of pretense or dissimulation, and bodily damage is also logically compatible with the absence of pain, since analgesic anesthesia is not only a coherent conceptual possibility but even, to our great good fortune, a *de facto* realizable one. Our judgments about other people's pains, (SIC) tells us, are consequently epistemically *gratuitous*. Given only the modes of epistemic legitimization acknowledged by neo-Humean empiricism, such beliefs cannot be epistemically warranted at all. That is the notorious "problem of other minds", so called since the pattern of reasoning plainly could be used to challenge not just the epistemic legitimacy of beliefs about other people's pains, but also the epistemic legitimacy of any beliefs regarding other people's *mental states* in general.

The key move in this reasoning, to put it in general terms, is the recognition that no *observations* entail the truth of any beliefs belonging to the family in question. This precisely echoes Hume's claim that particular problematic concepts and judgments cannot be derived from original impressions—in Kant's terms, they cannot be given an "empirical deduction"—and Hume's own reasonings can in fact be recast into this neo-Humean mold. If we limit what is "directly observable" to the proper and common sensible qualities and relations that are the admissible contents of Humean "impressions", then Hume's conclusion that we have no legitimate idea of *persisting substance*, for instance, rests on the recognition that no truths about qualitative similarity or indistinguishability entail any claims regarding the identity of objects across time. Nothing that is (in Hume's austere sense) directly observable, that is, can unfailingly distinguish between a second encounter with a single persisting item and a first encounter with an exact duplicate of a distinct item encountered earlier. Similarly, Hume's conclusion that we have no legitimate idea of *necessary connection* rests on the recognition that no "observational" truths about what *has* happened or what *is* happening entail any claims regarding what *will* happen. "The contrary of every matter of fact is still possible; because it can never imply a contradiction" (*Enq.* iv. 1).

As we have seen, however, the structurally parallel "problem of other minds" arises for neo-Humean empiricism despite its more relaxed conception of what is "directly observable", and other skeptical conclusions regarding the epistemic legitimacy of various families of beliefs can be generated here as well. The recognition that no truths about, to put it crudely, middle-sized objects and their perceivable properties entail any claims regarding, e.g., electrons, neutrinos, or quarks, for instance, issues in such a skepticism regarding beliefs about *theoretical entities*. And even the reasoning leading to *Cartesian demonic skepticism* can be recast in a neo-Humean mode, the key step being the recognition that no truths about the *contents* of experiences entail any claims about the *origins* of those experiences.

Anti-skeptical initiatives: strategic alternatives

What alternatives are available to a neo-Humean empiricist who is unhappy with such skeptical outcomes? The most straightforward one is to hold that some beliefs belonging to the problematic family *can* be logically warranted, i.e., to accept the Sophistry and Illusion Corollary, but then deny the key premise of the skeptical reasoning based on it. This strategy corresponds roughly to Hume's suggestion that we "mistake" certain epistemically legitimate ideas, which we in fact do have, for the epistemically problematic ideas, which we falsely believe ourselves to have. In this neo-Humean version, the suggestion is rather that what we are mistaken about is the *sense* or *cognitive content* of the problematic beliefs. Properly understood those beliefs actually "abbreviate" logically complex categorical and conditional commitments regarding observations. They can be *logically warranted by* observations because they are ultimately equivalent to, and so in principle *reducible to*, beliefs entirely about observable states of affairs. Some of what we are initially inclined to regard as evidential warrants, therefore, will actually *be* logical warrants. My claim that another person is feeling pain, for instance, can be logically warranted by my observations of that person's bodily states and overt behavior because my claim is ultimately equivalent, and so in principle reducible, to one that refers only to such bodily states and overt behavior. In essence, then, the *reductive* strategy, as I shall call it, proposes to reconstrue some presumptively evidential warrants as logical warrants by *narrowing the sense* of the judgments to be warranted.

Historically influential attempts to implement such a reductive strategy include phenomenalism, logical behaviorism, and instrumentalism. *Phenomenalists* responded to skepticism regarding the epistemic legitimacy of claims about persisting substances by suggesting that the sense of such claims can be fully explicated in terms of categorical and conditional claims about sensory impressions. A claim about ordinary material things, e.g., "There is a tasty red apple over there", the story went, can in principle be reduced to a collection of claims about "actual and possible sense data". Analogously, *logical behaviorists* responded to skepticism regarding the epistemic legitimacy of claims about other people's beliefs and desires by proposing to elucidate the sense of those claims in terms of categorical claims about "observable behavior" and conditional claims about "behavioral dispositions". And *instrumentalists* responded to skepticism regarding the epistemic legitimacy of claims about theoretical entities by suggesting that the sense of such claims is exhausted by categorical and hypothetical claims about measurements of observable properties.[5]

The difficulty with this strategy is not only that the in-principle reductions that it posits inevitably fail to be forthcoming in practice. The difficulty is that there are compelling reasons for concluding that such reductions are impossible. The locus of the problem lies in the nature of the *general conditionals* that would need to be true if it were possible to complete them. Intuitively speaking, each logical component of a successful "reducing" claim would have to *both* be formulated entirely in terms of epistemically unproblematic concepts *and* be true in just those circumstances in which the "reduced" claim was regarded as true. These two constraints, however, appear to be incompatible. Epistemically contentious concepts, i.e., those occurring essentially in non-observational judgments putatively standing in need of "reduction", evidently necessarily reemerge in the antecedents of the "reducing" conditionals.

A person whose body has been damaged, for instance, may perhaps wince or cry out whenever the damaged area is touched—but such behavior will be a manifestation of *pain* (rather than, for instance, an attempt to gain sympathy by exaggerating the extent of the injury) only if she has not been anesthetized, i.e., rendered insensible to pain, and, even then, only if the pain she feels is sufficiently intense to evoke such reactions. Reference to the occurrence and character of pains thus cannot be eliminated from the antecedents of the sort of true general conditionals about bodily

---

[5] The reductive response to Cartesian demonic skepticism, to complete the enumeration, is Berkeleian idealism. If nothing exists but minds and ideas in minds, then the *sense* of a claim about, for instance, "yon cherry tree" will be explicable entirely in terms of claims about perceptual experiences—ours and God's.

damage and behavior that would be necessary successfully to "reduce" claims about the occurrence and character of pains. When we restrict ourselves entirely to observational terms, the closest that we can come is a *qualified* general conditional: *Ceteris paribus*, a person whose body is damaged will wince or cry out whenever the damaged area is touched.

Analogously, I may perhaps experience sensations of red whenever I am facing in a particular direction—but only if my eyes are open, and the epistemic legitimacy of claims about eyes is precisely as problematic as that of claims about red apples, for eyes are also ordinary material things. Eliminating all explicit reference to any such persisting objects again leaves only a qualified general conditional: e.g., *ceteris paribus*, whenever I look over there, I experience sensations of red. And the same holds for the reductions envisaged by logical behaviorism. There are evidently no *unqualified* true general conditionals framed entirely in behavioral terms, i.e., without reference to either beliefs or desires, that would be adequate to "reduce" claims about either beliefs or desires. A person will, for instance, only *ceteris paribus* be disposed to carry an umbrella when she goes out—e.g., only if she believes that it will likely rain, that an umbrella will keep her dry in the rain, and so on, *and* if she wants to stay dry, doesn't want to keep both hands free, and so on.

The reductive strategy thus founders on what we might call the *surplus content* of the non-observational claims that neo-Humean empiricism finds epistemically problematic. The general conditionals formulated entirely in observational terms that might be supposed to occur in ostensible "reductions" of such claims inevitably turn out to be *qualified* conditionals, and when the conditions implicit in their *ceteris paribus* qualifications are made explicit, they turn out to include further epistemically problematic non-observational claims. The "reductions" needed to transform ostensible evidential warrants into actual logical warrants are arguably simply not possible.

In light of this failure of the reductive strategy, the natural temptation is to try to engage neo-Humean reservations regarding the epistemic legitimacy of various families of beliefs, as it were, "upstream" from the Sophistry and Illusion Corollary, i.e., to reject (SIC) itself, in effect by denying one of the premises from which it has been derived. This strategy has also been explored. One way of implementing it, for instance, is to hold that there are *two kinds* of evidential warrants.

On this view, the only kind of evidential warrant that we have so far been considering is that provided by *symptoms*, observations that we are warranted in judging to be correlated with a state of affairs because we have experienced the co-occurrence of the symptom and the state of affairs. That an ostensible *symptom* E is regularly correlated with the truth of the judgment J that such a state of affairs obtains, in other words, is something that we can come to know only "inductively", i.e., in the manner specified by premise (d):

> (d) We can warrantedly judge that J is often or always true when E occurs only if we can *discover* that the truth of J and the occurrence of E are regularly or reliably correlated.

In order to be warranted in judging that something is a symptom of a particular state of affairs, we must therefore be able to know independently of the occurrence of the symptom that the state of affairs obtains. That, of course, is essentially step (e) of our original neo-Humean reasoning, and, as originally pursued, it led directly to the skeptical Sophistry and Illusion Corollary. At this point, however, the alternative reasoning that we are now considering takes a different turn. It denies that premise (d) is true of *all* evidential warrants; that is, it rejects the assumption that all evidence consists of symptoms. Rather, the alternative argument runs, since we *do* sometimes know that a state of affairs of this or that epistemically troublesome sort obtains, and such knowledge cannot be *logically* warranted, there must be *another kind* of evidence, i.e., *non-symptomatic* evidence, something observable which, although its occurrence does not *entail* that such a state of affairs obtains, is nevertheless, as it was often put, *criterial* for its obtaining.

In his book *Individuals*, for example, P. F. Strawson constructs an anti-skeptical argument of just this form precisely in connection with two of the concepts whose epistemic legitimacy is called into question by the commitments of neo-Humean empiricism. He explicitly addresses concepts corresponding to different levels of epistemic stringency. One is the concept of a *persisting object*, which, as we have seen, is epistemically troublesome when what is understood to be (directly) observable is limited to the proper and common sensible contents of sense impressions. The other is the concept of *another person's experiences*, which turns out to be epistemically troublesome even on the more relaxed and accommodating interpretation of observability which allows for (direct) observations of bodily states and behavior.

Strawson's reasoning takes the form of a *reductio ad absurdum*. He begins by calling attention to certain of our epistemic *practices*. For example, we engage in the practice of "reidentifying" objects; that is, we in fact sometimes identify a given object as one which we have previously encountered. And we engage in the practice of "other-ascribing" experiences; that is, we in fact attribute experiences—for instance, pains—to other people. Our *concepts* of persisting objects and experiencing subjects, Strawson suggests, are in effect constituted by these practices. Something *is* a persisting object, for instance, just in case it is a potential focus of correct reidentifications. Our legitimate possession of those concepts thus presupposes the epistemic legitimacy of the corresponding practices.

Now, as we have seen, if only the proper and common sensible contents of sense impressions were observable, nothing we could observe would be sufficient to entail that a given object is one that we have previously encountered. Similarly, if only bodily states and behavior were observable, nothing we could observe would be sufficient to entail that some other person is in pain. Our original skeptical reasoning thus implies that, if all evidence consisted of "merely inductive" symptoms, such practices could not be legitimate. But, as even Hume recognized, we in fact ordinarily unreflectively, uncritically, and *unproblematically* engage in these practices, and, indeed, in everyday life we really have no choice but to do so. These epistemic practices, Strawson concludes, thus plainly *are* legitimate. Hence not all evidence can consist of merely inductive symptoms. Consequently, we not only necessarily regard ourselves as sometimes *warranted* in identifying a given object as one which we have previously encountered, and as sometimes *warranted* in ascribing pain to another person, but we are also epistemically *entitled* to do so. There must therefore exist, as Strawson himself puts it, "criteria" which are "logically adequate" to warrant such reidentifications of objects and other-ascriptions of pain.

What does this mean? What conditions would observations that served as "logically adequate criteria" for the obtaining of a particular sort of non-observational state of affairs have to satisfy? On the face of it, their connection with such a state of affairs would need to be both weaker than entailment and stronger than that of an inductively established symptom. What is crucial, however, is that, to secure its "logical adequacy", *every* occurrence of such a putative criterion would *necessarily* have to be correlated with an instance of the relevant sort of state of affairs. For suppose that such a correlation obtained only *sometimes* and *contingently*. Then, for each individual occurrence of the putative criterion, we could legitimately raise the question of whether we were warranted in judging that an appropriate correlative state of affairs obtained *then*, on *that* occasion. Such ostensible "criteria" would then differ epistemologically in no essential way from inductively established symptoms.

But if occurrences of "logically adequate criteria" for some non-observational state of affairs must be necessarily and universally correlated with instances of that state of affairs, then it is no longer clear why we should regard them as a second kind of *evidence*. We might just as well relax the notion of a *logical* warrant even further to include all observable items that are necessarily and universally connected with non-observational states of affairs—logically, conceptually, semantically, *or* "criterially". At least nominally, then, this second strategy would then become a variant of the first one, *accepting* the Sophistry and Illusion Corollary, but holding that some non-observational judgments *can* be logically warranted—now not because their sense is narrower than we intuitively took it to be, but because there are even more kinds of logical warrants than we intuitively took there to be.

Whatever terminological decision we might reach, however, it should by now be clear that we have parted company with the fundamental commitments of neo-Humean empiricism, for its leading idea was precisely that logical and evidential warrants *as originally conceived* constituted the only legitimate sorts of epistemic grounding relations. Whether we thought of "logically adequate criteria" as a special sort of (non-symptomatic) evidence or as a special sort of (non-entailing) logical warrant, however, they would still be an additional, *sui generis*, kind of epistemic warrant. Adding them to our inventory amounts to acknowledging a *third sort of epistemic grounding relation*, one distinct from *both* logico-semantic entailments and inductively established (symptomatic) evidence, and so parts company with both the letter and the spirit of neo-Humean empiricism.

The attentive reader will have noticed that the idea of "logically adequate criteria" has brought us around again to the sort of "every–must" judgments that Kant characterizes as synthetic *a priori*—unrestrictedly universal necessity judgments that cannot be (inductively) "derived from experience". An observable occurrence C will be a logically adequate criterion for the obtaining of a non-observational state of affairs N just in case *necessarily* N obtains *whenever* C occurs. And so far it seems that one cannot *both* be a neo-Humean empiricist *and* acknowledge the possibility of warrantedly believing such synthetic *a priori* judgments.

Indeed, the idea that there must be a third kind of epistemic warrant appears to be simply unavoidable. For our original neo-Humean reasoning evidently implies that we cannot otherwise warrantedly judge that any observable occurrences are even *symptoms* of the obtaining of non-observational states of affairs. An observable occurrence S, we recall, is a symptom of the obtaining of a non-observational state of affairs N just in case N *usually* obtains when S occurs and conversely, i.e., just in case instances of S are *generally* correlated with instances of N. But the original reasoning implied precisely that belief in such a regularity cannot itself ultimately be evidentially warranted, and the fact that S *can* sometimes occur *without* N's obtaining (and conversely) precludes the possibility of logical warrant. The belief that S *is* a symptom of N, then, can apparently be warranted only if we are prepared to abandon neo-Humean empiricism and acknowledge a third sort of epistemic grounding relation.

The claim that S is a symptom of N, we might say, expresses a sort of "weak" synthetic *a priori* judgment—synthetic because it cannot be logic-ally warranted, but *a priori* because it cannot be inductively "derived from experience". To put it another way, whenever we are dealing with states of affairs that are not themselves observable, neo-Humean empiricism apparently implies that we stand in need of "topic-specific" epistemic first principles, i.e., some way of warranting judgments to the effect that one or another sort of observable occurrence is non-logically related— "criterially" or symptomatically or *in any epistemically relevant way what-soever*—to the obtaining of such a state of affairs. We need some grounds for believing that, e.g., our experiencing sensations of red gives us *any* reason for judging that a red object is present, or that our observing bodily damage and certain sorts of behavior gives us *any* reason for judging that another person is in pain; but evidently no such grounds are available to a resolute neo-Humean empiricist.

Tertium quid rationalism *vs* Strategy K

The unavoidable conclusion seems to be that neo-Humean empiricism cannot account for the legitimacy of our *de facto* epistemic practices, in particular, for the legitimacy of the (strict Kantian or "weak" topic-specific) synthetic *a priori* principles on which those practices arguably rely. A neo-Humean empiricist apparently cannot successfully answer Kant's question: "How are synthetic *a priori* judgments possible?" A "transcendental deduction" of synthetic *a priori* principles evidently needs to appeal to a *sui generis* kind of epistemic warrant that is neither logical nor evidential, a third sort of epistemic grounding relation. Only a philosopher who acknowledges such a third kind of epistemic warrant—a *tertium quid rationalist*, as it were—could establish the epistemic legitimacy of synthetic *a priori* judgments. Or so it seems. But is Kant, then, just another *tertium quid* rationalist?

I think it is clear that this would be a disappointing result. If Kant's transcendental deduction turned out to rest on premises that could be justified only by appealing to a non-logical, non-evidential epistemic *tertium quid*, it would in essence *presuppose* the legitimacy of synthetic *a priori* judgments, i.e., the very epistemic legitimacy that it was ostensibly intended to secure. Kant would then be open to a charge of begging the question or, more charitably, of epistemic dogmatism. But is there any alternative?

We have several times stumbled across the idea that what we need is a strategy for justifying or legitimizing our acceptance of various epistemic *first principles*.

A priori principles bear this name not merely because they contain in themselves the grounds of other judgments, but also because they are not themselves grounded in higher and more general cognitions. Yet this property does not elevate them above all proof. (A148/B188)

From this perspective, the obvious difficulty lies in the fact that any such "proof" or justification must surely take the form of an *argument from premises*, and we will be justified in accepting the conclusion of such an argument only if we are justified in accepting its premises. The most that an argument from premises could show, consequently, is that a presumptive legitimacy can be transmitted from the premises to the conclusion. It could perhaps thereby establish the *derivative* legitimacy of its conclusion, but first principles are *first* precisely by virtue of possessing an *original*, non-derivative legitimacy.

What Kant in essence saw was that this reasoning itself rests on a presupposition that is so natural that it tends to be in effect invisible: namely, that any argument adequate to establish the legitimacy of accepting a given principle P must have P as its *conclusion*. Once this presupposition becomes salient, however, it is not too difficult to see that it is simply false. For the epistemic legitimacy of accepting a principle P would clearly be established by an acceptable argument whose conclusion instead *mentions* the principle and tells us something relevant *about* it, for instance: "Principle 'P' is epistemically legitimate."

Now this remark appears to have, in Bertrand Russell's memorable phrase, all the virtues of theft over honest toil—and, indeed, in this heavy-handed form, Kant's insight is hardly likely to seem helpful or illuminating. Nevertheless, it does suffice to suggest a further *strategy* for coming to grips with the problem of first principles and the synthetic *a priori*. For suppose that we could demonstrate, from unproblematic premises, that a candidate first principle, FP, had some significant characteristic, Φ, that was *related* in some straightforward way to the reasonableness of adopting or espousing that principle. The conclusion "Principle 'FP' has the significant characteristic Φ", which mentions 'FP' and says something about it, could then, if true, confer epistemic legitimacy on the principle which it mentions, without deriving that principle itself from others. Let's call this *Strategy K*. In briefest form, it looks like Figure 2.1.

This is all still very schematic, of course. But suppose that we could similarly *embed* the contentious *a priori* concepts and synthetic *a priori* principles in other judgments that (a) mention them and say about them that they have a suitable significant characteristic, which, (b) thereby confers epistemic legitimacy on the mentioned items, and crucially, (c) can themselves be derived from unproblematic premises, that is, can be shown to be epistemically legitimate *by neo-Humean standards*. Such an application of Strategy K would then give us a new way of bringing reason to bear on questions of epistemic legitimacy, but one that did *not* presuppose any new form of non-logical and non-evidential epistemic grounding relation. Kant's transcendental deduction relies precisely on Strategy K.

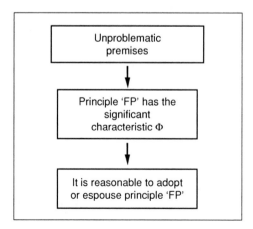

FIG. 2.1.   The basic idea of Strategy K

When it comes to our knowledge of the world, Kant is not a *tertium quid* rationalist but a neo-Humean empiricist.

What do Kant's embedding judgments look like? Let's abbreviate an expression that mentions an *a priori* concept—e.g., 'substance', 'causation'—by 'C_{AP}', and one that mentions a synthetic *a priori* judgment—e.g., 'Every event must have a cause', 'In every change, substance must be conserved'—by 'J_{SAP}'. In first approximation, Kant's Strategy K judgments will then have the forms

>   (K1)   The *a priori* concept 'C_{AP}' applies in the world.
>   (K2)   The synthetic *a priori* judgment 'J_{SAP}' is true of the world.

Although he doesn't put it quite this way, *these* judgments, Kant holds, are *logically* warranted—in fact, analytic—and if that is so, then they possess a neo-Humean epistemic authority that can in principle be transmitted to the more problematic concepts and judgments mentioned in them.

The significant characteristic ascribed to *a priori* concepts and synthetic *a priori* judgments in (K1) and (K2) is thus "applying in or being true of the world". Both formulations make use of a new notion: *the world*. How should it be understood? What world are we talking about? The answer that surely lies nearest at hand is: the *natural* world. In the *Prologomena*, however, Kant explains that, at least as far as its contents are concerned, *nature* is identical to *the totality of all objects of possible experience*, and that gives us a second, ultimately more useful, answer: the *experiencable* world.[6]

Kant himself, however, does not use the terms 'the world' and 'nature' in formulating his transcendental deduction. The expression that we find there is rather 'the synthetic unity of experience'. Here we need to recall that *experiences*, for Kant, are not the mere having of sense impressions, but rather consist in ostensible perceptual encounters with *objects in nature*, i.e., causally interacting individual substances in space and time, for that makes it pretty clear that 'the natural world', 'the experiencable world', and 'the synthetic unity of experience' all pick out essentially the same idea. One way that (K1) and (K2) actually get expressed in the text of the

---

[6] Besides having a content, nature of course has a *form*. Considered under its formal aspect, the word 'nature' adverts to the realm of empirical *lawfulness*: "Nature is the *existence* of things, so far as it is determined according to universal laws." See *Prolegomena*, 294–6. Kant also offers essentially equivalent explanations of the expressions 'world' and 'nature' in the First Critique—near the beginning of the Transcendental Dialectic (A418–19/B446–7)—but in terminology that is both more obscure and less helpful than the elucidations cited here.

First Critique in fact trades on this equivalence: What Kant explicitly ascribes to *a priori* concepts and synthetic *a priori* judgments is not epistemic legitimacy but "objective validity", i.e., their valid employment with respect to objects of experience. Most of the detailed work toward establishing such claims of objective validity, and so, in essence, in securing the analyticity of (K1) and (K2), occurs in a section of the book entitled "Systematic representation of all the synthetic principles of pure understanding".

An important feature of all three of these ways of expressing Kant's leading idea here—most explicit in the third variant—is their emphasis on *unity*. There is only *one* experienceable natural world, and all our many *separate* experiences of parts of it must consequently in principle "hang together" in a way that enables them to be parts of a single *comprehensive* experience of it. In this way Kant's question "How are synthetic *a priori* judgments possible?" becomes transmuted into the question "How is our unitary experience possible?" Correlatively, what we most frequently find in the *text* of the First Critique is neither explicit formulations of (K1) and (K2) nor an answer to the question in its original form, but rather an answer to the transmuted question: "Experience is possible only under the *categories*." The notion of "categories" is one of many ideas that Kant adapts from Aristotle. There's quite a bit to say about it, but at this point we can simply identify Kant's categories with what we have been calling *a priori* concepts, e.g., substance and causation. Our many separate experiences can be parts of a single comprehensive experience, in other words, only if *what* we experience is a unified natural world of causally interacting substances—i.e., only if we can validly apply such *a priori* concepts to objects of our experience and validly endorse the correlative synthetic *a priori* judgments with respect to them.

This brings into the foreground a theme that has already occurred a number of times in our search for Kant's transcendental deduction: namely, the idea that what ultimately stand in need of legitimization are various forms of epistemic *conduct*. The theme was already adumbrated in Hume's challenges to the epistemic legitimacy of particular habits or customs—e.g., our forming "causal" expectations on the basis of experiential regularities—and we found it echoed in Strawson's emphasis on the correlativity of the practice of reidentification to a legitimate conception of a persisting object. Just as a "jurisprudential" transcendental deduction would ultimately secure the original authority of the relevant legal codes and judicial rulings by legitimizing our particular *social practices* of investing certain persons in certain circumstances with conventional rights of use and disposition, so Kant's transcendental deduction is designed to secure the authority of *a priori* concepts and the synthetic *a priori* judgments correlative to them by legitimizing our particular *epistemic practices* with respect to them. That's part of what I had in mind when I formulated the outcome of Strategy K as a judgment to the effect that it is reasonable to *adopt* or *espouse* a particular principle.

It should be possible, then, to cast a transcendental deduction of epistemic first principles explicitly in the form of an argument that warrants such epistemic conducts as *applying* the problematic *a priori* concepts to objects of experience and *endorsing* the correlative synthetic *a priori* judgments as true of the world. In short, although Kant himself does not do so, we should be able to formulate such an argument as a piece of *practical* reasoning. If we hold to the natural and dominant paradigm of practical arguments, a transcendental deduction will then take on the general form of a piece of *means–ends* reasoning, in which the reasonableness of adopting or espousing a given principle is derived from a consideration of its unique role in realizing an end *that we in fact have*:

1. We shall achieve (a particular end) E^*.
2. A good way (the best way, the only way) to achieve E^* is to accept principles that have the significant characteristic Φ.
3. The (candidate first) principle 'P' has significant characteristic Φ.
4. So, we shall accept the principle 'P'.

Steps 1 and 4 here should be thought of, not as stating something true or false, but rather as expressing "imperatives" or, more clearly, *intentions*. The conclusion of this argument thus does not *say* that it is legitimate for us to accept the principle 'P'; but, if the argument is successful, it *shows* that, given our intention to achieve the end E^*, we are *authorized* to accept 'P' and so *warranted* in doing so. In this way, the conclusion of such an argument *confers* epistemic legitimacy on the principle mentioned in it.

In light of our recent discussion of Kant's use of Strategy K, we already have a pretty good idea of what could be substituted for the placeholder "Φ" in order to transform this schema into a transcendental deduction of *a priori* concepts and synthetic *a priori* judgments. The significant characteristic of such concepts and judgments, we have seen, is that, in Kant's terminology, they make it possible for our experience to be a synthetic unity, i.e., an experience of a unified natural world. That is precisely the point of (K1) and (K2), and they thus correspond to step 3 of such a means–ends argument. But what could serve as the end $\mathbf{E}^*$ that we are somehow committed to achieving, and that cannot be achieved (well, optimally, or at all) unless our experience has that form?

The experiencing subject: a constitutive end

This is the point at which it is crucial to pick up another thread that I have several times deliberately left dangling. Earlier, I traced the development of Kant's leading question, "How are synthetic *a priori* judgments possible?", into the transmuted question, "How is our unitary experience possible?", and the present practical reasoning is addressed to the ends served by our epistemic practices. The focus of the story of Kant's transcendental deduction, in other words, has shifted from experienced objects to experiencing *subjects*. What is at stake has turned out to concern the character of *our* experience and the nature of *our* epistemic ends. The time has consequently come to explore Kant's answer to this question: Who are *we*?

Descartes, of course, would answer: "*We* are thinking substances, *res cogitans*," but Hume's anti-dogmatic alarm clock had done its work well, and Kant consequently saw that the concept of a thinking substance was epistemically just as problematic as the concept of an extended one. What's more, if the answer is going to be of any use in developing our schematic practical reasoning into a plausible transcendental deduction, it will have to explain who *we* are without trivially identifying us as, for instance, would-be experiencers of a unified natural world of causally interactive substances. Any useful answer to the question "Who are *we*?", in other words, will need to be one that we could in principle formulate and understand without using any such problematic *a priori* concepts as substance and causation, and one that we could know to be correct without knowing anything about the unity of the experienced world. Kant's implicit answer satisfies these criteria. As far as his transcendental deduction is concerned, *we* are sensorily passive, temporally discursive apperceptive intelligences.

That sounds terribly complicated, but it is actually a collection of straightforward truisms. To say that we are sensorily passive is to say that we *find ourselves* with perceptual experiences. What we ostensibly encounter in experience doesn't depend on our choices, decisions, preferences, or desires, but only on the way in which our senses are affected. To say that we are intelligences, however, is to say that such experiential encounters are also structured by *concepts*. We don't just "have sense impressions"; we *take* something to *be*, e.g., black, blue, beige, or brown, or to *be*, e.g., a bush, a bear, a bicycle, a banana. Our ostensible perceptual experience is of instances of various kinds of things having various qualities. It is the sort of thing that can be expressed in a perceptual *judgment*, which can itself be true or false. That is why there can be perceptual error, why I can, for instance, mistake a harmless brown bush for a dangerous black bear.[7] To say that we are temporally discursive beings is to say that our many separate experiential encounters occur successively in time. For us, experience is just "one damn thing after another".[8] And, finally, to say that we are *apperceptive* beings is to say that we have the capacity to be aware of our own thoughts and experiences *as* our own. As Kant puts it, "The *I think* must *be able* to accompany all my representations. ... " (B131).

So far, we have largely been exploring what is involved in our being sensorily passive intelligences. Our focus, that is, has for the most part been on the objects of experience, and our question has been formulated as one concerning the legitimacy of applying *a priori* concepts to them and endorsing synthetic *a priori* judgments about them. The course of that exploration, however, has led us to refocus our attention directly on the experiencing subject, and here it becomes especially important to appreciate the implications of our being temporally discursive apperceptive beings. To this end, it is helpful to return to Descartes' original reflections regarding 'I think' and *res cogitans*.

Descartes is also sensitive to our temporal discursiveness, at least insofar as he observes in the Second Meditation that, as a thinking thing, he himself has *many* thoughts.

But what then am I? A thing that thinks. What is this? A thing that doubts, understands, affirms, denies, wills, refuses, and that also imagines and senses.

...Is it not the very same "I" who now doubts almost everything, who nevertheless understands something, who affirms that this one thing is true, who denies other things, who desires to know more, who wishes not to be deceived, who imagines many things even against my will, who also notices many things which appear to come from the senses? (AT 28–9 = CS 19)

---

[7] Or, much worse, mistake a dangerous brown bush for a harmless black bear.

[8] Technically speaking, that's just the "temporal" part of "temporally discursive". A *discursive* understanding is one that can represent a multiplicity of items (in Kant's terminology, a "manifold") only by representing them as standing in determinate relationships (in Kant's terminology, only by "synthesizing" it). The contrast is with an "intuitive understanding", e.g., God's "all-at-once" eternal omniscient grasp of what for us is always either past, present, or future.

What is important to notice about this remark is that it takes for granted the *unity* of the thinking and experiencing subject. Descartes, that is, proceeds immediately from observations having the form[9]

I think X & I think Y & I think Z

to a claim of the form:

the "I" who thinks X = the "I" who thinks Y = the "I" who thinks Z,

or, perhaps more perspicuously and explicitly introducing the temporal aspect,

I, who think X (at t_1) = I, who think Y (at t_2) = I, who think Z (at t_3).

Now Hume, we recall, quite properly observed that we never *encounter* any such persisting single subject of thoughts and experiences. The question thus arises how we *identify* the subject, the "I", who thinks this at one time as the same item (entity, being) as the subject, "I", who thinks that at another. What *entitles* us to the identities that Descartes takes for granted? Normally we determine whether the person who did one thing at one time is the same as the person who did another at another by appealing to particular empirical features—for instance, physical appearance or finger-prints or, more recently, DNA signatures—as *signs, tests, or criteria of personal identity*. But Hume's observation precisely implies that, when we're dealing with *ourselves* only as thinking and experiencing subjects, we can't do this. Considered just as an "I" who thinks this or that, the subject doesn't have any empirical features.

On Hume's official account, I am consequently *not* entitled to represent myself as a unitary thinking and experiencing subject. Rather, I "mistake" the dense succession of my contiguous and partially resembling, but numerically distinct, impressions and ideas for the experience of such a persisting subject. Just *formulating* these claims, however, already shows that Hume's story will not do. For *who is it* that supposedly makes the "mistake" of thus misrepresenting *just what* succession of impressions and

---

[9] This isn't quite right, of course. Descartes held that the mind is "transparent" to its own workings. Mental events occur *propria persona*. That is, when one has a "thought", one is also aware *that* one has it, what *kind* of thought it is, and what it is a thought *of*. Thus, for Descartes, the occurrence of *episodes* of thinking X, thinking Y, and thinking Z carries with it *awarenesses* of thinking X, thinking Y, and thinking Z, and it is these that collectively constitute the "observa-tions" which are *summarized* in the displayed conjunction.

ideas? The only possible answer is that *I* so misrepresent the succession of *my* impressions and ideas. The "I" who ostensibly misrepresents this succession *as* a unity, that is, is always necessarily thought as falling outside it.[10] So there is a genuine problem here, and neither Descartes nor Hume has a solution to this problem. Kant, however, had an ingenious idea, and it is this idea that lies at the very heart of his transcendental deduction. A homely analogy will help us to appreciate it.

Suppose that you are working the night shift at a delicatessen, and you discover that the stocks of sauerkraut, Swiss cheese, and corned beef are low. You straightforwardly conclude that, during the preceding day, someone ate some sauerkraut and someone ate some Swiss cheese and someone ate some corned beef—but you're obviously *not* entitled to conclude that the person who ate the sauerkraut is the same as the person who ate the Swiss cheese or that the person who ate the Swiss cheese is identical to the person who ate the corned beef. In short, from observations having the form

> someone ate sauerkraut & someone ate Swiss cheese & someone ate corned beef

you cannot legitimately conclude that

> the person who ate sauerkraut = the person who ate Swiss cheese = the person who ate corned beef.

One way of getting from the conjunctive premise to such identities would be by appealing to empirical signs or criteria of personal identity, and that's what we would usually do. For instance, if you somehow discovered that the person who ate the sauerkraut was a short stout redhead who walked with a limp, and that the person who ate the Swiss cheese was a short stout redhead who walked with a limp, and that the person who ate the corned beef was *also* a short stout redhead who walked with a limp, then you'd certainly have *some* evidence for concluding that

---

[10] The ostensible misrepresenting itself, however, is always necessarily thought as falling *within* it. A thinking and experiencing subject, that is, synchronically represents (thinks) its own *comprehensive* diachronic unity. Such a representation consequently, so to speak, reflexively subsumes itself. That's part of what's involved in Kant's notion of the *transcendental unity of apperception*. His immediate German Idealist successors, Fichte and Schelling, made a great theoretical fuss about it. Hume himself, by the way, eventually came to see that his own story of (our idea of) the self couldn't be right. See the Appendix to *THN*. We'll have more to say about all of this later, especially in connection with what Kant calls the "Paralogisms of Pure Reason".

you were actually dealing with just one person here. But there's another way it could go. For suppose that what you instead discovered was that

someone ate twelve Ruben sandwiches.

Since a Ruben sandwich consists of corned beef, Swiss cheese, and sauerkraut on rye (along with a little Russian dressing)—in Kant's terms, it is a *synthesis* of corned beef, Swiss cheese, and sauerkraut—this would be equivalent to discovering that

someone ate [sauerkraut + Swiss cheese + corned beef],

and that *would* imply that, at least in this instance,

the person who ate sauerkraut = the person who ate Swiss cheese = the person who ate corned beef.

The possibility of combining the three foodstuffs into a single "complex" comestible item, a Ruben sandwich, and making *it* the object of a *single* act of consumption, in other words, entitles you to assert the identity of the agents of the three original gustatory acts: eating sauerkraut, eating Swiss cheese, and eating corned beef.

Kant applies precisely this strategy to the problem of the unity of the thinking self. Given that

I think X & I think Y & I think Z,

what entitles me to conclude that

I, who think X (at t_1) = I, who think Y (at t_2) = I, who think Z (at t_3)

(Kant calls this the "analytic unity of apperception") is the possibility of combining the objects of the several acts of thinking into a single "complex" item, and making *it* the object of a *single* act of thinking:

I think [X + Y + Z].

(Kant calls this the "synthetic unity of apperception".) Here's how he puts it:

[The] empirical consciousness, that accompanies different representations is by itself dispersed and without relation to the identity of the subject. The latter relation therefore does not yet come about by my accompanying each representation with consciousness, but rather by my *adding* one representation to the other and being conscious of their synthesis. Therefore it is only because I can combine a manifold of given representations *in one consciousness* that it is possible for me to represent the *identity of the consciousness in these representations* itself, i.e., the *analytic* unity of apperception is only possible under the presumption of some *synthetic* one. (B133)

This is the key move in Kant's transcendental deduction. In our practical reasoning, it corresponds to step 2.

All that remains to do now is to put the various pieces of our picture together. For the "single complex item", $[X + Y + Z]$, that would in principle result from "conjoining" the "manifold" of our various separate perceptual encounters into a unitary "synthesis" of representations is precisely *the synthetic unity of experience*, i.e., the experiencable natural world. The possibility of our identifying ourselves as *single subjects of many experiences*, in other words, depends upon the possibility of our many separate experiences becoming parts of a single comprehensive experience, and that in turn, Kant argues, depends precisely on our ability validly to apply *a priori* concepts to objects of our experience and validly to endorse the correlative synthetic *a priori* judgments with respect to them. Such concepts and judgments are the '+'s in '$[X + Y + Z]$'. Figuratively speaking, they are the cognitive-epistemic "glue" that transforms a "manifold" of temporally disjoint experiences into parts of one comprehensive ongoing encounter with a *single unitary natural world*.

Correlatively, our being able to think of ourselves *as* single subjects of many thoughts and experiences is just the particular end $\mathbf{E}^*$ that we need to complete our practical reasoning, which, in light of our discussions, now looks like this:

1. We shall be able to think of ourselves as the unitary subjects of our diverse thoughts and experiences.
2. The only way to achieve this end is by deploying principles for combining temporally disjoint individual experiences into a unitary comprehensive experience.
3. The synthetic *a priori* judgments, 'J_{SAP}' (containing the *a priori* concepts 'C_{AP}') express just such principles of experiential unification. [(K1) and (K2)]
4. So, we shall endorse the synthetic *a priori* judgments 'J_{SAP}' (and thereby apply the *a priori* concepts 'C_{AP}').

And now we can also appreciate the way in which Kant's transcendental deduction can secure an *original* epistemic legitimacy. For my being able to think of myself as the single subject of many thoughts and experiences is not one of my *optional* ends, i.e., one that I might freely choose either to adopt or to eschew. It is, so to speak, a *constitutive* end. My doing so is a condition of there *being* an "I"—*one* active agent—who is able to consider and choose *at all*, among *many* optional ends.

Kant's transcendental deduction is thus an argument designed to establish that the conditions according to which the experienced world is constituted as an intelligible synthetic unity—that is, the conditions that entitle us to represent it as *one* mathematically lawful natural world—are *at the same time* the conditions by which an experiencing consciousness is itself constituted as a unitary self—that is, the conditions that make it possible for each of us to think of himself as *one* self-aware subject of many experiences. It's not just an accident that the sort of beings that *we are* represent what we ostensibly perceptually encounter as objects belonging to a system of causally interacting substances in space and time. Rather, our legitimately doing so is a condition of our being able to represent *ourselves* as single unitary subjects of such a multiplicity of ostensible perceptual encounters. In short, self and world—subject and object—are an inseparable "package deal". Like the north and south poles of a magnet, you can't have one without the other. (See Fig. 2.2.)

This completes our first encounter with Kant's transcendental deduction and, with it, my Big Picture of the constructive moment of the First Critique. Kant's solution to the Pythagorean puzzle turns out to include the surprising claim that the lawful orderliness of nature that we find manifested in the possibility of mathematical physics is something that in part depends upon us, upon who *we* are. Kant himself formulates this result very dramatically:

Thus we ourselves bring into the appearances that order and regularity in them that we call *nature*, and moreover we would not be able to find it there if we . . . had not originally put it there. (A125)

This is the positive consummation of Kant's proposed "Copernican experiment" in metaphysics: roughly, that we abandon the received idea that our empirical cognitions must conform to objects and try out instead

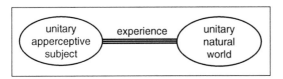

FIG. 2.2.   The Big Picture

the hypothesis that objects must conform to (the necessary conditions of) those cognitions (Bxvii–xviii).[11]

On Kant's account, we need to distinguish between things as they are *for us*, i.e., considered as possible objects of our experience, and things as they are *in themselves*, abstracting from the conditions of our possible experience of them. Trivially, then, we can have no *experience* of things as they are in themselves, i.e., apart from the conditions of our possible experience. Indeed, since, as we shall see, all empirical concepts, and, on Kant's view, even all mathematical concepts, derive their conceptual content from their relationships to sensory intuitions, Kant concludes that we cannot even have any *conception* of things as they are in themselves. Our experience of the world of nature is always and necessarily an experience of things as they are *for us*. Kant thus arrives at the striking conclusion that the world of nature is literally a world of *phenomena*, i.e., a world of *appearances*. This is the notorious thesis of "transcendental idealism".

The time has come, however, for us to put down the broad brush and, without fully abandoning our Dionysian élan, start to ease our way into the actual text of the First Critique. In light of the Big Picture, one thing that we should expect to find there is a detailed examination of the various ways in which the natural world constitutes a *synthetic unity*, and Kant does not disappoint us. His explicit topics in the first section of the book, the Transcendental Aesthetic, are two absolutely central principles of natural unity, *space* and *time*. The theme of transcendental idealism, however, will also be with us from the very beginning, and it will continue to accompany us along the way. The thesis that even space and time somehow depend upon *us* initially seems implausible, but, as we shall see, Kant indeed argues in support of it.

---

[11] More precisely and less paradoxically, the hypothesis "that all we cognize *a priori* about things is what we ourselves put into them" (Bxviii).

The World from a Point of View: Space and Time

3

When Kant finally gets down to business in the First Critique, he begins by emphasizing our sensory passivity, specifically, that *our* way of getting cognitively in touch with individuals is by way of *sensory intuitions.*

In whatever way and through whatever means a cognition may relate to objects, that through which it relates immediately to them . . . is *intuition.* This, however, takes place only insofar as the object is given to us; but this in turn, [at least for us humans,] is possible only if it affects the mind in a certain way. The capacity (receptivity) to acquire representations through the way in which we are affected by objects is called *sensibility.* Objects are . . . *thought* through the understanding, and from it arise concepts. But all thought, whether straightaway (*directe*) or through a detour (*indirecte*), must . . . ultimately be related to intuitions, thus, in our case, to sensibility, since there is no other way in which objects can be given to us. (A19/B33; the bit in brackets occurs only in B)

There follows a flurry of terminological distinctions: *sensation* is the effect of an object on our capacity for representation insofar as we're affected by it; an *empirical* intuition is one related to the object through sensation; and the indeterminate (i.e., generic) object of an empirical intuition is *appearance.* One shouldn't make too much of these introductory explanations. They're mostly addressed to traditional terms, some of which subsequently undergo changes, often dramatic ones, in Kant's hands. A few clarificatory and cautionary remarks are nevertheless in order.

To begin with, it's important not to confuse *intuitions* and *sensations.* Later, near the beginning of the Dialectic (A320/B376–7), Kant provides some helpful explicit terminological taxonomy (see Fig. 3.1). Recall that we could arrive at no clear verdict regarding whether Hume's "impressions" were or were not cognitive-epistemic items. Kant, on the contrary, is here decisive and explicit. When all the chips are down, intuitions *are* a species of cognition, and sensations are *not*. If sensations are the (immediate) results of the mind's being affected by objects, then intuitions are the results of the mind's being affected by (or, more actively put, processing) sensations.

Unfortunately, at the beginning of the First Critique all the chips aren't yet down, and especially there, Kant isn't always so decisive and explicit. In the Aesthetic, he proposes to

isolate sensibility by separating off everything that the understanding thinks through its concepts so that nothing but empirical intuition remains [and then] detach from the latter everything that belongs to sensation, so that nothing remains except pure intuition and the mere form of appearances, which is the only thing that the sensibility can make available *a priori*. (A22/B36)

Earlier he has told us that "that in the appearance which corresponds to sensation [is] its *matter*", whereas its *form* is "that which allows the manifold of appearance to be ordered in certain relations" (A20/B34). In describing the sort of "double abstraction" by which he will "isolate" sensibility, Kant plainly suggests that, once everything *conceptual* has been split off, what remains is still an *intuition*, an "empirical intuition", which owes its matter to sensation and its form to sensibility, but nothing at all to understanding. Later, we shall see that, by his own lights, this cannot be

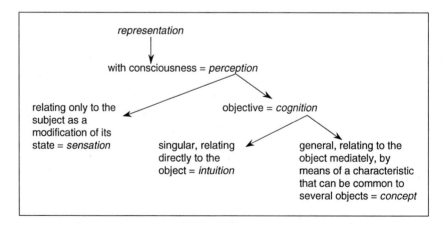

FIG. 3.1. Kant's classification of representations

right. The understanding turns out to be implicated in *all* cognition, singular as well as general. Kant, however, tends to remember more or less of this at different times, resulting in enough slippage in his usage of 'intuition' that some commentators have been moved to plump for a genuine systematic ambiguity: "intuition₁" here in the Aesthetic versus "intuition₂" later in the Analytic.[1] Here, however, we'll follow the more usual course of treating the term as univocal and allowing Kant this or that occasional expository infelicity.

The generic notion of an object of empirical intuition is what Kant calls *appearance*. Although the notion ultimately subsumes a bit more, to begin with it is most useful to think of Kantian "appearances" as the sorts of things that we prima facie encounter in experiences. 'Outer appearance' is thus roughly equivalent to our everyday expression 'physical object', while "appearances" in general subsume the empirical self as well, i.e., our own inner states insofar as they are experientially accessible to us through "introspection". The general idea is that appearances generate in us passive mental states, sensations, which get worked up into singular representations of items in space and time, intuitions.

Finally, it is important to be sensitive to the "-ing/-ed" ambiguity of such terms as 'sensation' (*Empfindung*), 'representation' (*Vorstellung*), and 'intuition' (*Anschauung*). A "representation", for instance, might be either a represent*ing* (act) or a represent*ed* (object); an "intuition", either an intuit*ing* (act) or an intuit*ed* (object). As we saw, it was structurally difficult for Hume to distinguish acts from contents, and consequently, he frequently wound up using such terms as 'perception' (another "-ing/-ed" ambiguous term, subsuming both impressions and ideas) and 'object' more or less interchangeably. Kant, in contrast, is basically clear about the distinction, but he continues to use the traditional and dangerously ambiguous vocabulary.[2]

---

[1] Footnote a to B160, e.g., can be read as supporting this interpretation.

[2] Kant is also quite clear that there is a related systematic ambiguity in such notions as "appearance" and "object", and later takes some pains to sort it out: "Now one can, to be sure, call everything, and even every representation, insofar as one is conscious of it, an object; only what this word is to mean in the case of appearances, not insofar as they are (as representations) objects, but rather only insofar as they designate an object requires a deeper investigation" (A189–90/B234–5).

Space, the form of outer sense

Consider an encounter with Wilfrid Sellars's favorite object, a pink ice cube. Kant's "double abstraction" thought experiment invites us to detach from our empirical intuition of it first "that which the understanding thinks about it, such as substance, force, divisibility, etc." and then "that which belongs to sensation, such as impenetrability, hardness, color, etc." (A20–1/B35). The concept of *ice* is the concept of a particular sort of substance having specific causal powers, so it is extracted during the first step. The second step eliminates such determinate sensory contents as coolness and pinkness. All that remain, Kant concludes, are "extension and form", a cubical region that was originally represented as filled with *ice*, subsequently with *cool* and *pink*, and now with nothing at all, i.e., "the *space* that was occupied by the body (which has now entirely disappeared)" (B5). Kant calls this a "pure form of sensibility" or, equivalently, "pure intuition".[3]

Despite having thus "isolated sensibility", however, Kant begins his story about space with what he calls (in B) a "Metaphysical Exposition" of the *concept* of space.[4] Nowadays we'd call it a "conceptual analysis". The contrast is with a subsequent "Transcendental Exposition" which, as we might expect, addresses the *epistemology* of space. Kant is first concerned, that is, with our ability to *think of* space.[5]

If you're a representative realist like Locke, then, even if you think that space has formal being, you're going to have trouble in explaining how we come to have a concept of it. The problem is that space is *causally impotent*. A pink ice cube can perhaps act on us to produce a representation of it (a Kantian "empirical intuition"), but the *space* occupied by the pink ice cube can't similarly act on us to produce a representation of *it* (a Kantian

---

[3] Many of the claims discussed in this section with respect to space (and the corresponding claims with respect to time) will in retrospect assume very different emphases or carry additional significant implications, i.e., after exploring Kant's related work in the Analytic, especially the "Axioms of Intuition", and in the Dialectic, especially the Antinomies.

[4] Besides introducing an explicit distinction between metaphysical and transcendental expositions in B, Kant made a number of further expository changes to the A version of the Aesthetic, including renumbering and relocating, as well as partially modifying, several arguments. Some additional clarity was indeed gained thereby, although his substantial views and theses remained basically the same. For the most part my account will follow the later version.

[5] But it is important to Kant's story that space and time themselves are *individuals*, i.e., given in *intuitions*, singular representations, and not "mere concepts". In this connection, see also his footnote to B136.

"pure intuition"). Locke's solution was to hold that material objects cause not only sense impressions of themselves, but also representations of *instances* of concepts of basic spatial characteristics (determinate shapes and sizes, determinate relationships of direction, adjacency or distance, etc.). From these we can proceed to complex concepts of spatial characteristics, and these in turn are mobilized to form the concept of *space*.

Kant argues that this sort of account cannot be correct. "Space is not an empirical concept that has been drawn from outer experiences" (A23/B38).[6] You can't get to the concept of *space* simply by piling up concepts of spatial characteristics. Concepts of spatial characteristics are *systematic*, and the center of focus of this systematicity is the concept of a three-dimensional spatial continuum. The systematic structure of the family of concepts of spatial characteristics, that is, *presupposes* the concept of the unitary individual, space. One can't think of a point, line, plane, or solid except as a point, line, plane, or solid *in space*. But to be located in space at all is to be in one place *rather than another*, and so the *whole* of space is implicit in every spatial experience (see Fig. 3.2).

Furthermore, spatiality isn't an *optional* feature of our outer experiences. We can't represent outer things (i.e., things distinct from us) without space, and we "can never represent that there is no space" (A24/B38).[7] Contrary to a thesis of Hume's, there couldn't be a "world" consisting of a single representing of a red dot and nothing else. Even a red dot must be represented *as* in a spatial (and temporal) world that is, so to speak, already sketched in, however vaguely and schematically, and that can't ever be filled in completely. The fundamental theme of Kant's first two arguments in B, then, is that the representation of space holds universally and necessarily of outer experience, and so is *a priori*. "Space is a necessary representation, *a priori*, that is the ground of all outer intuitions" (A24/B38).

You can't have this: without having this:

Fig. 3.2. Outer objects are necessarily represented as in space

---

[6] "Outer" experiences are experiences of things distinct from oneself (the experiencing subject), paradigmatically, ostensible perceptual encounters with objects.

[7] This is true of us human beings, but it may be different for other beings. "For we cannot judge at all about whether the intuitions of other thinking beings are bound to the same conditions that limit our intuition and that are universally valid for us" (A27/B43). Cf. A42/B59.

The fundamental theme of his third and fourth arguments in B, on the other hand, is that the representation of space is an *intuition*, a singular representation. "Space is not a discursive or, as is said, general concept of relations of things in general, but a pure intuition" (A25/B39). There's only *one* space[8]—"if one speaks of many spaces, one understands by that only parts of one and the same unique space"—and the concept of space is a basic one. It's not a representation of the form "the F", i.e., a "definite description" that is mediated by the concept of a *kind* or *sort* of thing. Hence, it's not "discursive" in the sense of having the kind of internal conceptual complexity that could make it possible for propositions of geometry to be (as Leibniz held) in principle analyzable down to the analytic 'All AB is A' form.

On the other hand, since we can think coherently of *empty* space, the concept of space is not the concept of a characteristic (quality or relation) which needs to be exemplified to be present. The concept of *space* is not the concept of something adjectival on things-in-space. The concept of space is the concept of an individual.[9] Whether considered in relation to its contents or in relation to its parts, space is essentially a *one* in contrast to a *many*, but this one–many contrast is not the contrast between a characteristic and its instantiations (which exemplify it) or a concept and its instances (which fall under it). The many outer *objects* and the (infinitely) many *parts* of space (spatial locations) neither exemplify space nor fall under it, but rather are *in* it. "Therefore the original representation of space is an *a priori intuition*, not a *concept*" (B40).

---

[8] Kant's assertion of the *necessary unity* of space (and time) has in fact been challenged, but not, I think, effectively. One can, of course, characterize the spatial (or temporal) relationships among one group of objects without *mentioning* any of a second group of objects and their respective spatial (or temporal) relationships, and conversely. But, if we are talking about potential objects *of experience*—i.e., not just telling a story, but telling a story that could be *true*—it is arguably incoherent to add that *no* object in the first group stands in any spatial (or temporal) relation to *any* object in the second group, which is presumably what it would take for the two groups of objects to be the contents of "two distinct spaces (or times)". For we ourselves, and *a fortiori* our experiencings, are located in space and time. The members of *both* groups are potential objects of *our* experience only insofar as they are able to affect our sensibility, and consequently only insofar as they stand in some spatial and temporal relationship *to us* and *ipso facto* thereby to each other. The necessary unity of space and time is of central importance for Kant's later treatment of substance and causation in the Analogies, and I shall have more to say about it on that occasion.

[9] The *conceptual* representation of space gets rather short shrift in the Aesthetic. "Space is represented as an infinite *given* magnitude" (A25/B40). The skeletal story gets partially fleshed out later, in the Analytic.

Finally, the fundamental theme of the Transcendental Exposition of the concept of space is to emphasize the point, already made earlier, that geometry, although consisting of a body of universal and necessary truths, is *ampliative*; i.e., the propositions of geometry are not analytic but synthetic. This becomes especially important here, for, on Kant's view, what geometry is *about* is precisely the unitary individual *space*. "Geometry is a science that determines the properties of space synthetically and yet *a priori*" (B40; cf. A24). To cite a few examples, no analysis of the concepts of a *point* or a *straight line* or a *triangle*, of *perpendicularity* or *summation*, suffices to establish that one can always construct a line perpendicular to both of two mutually perpendicular lines (i.e., that space has three dimensions), that only one straight line lies between two points, that two straight lines cannot enclose an area, or that the interior angles of a triangle sum to two right angles. (See also A47–8/B65.) But neither are these ordinary empirical claims, judgments of experience, for "what is borrowed from experience always has only comparative universality, namely through induction" (A25), while "geometrical propositions are all apodictic, i.e., combined with consciousness of their necessity" (B41; see also A48/B65). The science of space is thus a locus of synthetic *a priori* judgments, and any account of what space *is* must show how this is possible.

So what *is* space? Kant found two theories on offer. On the Newtonian account, space—and, to anticipate, likewise time—is a sort of quasi-substance, a "container" for goings-on in the world. Advocates of this theory of *absolute* space (and time), as Kant saw it,

must assume two eternal and infinite self-subsisting non-entities [*Undinge*] (space and time) which exist (yet without there being anything real) only in order to encompass everything real within themselves. (A39/B56)

In contrast, on the Leibnizian account, space (and likewise time) resembles a set of attributes of physical objects. It depends on objects in the way that relations depend on their terms—cancel out the objects, and there is no space. Leibnizians thought of space on the model of a *family*. The existence of the family depends on the obtaining of relations ("father of", "mother of", "brother of", "sister of") among individual persons. Cancel out the persons, and there is no family. Advocates of this *relational* theory of space (and time), that is,

hold space and time to be relations of appearances (next to or successive to one another) that are abstracted from experience though confusedly represented in this abstraction. (A40/B56–7)

It is clear that Kant cannot consistently subscribe to either of these accounts.

The problem with the Newtonian theory is essentially that a quasi-substantial space would not *consist* of anything. Since our intuition is sensible, if space were such a quasi-substance (an *Unding*), it could be given to us in experience only as a sensory *content*. But, as we have seen, we arrive at the pure intuition of space precisely by "eliminating" (in thought) all sensory contents, and we cannot thus "eliminate" space from any outer intuition. Space isn't a part of the *content* (the "matter") of any intuition, but something independent of such contents in that, unlike them, it itself doesn't cause any representations.

The fundamental problem with the *received* Leibnizian relational theory, on the other hand, is that it cannot account for the possibility of synthetic *a priori* geometrical propositions.

[Empirical concepts], together with that on which they are grounded, empirical intuition, cannot yield any synthetic proposition except one that is also merely empirical, i.e., a proposition of experience; thus it can never contain necessity and absolute universality of the sort that is nevertheless characteristic of all propositions of geometry. (A47/B64)

But, since geometrical propositions, although *a priori*, are not analytic, in forming the synthetic cognitions to which they pertain, one is "forced to take refuge in intuition, as indeed geometry always does" (A47/B65). Since this cannot be an empirical intuition, "you must therefore give your object *a priori* in intuition, and ground your synthetic proposition on this" (A48/B65). The intuitive representation of space must consequently itself be *a priori*, i.e., not produced by appearances ("physical objects") but, so to speak, by the mind. What Kant concludes is that space must be the *form* of *outer sense*.

Now how can an outer intuition inhabit the mind that precedes the objects themselves, and in which the concept of the latter [i.e., the objects] can be determined *a priori*? Obviously not otherwise than insofar as [this outer intuition] has its seat merely in the subject, as its formal constitution for being affected by objects and thereby acquiring *immediate representation*, i.e., *intuition*, of them, thus only as the form of outer *sense* in general. (B41)

Space is nothing other than merely the form of all appearances of outer sense, i.e., the subjective condition of sensibility, under which alone outer intuition is possible for us. (A26/B42)

If...space (and time as well) were not a mere form of your intuition that contains *a priori* conditions under which alone things could be outer objects for you, . . . then you could make out absolutely nothing synthetic and *a priori* about outer objects. (A48/B66)

On Kant's view, there is consequently something right about Leibniz's relational theory after all. Since space is a *form*, and so essentially correlative to contents, although space can be *thought* empty of matter (sensory contents), space couldn't *be* empty of matter. But that does not show, as the Leibnizian account has it, that the reality of space consists entirely in relationships among the objects in it. On the contrary,

if we depart from the subjective condition under which alone we can acquire outer intuition, namely that through which we may be affected by objects, then the representation of space signifies nothing at all. This predicate is attributed to things only insofar as they appear to us, i.e., are objects of sensibility. (A26–7/ B42–3)

This is the thesis of the *transcendental ideality* of space, "i.e., that it is nothing as soon as we leave aside the condition of the possibility of all experience, and take it as something that grounds the things [as they are] in themselves" (A28/B44). At first encounter, the thesis is likely to strike one as implausible, and shortly we will take a much closer look at it, but first we need to take a look at Kant's story about time.

Time, the form of inner sense

In essence, Kant's account of time exactly parallels his account of space. In a "metaphysical exposition" of the concept of time (A30–2/B46–8), he argues, first, that the representation of time holds universally and necessarily of experience, and so is not derived from experience but rather given *a priori*, and, second, that it is not a discursive or general concept but rather an *intuition*, a singular representation. In short, like space, time is a necessarily unitary intuition. (That's why time can be represented *spatially*, by a straight line whose properties are isomorphic to those of time "with the sole difference that the parts of the [line] are simultaneous but those of [time] always exist successively" (A33/B50). The "transcendental exposition" of the concept of time is only nominally separated out (in B) from the arguments of the metaphysical exposition, but its theme is that, just as there are synthetic *a priori* truths constituting a science of space, geometry, there are likewise synthetic *a priori* truths constituting, as it were, a science of time, what we might call "*a priori* chronometry", e.g., that time has only one dimension, and that different times are not simultaneous but successive (A31/B47). This last principle, Kant adds, is particularly important, because it makes comprehensible the possibility of an *alteration,*

i.e., of a combination of contradictorily opposed predicates . . . in one and the same object. Only in time can both contradictorily opposed determinations in one thing be encountered, namely *successively.* Our concept of time therefore explains the possibility of as much synthetic *a priori* cognition as is presented by the general theory of motion, which is no less fruitful. (B48–9)

Kant concludes, then, that, just as in the case of space, time is neither a (Newtonian) container nor a (Leibnizian) collection of empirical relationships among events, but the form of *inner* sense.

Time is nothing other than the form of inner sense, i.e., of the intuition of our self and our inner state. (A33/B49)

Since our "inner state" includes all our representations of "outer things", however, time turns out to be an *a priori* condition of all appearance in general, "the immediate condition of inner intuition . . . and thereby also the mediate condition of outer appearances".

If I can say *a priori*: all outer appearances are in space and determined *a priori* according to the relations of space, so from the principle of inner sense I can say entirely generally: all appearances in general, i.e., all objects of the senses, are in time, and necessarily stand in relations of time. (A34/B51)[10]

Kant's talk of "inner sense" concerns our knowledge of ourselves as other than purely rational beings, i.e., as beings who have an *experiential history.* This adds an important dimension of complexity to his story. Recall that Hume subscribed to the thesis that the representation of a succession is a succession of representations. The Humean picture of an experience of a person raising his arm, then, would look something like Figure 3.3. Each step in the succession of representations includes both a "vivid" impression of the arm in its then-and-there orientation and in-

---

[10] Time, we can therefore say, is a form of both inner and outer *intuitions,* i.e., intuiteds. But it isn't on that account quite right to say that time is a form of both inner and outer *sense.* Outer sense is our ability to be affected by objects *distinct from us;* inner sense, our capacity to be affected by *states of ourselves.* This is a logical dichotomy, i.e., a mutually exclusive and jointly exhaustive classification of our receptive faculties, and correlatively space and time are mutually exclusive and jointly exhaustive *forms of our sensibility.*

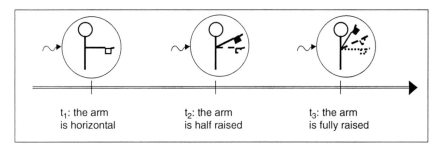

| t₁: the arm is horizontal | t₂: the arm is half raised | t₃: the arm is fully raised |

FIG. 3.3. Humean representation of a temporal sequence

creasingly "faint" "lingering representations" of preceding orientations of the arm. The degree of "faintness" or "vividness" corresponds to the time that has elapsed between an original impression (given in visual perception) and subsequent ideas of it (retained and reproduced in short-term memory). That is ostensibly what makes this sequence of representations the representation of an experienced *temporal* sequence, i.e., of the position of the arm *changing*, rather than, for instance, of an experience of successively noticing that each of three identical triplets is pointing in a different direction.

Kant saw very clearly, however, that temporality couldn't simply be, so to speak, a matter of *brightness* and *dimness* (or, for that matter, any other such *empirical* feature of impressions and ideas). There are lots of ways of generating similar sequences of representations which are not representations of a temporal sequence. Wilfrid Sellars invites us,[11] for instance, to imagine the same sequence of impressions as instead resulting from attending to various simultaneously existing parts of a multi-armed Hindu statue under changing conditions of illumination (see Fig. 3.4).

Nevertheless, there's surely something right about the notion of "lingering representations" of earlier stages or phases of a temporal process. The earlier stages of the process must leave *traces* that are somehow different and related to one another in a way that enables us to be conscious of a temporal sequence. That is, our (non-conceptual) *sensations*—the way in which we are successively *affected*—must stand in a field of relations that are appropriately *analogous* to (conceptually) represented temporal relations. Call them τ-*relations*. In other words, when we represent a sequence

---

[11] In *Science and Metaphysics* (London and New York: Routledge & Kegan Paul, 1968), 214. Like these pictures, my discussions of Kant's accounts of space and time are deeply indebted to Sellars's treatment of the same themes.

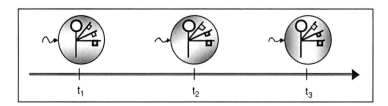

FIG. 3.4. Simultaneous states Humeanly represented as successive

of events in time, e.g., "First there was X, then Y, and then Z", the representation is evoked by a cluster of *compresent*[12] τ-related sensations corresponding to representations of X, Y, and Z. And now we can add that the same point holds with respect to *spatial* relations. That is, our (non-conceptual) sensations must also stand in a field of relations—*σ-relations*—that are appropriately analogous to (conceptually) represented spatial relations. When we represent an arrangement of items in space, e.g., "X is below Y and to the left of Z", the representation is evoked by a cluster of σ-related sensations corresponding to representations of X, Y, and Z, itself the result of our being affected by the disposition of things as they are in themselves ("*espace*", about which more later) (see Fig. 3.5).

Kant's picture of spatio-temporal experiences thus includes both a conceptual level in which objects are intuited, i.e., represented *as* in space and time, and a non-conceptual level of affectedness—"the manifold of sense"—whose σ- and τ-related items (sensations) evoke those intuitions. (Here I limit myself to depicting just the rising arm, and omit the formally real disposition of things, "*espace*", which affect us to produce σ-related sensations (see Fig. 3.6). More about "*dureé*" later.)

It's important to be clear that we shouldn't expect to *find* such manifolds of σ- and τ-related sensations by introspection. In Kant's story, they are, so to speak, theoretical posits. He is not engaged in phenomenological reporting, and the pictures we are developing here are consequently not meant to be dispatches from the introspective front lines. This becomes clear when we turn to Kant's own account of introspection, i.e., to the story of *inner sense*.

---

[12] *Not* 'simultaneous'. If Kant is right about the transcendental ideality of time, formally real sensations (sensations as they are in themselves) can't coherently be thought to stand in temporal relationships. The question of whether one can think or say *anything* intelligible about things as they are in themselves will explicitly exercise us shortly.

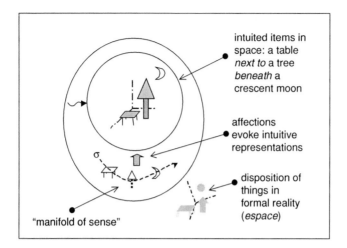

FIG. 3.5. Kantian representation of spatially related items

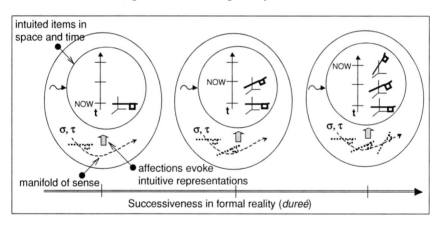

FIG. 3.6. Kantian representations of a temporal sequence

So far, we've been talking about representations of temporal relationships among outer occurrences, i.e., representations involving representations of objects in the world. But, on Kant's account, the *same* story applies
to our representations of the temporal structure of inner occurrences, i.e.,
representations involving representations of *our own representations*. Kant
maintains that the fact that we *have* representations does not imply that
we're (automatically) aware of them *as* representations. Just as things
distinct from me must affect me, producing a manifold of (σ- and τ-
related) sensations to which I respond with (conceptual) representations
of spatio-temporally related *objects*, the manifold of my inner states must

affect me to produce a manifold of (τ-related) items to which I *respond* with a (conceptual) representation of temporally related *representations* (perceivings, thinkings, rememberings, etc.). Representations must, as it were, be "reported to the mind" by a faculty of *inner* sense, analogous to the way in which objects are "reported to the mind" by a faculty of outer sense.

In human beings this consciousness [of inner states] requires inner perception of the manifold that is antecedently given in the subject, and the manner in which this is given in the mind without spontaneity [i.e., passively] must be called sensibility on account of that difference. If the faculty for becoming conscious of oneself [i.e., inner sense] is to seek out (apprehend) that which lies in the mind, it[13] must affect [the mind], and it can only produce an intuition of itself in such a way ....(B68)

In direct contrast to Descartes, in other words, Kant insists that one can be aware of a representation (thought) only by means of *another*, numerically distinct, representation *of* it—so to speak, a "meta-representation" (meta-thought)—and the original representation must be *responsible for* that meta-representation (see Fig. 3.7).

Kant's account of inner sense thus combines an anti-Humean thesis with an anti-Cartesian thesis. Contrary to Hume's view, the representation of a sequence cannot simply be a sequence of representations, but rather involves my actively responding to a *compresent* sensory manifold and representing states of affairs *as* successive in time by *adding* a representation of time (see Fig. 3.8). Contrary to Descartes' view, the mind is not transparent to its own workings. Inner states do not occur *propria persona*, but consciousness or awareness of a representing occurs only in the form of a numerically distinct meta-representing (see Fig. 3.9). These two theses come together in Kant's "Elucidation" of his theory of time (A36–8/B53–5).

The Elucidation is addressed to an objection to Kant's conclusion that time, like space, is transcendentally ideal, an objection "which must naturally occur to every reader who is not accustomed to these considerations".

---

[13] This is an excellent point at which to highlight one sort of problem that confronts a translator of Kant's work. The anaphoric ambiguity of the pronoun 'it' here—is the intended antecedent 'faculty', 'mind', or 'that which lies in the mind'?—reproduces precisely a corresponding ambiguity of the original text. Kemp-Smith, Pluhar, and Guyer–Wood all elect to retain the ambiguity—and, to make possible this pedagogically useful footnote, I've done so as well. But I take Kant's meaning to be that, in order for us to become conscious of it, *what lies in the mind* must affect the mind.

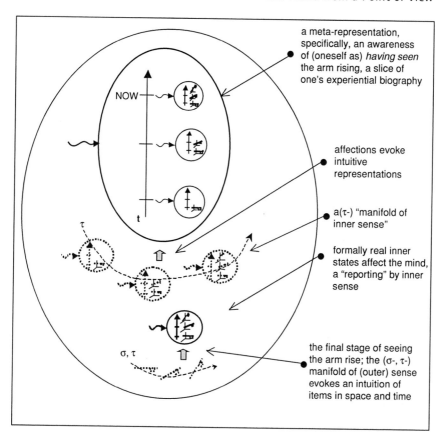

a meta-representation, specifically, an awareness of (oneself as) *having seen* the arm rising, a slice of one's experiential biography

affections evoke intuitive representations

a(τ-) "manifold of inner sense"

formally real inner states affect the mind, a "reporting" by inner sense

the final stage of seeing the arm rise; the (σ-, τ-) manifold of (outer) sense evokes an intuition of items in space and time

FIG. 3.7. Inner sense at work: an awareness of awarenesses

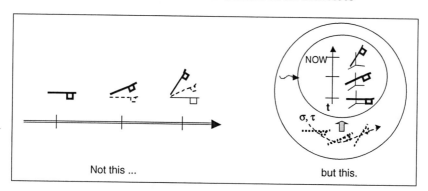

Not this ...

but this.

FIG. 3.8. Kant's anti-Humean thesis

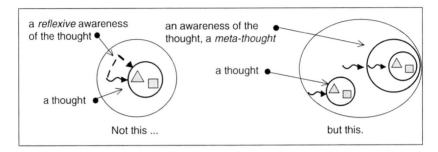

FIG. 3.9.   Kant's anti-Cartesian thesis

It goes thus: Alterations are real (this is proved by the change of our own representations, even if one would deny all outer appearances together with their alterations). Now alterations are possible only in time, therefore time is something real. (A36–7/B53)

Kant's response is initially astonishing: "There is no difficulty in answering," he writes, "I admit the entire argument." But, as you might expect, it turns out that he admits it only with a distinctively Kantian twist: "Time is certainly something real, namely, the real form of inner intuition" (A37/B53). It is true that I necessarily *represent* my own inner states as successive in time. But this requires that I actively respond to the manifold of my inner states and represent them (*contra* Descartes) *in a distinct meta-thought* as successive in time (*contra* Hume) *by adding a representation of time.*

I can, to be sure, say: my representations succeed one another; but that only means that we are conscious of them as in a temporal sequence, i.e., according to the form of inner sense. Time is not on that account something in itself, nor any determination objectively adhering to things. (A37/B54 n.)

The *reason* that this objection so readily occurs even to readers who are relatively philosophically unsophisticated, Kant suggests, is not far to seek.

They did not expect to be able to demonstrate the absolute reality of space apodictically, since they were confronted by idealism, according to which the reality of outer objects is not capable of any strict proof: on the contrary, the reality of the object of our inner sense (of myself and my state) is immediately clear through consciousness. The former could have been a mere illusion, but the latter, according to their opinion, is undeniably something real. (A38/B55)

In other words, Descartes had (ostensibly) shown that there might be *nothing at all* formally real in space, i.e., that the existence of extended substance might be a demonic deception. So space (that is, extension) might after all be transcendentally ideal, i.e., have no existence independently of our sensible intuitions. But my own representations ("thoughts"), about which (as Descartes had also shown) I cannot be deceived, are successive in time. Since those representations (*qua* inner states) have *formal* being, time must also have formal being, i.e., exist as a determination of things as they are in themselves, independently of our sensible intuition.

What such objectors forget, Kant tells us, is that *both* outer *and* inner experiences are instances of something's appearing somehow *to us*, and such an episode can always be regarded from two perspectives:

one where the object is considered in itself (without regard to the way in which it is to be intuited, the constitution of which however must for that very reason always remain problematic), the other where the form of the intuition of this object is considered, which must not be sought in the object in itself but in the subject to whom it appears, but which nevertheless really and necessarily pertains to the appearance of this object. (A38/B55)[14]

That I necessarily *represent* my inner states *as* successive in time is a remark made from the second perspective, but I cannot legitimately infer from this that those states as they are in themselves are successive in time. Our intuition is sensible, not intellectual, and so my inner states are given to me in experience only insofar as I am affected by them.

But if I or another being could intuit myself without this condition of sensibility, then these very determinations, which we now represent to ourselves as alterations, would yield us a cognition in which the representation of time and thus also of alteration would not occur at all. . . . If one removes the special condition of our sensibility from [our inner intuition], then the concept of time also disappears, and it does not adhere to the objects themselves, rather merely to the subject that intuits them. (A37–8/B54)

The transcendental ideality of space and time

As Kant was well aware, the claim that the spatial and temporal character of our experience is something that in some way depends on *us* initially seems rather implausible. He is consequently anxious to head off various potential misunderstandings of his thesis.

---

[14] I here depart slightly from the Guyer–Wood translation. They have "the representation of this object", but the German *Erscheinung dieses Gegenstandes* clearly requires 'appearance', even according to their own conventions of translation.

If I say: in space and time intuition represents both outer objects as well as the self-intuition of the mind as each affects our senses, i.e., as it *appears*, that is not to say that these objects would be a mere *illusion*. (B69)

Kant here envisions an objector who believes that the only alternative to space and time being *transcendentally* real (having formal being) is that they are *illusory*. Kant, however, is working with a richer set of distinctions, one which separates transcendental ideality from empirical illusion. His distinction between *things in themselves* and *appearances* should not be mistaken for the distinction between veridical and illusory experiences. The latter contrast falls *within* the domain of "appearances", i.e., our experiential encounters with empirically real objects in nature.

Thus I do not say that bodies merely *seem* to exist outside me or that my soul [inner states] only *seems* to be given [in my self-consciousness] if I assert that the quality of space and time—in accordance with which, as a condition of their existence, I posit both of these—lies in my kind of intuition and not in these objects in themselves. (B69; see also A45–6/B62–3)

It is also tempting to interpret Kant's Transcendental Idealism as a story about *two worlds*: a knowable world of "appearances", i.e., the encountered natural world of phenomena, and a hidden uncognizable world of "things in themselves"—but this is also a mistake. Kant's contrast is fundamentally epistemological, a contrast between the world as *we* necessarily experience it—things as they are *for us*—and that same world considered apart from the conditions of *our* possible experience of it, so to speak, as *God* might experience it—things as they are in themselves. The crucial consequence is that things as they are for us and things as they are in themselves are the *same* things.[15]

The point of calling the things we experience 'appearances' is related to the point that we make nowadays by insisting that "there is no given" or that "all language is theory-laden" or that "all perception is perception *as*". What Kant understood was that formal reality is not somehow "self-intimating" or "self-disclosing". It is accessible *to us* only through our experiences, and so, ultimately, only through "our kind of outer as well as inner intuition",

which is called sensible because it is *not original*, i.e., one through which the existence of the object of intuition is itself given (and that, as far as we can have

---

[15] As Wilfrid Sellars once put it, the world of things in themselves must contain dollar bills; otherwise we couldn't pay our debts.

insight, can only pertain to the original being); rather it is dependent on the existence of the object, thus it is possible only insofar as the representational capacity of the subject is affected through [it]. (B72)

An "original" intuition, as Kant is thinking of it here, would be an *originating* intuition, i.e., the power to bring objects into existence by having singular representations of them. To the extent that we can make sense of this, Kant remarks, only "the original being" (*Urwesen*), that is, God, could have such a power. We human beings, however, can intuit only items that *already* exist, independently of our representing them, and then only to the extent that we are affected by them.[16] Consequently,

the things that we intuit are not in themselves what we intuit them to be, nor are their relations so constituted in themselves as they appear to us; and if we remove our own subject or even only the subjective constitution of the senses in general, then all constitution, all relations of objects in space and time, indeed space and time themselves would disappear. . . . What may be the case with objects in them-selves and abstracted from all this receptivity of our sensibility remains entirely unknown to us. We are acquainted with nothing except our way of perceiving them, which is peculiar to us, and which therefore does not necessarily pertain to every being, though to be sure it pertains to every human being. (A42/B59)

Notice that Kant here explicitly refers to relations among things as they are in themselves. When Kant denies that things as they are in themselves are spatial or temporal, in other words, this does not imply that they are *punctiform* or *static*, for those are themselves notions that make sense only for spatio-temporal items. Rather, formal reality must be thought of as structured and dynamic in some sense *analogous to* the spatio-temporal character of experienced objects. Formally real persons, for instance, may not be temporal, but they are nevertheless *active*.

As we have seen, Kant suggests (A37/B54) that if, *per impossible*, our experience were not subject to the conditions of sensible intuition, neither objects in the world nor our own inner states would appear to us as undergoing alterations in time. Much the same thought also occurs later in the text, in the B version of the Transcendental Deduction:

Thus if one assumes an object of a *non-sensible* intuition as given, one can certainly represent it through all of the predicates that already lie in the presupposition that *nothing belonging to sensible intuition pertains to it*: thus it is not extended, or in space,

---

[16] "It may well be," Kant adds, "that all finite thinking beings must necessarily agree with human beings in this regard," although that is something that we are not in a position to determine (B72).

that its duration is not a time, that no alteration (succession of determinations in time) is to be encountered in it, etc. But this is not yet a genuine cognition. . . . (B149)

What is especially interesting here is Kant's reference to a "duration" that is "not a time". The full-dress version of Kant's story of temporal experience, pictorially reconstructed in Figure 3.6, contains three "time-like" structures:

(a)   represented temporal relationships among intuited states of affairs;
(b)   τ-relationships among compresent sensations;
(c)   the successiveness of representings in formal reality (the "duration" that is "not a time", for which I have borrowed Henri Bergson's term '*dureé*').

Similarly, we can distinguish in the full-dress version of Kant's story of spatial experience, pictorially reconstructed in Figure 3.5, three "space-like" structures:

(a)   represented spatial relationships among intuited objects;
(b)   σ-relationships among compresent sensations;
(c)   the disposition of things in formal reality, (which I have correspond-ingly called '*espace*').

The thesis of transcendental idealism is that the only spacelike and time-like structures that *we* have, the only ones available to us in experience, are those listed under (a). The relationships listed under (b) and (c) are relationships among things as they are in themselves, and so necessarily not possible objects of our experience, and, as we shall see, given Kant's theory of cognition, consequently not even literally cognizable by us.[17] That is, we cannot have "scientific" knowledge of them, the kind of knowledge that we have of the natural world. Any attempt to literally characterize objects independently of our modes of sensible intuition, e.g., as given to a "non-sensible" intuition, collapses into a *via negativa*. We can merely indicate what such an intuition of the object *is not* (B149).

But all this is compatible with the view that we can have a different sort of idea of things as they are in themselves, the *analogical* kind of idea that Kant, for instance, agrees with medieval philosophers in ascribing to us

---

[17] In this connection, see A770–1/B798–9. "We also cannot conceive of any community of substances that would be different from anything that experience provides; no presence except in space, no duration except merely in time."

with respect to God. *Can* we assume "a unique wise and all-powerful world author"? he asks.

Without any doubt. . . . But then do we extend our cognition beyond the field of possible experience? *By no means.* For we have only presupposed a Something, of which we have no concept at all of what it is in itself . . . ; but . . . we have thought this being, which is unknown to us, only *in accordance with the analogy* with an intelligence (an empirical concept) . . . . (A697–8/B725–6)

Similarly, then, we can think (b) relationships among sensations—σ- and τ-relations—and (c) relationships among things as they are in themselves—"dureé" and "espace"—*in accordance with the analogy* with spatial and temporal relationships among experienced items, i.e., our sensible forms of empirical intuition.

It's admittedly hard to get an informal "feel" for the thesis that space and, especially, time are only empirically real, but transcendentally ideal. One technique that some students of Kant have found useful is to construct a *model* of the (posited, philosophico-theoretical) relationship between "dureé" and temporal relations *within* the domain of "appearances", i.e., by using the *empirical* contrast between veridical and illusory time-order. Herewith, then, the description of a temporal illusion.

It begins with the so-called "phi-phenomenon", an illusion of apparent motion. When two red lights (left and right), at the same height but separated by an appropriate distance, are alternately flashed at particular intervals in a dark room, an observer has the experience of *one* red light moving continuously back and forth. The mind, so to speak, "fills in" the spatial and temporal gaps between the actual flashes (see Fig. 3.10).

It was the philosopher Nelson Goodman who first asked what would happen if one held the distances and intervals constant, but used a red light on the left and a *green* light on the right. The answer could hardly have been anticipated. What observers in fact experienced turned out to be one light in continuous oscillatory motion that changed color *midway* between its left and right limiting positions. This is the phenomenon of "color phi" (see Fig. 3.11).

Now think of the observer's conscious experience during the interval t_1–t_2 as a sort of movie, composed of many brief "frames", and imagine a "close-up" of what this film must be like in the immediate vicinity of the experienced change of color. A series of frames—A, B—representing a red light will be directly followed by a series of frames—C, D—representing a green light. Since frames C and D are *experienced* as occurring *before* the

81

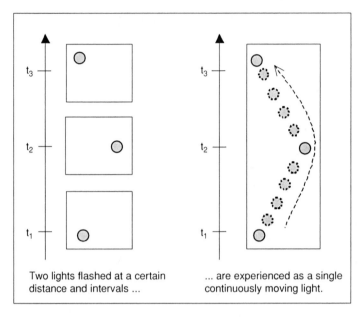

FIG. 3.10. The phi-phenomenon: apparent motion

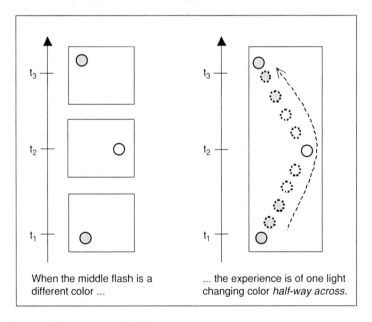

FIG. 3.11. The "color phi" phenomenon

moving light reaches its rightmost position—represented, let us suppose, in frame E—they are experienced as occurring during an interval when *in fact* the red light is on and the green light off (see Fig. 3.12).

But frames C and D clearly couldn't have been *created* until the red light had switched off and the green light switched on. The experience that's represented in frame E, in other words, actually occurred *before* the creation of frames C and D and their "insertion" into the experiential film. The (subjective, conscious) *experienced* time-order of events is consequently different from the (causal, objective) time-order of their *experiencings*. Color phi is a temporal illusion.

It is important to be clear that this is only a model. Kant is *not* claiming that temporal or spatial experience as such is illusory, i.e., that objects experienced *as* in space and time only *seem* to be in space and time. His thesis is only that space and time are not identical to the (unknown and uncognizable) structures of things as they are in themselves—what I have called "espace" and "dureé"—which *affect* us in a manner that results in sensations to which we *respond* by intuiting items as in space and time.

Is Kant right about space and time?

Kant's claim that space and time are transcendentally ideal perhaps becomes less puzzling when we consider in exactly what *way* the

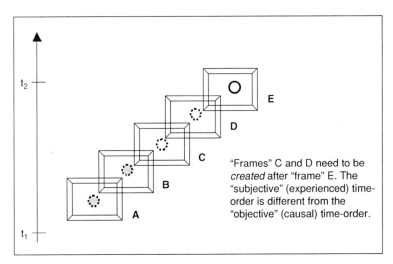

"Frames" C and D need to be *created* after "frame" E. The "subjective" (experienced) time-order is different from the "objective" (causal) time-order.

FIG. 3.12.   Color phi is a *temporal illusion*

experienced world is spatially and temporally structured. To put it briskly, we experience the world *perspectivally*, from a spatio-temporal *point of view*. The space that we *experience* is structured in terms of left and right, up and down, above and below, in front of and behind, and the time that we *experience* has a direction and is structured in terms of past, present, and future. The "space" and "time" that are posited by contemporary mathematical physics make no use of any such perspectival contrasts.[18]

Now it is arguably not an *accident* that the spatial and temporal forms of our sensibility have this sort of "egocentric" perspectival or, as philosophers sometimes call it, *indexical* character. To see this, it will be necessary to return to the theme of ones-*versus*-manys and the thought that *we* are concept-users.[19]

As we shall see, Kant himself emphasizes that the most fundamental form of judgment, whether expressed in thought or speech, involves the subsumption of an individual item under a general concept. Any general concept is a one that contrasts with the many constituted by its (actual and possible) instances, i.e., items that do or could fall under that concept, and every *de facto* application of such a concept thus presupposes the notion of such a plurality of instances. A general concept is essentially a principle of unity for its instances and so, *a fortiori*, cannot also be the ground of their plurality or multiplicity. Our use of general concepts in judgments, in other words, does not give rise to the notion of the (actual or possible) plurality of such instances, but rather presupposes some distinct "pre-conceptual" principle of multiplicity. To say this, however, is just to say

---

[18] It is perhaps not entirely misguided to think of the "space" and "time" of contemporary physics as playing the roles of "espace" and "dureé" in Kant's full-dress picture of spatio-temporal experience. In a way that Kant could not anticipate, in fact, the idea that things as they are in themselves might be significantly different from things as they are for us has become a commonplace of our contemporary world-picture, for that's just what our most sophisticated physical science has been saying for quite a while. Quantum physics tells us that what appears to us as a world composed of causally interactive persisting middle-sized homogeneous colored solid objects is actually a manifestation of vast swarms of curiously behaving submicroscopic entities that answer to a mathematics radically different from Newton's familiar laws. If that is right, then the world as it really is, in itself, is very different indeed from the world as it is for us, i.e., as it appears to us in our innumerable mundane encounters with it outside the laboratory.

[19] The line of thought that I am about to pursue was originally developed in elegant detail by Anton Friedrich Koch in his admirable book *Subjektivität in Raum und Zeit* (*Subjectivity in Space and Time*) (Frankfurt am Main: V. Klostermann, 1990). Koch himself was working out the implications of considerations originally adduced by P. F. Strawson in his *Individuals* (London: Methuen, 1959). The exposition that I give here draws on my own extensive discussion in "On a Certain Antinomy: Properties, Concepts and Items in Space", in J. Tomberlin, ed., *Philosophical Perspectives, X: Metaphysics* (Cambridge, Mass. and Oxford: Blackwell Publishers, 1996), 357–83.

that *general concepts do not individuate*, i.e., that it is possible for *distinct* individuals to fall under all and only the *same* general concepts.

(C)   There could be items, *a* and *b*, such that $a \neq b$, and (nevertheless), for every general concept C, *a* falls under C if and only if *b* falls under C.

On the other hand, it is surely intuitively plausible to insist that distinct individual items cannot *simply differ* (period), but must necessarily differ *in some respect*. This idea is captured in Leibniz's principle of the "identity of indiscernibles": If *every* property of the item picked out by '*a*' is also a property of the item picked out by '*b*', and conversely, then '*a*' and '*b*' pick out one and the same item, i.e., $a = b$.

(L)   Necessarily, if every property of *a* is a property of *b*, and conversely, then $a = b$. (Equivalently, if $a \neq b$, then either *a* or *b* has some property that the other lacks.)

When we put these two principles, (C) and (L), together, however, we can see that there must be a difference between an individual item's *having a property* and its *falling under a general concept*; for if we add the principle

(P)   For every property, P, there is a general concept, C, such that any item, *x*, has the property P if and only if *x* falls under the concept C, and conversely,

the result is an inconsistent triad, that is, (C), (L), and (P) together imply a contradiction. Hence if, as seems reasonable, we accept (C) and (L), then we must reject (P).

Now, although general concepts don't individuate the items that fall under them (C), it's clear enough what presumably *should* individuate them, namely, *space* and *time*. One individual is ultimately distinguished from all other (actual and possible) individuals by virtue of its unique spatio-temporal location.[20] The most basic properties with respect to which distinct individuals necessarily differ, (L), in other words, are *spatial* and *temporal* properties. It follows that some spatial and temporal properties must not correspond to general concepts. What could they be?

At this point it's useful to imagine that the world might be thoroughly and dramatically spatially symmetric—Strawson offers us the picture of a "chessboard universe"—and temporally repetitive—Nietzsche offers us

---

[20] Kant himself mobilizes this observation in his critique of Leibniz's philosophy in the "Amphiboly". See A272/B328.

the idea of "eternal recurrence". In that case how might I nevertheless uniquely individuate, say, the coffee cup on my desk? It should be clear that any description of the cup formulated entirely in terms of general concepts, including general spatial and temporal concepts, will not do. If the universe happens to be thoroughly spatially symmetric, nothing like "the one and only white-and-blue-striped cylindrical ceramic cup situated on a black wood surface 12 inches from a notebook computer and 4 inches from an ink jet printer" will be available, since there will always be at least *two* items satisfying such a description. Nor can we have recourse to anything like "the one and only cup from which, on 1 November 2002 at 12:47 p.m., a 60-year-old male philosopher took a sip of coffee just before typing the words 'ink jet printer'", since if the universe happens to be thoroughly temporally repetitive, an infinite number of distinct events will satisfy such a description. But is there any alternative?

Of course there is. *Whether or not* the universe happens to be symmetric and repetitive, I can always uniquely individuate the coffee cup on my desk *demonstratively*, that is, by direct *indexical* localization. It is *that cup here and now over there, in front and slightly to the right of me.* Even if the world happens to be radically spatially symmetric and temporally repetitive, in other words, a cognizing subject could still gain a differentiating ground for two descriptively identical spatio-temporal items (i.e., two items which fall under all the same *general* concepts) by representing them in their indexical (perspectival) relationships to *himself*, i.e., relative to his *here* and *now* (and *only* by doing so). The indexical properties *being here* and *occurring now*, in short, are the spatial and temporal properties that we have been looking for, the properties that do not correspond to general concepts.

The thesis of the transcendental ideality of space and time is the thesis that, insofar as space and time can function as secure principles of individuation, such indexical spatial and temporal properties, or, equivalently, our "egocentric" and perspectival systems of spatial and temporal representation, are basic or fundamental. This is not to say that we cannot operate with purely formal representations of "space" and "time" as contemporary mathematical physics does. But it is to claim that we can do so only by abstracting from something essential to space and time as such.

A *non*-indexical "space" or "time" can *individuate* items only if it is *coordinatized*. That, however, requires that it be possible to fix an *origin* for the system of coordinates, and, since any such "space" or "time" will be causally impotent and so not itself independently perceivable, the possibility of fixing such an origin will depend upon the possibility of uniquely picking out some item *in* that "space" and "time".[21] Coordinatizing a non-indexical "space" and "time", in other words, *presupposes* the possibility of individuating "spatio-temporal" items, and so presupposes the only principles we have for individuating items at all, namely, the *indexical* and *perspectival* space and time of our experience.

Perhaps surprisingly, then, when his claim is properly interpreted, there turn out to be good reasons for concluding that Kant is indeed right about the transcendental ideality of space and time. We have, however, by no means thereby exhausted the implications of his thesis of transcendental idealism. It will continue to play a central role as we move from the Transcendental Aesthetic into the Transcendental Analytic, and the focus of our attention correlatively shifts from Kant's story of the sensibility to his account of the understanding.

---

[21] That time, in particular, cannot be perceived will play a crucial role later in the First Critique, in Kant's arguments for substance and causation in the "Analogies of Experience".

Concepts and Categories: 4
Transcendental Logic and the
Metaphysical Deduction

In Kant's systematic conception of the First Critique, the "Transcendental Aesthetic" is the first main division of the "Transcendental Doctrine of Elements"; the second main division is the "Transcendental Logic". The two divisions correspond to the two aspects of our being sensorily passive intelligences, and Kant opens the Transcendental Logic with a clear statement of his "doctrine of two sources". All our cognitive achievements, and so, in particular, our experiences of the natural world, arise from the conjoint exercise of two complementary faculties, "the reception of representations (the receptivity of impressions)" issuing in "intuitions", through which objects are *"given"*, and the "faculty for cognizing an object by means of these representations (spontaneity of concepts)", through which objects are *"thought"* (A50/B74).[1]

If we will call the *receptivity* of our mind to receive representations insofar as it is affected in some way *sensibility*, then on the contrary the faculty for bringing forth representations itself, or the *spontaneity* of cognition, is the *understanding*.... Neither of these properties is to be preferred to the other. Without sensibility no object would be given to us, and without understanding none would be thought. Thoughts without content are empty, intuitions without concepts are blind. It is thus just as necessary to make the mind's concepts sensible (i.e., to add an object

---

[1] Kant is here building on his earlier distinction between two forms of intuition—one pertaining to our being affected by things outside us, the other to affections arising from our own activity. This "outer"/"inner" dichotomy is logically exhaustive and, *inter alia*, explains why space and time are all the forms of intuition that we have or need.

to them in intuition), as it is to make our intuitions understandable (i.e., to bring them under concepts). (A51/B75)

Kant here makes clear his disagreements with both Descartes and Hume. Contrary to Descartes' views, Kant concludes that reason *alone* cannot yield any sort of knowledge of the natural world, that is, the world that we encounter in experience. Without sensory intuitions to give our concepts empirical *content*, our thoughts could not be *about the world*. They would be "empty". But experience is also not, as Hume thought, simply a matter of passively receiving sensory impressions. Rather, we ourselves contribute something *to* both aspects of our experiences: On the sensory *content* of our intuitions, we impose a spatio-temporal *form*, and to the cognitions of objects and events in the world evoked by those sensory impressions, we contribute a conceptual structure without which those intuitions would be "blind".

Hence we distinguish the science of the rules of sensibility in general, i.e., aesthetic, from the science of the rules of understanding in general, i.e., logic. (A52/B76)

Transcendental logic

True to his system-building inclinations, Kant proceeds to break down the genus *logic* into various subspecies. Logic, he tells us, can concern either the *general* use or *particular* (specialized) uses of the understanding, and each sort of logic can, in turn, be either *pure* or *applied*. General logic is, so to speak, "all-purpose" or "topic-neutral" logic. It "contains the absolutely necessary rules of thinking, without which no use of the understanding takes place at all". The logic of a particular or specialized use of the understanding, in contrast, concerns "the rules for correctly thinking about a certain kind of objects" (A52/B76). Contemporary examples of the sort of thing that Kant has in mind might be, for instance, *deontic* logic (concerning rules for reasoning about obligations and permissions) or *tense* logic (concerning rules for reasoning about perspectival temporal relationships).

Nowadays we sometimes call such specialized logics 'applied', but Kant's "pure" vs. "applied" distinction is a different one. Logic is pure, he tells us, if it abstracts from

all empirical conditions under which our understanding is exercised, e.g., from the influence of the senses, from the play of imagination, the laws of memory, the power of habit, inclination, etc., hence also from the sources of prejudice, indeed, in general from all causes from which particular cognitions arise or may be alleged to arise .... (A53/B77)

As Kant understands matters, to put it slightly differently, what makes logic *pure* and *formal* is that it concerns only *relations among concepts* (e.g., subordination, coordination), independently of the *content* of those concepts. This is essentially the traditional Aristotelian conception that lies at the basis of classical *syllogistic* logic, which is the Kantian paradigm of pure general logic.[2]

In contrast, "applied logic", in Kant's sense, is in essence a branch of empirical psychology, concerned with the way we *actually* reason. "It deals with attention, its hindrance and consequences, the cause of error, the condition of doubt, of reservation, of conviction, etc." (A54/B79). In a contemporary idiom, Kant's "applied logic" is a (descriptive) theory of our logical *performance*; his "pure logic", a (normative) theory of our logical *competence*.

Pure general logic thus "abstracts ... from all content of cognition, i.e., from any relation [*Beziehung* = 'reference'] of it to the object, and considers only the logical form in the relation [*Verhältnis* = 'relationship'] of cognitions to one another, i.e., the form of thinking in general" (A55/B79). Transcendental logic, on the other hand, is a species of pure *specialized* logic. In transcendental logic, Kant tells us,

we isolate the understanding (as we did above with sensibility in the transcendental aesthetic), and elevate from our cognition merely the part of our thought that has its origin solely in the understanding. The use of this pure cognition, however, depends on this as its condition: that objects are given to us in intuition, to which it can be applied. For without intuition all of our cognition would lack objects, and therefore remain completely empty. (A62/B87)

In essence, then, transcendental logic is concerned with the most general principles of our thinking about objects experienced as in space and time. Kant's idea is that, just as there are *a priori* constraints on humanly possible *intuitions* of objects—i.e., *we* can experience individual objects only as spatio-temporally located—there are also *a priori* constraints on

---

[2] More precisely, Kant's paradigm is *extended* classical syllogistic logic, including hypothetical, disjunctive, and modal syllogisms alongside the traditional categorical forms. For a provocative and illuminating defense of the priority of such classical syllogistic over Boolean and Fregean alternatives, see Michael Wolff, *Abhandlung über die Prinzipien der Logik*, (*A Treatise on the Principles of Logic*) (Frankfurt am Main: V. Klostermann, 2004).

humanly possible *conceptions* of experienced objects—i.e., *we* necessarily represent such objects (he intends to show) as causally interactive substances. For this reason, we might usefully think of transcendental logic as "the logic of traditional metaphysics".[3]

Kant calls the constructive part of a logical theory—the part which delineates the relevant rules for correct thinking—an *analytic*. The correlative critical part—the part which identifies and exposes various forms of fallacious thinking—is a *dialectic*. The distinction applies both to general logic and to specialized logics, and so carries over to transcendental logic. The first division of Kant's Transcendental Logic is thus the "Transcendental Analytic"; the second, the "Transcendental Dialectic". The former concerns the most general *forms of concept* which structure our *experience* of objects and so presupposes that those objects are "given" to us in (sensible) intuition. The latter concerns the "dialectical illusions" that arise when we fail to observe these restrictions and surrender to the "very enticing and seductive" temptation to "make use of these pure cognitions of the understanding and principles by themselves, and even beyond all bounds of experience", "judging without distinction about objects that are not given to us, which perhaps indeed could not be given to us in any way" (A63/B87–8).

A new theory of concepts

Just as he earlier undertook to identify the contributions to our experience which flow from our capacity for sensible intuition, Kant now proposes to identify the contributions to our experience which flow from our capacity for conceptual thought. His point of departure for this project is a radically new *theory of concepts*, which, in turn, rests on two fundamental insights:

(1) Concepts are *principles of unity*.
(2) All consciousness that something is the case is *judgmental* consciousness; it has *propositional form*.

---

[3] Alternatively, just as we earlier borrowed from contemporary linguistics the distinction between competence and performance to model Kant's distinction between pure and applied logic, so too we might borrow the distinction between (abstractly characterized) representational systems in general and "humanly possible languages" to model his distinction between general and transcendental logic.

The first of these theses develops Kant's crucial observation that we are *discursive intelligences*. A *discursive* being is one who can think a manifold only by thinking its elements as in relation to one another. Unlike God, who can, so to speak, grasp a manifold of elements "all at once" in its full multiplicity, simply as such, a discursive being needs to "collect" and "relate" the elements to form a thinkable unity. A discursive being, in short, is a *synthesizer*. A discursive *intelligence*, in turn, is a *conceptual* synthesizer.

Synthesis consists in the "action of putting different representations together with each other and comprehending their manifoldness in one cognition" (A77/B103). Kant calls the principle of *unity* of the action of "ordering different representations under a common one" a 'function' (A68/B93). In principle, this is a very general notion, applying, for instance, to acts assigning

(a) multiple *instances* to a single *concept* [$x, y, z, \ldots$ are all F],
(b) multiple *encounters* to a single *object*,
(c) multiple *experiences* to a single *subject* [I think x, y, z].

All of these "unities of manifolds" will turn out in the end to be interdependent upon one another. In the first edition of the Critique, Kant's emphasis in the Transcendental Deduction is on (b); in the second edition, on (c). In both editions, however, Kant's point of departure is (a), and he begins by setting himself in strong opposition to a received tradition. And this brings us to his second thesis.

What Kant saw was that the form of a *judgment* cannot be accounted for in terms of a Lockean "mental chemistry". *Propositional form* is not the same thing as a *complex idea*. By collapsing the distinction between complex ideas and propositional judgments into a "modes of being" contrast between the 'is' of "identity" and the 'is' of "predication", the received model *conceals* judgmental or propositional form.

> Being red + being square = being red & square [a complex idea].
> Being Socrates (IDENTITY) + being wise (PREDICATION) = Being Socrates & wise.

This confusion was aided and abetted by Descartes' account of judgment as the willed affirmation or denial of a content presented by the intellect or understanding, according to which the judgment that Socrates is wise has a canonical form something like in Figure 4.1.

Kant, however, saw that a judgment is not simply an affirmed conjunction of ideas. Judgments have *various logical forms*. He issues his manifesto

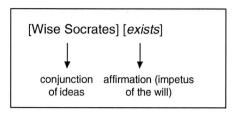

FIG. 4.1. Descartes' theory of judgment

at A68/B93: "[The] understanding can make no other use of... concepts than that of judging by means of them." What follows embodies a dramatically new understanding of both concepts and judgments.

The understanding is a faculty for thinking (i.e., *having* an understanding is *being able to* think); thought is cognition through concepts; and concepts are terms of possible judgments. Hence, the understanding is a faculty for judging. Since only intuitions (i.e., sensations) are immediately related to objects, in a judgment a concept is related to objects only indirectly, by being immediately related to some other representation of the object (a sensory intuition or another concept).[4] Judgments are thus "functions of unity among our representations". Instead of cognizing an object by means of some sort of "direct apprehension", we do so by means of a representation relating this representation of the object to others (A69/B94). We draw many possible cognitions together into one, e.g.:

> All bodies are divisible ← This body is divisible, That body is divisible, That other body is divisible,...

The concept of body, in turn, here occurring in the subject term of judgments, signifies something that can be cognized through it, e.g., metal. As Kant emphasizes, it is a concept *only because* there are "contained under it" other representations by means of which it can (ultimately) be related to objects, i.e., only because it also has a *predicative* use (A69/B94). The concept of body, for instance, is the predicate of the possible judgment that every metal is a body.

This is a rudimentary "inferential role" theory of concepts,[5] and also shares certain elements with Frege's account. Insofar as they are

---

[4] The ambiguities surrounding Kant's use of 'intuition' are actively at work in this remark. Shortly we will make an effort to sort them out.

[5] In this connection, see also Kant's discussion of the "qualitative" unity, plurality, and completeness of concepts at B114–15.

ultimately essentially predicative items, concepts are "unsaturated" and have "logical form". The mastery of any concept is the mastery of its use in judgments. All concepts, including individual concepts, already embody the logical form of a judgment. Judgmental forms are involved *whenever* concepts are realized, mobilized, or applied. This is a revolutionary move.

> The concept *wisdom* = ——is wise.
> The concept *Socrates* = Socrates is . . . .

Kant also retains, however, the traditional view according to which concepts track with *mental abilities*, i.e., one's *having* a concept consists in the ability to deploy it in thoughts, i.e., to think in terms of it. This holds at all levels of generality. Thus there is an extremely general concept: —— *is* . . . , possession of which consists in the ability to have thoughts of that logical form (i.e., subject–predicate thoughts): "Socrates is wise", "Plato is wise", "Meno is pale", etc.

For Kant, the "unsaturated" judgmental logical form 'Fx' is the *fundamental* unity. Thus the logical *subjects* of judgments also presuppose judgmental forms; e.g., 'This piece of metal' implicitly embodies the 'Fx' form 'This *is* a piece of metal'. But what, then, are we to make of the 'x', that is, the 'this'? The question leads us back into a complex of issues centered on Kant's still somewhat blurry notion of *intuitions*.

Intuitions revisited: Cartesian perception and Kantian perception

Recall our earlier full-dress Cartesian story about human perception which distinguished among (a) a sense impression, the "confused" thought evoked in the mind by the action of an object on the brain; (b) an immediate spontaneous judgment, e.g., "This stick half-immersed in water is bent"; and (c) a learned critical judgment, e.g., "This stick half-immersed in water only looks bent (since partially immersing a straight stick in water doesn't cause it to bend)" (see Fig. 4.2).

The attentive reader will notice that I have inserted a bit of our earlier picture of Kant's account of spatio-temporal experience into this picture of Cartesian perception, thereby introducing a certain tension at the middle level. This tension corresponds to some unresolved residual ambiguities in Kant's conceptions of receptivity and intuitions. What Kant explicitly tells us is that *three* things are required for cognition of an object:

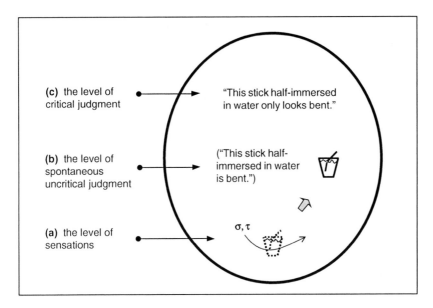

FIG. 4.2. Cartesian perception

The first thing that must be given to us . . . is the *manifold* of pure intuition; the *synthesis* of this manifold by means of the imagination is the second thing, but it still does not yield cognition. The concepts that give this pure synthesis *unity* . . . are the third thing necessary for cognition of an object that comes before us, and they depend on the understanding. (A78–9/B104)

On the interpretation that I want to suggest, the "manifold of pure intuition" here is the manifold of *sense*, i.e., the non-cognitive (σ, τ) structure of sensations that results from our being affected by objects and evokes a perceptual experience of them. One of Kant's leading ideas, then, will be that such "intuitions", i.e., *sensations*, need to be synthesized into an "intuition", i.e., a *singular representation* (of an item in space and time). Kant here ascribes this activity of synthesis to "the imagination", which, just a bit earlier, he obscurely characterizes as "a blind though indispensable function of the soul" (A78/B103). Since he has just told us (A68/B93) that the receptivity of sensibility and the spontaneity of understanding exhaust the faculties that we bring to cognition, it is rather surprising to find "the imagination" popping up here, but Kant's terminology should not mislead us into supposing that he has suddenly changed his mind. A *function*, we recall, is "the unity of the action of ordering different representations under a common one", and insofar as *we* are active and spontaneous in cognition, functions belong to the understanding. As it will later become clear, "the imagination" (more precisely, what Kant will call the "productive imagination") just *is* the understanding, playing a particular role in guiding the synthesis of sensory raw materials.[6] The point of speaking in terms of "imagination" is to stress the *imagistic* (i.e., sensory) character of the products of this synthesis, but what is actively at work is still the understanding, i.e., the faculty of *concepts* and *judgments*.

On Kant's view, in short, the understanding plays both an *analytical* role—answering questions about similarity and difference, classification and kinds, veridicality and illusion, and so on—and a *synthetic* role—guiding the processing of the raw materials of (non-conceptual) sensations in order to generate the framework of items (presented as in space and time) which the same understanding in its analytical role engages in judgments.

The same function that gives unity to the different representations *in a judgment* also gives unity to the mere synthesis of different representations *in an intuition*, which, expressed generally, is called the pure concept of the understanding. The same understanding, therefore, and indeed by means of the same actions through which it brings the logical form of a judgment into concepts by means of the analytical unity, also brings a transcendental content into its representations by means of the synthetic unity of the manifold in intuition in general.... (A79/B104–5)

It's clear enough that the "intuitions" which *result* from the synthetic operations of the understanding cannot be identical to the "intuitions" that are the immediate products of our being affected, i.e., the non-cognitive sensations that are the *inputs* to those same operations. On the other hand, it is equally clear that these "intuitions" are not themselves judgments or conceptual constituents of judgments. So Kant's picture of perceptual experience evidently introduces a level of theoretical analysis *between* the level of sensations and the level of judgments proper, whether spontaneous and uncritical or critical and reflective.

Now we can get a better handle on Kant's claim that

judgment is... the mediate cognition of an object, hence the representation of a representation of it. In every judgment, there is a concept that holds of many, and that among this many also comprehends a given representation, which is then related immediately to the object. (A68/B93)

---

[6] And, indeed, in Kant's handwritten marginalia to his own copy of the A edition of the First Critique, he replaces the phrase 'of a blind but indispensable function of the soul' with 'of a function of the understanding'.

Here it is especially important to be careful about the "-ing/-ed" ambiguity of 'intuition'. An "intuition", that is, can be either the act of intuit*ing* some item or the intuit*ed* item that is the object of such an act. In any case, intuitions are *singular representations*, so an "intuition" will be either a singular represent*ing* of an item or the individual item thereby represent*ed*. Now, since "thoughts without content are empty" and it is consequently "necessary to make the mind's concepts sensible (i.e., to add an object to them in intuition)", the most fundamental form of judgment for Kant will be one in which some item is *intuited under a concept*, i.e., a judgment containing a singular conceptual representing (an intuit*ing*) of an item located in space and time (an intuit*ed*). In short, it will be a *perceptual* judgment, that is, the judgmental aspect of just the sort of perceptual experience that we have been exploring.

Such a judgment will have both a logical subject (subject term) and a logical predicate (predicate term). The logical predicate will be the "concept that holds of many", and that also "comprehends a given representation, which is then related immediately to its object". This "given representation", in turn, will be the logical subject. Since "no representation pertains to the object immediately except intuitions alone" (A68/B93), the logical subject of a perceptual judgment will itself be an "intuition", i.e., an intuit*ing* (singular representing) of "its object", a particular kind of item, K, intuit*ed* as located *here* and *now* in space and time: '*this K*'. Kant's full-dress theoretical picture of a perceptual experience will consequently look something like Figure 4.3.

The Forms of Judgment

This picture also gives us what we need to interpret the so-called Metaphysical Deduction, i.e., the reasoning through which Kant arrives at an enumeration of the *a priori* concepts that form the subject matter of his subsequent Transcendental Deduction.[7] In particular, it gives us the key

---

[7] Kant gave it this title only in the B edition, and even there only later in the text, at B159: "In the *metaphysical deduction* the origin of the *a priori* categories in general was established . . . ." The contrast between metaphysical and transcendental *deductions* in the Analytic parallels that between the metaphysical and transcendental *expositions* of the concepts of space and time in the Aesthetic. In each case, the former concerns the analysis of concepts; the latter addresses epistemological issues.

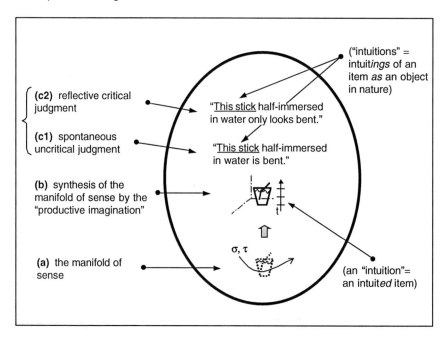

FIG. 4.3. Kantian perception

that we need in order to decipher what Kant calls "the clue to the discovery of all pure concepts of the understanding", i.e., what we need to understand his Table of Categories and its relationship to the Table of Forms of Judgment, more precisely, of "functions of unity in judgments" that precedes it.[8] "Functions of unity in judgments", of course, are manifested in the application of concepts, and Kant's first table is consequently an enumeration of the ways in which concepts can function as terms in judgments, in particular, of the way in which, in judgments, *concepts can be related to objects*. Now, as we have just seen,

a concept is...never immediately related to an object, but is always related to some other representation of it (whether that be an intuition [i.e., an intuit*ed* or an intuit*ing*] or itself already a concept). (A68/B93)[9]

---

[8] The following discussion is deeply indebted to the elegant Apollonian treatment by Michael Wolff, *Die Vollständigkeit der Kantischen Urteilstafel* (*The Completeness of Kant's Table of Judgments*) (Frankfurt am Main: V. Klostermann, 1995).

[9] The handwritten marginalia in Kant's personal copy of the A edition are again helpful. There he replaces what here occurs in parentheses with the unparenthesized phrase 'which itself contains intuition only mediately or immediately'.

If, for instance, we begin with the general judgment "All bodies are divisible", Kant explains,

the concept of the divisible is related to various other concepts; among these, however, it is here particularly related to the concept of body,

i.e., not to an intuition but to another concept. But, Kant continues, the concept of a body "in turn is related to certain appearances that come before us", i.e., ultimately to various intuit*ed* objects, by means of corresponding intuit*ings* in perceptual judgments: 'This body . . .', 'That body . . .', etc. In each of these judgments, whether particular or general, the concept *body* occurs as a constituent of the logical subject. But, as we have already seen, concepts are essentially predicative, and Kant explicitly observes that this is equally true of the concept *body*. It is the predicate, for instance, of the possible judgment "Every metal is a body". This, in turn, suggests yet another way in which a concept can be related to *objects*, namely, by way of an *inferential* relationship among judgments. The general judgments "All bodies are divisible" and "Every metal is a body", for example, establish a mediate relationship between the concepts *metal* and *divisible*, and thereby a still more mediate relationship between the concept *divisible* and items intuited as, e.g., 'this piece of metal'. It turns out, then, that a concept can be related to objects in any of *four* different ways (see Fig. 4.4).

1. The way in which the concept *body* relates to an object in the judgment "This *body* is divisible". (As a constituent of an intuit*ing*, in the *subject term* of a judgment about an intuit*ed* individual object.)
2. The way in which the concept *divisible* relates to an object in the judgment "This body is *divisible*". (As the *predicate term* of a judgment about an intuited object.)

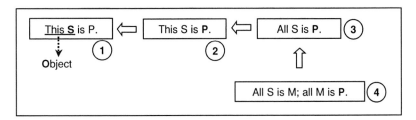

Fig. 4.4. Logical functions of unity: how a concept can relate to an object

3. The way in which the concept *divisible* relates to objects in the judgment "All bodies are *divisible*". (By being directly related *in a judgment* to another concept which is indirectly related to intuited objects.)

4. The way in which the concept *divisible* relates to metal objects through the judgments "Every metal is a body" and "All bodies are *divisible*". (By being indirectly related through a relationship between judgments *in an inference* to a concept which is indirectly related to intuited objects.)

These four possibilities correspond to the main headings of Kant's Table of Forms of Judgment (see Fig. 4.5). The three "moments" under each rubric in turn correspond, roughly, to subordinate contrast classes suggested by each heading. Under "Quantity", we consider *how many* of the objects falling under its concept the logical subject of a judgment might relate to: all of them, some of them, or one in particular (*this* one). Under "Quality", we consider *how* a concept might be logically predicated of the objects picked out by a judgment's logical subject: affirmatively or negatively or "infinitely" (about which more in a moment). Under "Relation", we consider how concepts might be related in a simple or complex judgment *to each other*: categorically, conditionally, or as mutually exclusive. Finally, under "Modality", we consider whether an inference establishes the relationship of a given concept to an object to be possible, actual, or necessary.[10]

---

1. Quantity of Judgments
Universal [All S is P]
Particular [Some S is P]
Singular [This S is P]

2. Quality	**3. Relation**
Affirmative [A is B]	Categorical [All A is B]
Negative [A is not B]	Hypothetical [If A is B, then C is D]
Infinite [A is non-B]	Disjunctive [Either A is B, or else A is C]

4. Modality
Problematic [A is possibly B]
Assertoric [A is B]
Apodictic [A is necessarily B]

FIG. 4.5. Table of Forms of Judgment (A70/B95)

[10] Kant unfortunately tends to confuse *necessary* judgments, i.e., judgments that are *themselves* necessary, with *necessity* judgments, i.e., judgments to the effect *that* something (else) is necessary. Cf. A75–6/B100–1.

From our contemporary perspective, there's clearly a certain amount of arbitrariness about all this. In large measure, Kant is simply adapting to his own ends classifications that he has received from earlier logical tradition. This is surely the case regarding the subdivisions under "Relation", according to which

all relations of thinking in judgments are those *a*) of the predicate to the subject, *b*) of the ground to the consequence, and *c*) between the cognition that is to be divided and all of the members of the division (A73/B98),

a division that, Kant stresses, should establish a certain "community of cognitions" by reflecting relations of "logical opposition" among disjoined predicate concepts that are mutually exclusive and conjointly exhaustive. (His elegant example is: "The world exists either through blind chance, or through inner necessity, or through an external cause" (A74/B99))

While, as we have seen, Kant's explicit acknowledgment of singular judgments—which, as he notes, the received tradition treats as universal (A71/B96)—is a significant theoretical contribution, his interpolation of "infinite" judgments under "Quality", in contrast, is frequently regarded as reflecting only his fondness for architectonic system building. His example is "The soul is immortal"—which the tradition classifies as affirmative, in contrast to the genuinely negative judgment "The soul is not mortal"—but his own attempt to explain his alternative classification and the appropriateness of the term 'infinite' is hardly especially lucid. One way to highlight Kant's distinction is that, whereas negative judgments are *exclusionary*, "infinite" judgments are *predicational*. The negative judgment, that is, simply excludes its subject (e.g., the soul) from the class of items to which the predicate term truly applies (e.g., mortal beings). Thus it would be equally correct to judge that *a stone* or *the number six* is not mortal. The corresponding "infinite" judgment, in contrast, itself predicates a determinate property (immortality) of its subject (the soul), a property that it would not be equally correct to predicate of a stone or the number six. Later, in the Dialectic, we will see that the distinction in fact carries significant critical implications.

The Table of Categories

Notice that, as an enumeration of *functions*, the Table of Forms of Judgment operates at an extremely high level of abstraction. A classification of ways in which concepts can relate to objects is itself *meta*-conceptual; that is, it equips us to sort *concepts* according to the ways they do or can function in judgments. It is important to understand that this is also true of the "pure concepts of the understanding" enumerated in the subsequent Table of Categories. Unlike ordinary empirical concepts, that is, categories do not straightforwardly conceptually sort or classify items in the natural world. In the first instance, they sort or classify *other conceptual items*, and do so according to their most general logical and epistemic roles. Classifications in terms of the categories are fundamentally *meta*-conceptual classifications.

This becomes fully clear only in the Analytic of Principles, but it is already indicated by Kant's treatment (added in B) of the medieval "categories" *unum*, *verum*, and *bonum*, i.e., *one*, *true*, and *good*.

These supposedly transcendental predicates of *things* are nothing other than logical requisites and criteria of all *cognition of things* in general, and ground it in the categories of quantity, namely the categories of *unity*, *plurality*, and *totality*; yet these categories must really have been taken as material, as belonging to the possibility of things itself, when in fact they should have been used in a merely formal sense, as belonging to the logical requirements for every cognition .... (B113–14)

In other words, although medieval philosophy taught that every *being* is one, true, and good, this traditional doctrine is properly interpreted meta-conceptually, as reflecting functional constraints on concepts that are already embodied in (some of) Kant's own categories.

Thus the criterion of the possibility of a concept (not of its object), is the definition, in which the *unity* of the concept, the *truth* of everything that may initially be derived from it, and finally the *completeness* of everything that is drawn from it, constitute everything that is necessary for the production of the entire concept .... (B115)

In first approximation, Kant's categories simply *are* the forms of judgment, specialized to cognitions of sensibly intuited objects (see Fig. 4.6). More precisely, given the forms that judgments can take, the categories (collectively) functionally specify the sorts of concepts of sensibly intuited items that are suitable to serve as the subjects of judgments about objects in space and time. As Kant puts it: "They are concepts of an object in general, by means of which its intuition is regarded as *determined* with regard to one of the *logical functions* for judgments" (B128). The Table of Categories thus reflects operations of the understanding in its *synthetic*

```
┌─────────────────────────────────────────────────────────────────────────┐
│                         1. Of Quantity                                    │
│                            Unity                                          │
│                            Plurality                                      │
│                            Totality                                       │
│                                                                           │
│   2. Of Quality                        3. Of Relation                     │
│      Reality             Of Inherence and Subsistence (substantia et accidens) │
│      Negation            Of Causality and Dependence (cause and effect)   │
│      Limitation          Of Community (reciprocity between agent and patient) │
│                                                                           │
│                         4. Of Modality                                    │
│                      Possibility–Impossibility                            │
│                      Existence–Non-existence                              │
│                      Necessity–Contingency                                │
└─────────────────────────────────────────────────────────────────────────┘
```

FIG. 4.6. Table of Categories (A80/B106)

role. Since, as we have seen, Kant holds that "the same function that gives unity to the various representations *in a judgment* also gives unity to the mere synthesis of various representations *in an intuition*" (A79/B104–5), the Table of Categories just *is* the Table of Forms of Judgment, that is, an enumeration of the same *functions*, but considered from a different theoretical perspective, in a different *role*.

Thus the function of the *categorical* judgment [under "Relation" in the Table of Forms of Judgment] was that of the relation of the subject to the predicate, e.g., "All bodies are divisible." Yet in regard to the merely logical use of the understanding it would remain undetermined which of these two concepts will be given the function of the [logical] subject and which will be given that of the [logical] predicate. For one can also say: "Something divisible is a body." Through the [corresponding] category of substance [under "Of Relation" in the Table of Categories], however, if I bring the concept of a body under it, it is determined that its empirical intuition in experience must always be considered as subject, never as mere predicate; and likewise with all the other categories. (B128–9)[11]

[11] As we shall see later, the question of the relationship between the Table of Categories and the Table of Forms of Judgment is further complicated by the fact that the categories themselves may be, as Kant puts it, either *pure* or *schematized*, and that there is a sense in which *un*schematized categories remain, so to speak, purely logical. "In fact, even after abstraction from every sensible condition, significance, but only a logical significance of the mere unity of representations, is left to the pure concepts of the understanding [i.e., the categories], but no object and thus no significance is given to them that could yield a concept of the object. Thus, e.g., if one leaves out the sensible determination of persistence, [the concept of] substance would signify nothing more than a something that can be thought as a subject (without being a predicate of something else). . . . Without schemata, therefore, the categories are only functions of the understanding for concepts, but do not represent any object" (A147/B186–7).

Because (he is convinced) the Table of Forms of Judgment was constructed systematically, according to principles that guaranteed its completeness, Kant can then straightaway conclude that the Table of Categories gives an exhaustive enumeration of all the basic "pure concepts of the understanding". Unlike Aristotle's list of categories, from which Kant borrows the term, it "has not arisen rhapsodically from a haphazard search for pure concepts, of the completeness of which one could never be certain" (A81/B107).

While the Table of Categories thus lists all the *basic* elements of the pure cognition of the understanding, thereby satisfying the condition of completeness that Kant lays down as a methodological criterion of adequacy at the start of the Transcendental Analytic (A64/B89), Kant makes it clear that a fully developed systematic working out of the metaphysics of nature would also locate, enumerate, and characterize a goodly number of *derivative* pure concepts of the understanding.[12] Although compiling a complete catalogue would be, he says, "useful and not unpleasant", given his present critical purposes, it is also "dispensable", and he consequently here contents himself with listing

under the category of causality, ... the predicables of force, action, and passion [undergoing]; under that of community, those of presence and resistance; [and] under ... modality, those of generation [coming to be], corruption [passing away], alteration, and so on. (A82/B108)

Despite Kant's disclaimer, we shall later in fact encounter a few of these derivative categories in more detail.

In the B edition, Kant concludes his chapter on the discovery of all the pure concepts of the understanding with a few structural observations regarding the Table of Categories at which he has arrived. The most significant of these is that the four groups of categories divide into two classes,

the first of which is concerned with objects of intuition (pure as well as empirical), the second of which, however, is directed to the existence of these objects (either in relation to each other or to the understanding). (B110)

The former, consisting of the categories of Quantity and Quality, he designates as *mathematical*. The latter subsumes the categories of Relation

---

[12] Kant, in fact, produced such a systematic treatment in his own *Metaphysical Foundations of Natural Science*, published in 1876, between the A and B editions of the First Critique, i.e., early enough for him to be able to refer to it explicitly at B110.

and Modality and is called *dynamical*. Apart from remarking that, "as one sees", the first of these "has no correlates, which are to be met with only in the second class," Kant here offers no further elucidation of this distinction. (The remark itself simply calls our attention to the fact that leading concepts are paired with contrasting ones only in the dynamical categories—substance vs. accident, cause vs. effect, agent vs. patient, possible vs. impossible, existent vs. non-existent, and necessary vs. contingent.) It will surface again, however, within his "systematic representation of the *principles* of pure understanding" following the Transcendental Deduction, and there it will become much clearer what Kant in fact has in mind.

Finally, Kant observes that the three entries under the main headings in the Table of Categories in each case themselves stand in an interesting relationship, namely, that "the third category always arises from the combination of the first two in its class" (B110). Thus he suggests that when we regard a plurality as a unity, we treat it, so to speak, under the aspect of *totality* (i.e., in its totality). When reality is combined with negation, what results is *limitation*—the limits or boundaries of something real are marked by its absence, i.e., where it's *not*. *Community* is the reciprocal causal determination of substances by each other. (Here Kant offers the intriguing example of the parts of a body "which reciprocally attract yet also repel each other" (B112). The idea that Newtonian matter manifests this kind of balancing of forces—attraction, i.e., gravitation, and repulsion, i.e., impenetrability—is worked out in considerable detail in his metaphysics of natural science.) And finally, "*necessity* is nothing but existence that is given by possibility itself" (B111).[13] Kant insists, however, that these relationships do not make the third concept "merely derivative", since "the combination of the first and second in order to bring forth the third concept requires a special act of the understanding"

---

[13] Kant here anticipates a relatively contemporary version of the ontological argument. The concept of God is the concept of a necessary being, i.e., one which, *if* it exists, necessarily exists. That is, abbreviating 'God exists' by 'G', we have $G \rightarrow \Box G$. Contraposing yields $\sim\Box G \rightarrow \sim G$, and, substituting '$\sim G$' for G, $\sim\Box\sim G \rightarrow \sim\sim G$, or, using standard equivalences, $\Diamond G \rightarrow G$, i.e., if it's possible that God exists, then God exists. Since, the argument continues, it's surely *possible* that God exists, it follows that God *does* exist. Correlatively, a being whose actual existence thus follows from its possible existence will be a necessary being. For, if $\Diamond G \rightarrow G$, the supposition that God exists, but not necessarily, i.e., that $G \& \sim\Box G$, will imply a contradiction. The second conjunct, $\sim\Box G$, implies $\Diamond\sim G$, and since (by substitution) we have $\Diamond\sim G \rightarrow \sim G$, we can derive $\sim G$, contradicting the first conjunct. Kant himself, parenthetically, argues in the First Critique (A590/B618 ff.) that the concept of such a necessary being is itself a dialectical illusion, and that, although it is a necessary postulate of *practical* reason, God's existence cannot be proved by any form of argument.

(B111).[14] (At this point the reader must conduct his own thought experiments.)

With his Table of Categories, Kant has arrived at a systematic enumeration of the *a priori* concepts whose epistemic legitimacy constitutes the theme of the Transcendental Deduction. More importantly, by explicitly grounding the origins of those "pure concepts of the understanding" in our nature as sensorily passive conceptual synthesizers, he has already laid the groundwork for the *strategy* of the Transcendental Deduction, Strategy K.

In particular, two epistemic tasks can now be placed on Kant's agenda. He needs to show, first, that

> (I)   our conceptual intuit*ings* necessarily *embody* the categories,

i.e., recalling that the categories are meta-conceptual classifications, that the concepts under which we intuit spatio-temporal items *belong to* the classes of concepts functionally picked out by the categories. And he needs to show, second, that

> (II)   our sensory intuit*eds* necessarily *fit* (or: *answer to*) the categories,

i.e., that all the items which we intuit as in space and time in fact *fall under* concepts belonging to the classes picked out by the categories. These two tasks are most explicitly sorted out in the B edition, in Kant's transition from a first part of the Deduction, in which

> (I)   the "possibility [of the categories] as *a priori* cognitions of objects of an intuition in general",

is established to a second part in which

> (II)   "the possibility of cognizing *a priori thorough categories* whatever objects *may come before our senses*"

remains to be secured (B159–60).

We already command a general strategic overview of Kant's plan for discharging these two tasks. In the course of the next chapters, we will boldly enter the thickets of the *text* of Kant's Transcendental Deduction

---

[14] Some readers will be tempted to see here an anticipation of the notorious "Hegelian three-step"—thesis/antithesis/synthesis. The temptation should probably be resisted, if for no other reason than that Hegel himself never used the "thesis/antithesis/synthesis" formula, and, indeed, it arguably misrepresents the actual structure of his thought. But that is a topic for another book: e.g., Terry Pinkard's outstandingly erudite and readable *Hegel: A Biography* (Cambridge and New York: Cambridge University Press, 2000).

and try to find there evidences of the execution of that plan. Some of its footprints will be clearer in the A Deduction; others, in B. But our search, in fact, will not be completely finished until we have passed through the Transcendental Deduction proper and moved from the "Analytic of Concepts" into the "Analytic of Principles", i.e., from consideration of the role of *a priori* concepts in perceptual synthesis to explicit consideration of their employment in legitimate "every–must" synthetic *a priori* judgments. Let us set to work!

Perceptual Synthesis: From   5
Sensations to Objects

In his Introduction to the first edition, Kant writes that the inquiry culminating in his "Deduction of the Pure Concepts of the Understanding" has two sides.

> One side refers to the objects of the pure understanding, and is supposed to demonstrate and make comprehensible the objective validity of its concepts *a priori* . . . . The other side deals with the pure understanding itself, concerning its possibility and the powers of cognition on which it itself rests; thus it considers it in a subjective relation, ... (Axvi–xvii)

The first of these projects, showing *that* the categories necessarily apply to all possible objects of experience, Kant calls the "objective deduction"; the second, in essence the project of showing *how* the categories can apply to objects of experience, the "subjective deduction" (Axvii). Since the categories have already been identified with the "pure concepts of the understanding", the fundamental job of the subjective deduction is to explain the role of the understanding in experience. In particular, we need to explore the way in which the understanding "brings a transcendental content into its representations by means of the synthetic unity of the manifold in intuition in general" (A79/B105). This task is writ especially large in the A Deduction.

At the beginning of the A Deduction, however, the understanding seems not to be present at all. Although Kant has already told us (A51/B75) that experience arises only through the cooperation of the sensibility and the understanding, he now appears to embark on a prima facie different account:

> There are...three original sources (capacities or faculties of the soul) which contain the conditions of the possibility of all experience, and cannot themselves be derived from any other faculty of the mind, namely *sense, imagination*, and *apperception*. On these are grounded (1) the *synopsis* of the manifold *a priori* through sense; (2) the *synthesis* of this manifold through the imagination; finally (3) the *unity* of this synthesis through original apperception. (A94–5; cf. A115)

We have, in fact, encountered something like this three-aspect account before, at A78–9/B104, and we used it to draw some morals regarding Kant's use of the term 'intuition'. But what we had there were not sense, imagination, and apperception, but rather "the manifold of pure intuition", its "synthesis...by means of the imagination", and "the concepts that give this pure synthesis unity" which, Kant there told us, "depend on the understanding". On the face of it, then, there are significant differences between these two enumerations, and we shall need to try to sort them out, especially the relationship between the understanding and "original apperception". This will, in fact, bring us directly to the heart of the subjective deduction.

A phenomenology of perception

It has become commonplace in certain philosophical circles[1] to dismiss much of what goes on in the A Deduction as presupposing a naïve and outmoded psychological theory of "mental faculties", and there is no denying that this is indeed Kant's expository idiom. It would be a mistake, however, to suppose that Kant actually regards the various "sources" and "activities of synthesis" into which he dissects experience as separate, structurally isolatable, sequentially operative input–output mechanisms. (Kant himself, for instance, speaks of different "syntheses" as being "inseparably combined" (A102).) It is more fruitful to think of them as elements of a *phenomenological analysis* of various aspects and conditions of perception, i.e., as philosophically useful "distinctions of reason" (to adopt a notion from Hume) that need not correspond in any straightforward way

---

[1] P. F. Strawson's important book *The Bounds of Sense* contains probably the most influential instance of such an interpretation.

to the classifications and explanatory accounts of a psychological or psycho-physical *theory* of perceptual experience.

We can begin to get a sense of what Kant is up to here by exploring one of our own perceptual experiences. My gaze, for instance, momentarily lights on my copy of the German text of the First Critique—a substantial tome, bound in green—and I spontaneously think, "This thick green book is difficult reading." The demonstrative 'this' marks the thought as a *perceptual* judgment. It is about something that is here and now sensorily present in my visual field, an object that I *take* to be a thick green book, since that is the concept that I apply. In this case, my perceptual experience is veridical; that is, what I see is *in fact* a thick green book. I see it *as* a thick green book (for that is what I take it to be), and I judge *of* it that it is difficult reading.

But while it's correct to say that I see a thick green book and that I see it *as* a thick green book, it's also correct to say that I don't see *all* of the book. What I see *of* it, for instance, is only its green spine and front cover. I see it *as* a thick green book, and so *as* also having a green back cover and many black-and-white inside pages, but what I see *of* it doesn't include its inside pages and back cover. How, then, do the inside pages and back cover get into my perceptual experience?

One possible answer, of course, is that they don't get into my *perceptual* experience at all. All that I "strictly speaking" see are "surfaces", which can properly be characterized in terms of color and shape and perhaps curvature ("bulginess"), but which have no "thickness", and so no "back" and no "insides". On this sort of "sense datum" account, the green back cover and black-and-white inside pages of the book are related to my perceptual experience only by corresponding to *unactualized perceptual possibilities* that I might *infer* from it. Correlatively, the only sense in which it would be correct to say that I see what I do *as* having a back cover and inside pages is the sense in which it would also be correct to say, for example, that I see what I do *as* being inflammable or non-magnetic, for these properties can also be associated with families of unactualized perceptual possibilities.

As we have already observed, Kant rejects such austere "Humean" strictures on descriptions of our perceptual experience. What we see are *objects*, e.g., books. When I see a book, I see it *as* a complete substantial object, and so as having parts other than what I see *of* it. Those parts are consequently (somehow) present *as actualities* in my perceptual experience, even though they're not strictly speaking *seen* (where what I "strictly speaking *see*" is what I see *of* the book that I see). If what I see *of* the book corresponds, as seems plausible, to what is "present in intuition" in the sense of being present as elements in *sensation*, then what I need in order to be able to see the book *as* a book, and so *as* having parts other than what I see *of* it, is a way of making those further parts, although not in that sense "present in intuition", nevertheless present (as actualities) in *perception*. Precisely this, Kant tells us, is the job of the *imagination*.

Imagination is the capacity to represent an object even *without its presence* in intuition. (B151)[2]

On Kant's account, in other words, the parts of the book over and above what I see *of* it are present in my perceptual experience as *imagined*.

Now it is important to be clear that being "present as imagined" does not imply being *presented* as imagined. To the extent that I am aware of my experience as such, that is, I am aware of it simply as a unitary experience of *seeing a book*. The philosophically useful "distinctions of reason" that we are in the process of drawing, that is, are not distinctions that can be, so to speak, introspectively "read off" from our perceptual experiences merely by suitably directing our attention to them. This is part of what Kant had in mind when he called imagination "a blind although indispensable function of the soul, without which we would have no cognition at all, but of which we are seldom even conscious" (A78/B103).

Imagination thus turns out to be an essential aspect of perception *per se*. As Kant recognizes, this is an innovative view.

No psychologist has yet thought that the imagination is a necessary ingredient of perception itself. This is so partly because this faculty was limited to reproduction, and partly because it was believed that the senses do not merely afford us impressions but also put them together and produced images of objects, for which without doubt something more than the receptivity of impressions is required, namely a function for the synthesis of them. (A120n.)

This is the function that Kant calls "the synthesis of apprehension in the intuition" (A98ff.).

---

[2] The translation offered here echoes an ambiguity in the original text: viz., the question of whether 'in intuition' modifies 'represent' or 'presence'. I take Kant to mean that the imagination is the power of *presenting in* (a sensible) *intuition* (parts or aspects of) objects that are not present (in the manifold of sense). Pluhar adopts essentially this reading; Guyer–Wood retains the ambiguity.

The "threefold synthesis"

The synthesis of apprehension is one of three "syntheses" that figure centrally in the A Deduction. The other two Kant calls "the synthesis of reproduction in the imagination" and "the synthesis of recognition in the concept". The imagination thus has *two* jobs to do in Kant's story. On the one hand, it functions to pull together a synchronic manifold of sensations into what Kant calls an *image*. "It must therefore antecedently take up the impressions into its activity, i.e., apprehend them" (A120)—hence, "the synthesis of apprehension". (See also A98–100.)

On the other hand, since, as Hume observed, "our eyes cannot turn in their sockets without varying our perceptions" (*THN* I. iv. 6; 252), to secure anything like a stable image, we also need to be able to pull together the sensory manifold *diachronically*, and so somehow to "carry over" its earlier elements. As Kant puts it:

It is, however, clear that even this apprehension of the manifold alone would bring forth no image and no connection of the impressions were there not a subjective ground for calling back a [representation[3]], from which the mind has passed on to another, to the succeeding ones . . . i.e., a reproductive faculty of imagination . . . . (A121)

This is the "synthesis of reproduction". (See also A100–2.)

In the B Deduction, these syntheses of apprehension and reproduction are bundled together as the *figurative* synthesis of the manifold of sensible intuition (*synthesis speciosa*), which Kant contrasts with an *intellectual* synthesis (*synthesis intellectualis*), "without any imagination merely through the understanding" (B152).

That the syntheses of apprehension and reproduction are both *unifying activities* plainly disqualifies them from being functions of our purely receptive sensibility.

The manifold of representations can be given in an intuition that is merely sensible, i.e., nothing but receptivity. . . . Yet the *combination* (*conjunctio*) of a manifold in general can never come to us through the senses . . . for it is an act of the spontaneity of the power of representation . . . . (B129–30)

---

[3] Kant's text literally has "calling back a perception" (*Wahrnehmung*), but his point is more general, and, indeed, in the very next paragraph his discussion continues in terms of the reproduction and association of representations (*Vorstellungen*).

If Kant is going to remain true to his account of experience as arising from the collaboration of the passive sensibility with an active understanding, then, the functions here ascribed to the imagination should turn out to be activities of the understanding—and so they do. The imagination, so to speak, has one foot in each camp. It is, in essence, the understanding *as it relates to* the sensibility.

Now since all of our intuition is sensible, the imagination on account of the subjective condition under which alone it can give a corresponding intuition to the concepts of understanding, belongs to *sensibility*; but insofar as its synthesis is still an exercise of spontaneity, ... the imagination is to this extent a faculty for determining the sensibility *a priori*; and its synthesis of intuitions, *in accordance with the categories*, must be the transcendental synthesis of *imagination*, which is an effect of the understanding on sensibility and its first application ... to objects of the intuition that is possible for us [i.e., to sensations]. (B151–2)

In the B Deduction, "insofar as imagination is spontaneity", Kant tells us, he occasionally speaks of it as the *productive* imagination,[4] in contrast to the *reproductive* imagination, "whose synthesis is subject solely to empirical laws, namely those of association, and therefore contributes nothing to the explanation of the possibility of cognition *a priori*" (B152). It is important to be clear, however, that the productive imagination also exercises a reproductive *function*, without which no "image" and no "connection of impressions" would be possible.

Kant elucidates this dual function of the imagination, apprehension and reproduction, in his example of "drawing a line in thought" (A102). In the first instance, 'drawing' is Kant's generic term for the activity of producing a representation of *something in space*, although we will see that it gradually acquires a broader sense as he proceeds.

[In] order to cognize something in space, e.g., a line, I must *draw* it, and thus synthetically bring about a determinate combination of the given [sensory] manifold .... (B137–8)

We cannot think of a line without *drawing* it in thought; we cannot think of a circle without *describing* it [i.e., tracing out its shape]; we cannot represent the three dimensions of space without *placing* three lines perpendicular to each other at the same point ... (B154)

Let us reflect for a moment on what is involved in drawing a line in thought. The operation proceeds methodically from stage to stage. It's

---

[4] In A, Kant rather speaks of the *productive synthesis* of the imagination. Cf. A118.

clear that, although the line has been "drawn" bit by bit, and so is always "decomposable" into parts, at each stage I need to hold it together, so to speak, as a single intuitable item. That's the synthesis of apprehension. From the standpoint of what I earlier called *dureé*, the process looks something like Figure 5.1.

But it's also clear that, in order to be *extending* the line bit by bit in "drawing" it, I need to *retain* the results of the earlier stages of the process and carry them over into the later stages. That's the synthesis of reproduction. Here's how Kant formulates it:

Now it is obvious that if I draw a line in thought, or think of the time from one noon to the next, or even want to represent a certain number to myself, I must necessarily first grasp one of these manifold representations after another in my thoughts. But if I were always to lose the preceding representations (the first parts of the line, the preceding parts of the time, or the successively represented units) from my thoughts and not reproduce them when I proceed to the following ones, then no whole representation and none of the previously mentioned thoughts, not even the purest and most fundamental representations of space and time, could ever arise. (A102)

As we earlier put it, what we need is not just a sequence of representations, but the representation of a sequence. In short, we need to get *time* into the picture. Enhancing our original picture to take these considerations into account, we now have Figure 5.2.

"The synthesis of apprehension is therefore inseparably combined with the synthesis of reproduction" (A102).

What Kant says here about space and time is worth emphasizing. In the Transcendental Aesthetic, space and time were, so to speak, just *given* as two unitary and indissoluble "forms of intuition" (of outer and inner

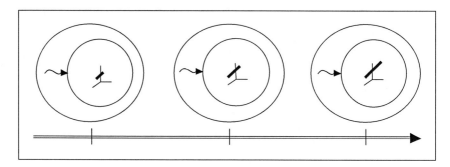

FIG. 5.1.   Successive stages of drawing a line in thought (apprehension)

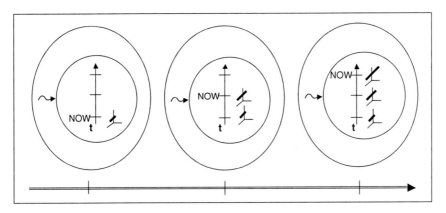

FIG. 5.2. Successive stages of drawing a line in thought (with reproduction)

sense). But both space and time can also be represented as objects which contain manifolds, e.g., of points or instants—Kant calls such representations "formal intuitions"—and then they need a function for their synthesis. The understanding (*qua* productive imagination) is thus implicated in the "most fundamental representations of space and time", i.e., even in *pure* (mathematical) chronometric and geometric representations.

Space, represented as *object* (as is really required in geometry), contains more than the mere form of intuition, namely the *comprehension*[5] of the manifold given in accordance with the form of sensibility in an *intuitive* representation, so that the *form of intuition* merely gives the manifold, but the *formal intuition* gives the unity of the representation. In the Aesthetic I ascribed this unity merely to sensibility, only in order to note that it precedes all concepts, though to be sure it presupposes a synthesis, which does not belong to the senses but through which all concepts of space and time first become possible.[6] (B160–1 n)

What Kant realized, however, was that, even when we have integrated time into our picture of perception, there is still something absolutely essential missing from this account. Crucially, I must also be able to

[5] The Guyer–Wood translation here is arguably infelicitous, but it's hard to find a significantly better one. The German is *Zusammenfassung*, literally a form of "grasping and holding together". (In contemporary German, *eine Zusammenfassung* is a *summary*.) Kemp-Smith has '*combination*' (which Guyer–Wood reserve for *Verbindung*); Pluhar has '*amalgamation*'.

[6] The third of Kant's three syntheses also turns out to be a condition of pure representations of space and time. As we shall see, this third synthesis itself depends upon what Kant calls *transcendental apperception*, and "that it deserves this name", he writes, "is already obvious from this, that even the purest objective unity, namely that of the *a priori* concepts (space and time) is possible only through the relation of the intuitions to it" (A107).

recognize what's going on at each later stage as a *continuation* of something that I have been continuously up to, a *single* ongoing activity that I was also engaged in at the earlier stages, or I am not drawing a line. Thus Kant:

Without consciousness that that which we think is the same as what we thought a moment before, all reproduction in the series of representations would be in vain. For it would be a new representation in our current state, which would not belong at all to the act through which it had been gradually generated, and its manifold would never constitute a whole . . . . If, in counting, I forget that the units that now hover before my senses were successively added to each other *by me*, then I would not cognize the generation of the multitude through this successive addition of one to the other, and consequently I would not cognize the number . . . . (A103; my emphasis)

Kant is here thinking of counting on the model of keeping a *tally* in which each added stroke is a "unit". When I reach, say '| | | |', my earlier accomplishments—'| | |', '| |', and '|'—must, as it were, still be in the picture. Unless I represent myself as having *arrived at* '| | | |' *by way of* '|', '| |', and '| | |', I am not counting.

What Kant saw, in short, is that we need to get *self-consciousness* into the picture. In his terminology, what we need to add to the contributions of the imagination is *transcendental apperception* (A107). I need a consciousness of *myself* as having begun to draw the line and then extending it further bit by bit in an orderly way, or as having begun keeping a tally and then systematically successively adding new units to it. This is a consciousness of myself *as active*, i.e., as thinking, in time. It is different from my consciousness of myself as passive, receptive, or affected, i.e., as having sense impressions.

[It] is this *one* consciousness that unifies the manifold that has been successively intuited, and then also reproduced, into one representation. This consciousness may often only be weak, so that we connect it with the generation of the representation only in the effect, but not in the act itself, i.e., immediately; but regardless of these differences one consciousness must always be found, even if it lacks conspicuous clarity, and without that concepts, and with them cognition of objects, would be entirely impossible. (A103–4)

Once again, that is, as Kant's cautionary remarks remind us, we should not expect simply to stumble introspectively across such a consciousness of oneself in the unity of action lying at the ground of perceptual experience. It is not a *datum* but rather a condition of the possibility of my thinking of myself as, e.g., drawing a line or keeping a tally that first comes properly into view in philosophical reflection on such activities. I shall represent the role of transcendental apperception in our schematic diagrams by connecting the various stages of the depicted activity to a capital letter 'I' (see Fig. 5.3).

Perhaps surprisingly, we have now also arrived at Kant's third synthesis, "the synthesis of recognition in the concept". When we understand how and why, we will have gained an essential insight into the Transcendental Deduction as a whole.

Transcendental apperception, rules, and concepts

I have several times mentioned the fact that such activities as drawing a line in thought and counting (keeping a tally) proceed in an *orderly* or *methodical* or *systematic* way. Kant speaks in this connection of the *unity of a rule* (A105). Consider again the example of counting. The rule "*add a stroke*" governs each transition from stage to stage: $| \rightarrow | | \rightarrow | | | \rightarrow | | | |$, etc. In thinking of what I am doing as keeping a tally, I represent each stage as something that *I* produce by applying the (same) rule to what *I* produced in the preceding stage. Thereby I necessarily presuppose that

the I who writes '|' = the I who writes '| |' = the I who writes '| | |' = the I who writes '| | | |'.

There is, in other words, an essential interplay between apperceptive self-consciousness and the activity of carrying out a construction according to a rule. Kant's Strategy K is beginning to emerge.

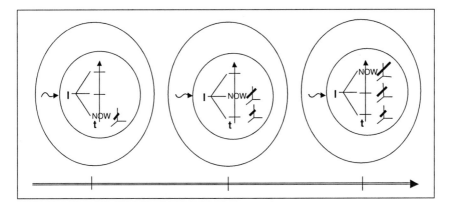

FIG. 5.3. Successive stages of drawing a line in thought (with apperception)

Drawing a line is also a construction carried out according to a rule. What rule? Kant's answer is: *the concept of a line*. "As far as its form is concerned," Kant tells us, a concept, "is always something general, and something that serves as a rule" (A106). I am "guided by a rule" insofar as I "act under a concept". As Wittgenstein has reminded us, I do not *consult* the concept (*qua* rule) (*Philosophical Investigations PI*, §§217–19). Rather I represent my activity *in terms of* the concept, i.e., *as* drawing a line, and I thereby "know how to go on". In Wittgenstein's well-known example, insofar as I represent myself as "counting by two's" and "know how to go on"—2, 4, 6, 8, 10, . . . —it is the rule '{+2}' that determines what I say next (*PI*, §§185 ff.).

The key point for understanding the subjective deduction is that, on Kant's account, a consciousness of oneself as *passive*, as having perceptions, *also* requires this kind of rule-guided, concept-structured activity.

The objective unity of all (empirical) consciousness in one consciousness (of original apperception) is . . . the necessary condition even of all possible perception . . . . (A123)

To be perceptually aware of determinate intuitable items, we need to "draw them in thought", i.e., to construct appropriate "images" from the raw materials of the sensory manifold according to concepts *qua* rules. The mere representation of items in space, that is, presupposes a synthesis of representations across time (and conversely, as the Refutation of Idealism will demonstrate).

Thus the concept of body serves as a rule for our cognition of outer appearances by means of the unity of the manifold that is thought through it. However, it can be a rule for intuitions only if it represents the necessary reproduction of the manifold of given [appearances[7]], hence the synthetic unity in the consciousness of them. Thus in the case of the perception of something outside of us the concept of body makes necessary the representation of extension, and with it that of impenetrability, of shape, etc. (A106)

That is how Kant's third synthesis, the "synthesis of recognition in a concept", is related to the role of apperceptive self-consciousness in perception. "It is this apperception that must be added to the pure imagination in order to make its function intellectual" (A124). And with the emergence of an indispensable role for concepts in perception, we

---

[7] Guyer–Wood here has 'intuitions', but the German *Erscheinungen* clearly requires 'appearances'.

have finally made contact with Kant's characterization of experience as arising from the cooperation of a passive sensibility and an active understanding. For we are now in a position to elucidate the relationship between this earlier "doctrine of two sources" and the present account of "an experience in general and cognition of its objects" as resting on "three subjective sources of cognition: *sense, imagination*, and *apperception*" (A115). For if 'sense' still adverts to the contribution of the receptive sensibility, i.e., the sensory manifold that is the first product of our being affected, then the contribution of the spontaneous understanding must be the "threefold synthesis" which results from the operations of 'imagination' and 'apperception'—and so it is.

The unity of apperception in relation to the synthesis of the imagination is the *understanding*. (A119)

Consequently, we can now relatively straightforwardly at least *locate* the threefold synthesis with respect to our earlier picture of Kantian perception. The understanding in the role of the productive imagination determines the way in which I take up the manifold of sense into an "image", i.e., a singular representation of an object in space. As the concept of a line functions as a rule guiding the activity of "drawing a line in thought", when I perceive, e.g., a thick green book, the *concept of a book* functions as a rule guiding the activity of constructing the singular representation of an object in space which is my "image" of the book. Bracketing temporarily the important details regarding time and apperception, yields the picture shown in Figure 5.4.

The idea that a *concept* can determine an *image* may initially seem implausible. Here it is useful to consider such "ambiguous figures" as the Necker Cube or Jastrow's "duck–rabbit" (Fig. 5.5). A little experimentation will confirm that the deliberate decision to see the figure one way rather than another—i.e., thinking of it in terms of one concept rather than another—can appreciably change the "look" of the printed image, despite the fact that it, of course, does not undergo any *physical* change on the page.

So far we have seen only that, insofar as apperception secures an essential role for the understanding in perceptual synthesis, "appearances", as Kant puts it—that is, objects as we encounter them in perception—"have a *necessary relation to the understanding*" (A119). Consequently we next need to explore in more detail the way in which apperceptive self-consciousness is related to concepts and the understanding. As Kant

Perceptual Synthesis

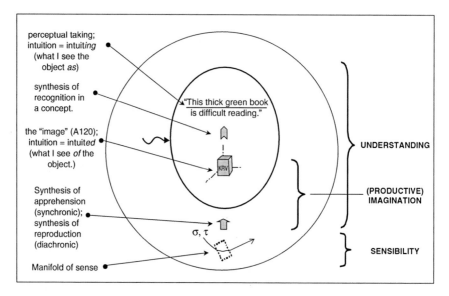

FIG. 5.4. Kantian perception and the "threefold synthesis"

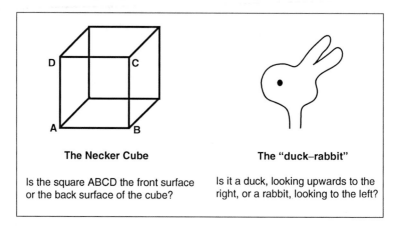

FIG. 5.5. Ambiguous figures: concepts can determine images

himself reminds us, he has already explained the understanding in a variety of ways

through a spontaneity of cognition (in contrast to the receptivity of the sensibility), through a faculty for thinking, or a faculty of concepts, or also of judgments,

explanations which, he adds, are essentially equivalent when properly interpreted. Now, he continues, we can characterize it as the *faculty of rules*. This designation is more fruitful and comes closer to its essence. Sensibility gives us forms (of intuition), but the understanding gives us rules. (A126)

Earlier, when we were exploring Kant's innovative account of concepts, we originally met the understanding in the form of a faculty for thinking. Since thinking is cognition through concepts, and concepts are predicates of possible judgments, the understanding was also identified as a faculty for judging, and the categories, i.e., the pure concepts of the understanding, first emerged in the guise of *forms of judgment*. From the present perspective, in contrast, we can think of the categories as the most general *rules for generating perceptual takings*, i.e., for making something "an object of representations" (A104).

The *a priori* conditions of a possible experience in general are at the same time conditions of the possibility of the objects of experience. Now I assert that the *categories* [enumerated earlier] are nothing other than the *conditions of thinking in a possible experience*, just as *space* and *time* contain the conditions of the *intuition* for the very same thing. They are therefore also fundamental concepts for thinking objects in general for the appearances, and they therefore have *a priori* objective validity, which was just what we really wanted to know. (A111; cf. A158/B197)

To come at the central point from another angle, what Kant saw was that to think of oneself as, for instance, seeing a thick green book is, first, to think of *what* one sees (the "object of representations") as an item with its own spatio-temporal history, i.e., an item *in nature*, and consequently, crucially, to think of one's ostensible perceptual encounter with this item as an episode in *two* histories, namely, *its* history and *one's own* history, i.e., to think of oneself as being *affected by* an item in nature.

We can consequently say that, at a certain very high level of generality, every perception has the *same* form, the form of an *encounter* between a subject and an object. To think of something present in intuition *as* an object of representation is, however schematically, to commit oneself to the in-principle possibility of filling in both *its* history as an item in nature, i.e., in a lawful system of spatio-temporal items, and *one's own* history as an experiencer of this nature here and now in perceptual encounter with it.[8] That is what Kant means when he writes that

---

[8] Contemporary phenomenologists speak in this connection of perceptual experiences as having "horizons".

There is only *one* experience in which all perceptions are represented as in thoroughgoing and lawlike connection, just as there is only one space and time, in which all forms of appearance and all relation of being or non-being take place. If one speaks of different experiences, they are only so many perceptions insofar as they belong to one and the same universal experience. The thoroughgoing and synthetic unity of perceptions is precisely what constitutes the form of experience, and it is nothing other than the synthetic unity of the appearances in accordance with concepts. (A110)

The form of experience, at least as far as this part of the First Critique is concerned, in other words is: an identical self persisting through time in relation to a systematic world of spatio-temporal items that affect it. Let's consider an example. In Figure 5.6 we see one experience of several successively perceived items. My productive imagination is busily react-

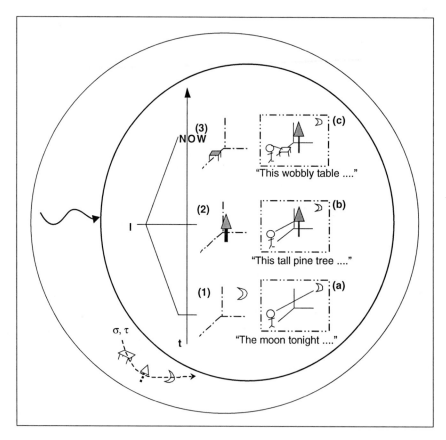

FIG. 5.6. A complex perceptual experience: taking in a scene

ing to the manifold of sense. First I notice the lovely crescent moon, then the stately pine tree, and now I am observing the wobbly table beneath it. I represent (1), (2), and (3) as encounters with objects in nature—the moon, a tree, a table—and so now think of myself as being in the situation depicted in the cartoon (c).

Now in order for me to pull together (1), (2), and (3) into a perceptual encounter with a complex scene, I need to be able to think them all as *my* successive perceptions. I must be able, that is, to form something like the representation

I perceive [(1) and then (2) and then (3)],

e.g., "I see the crescent moon shining on a stately pine tree next to a wobbly table". This is an instance of what Kant calls "the principle of the necessary unity of apperception" (B135), namely, that

the manifold representations that are given in a certain intuition would not all together be *my* representations if they did not all together belong to one self-consciousness; i.e., as my representations (even if I am not conscious of them as such) they must yet necessarily be in accord with the condition under which alone they *can* stand together in a universal self-consciousness, because otherwise they would not throughout belong to me. (B132–3)

This is in essence just the proposition that it must be possible for *me* to think all *my* representations collectively as *mine*, and it is in one sense, Kant tells us, as uninformative as it sounds. It is "itself identical, and thus an analytical proposition" (B135); that is, it is *analytic.*

What Kant saw, however, was that this prima facie uninformative analytic proposition is actually the key that unlocks the whole Transcendental Deduction, for, unlike Descartes, he explicitly recognized that it is a *different* analytic proposition from the principle that it must be possible for me to think *each* of my representations *severally* as mine.

The *I think* must *be able* to accompany all my representations, for otherwise something would be represented in me that could not be thought at all, which is as much as to say that the representation would either be impossible or else at least nothing for me. (B131–2)[9]

This proposition tells us only that, if I successively perceive (1), (2), and (3), then I must be able to form something like the representations

---

[9] Cf. "All intuitions are nothing for us and do not in the least concern us if they cannot be taken up into consciousness, whether they influence it directly or indirectly, and through this alone is cognition possible" (A116).

I perceive (1); I perceive (2); I perceive (3).

But, as we observed earlier, the proposition

(I) I think X & I think Y & I think Z

does not by itself imply the "analytical unity of apperception"

(II) I, who think X = I, who think Y = I, who think Z.

For the empirical consciousness that accompanies different representations is by itself dispersed and without relation to the identity of the subject. The latter relation therefore does not yet come about by my accompanying each representation with consciousness . . . . (B133)

When Descartes unreflectively treated (I) as sufficient to establish (II), he was, Kant realized, making exactly the same sort of mistake that Hume made when he treated the fact that

(i) a representation of α is followed by a representation of β

as sufficient to establish that

(ii) α is followed by β.

Just as a succession of representations, (i), is not yet what is required in order to ground (ii), namely, the representation of a succession,

(iii) a representation of [α followed by β],

so, too, the possibility of *separate* self-ascriptions, (I), does not suffice to ground the thoroughgoing identity of the self, (II). Rather, "the *analytical* unity of apperception is possible only under the presupposition of some *synthetic* one" (B133), that is, schematically, the possibility of

(III) I think [X + Y + Z].

[It] is only because I can combine a manifold of given representations *in one consciousness* that it is possible for me to represent the *identity of the consciousness in these representations* . . . . (B133)

Only if (III) is possible, will (II) follow from (I). (See Figure 5.7.)

Notice that this is a claim in the mode of possibility. "All representations have a necessary relation to a *possible* empirical consciousness" (A117n.). I do not need to actually *be* conscious of my representations *as mine*, but if they *are* mine, then it must be possible for me to think them *as* mine. And from this it follows that those representations themselves

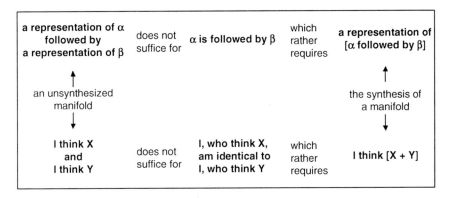

FIG. 5.7. Hume's time and Descartes' self: parallel mistakes

must satisfy the necessary conditions of my so thinking them—whatever those necessary conditions might turn out to be (B132–3).

It is also worth noticing that Kant explicitly restricts his conclusion to creatures like us, whose intuitable manifolds are all *passively* given, through a receptive sensibility.

This principle . . . is not a principle for every possible understanding, but only for one through whose pure apperception in the representation *I am* nothing manifold is given at all. That understanding through whose self-consciousness the manifold of intuition would at the same time be given . . . would not require a special act of synthesis of the manifold for the unity of consciousness, which the human understanding . . . does require. (B138; cf. B145)

For it is precisely because we have no *intuition* of the experiencing self, because *I am* contains no intuitable manifold—"This *representation* is a *thinking*, not an *intuiting*" (B157)—that we cannot appeal to "criteria of personal identity" to mediate the inference of (II) from (I).

Objects of representation

Kant concludes, then, that the *modes of synthesis* represented by the '+'s in (III) are necessarily prior to and presupposed by the *unity of the subject* represented by the '='s in (II).

The thought that these representations given in intuition all together belong *to me* means . . . the same as that I unite them in one self-consciousness, or at least can unite them therein, and although it is itself not yet the consciousness of the *synthesis* of the representations, it still presupposes the possibility of the latter;

i.e., only because I can comprehend[10] their manifold in a consciousness do I call them all together *my* representations, for otherwise I would have as multicolored, diverse a self as I have representations of which I am conscious. Synthetic unity of the manifold of intuitions . . . is thus the ground of the identity of apperception itself, which precedes *a priori* all *my* determinate thinking. (B134)

But what are those modes of synthesis? What Kant proceeds to argue is that there is really only one most generic and most fundamental mode of synthesis, and that is the synthesis of intuitions *under the categories*, i.e., a synthesis guided by the concept of an *object*. Our next job, therefore, is to understand *why* and *how* the fact that my representations must satisfy the necessary conditions of my thinking of them *as* mine implies that my experience must be of categorially structured objects.

To this end, the first point that we need to remember is that the fundamental activity of the mind, so to speak, is perceptually representing *determinate individuals*. "[T]he representations of *outer sense* make up the proper material with which we occupy our mind . . . ." (B67).[11]

The synthetic unity of apperception is the highest point to which one must affix all use of the understanding, even the whole of logic . . . . (B134 n).[12]

In particular, the nature and function of *concepts* can be understood only in relation to intuitive representations of determinate individuals.

It is entirely contradictory and impossible that a concept should be generated completely *a priori* and be related to an object although it neither belongs itself within the concept of possible experience nor consists of elements of a possible experience. For it would then have no content, since no intuition would corres-

---

[10] This is one of those places where a bit of German is helpfully suggestive. What is here translated as 'comprehend' is *begreifen*, the verb corresponding to the noun *Begriff*, i.e., concept.

[11] Cf. B147: "[All] mathematical concepts are not by themselves cognitions, except insofar as one presupposes that there are things that can be presented to us only in accordance with the form of that pure sensible intuition. *Things in space* and *time*, however, are given only insofar as they are perceptions (representations accompanied with sensation), hence through empirical representation. The pure concepts of the understanding, consequently, even if they are applied to *a priori* intuitions (as in mathematics), provide cognition only insofar as these *a priori* intuitions . . . can be applied to empirical intuitions." In other words, even pure mathematics depends on the possibility of perceptual representations of determinate individuals in space and time.

[12] The sentence, and thereby the footnote, concludes with the provocative remark that "indeed this faculty [i.e., apperception] is the understanding itself". In a later footnote, in contrast, we find: "It is one and the same spontaneity that, there under the name of imagination and here under the name of understanding, brings combination into the manifold of intuition" (B162 n.). And, in A, we have already noted Kant's claim that "*The unity of apperception in relation to the synthesis of the imagination* is the *understanding*" (A119). It is clearly not easy to bring all these claims about the identity of the understanding together into one coherent story.

pond to it although intuitions in general... constitute the field... of possible experience. An *a priori* concept that was not related to [possible experience] would be only the logical form for a concept, but not the concept itself through which something would be thought. (A95; cf. A135–6/B175)

If I think of "*red* in general", I represent something that is in the first instance a property of intuited items: this red book, pencil, sweater, apple, etc. That is, in thinking "*red* in general", I represent something that I, as a unitary *subject*, could experientially encounter on multiple occasions in various circumstances:

I thereby represent to myself a feature that (as a mark) can be encountered in anything, or that can be combined with other representations; therefore only by means of an antecedently conceived possible synthetic unity can I represent to myself the analytical unity. (B134n.)

Correlatively, the ability to think general thoughts, e.g., "All bodies are heavy", presupposes the ability to represent the properties thereby thought as universally related to each other as combined in an individual object, e.g., "This heavy body..." (B142). On Kant's view, we recall, concepts are *essentially* judgmental in form. The basic function of a concept, as a principle of unity, is to be the sort of thing that multiple items can be *predicatively* brought under as instances. Hence, the application of concepts presupposes the availability of logical subjects, and ultimately *determinate* logical subjects.

The second point that we need to emphasize is that, at least for us human beings, representing determinate individuals is a *perspectival* business. Objects in space and time are seen or imagined from a *point of view*. To represent an intuited item in a perceptual judgment, e.g., "This K...",

---

Here it is perhaps useful to recall Kant's first characterization of the imagination as "a blind but indispensable function of the soul" (A78/B103). Given that, in formulating his "doctrine of two sources", Kant notoriously observed that "intuitions without concepts are blind" (A51/B75), we might interpret this later reference to the "blindness" of the imagination as the claim that the syntheses of imagination alone can't yield *cognitions*. For this, the third element of the "threefold synthesis" is needed, i.e., "the synthesis of recognition in the concept", and that, as we have seen, crucially depends on the faculty of apperception, i.e., the ability to think of *oneself* as a unitary subject. When Kant writes in B that "the transcendental synthesis of *imagination*,... is an effect of the understanding on sensibility" (B152), then, his thought seems to be that, although considered entirely apart from the conditions of human sensibility, the understanding would just *be* apperception, in relation to human sensibility, it necessarily also plays the synthesizing role of the imagination.

I must, so to speak, present myself with a referent for the '*This*' by "drawing" it in thought.[13] A *determinate* intuition

is possible only through the consciousness of the determination of the manifold through the transcendental action of the imagination (synthetic influence of the understanding on the inner sense) which I have named the figurative synthesis. (B154)

When we put these two points together, we are led to a stratum of perceptual representings in which the synthesis of the manifold of sense "pulls together" many diverse *views* or *aspects* of a single *object*.

Let's explore Figure 5.8. To begin with, although books are necessarily *seen* or *imagined* from a point of view, there is nothing perspectival about books as such. Each "image" is perspectival—an image of a-book-from-a-point-of-view—but the object *conceived* is not perspectival. To perceive the book *as* a book, I need to take up the manifold of sense—(a), (b), (c)—in such a way that what results are the images (1), (2), (3) and their associated judgments. My productive imagination must react to the manifold of sense by "drawing", i.e., constructing, the "images" (1), (2), (3) and conceiving them *as* aspects of (views of, encounters with) *one* object, a thick green book.

In B, Kant calls the way in which (1), (2), and (3) "hang together" the "synthesis of apprehension".

[By] the *synthesis of apprehension* I understand the composition of the manifold in an empirical intuition through which perception, i.e., empirical consciousness of it (as appearance), becomes possible. (B160)

As we have seen, this synthesis of apprehension arises from two sources: the passive receptivity of sensibility, which provides the sensory "raw materials" that constitute the "matter" of the intuited items, and the active spontaneity of understanding, which accounts for the sort of *intelligibility* manifested by the succession of images (1), (2), (3), i.e., their "form". In A, Kant calls this intelligible form the *affinity* of the intuited manifold.

There must . . . be an objective ground . . . on which rests the possibility . . . of a law extending through all appearances, a law, namely, for regarding them throughout

---

[13] It is perhaps worth noticing that the German word here translated as 'drawing' is not *zeichnen* (sketching or drafting), but *ziehen*, whose basic meaning is *pulling*. Kant's root metaphor for "drawing a line", we might say, is something like "drawing *out* (stretching, elongating) a given (starting) point". Correlatively, we metaphorically "draw" an object of intuition by "drawing (pulling) *together* a manifold of sensations" into a unified image.

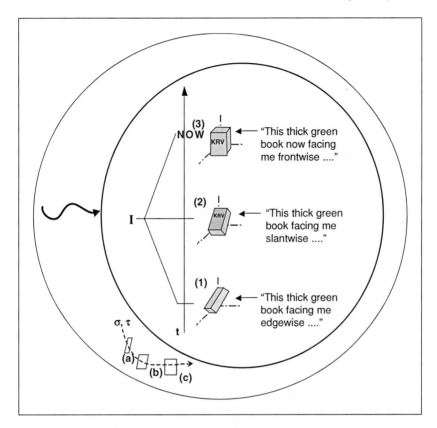

FIG. 5.8. Perceptual synthesis: various views of a single object

as data of sense that are associable in themselves and subject to universal laws of a thoroughgoing connection in reproduction. I call this objective ground of all association of appearances their *affinity*. (A122; cf. A113)

The affinity of the images (1), (2), (3), in other words, consists in their "hanging together" perspectively in such a way that they are "associable" *as* multiple views of a single thick green book. What accounts for this affinity, Kant tells is, is that the images have been constructed in accordance with a *rule*, namely, the *concept* of a book.[14]

---

[14] This is not to say that the world doesn't also need to be suitably cooperative. Kant has, in fact, mentioned this a bit earlier, in his remarks about cinnabar at A100–1; but the clearest formulation of the point actually comes much later, in Kant's discussion of "the logical law of genera" at A653–4/ B681–2. He there concludes that "the logical principle of genera ... presupposes a transcendental one if it is to be applied to nature (by which I here understand only objects that are given to us). According to that principle, sameness of kind (*Gleichartigkeit*) is necessarily presupposed in the

Think of a jigsaw puzzle. The colors and shapes of the individual puzzle pieces correspond to the diverse images (the intuit*eds*) in our example; the pictorial motif of the puzzle, to their conceptual representation in judgments (the intuit*ings*). It is only because the colors and shapes of the puzzle pieces "hang together" in the right way that we are able to "synthesize" the pictorial motif of the puzzle out of them. Similarly, it is only because the diverse images "hang together" in the right way that I am able to conceive them *as* views of *one* thick green book. Now the shapes and colors of the puzzle pieces *do* hang together in the right way, and the *reason* that they do, of course, is that we made the pieces by cutting up the picture. The pictorial motif of the puzzle thus functions to *determine* the colors and shapes of the pieces in such a way that it is subsequently possible to assemble them into just that picture. Kant's thesis, analogously, is that *the concept of a book* functions to *determine* the images that I "draw" when responding to the manifold of sense in such a way that it is possible to conceive of them as aspects of just that object. His own example is not a book but a house.

Thus if, e.g., I make the empirical intuition of a house into perception through apprehension of its manifold, my ground is the *necessary unity* of space and of outer sensible intuition in general, and I as it were draw its shape in agreement with this synthetic unity of the manifold in space. This very same synthetic unity, however, if I abstract from the form of space, has its seat in the understanding.... (B162)

In other words, when I take up a sensory manifold as a perception of a house, I construct a *perspectival* image of a house as situated thus-and-so in space. If, however, I "abstract from the form of space", that is, consider only the *non*-perspectival *predicative* concept of a house, I find that "this very same synthetic unity" "has its seat in the understanding". That is, the non-perspectival concept 'house' *both* functions as a rule guiding the construction of the perspectival image *and* is mobilized in the corresponding perceptual *judgment*.[15]

manifold of a possible experience (even though we cannot determine its degree *a priori*), because without it no empirical concepts and hence no experience would be possible" (A654/B682). I am grateful to Kenneth Westphal for calling my attention to these passages.

[15] In this connection it is perhaps also useful to consider the way in which the construction of a house can be guided by blueprints, or the ways in which an object can both determine and be determined by the various views or "elevations" produced by a draftsman at his drawing board.

Parenthetically, in the balance of the cited passage, Kant himself concludes that what "has its seat in the understanding" is "the category of the synthesis of the homogeneous in an intuition in general, i.e., the category of *quantity*" (B162). His account thus clearly operates at a higher level of abstraction than my own, but, as we shall see when we come to discuss the "Axioms of Intuition", our conclusions are entirely compatible.

At this point, it is dangerously tempting to interpret Kant "reductively", as the sort of analytical *phenomenalist* for whom the object, e.g., the book, *consists of* the intuited items (the perspectival "images") which do or would occur in such perceptual experiences. This would be a serious mistake. The conceptual content 'book' indeed functions in the *determination* of those sequences of representings (mental acts) which count as perspectival perceptual encounters with a book. But the *object* of such perceptual representations of a book is *not* itself such a sequence of representings (actual or possible), and, correlatively, the *concept* of a book is not the concept of a mental content or sequence of mental contents, but rather the concept of such an object of representations. This, Kant tells us, is why the content of a perceptual experience can be articulated in the form of a *judgment*, since "a judgment is nothing other than the way to bring given cognitions to the *objective* unity of apperception" (B141).

Insofar as successive apprehensions are experienced as encounters with (views or aspects of) a single object of representation, that is, they are *necessarily* related to each other.

Only in this way does there arise from this relation a *judgment*, i.e., a relation that is *objectively valid*, and that is sufficiently distinguished from the relation of these same representations in which there would be only subjective validity, e.g., in accordance with the laws of association. In accordance with the latter I could only say "If I carry a body, I feel a pressure of weight," but not "It, the body, *is* heavy," which would be to say that these two representations are combined in the object, i.e., regardless of any differences in the condition of the subject, and are not merely found together in perception (however often as that might be repeated). (B142)

Analytical phenomenalism, in short, precisely cannot account for the *necessity* attaching to the belonging-together *in perception* of what is combined *in an object*.

But what does it mean to say, for instance, that the book is an object of representations? Kant himself explicitly raises the question at A104, and he begins by observing that the thesis of transcendental idealism evidently renders the matter particularly acute.

We have said above that appearances themselves are nothing but sensible representations, which must not be regarded in themselves . . . as objects (outside the power of representation). What does one mean, then, if one speaks of an object corresponding to and therefore also distinct from the cognition? (A104)

The question is a central one, which accompanies Kant throughout the First Critique, reappearing later, for example, (along with the example of the house) in connection with his discussion of causation in the Second Analogy.

Now one can, to be sure, call everything, and even every representation, insofar as one is conscious of it, an object; only what this word is to mean in the case of appearances, not insofar as they are (as representations) objects, but rather only insofar as they designate an object, requires a deeper investigation. (A189–90/B234–5)

The answer that he gives at both places is the same. The object is that aspect of the contents of perceptual experience which contains "the condition of [a] necessary rule of apprehension" that "makes one way of combining the manifold necessary" (A191/B236). Somewhat more clearly:

We find . . . that our thought of the relation of all cognition to its object carries something of necessity with it, since namely the latter is regarded as that which is opposed to our cognitions being determined at pleasure or arbitrarily rather than being determined *a priori* in a certain way, since insofar as they are to relate to an object our cognitions must also necessarily agree with each other in relation to it, i.e., they must have that unity that constitutes the concept of an object. (A104–5)

The basic point being made at both places is that the concept of an object of representations is the concept of something that *explains* something. The concept of a book, for instance, insofar as a book is an object of representations, is *not* the concept of an intelligible and coherent series of (actual and possible) apprehensions, but rather the concept of something which *explains* the intelligibility and coherence of such a series of apprehensions. *What* is explained is the intelligible perspectival hanging-together of successively intuited items *in the subject* that makes possible the perceptual synthesis which is the most fundamental condition of the unity of apperception, the thoroughgoing identity of the 'I' who experiences and thinks.

[The] unity that the object makes necessary can be nothing other than the formal unity of the consciousness in the synthesis of the manifold of representations. (A105)

It is important to appreciate both the ingenuity and the implications of Kant's analysis here. He is carefully steering a course between the Scylla and Charybdis of two wrong answers to the question "What is the object X that is the object of a series of representations?":

(A) *Analytical Phenomenalism*: The object X *consists of* the series of actual representings, along with other (conditionally determinate) possible representings.

(B) *Representative Realism*: The object X is something formally real (existing in itself) that *corresponds to* the series of actual representings.

As we have seen, however, Kant is quite clear that, *contra* (A), the concept of an object of representations is the concept of "an object corresponding to and therefore also distinct from the cognition" (A104). And he also argues that, *contra* (B), since "we have to do only with the manifold of our representations", a *formally real* X which was supposed to correspond to them would be "nothing for us" (A105).

Kant himself rejects the question, at least when it is posed in the form that leads to such traditional answers. We should not try to say what the object of a series of representations *is*.

It is easy to see that this object must be thought of only as something in general = X, since outside of our cognition we have nothing that we could set over against this cognition as corresponding to it. (A104)

We must rather explain what it means to say that particular representations are "of an object". What we need to understand, in other words, is the *concept* of an object of representations. It is the concept of an item which explains something, namely, the synthetic unity of apprehension in the subject.

An *object* . . . is that *in the concept of which* the manifold of a given intuition is *united*. (B137, 2nd emphasis mine)

What Kant proposes to elucidate, in short, is not the "metaphysical/ontological" predicate 'is an object of representations' but rather the "semantic/epistemic" predicate 'is the *concept of* an object of representations' or, as I shall put it for the sake of brevity, 'is an *object-concept*'. He explains this *meta*-conceptual notion, in turn, with reference to the *synthesizing role* of such concepts, i.e., their function as principles of the unity of apprehension in the most fundamental sort of perceptual synthesis which is a condition of the possibility of the unity of apperceptive consciousness in the experiencing subject.

Thus the original and necessary consciousness of the identity of oneself is at the same time a consciousness of an equally necessary unity of the synthesis of all appearances in accordance with concepts, i.e., in accordance with rules that not only make them necessarily reproducible, but also thereby determine an object for their intuition, i.e., *the concept of something in which they are necessarily connected* . . . . (A108, my emphasis)

Thus a book is the object of the series of representings (1), (2), (3) in Figure 5.8 above by virtue of its *concept* being that aspect of the corresponding perceptual takings—"this thick green *book* facing me edgewise (slantwise, frontwise)"—that, together with other factors, explains the belonging-together of these apprehensions as states of the perceiving subject. The concept of a book is the concept of an item which determines the way in which the apprehensions hang together. By reference to the way in which the conceptual content *book*, together with other factors, functions as a rule guiding the construction of the intuited images, we can explain the *necessity* of just this sequence of perspectival perceptual takings.

The "other factors" entering into such an explanation are, of course, the relationships between the experienced object and the perceiving subject. What yields perspectival individual concepts of the form "this book in such-and-such determinate relations to me (the subject)", in other words, is the content *book* together with a conception of myself as a *co-participant in nature* (the world). My consciousness of the way in which the apprehensions—(1), (2), and (3)—hang together requires that I am simultaneously conscious of them both as *mine* and as aspects of an object in nature (i.e., views of a book). My consciousness of myself as passive, as having perceptual experiences, requires (a) a consciousness of objects in nature, which requires (b) that I "draw" such objects in accordance with their concepts functioning as rules, which in turn requires (c) a consciousness of myself as *active.*

[F]or the mind could not possibly think of the identity of itself in the manifoldness of its representations . . . if it did not have before its eyes the identity of its action, which subjects all synthesis of apprehension (which is empirical) to a transcendental unity. . . . (A108)

The relation of the object of representation to an experiencer's perceptual representings of it is thus what C. S. Peirce termed *abductive.* The object is a necessarily *postulated* item whose actuality *explains* the coherence and intelligibility of the apprehended manifold in the perceiving subject. The most general concept of such an object is thus the "concept of something in which [appearances] are necessarily connected" (A108).

The pure concept of this transcendental object (which in all our cognitions is really always one and the same = X) is that which in all our empirical concepts in general can provide relation to an object, i.e., objective reality. Now this concept cannot contain any determinate intuition at all, and therefore concerns nothing but that unity which must be encountered in a manifold of cognition insofar as it stands in relation to an object. This relation, however, is nothing other than the necessary unity of consciousness, thus also of the synthesis of the manifold through a common function of the mind for combining it in one representation. (A109)

What Kant is saying here is that there is one *generic* concept of an object of which all our *empirical* object-concepts, i.e., concepts of particular *kinds* of objects (books, houses, trees, pencils, etc.), are specifications. When we abstract from the specific differences of our concepts of kinds of objects, we also abstract from all *determinate* sensory content and perspectival orientation. What remains is the concept of something that explains the perspectival hanging-together of *any* sensory manifold insofar as it can be perceptually synthesized into a representation of *one (spatio-temporal) item* (in nature), multiply encountered by *one self-identical subject.*

I have several times represented Kant as arguing that this most fundamental sort of perceptual synthesis is a condition of the possibility of the unity of apperceptive consciousness in the experiencing subject. In fact, however, his thesis is a significantly stronger one, namely, that this sort of perceptual synthesis is *the* condition of the possibility of the transcendental unity of apperception. That is, Kant in essence seems to be claiming that the *only* way to validate the inference from, (I), "I think X & I think Y & I think Z" to, (II), "I, who think X = I, who think Y = I, who think Z" is by a synthesis, (III), "I think [X + Y + Z]" in which X, Y, and Z are synthesized *as* multiple encounters with a single item. But that isn't quite right.

Consider, for example, (P), "I felt [an itch followed by a twinge followed by an ache]". Here we plainly have "a manifold of representations combined in one consciousness" (B133) in a way that posits no single, multiply encounterable object of representations. Such syntheses of representations of *inner* sense are clearly possible, and we might consequently wonder whether, at least in principle, *all* the syntheses required for the thoroughgoing unity of apperception could be of this sort, that is, syntheses in which the apprehended items are conceptually represented as *states of the experiencing subject.*

Kant's answer is: "No". That what we really experience are only ("mind-dependent") states of ourselves is the thesis of *empirical idealism,* and Kant not only rejects it but, as we will see, also explicitly undertakes to refute it. The crucial point, to anticipate, is that the temporal synthesis in (P) presupposes a determinate *objective* time-order. What Kant will argue is that securing such a time-order requires that there be *some* manifolds of apprehension which are synthesized under *object-concepts*, i.e., *as* multiple encounters with one "mind-independent" object. That is not the *only* way that we relate apprehensions in a synthesis, but it is the *basic* or *fundamental* way that we do so, and the possibility of other sorts of synthesis, e.g., of "inner" manifolds, depends on and presupposes it.

This will become fully clear, however, only after we have explored the Analogies of Experience. Their fundamental theme will be that *time is not perceived*. Time-order consequently cannot be "extracted from" experience, but must be "read into" it. I need to *construct* a unitary objective time-order by appealing to *causal laws* pertaining to *persisting substances* in systematic interaction. Although I have now essentially completed my discussion of the A and B texts of Kant's Transcendental Deduction, then, the Transcendental Deduction itself won't be complete until we have worked through the Analogies and the Refutation of Idealism.[16] This is a good time, therefore, for us to move on into the Analytic of Principles, and so—after one more short digression—that is what I shall do.

Apperception and inner sense

The short digression concerns Kant's somewhat difficult discussion, near the end of the B Deduction, of

the paradox that must have struck everyone in the exposition of the form of inner sense: namely how this presents even ourselves to consciousness only as we appear to ourselves, not as we are in ourselves . . . . (B152)

The account offered in the Aesthetic based this conclusion on our sensory *passivity*, arguing that "we intuit ourselves only as we are internally *affected*", but this, Kant now observes, "seems to be contradictory, since

---

[16] i.e., the Transcendental Deduction in the sense of the Big Picture that I sketched in Ch. 2. Strictly speaking, of course, 'the Transcendental Deduction' picks out only a particular stretch of text in the First Critique (A95–130, B129–69). But then one can get *really* fussy, and notice that the heading for §26 in the B Deduction (B159) reads "Transcendental deduction of the universally possible use of the pure concepts of the understanding in experience"—which suggests that the Transcendental Deduction *per se* is about to be presented—and also that, in the very first paragraph of that section, Kant writes that "in the *transcendental deduction* [the possibility of the categories] as *a priori* cognitions of objects of an intuition in general was exhibited (§§20, 21)"—which surely suggests that at least *a* Transcendental Deduction has *already* been presented. Such observations are the lifeblood of Apollonian Kant scholarship, but, given the Dionysian spirit of the present work, we won't trouble ourselves with them here.

we would have to relate to ourselves passively" (B153). The result, he says, is that it has become customary in systems of psychology to *identify* inner sense and apperception—and that is a mistake. Kant consequently proposes to revisit the topic of inner sense in light of his newly won insights into the role of the understanding in experience.

Inner sense is the capacity to be affected by states of oneself in such a way that one can come to represent them *as* states of oneself. It contains, Kant tells us,

the mere *form* of intuition, but without combination of the manifold in it, and thus it does not contain any *determinate* intuition at all .... (B154)

"The mere form of intuition" contained in inner sense is, in first approximation, *a sequence of representations of representations* (*as* representations). Pictorially, we have Figure 5.9.

The crucial point is that this "mere form" doesn't yet tell us what the represented representations *themselves* represent, i.e., what they are representations *of*. For that, we would need to fill in the little "thought balloons", ultimately with representations of *outer* sense, that is, of items in space. For even though applications of inner sense can be iterated, i.e., we can also have (meta-meta-) representations of (meta-) representations of representations, a *determinate* "inner" experience couldn't, as it were, "bottom out" in empty balloons.

Apperception, in contrast, "applies to all sensible intuition of objects in general, to the manifold of *intuitions in general*". That is, the synthetic unity

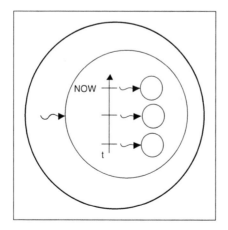

FIG. 5.9. A "mere form of intuition"

of apperception necessarily characterizes *both* outer *and* inner experiences. Both families of representations must satisfy the necessary conditions for being combined in *one* consciousness, i.e., for being *my* representations (see Fig. 5.10).

In both OS and IS, the understanding (*qua* productive imagination) is *actively* responding to an instance of being *passively* affected. In each case, we have a "figurative synthesis", i.e., a "determination of the manifold through the transcendental action of the imagination" (B154). OS is a perceptual experience. The productive imagination is apprehending a manifold of outer sense, i.e., of sensations, and constructing images of objects in space. IS, in contrast, is an *introspective* experience. The productive imagination is apprehending a manifold of inner sense, i.e., of representations, and constructing representations of mental episodes (representings) as occurrences in time.

In each case, however, the understanding is *active*, and, in each case, "since in us humans the understanding is not itself a faculty of intuitions", "it exercises that action on the *passive* subject, whose *faculty* it is" (B153). In introspective experience, consequently, just as in perceptual experience,

the understanding ... does not *find* some sort of combination of the manifold already in inner sense, but *produces* it, by *affecting* inner sense. (B155)

That is why "through inner sense we intuit ourselves only as we are internally affected *by our selves*, i.e., ... we cognize our own subject only

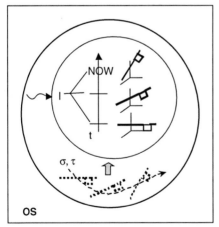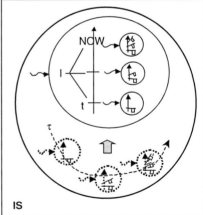

FIG. 5.10.   OS: outer sense at work; IS: inner sense at work

as appearance" (B156). And that is also why, once it is properly distinguished from inner sense, even with respect to introspection, the synthetic unity of apperception remains "the highest point to which one must affix all use of the understanding" (B134n.).

This completes our short digression. It is finally time to secure some "every–must" judgments. Onward into the Analytic of Principles!

Schemata and Principles: 6
From Pure Concepts to
Objective Judgments

Kant begins the Analytic of Principles by reminding us of the classical division of *logic* into the theories of concepts, judgments, and inferences, corresponding to a division of "the higher faculties of cognition" into "understanding, the power of judgment, and reason", all three of which "are comprehended under the broad designation of understanding in general", i.e., that sense of "understanding" in which its activities are contrasted with the receptivity of sensibility (A130–1/B169). Summarizing the results of the B Deduction, Kant has just told us that he there exhibited

> the pure concepts of the understanding... as principles of the possibility of experience, ... the latter as the *determination* of appearances in space and time *in general*—and the latter, finally, from the principle of the *original* synthetic unity of apperception, as the form of the understanding in relation to space and time, as original forms of sensibility. (B168–9)

That is, although, as we recall, on Kant's account, the (propositional) forms of judgment are implicated *whenever* concepts are in play, the focus of the Transcendental Deduction has been on the role of the understanding (in the broad sense) as a faculty of concepts primarily insofar as they function as rules guiding perceptual synthesis. While it has been continually implicit in Kant's story, in other words, the specifically predicative role of concepts in determinate *objective judgments* about items in nature, and especially in synthetic judgments *a priori*, has so far remained very much in the background. Now it moves to center stage.

It is in judgments that concepts, including the pure concepts of the understanding, are *predicatively* applied. The Analytic of Principles will consequently be

a canon for the *power of judgment* that teaches it to apply to appearances the concepts of the understanding, which contain the condition for rules *a priori*. (A132/B171)

Correspondingly, the power of judgment is

the faculty of *subsuming* under rules, i.e., of determining whether something stands under a given rule . . . or not. (A132/B171)

Kant neatly anticipates Wittgenstein's conclusion that pure general logic cannot give us any precepts for exercising the power of judgment, i.e., any *general* rules for applying rules to cases. For

if it wanted to show generally how one ought to subsume under these rules, i.e., distinguish whether something stands under them or not, this could not happen except once again through a rule. But just because this is a rule, it would demand another instruction for the power of judgment, and so it becomes clear that . . . the power of judgment is a special talent that cannot be taught but only practiced. (A133/B172)

With respect to *transcendental* logic, however, the situation is quite different, for

in addition to the rule (or rather the general condition for rules), which is given in the pure concept of the understanding, it can at the same time indicate *a priori* the case to which the rules ought to be applied. (A135/B174–5)

Transcendental logic, we recall, is a pure *specialized* logic. In essence, it is the general theory of humanly possible conceptualizations of *objects given in intuition*. The Analytic of Principles will consequently begin with an account of "the sensible condition under which alone the pure concepts of understanding can be employed" and then deal with "those synthetic judgments that flow *a priori* from pure concepts of the understanding under these conditions" (A136/B175). In this chapter, we shall explore the first of these topics. Kant calls it "the schematism of the pure concepts of the understanding".

The unity of perception

According to Kant's "doctrine of two sources", a perceptual experience has two theoretically distinguishable elements or aspects: an "image", constructed out of the raw materials of the manifold of sense by the understanding in its role as the productive imagination, and a propositional indexical "taking" in which such an "appearance" is conceived under object-concepts. A perceptual experience thus combines a sensory presentation with a singular judgment, and the question naturally arises how two such prima facie disparate items can be *unified*. We need, in other words, to understand the *unity* of a perceptual act. What sort of unity is it, and how does it come to be?

In the Schematism, Kant formulates this question as a problem regarding the *homogeneity* of concepts and the objects subsumed under them.

In all subsumption of an object under a concept the representations of the former must be *homogeneous* with the latter, i.e., the concept must contain that which is represented in the object that is to be subsumed under it.... (A136/B176)

In perception, the "representations of the former" are the items that are intuit*ed*, i.e., the "images"; their subsumption under a concept is their intuit*ing* in a perceptual judgment.[1] Now if the individuality of an intuited item could be understood on Leibniz's model, there would be no problem regarding the homogeneity of the objects given in intuition and the general predicative concepts under which those objects are subsumed in perceptual judgments. Kant's homogeneity requirement is trivially satisfied when the intuitive representation of a determinate object takes the form of an infinitely conjunctive Leibnizian individual concept. The predicative general concept *itself* (or its negation) is necessarily contained as a conjunct in any such representation of an object.

One of the fundamental insights shaping Kant's philosophical story, however, is that *our* intuition is sensory, and that sensation is *not* just a "confused" mode of conceptual thinking. It follows, however, that in particular

the pure concepts of the understanding, ... in comparison with empirical (indeed in general sensible) intuitions, are entirely unhomogeneous, and can never be

---

[1] In the example that immediately follows, however, Kant predicates homogeneity of a pair of *concepts*: "Thus the empirical concept of a *plate* has homogeneity with the pure geometrical concept of a *circle*...". That seems clear enough, until one reads the rest of the sentence: "for the roundness that is thought in the former can be intuited in the latter" (A137/B176). Since it is plainly difficult to make sense of roundness being *intuited* in a pure geometrical *concept*, the final clause offers an occasion for substantial exegetical creativity. For example, although it's not really clear how much it would help, Hans Vahinger once proposed *interchanging* 'the former' and 'the latter'. In any event, Kant's text evidently needs some sort of tidying up, and the interpretation that I'll be offering is, I think, at least as plausible as any other currently in circulation.

encountered in any intuition. Now how is the *subsumption* of the latter under the former, thus the *application* of the category to appearances possible, since no one would say that the category, e.g., causality, could also be intuited through the senses and is contained in the appearance? (A137–8/B176–7)

Answering this question is the fundamental task of the Schematism chapter of the First Critique, but the notion of a *schema* is broader than the specific *temporal* notions that Kant will bring to bear on this issue of *categorial* homogeneity. It will consequently be useful first to tell the story of schemata in connection with *empirical* concepts and *space*, and only later to return to the topic of the *pure* concepts and time.

Schemata: some puzzles

The Schematism chapter offers a good case study for the challenges in reading and interpreting the First Critique. One commentator was in fact moved to write that it

probably presents more difficulty to the uncommitted but sympathetic reader than any other part of the *Critique of Pure Reason*. Not only are the details of the argument highly obscure (that, after all, is a common enough experience in reading Kant, though one is not often so baffled as one is here): it is hard to say in plain terms what general point or points Kant is seeking to establish.[2]

Since the central virtue of an exegetical hypothesis is its ability to solve interpretive problems, it will perhaps prove helpful to begin our own exploration of the Schematism with a look at some of these difficulties.

What we need to solve a homogeneity problem, Kant tells us, is a particular sort of *mediating representation*. On the face of it, however, the conditions that such a "transcendental schema" would need to satisfy seem to be mutually incompatible.

Now it is clear that there must be a third thing, which must stand in homogeneity with the category [concept] on the one hand and the appearance [intuited object] on the other, and makes possible the application of the former to the latter. This mediating representation must be pure (without anything empirical) and yet *intellectual* on the one hand and *sensible* on the other. Such a representation is the *transcendental schema*. (A138/B177)

---

[2] W. H. Walsh, "Schematism", in *Kant-Studien*, 49 (1957), repr. in Robert Paul Wolff, ed., *Kant: A Collection of Critical Essays* (Garden City, NY: Anchor Books, 1967), 71–87, at 71.

In light of Kant's principled separation of sensibility and understanding, it is surely hard to see how any *one* representation could be both intellectual and sensible. But this is not the only place in the First Critique that we find such prima facie incoherent requirements.

We meet a similarly paradoxical characterization, for instance, late in the Dialectic in Kant's discussion of *mathematical* knowledge. Construction of a mathematical concept, he tells us, requires a "*non-empirical intuition*", which "as intuition, is an individual object", but, since concepts are general representations, must nevertheless "express in the representation universal validity for all possible intuitions that belong under the same concept" (A713/B741). Kant proceeds to supply an example of such a "construction" *a priori*:

Thus I construct a triangle by exhibiting an object corresponding to this concept, either through mere imagination, in pure intuition, or on paper, in empirical intuition, but in both cases completely *a priori*, without having had to borrow the pattern for it from any experience. (A713/B741)

(A triangle "constructed" only in imagination would be an instance of the sort of "formal intuition" mentioned at B160 n., the synthesis of an envisioned pure spatial manifold.)

The example in fact echoes one given in the Schematism, but there is a prima facie tension between them. In the Dialectic, it is apparently the constructed figure itself which is supposed to express the geometrical concept—"The individual drawn figure is empirical, and nevertheless serves to express the concept without damage to its universality...." (A714/B742)—but the point of the corresponding example in the Schematism is precisely to *distinguish* the schema from an image.

In fact it is not images of objects but schemata that ground our pure sensible concepts. No image of a triangle would ever be adequate to the concept of it. For it would not attain the generality of the concept, which makes this valid for all triangles, right or acute, etc.... The schema of the triangle can never exist anywhere except in thought.... (A140–1/B180)

Thus although, like the mathematician's formal intuition of a triangle, a schema is "in itself always only a product of the imagination", nevertheless "the schema is to be distinguished from an image" (A140/B179). A schema, Kant suggests, is rather the representation of a *method* or a *procedure*, a "rule of the synthesis of the imagination" (A141/B180) which "can never exist anywhere except in thought".

Even less does an object of experience or an image of it ever reach the empirical concept, rather the latter is always related immediately to the schema of the imagination, as a rule for the determination of our intuition in accordance with a certain general concept. The concept of a dog signifies a rule in accordance with which my imagination can specify the shape of a four-footed animal in general, without being restricted to any single particular shape that experience offers me or any possible image that I can exhibit *in concreto*. (A141/B180)[3]

As we recall, the *faculty* of rules is precisely the faculty of concepts, i.e., the understanding (A126). But if schemata exist only in thought and, *qua* rules, specifically in the understanding, it is hard to see how a schema could also be *sensible*. Schemata will simply *be* concepts, and, if so, it is not at all clear how Kant's appeal to them offers any advance on the homogeneity problem that it is intended to resolve. But as the section on the Schematism draws to a close, we indeed find Kant himself speaking of schemata precisely as *sensible concepts*:

[The] schema is really only the phenomenon, or the sensible concept of an object, in agreement with the category. (A146/B186)

Finally, on first encounter, what Kant says about the relationship between schemata and the *imagination* appears equally problematic. On the one hand, as we have seen, he tells us that the schema is "in itself always only a product of the imagination". Yet, in the very same paragraph, he concludes that a schema of a concept is a representation of "a general procedure of the imagination for providing a concept with its image" (A140/B179–80), i.e., a representation of the *process* rather than its product. And sometimes Kant talks about schemata in terms that resonate with what he says elsewhere (A78/B103) about the imagination itself:

This schematism of our understanding with regard to appearances and their mere form is a hidden art in the depths of the human soul, whose true operations we can divine from nature and lay bare before our eyes only with difficulty. (A141/B180)

---

[3] It is instructive to compare Wittgenstein's remarks on the practice of defining the names of colors by pointing to samples and saying "This colour is called 'blue'", etc.:

[T]his case can be compared ... to putting a table in my hands, with the words written under the colour-samples.—Though this comparison may mislead in many ways.—One is now inclined to extend the comparison: to have understood the definition means to have in one's mind ... a sample or picture. So if I am shewn various different leaves and told "This is called a 'leaf' ", I get an idea of the shape of a leaf, a picture of it in my mind.—But what does the picture of a leaf look like when it does not shew us any particular shape, but 'what is common to all shapes of leaf'? Which shade is the 'sample in my mind' of the colour green—the sample of what is common to all shades of green? (*PI* §73)

Schemata: some solutions

As it turns out, however, we already have on hand almost all the distinctions and insights that we need in order to resolve most of these interpretive puzzles. What we basically need to do is just to review and apply what we have learned about Kant's theory of perceptual synthesis from our explorations of the A and B Deductions. And, to begin with, this means that we need to recall that what Kant calls "the imagination" turned out to be the same faculty as what he calls "the understanding".

[The] synthesis of apprehension, which is empirical, must necessarily be in agreement with the synthesis of apperception, which is intellectual .... It is one and the same spontaneity that, there under the name of imagination and here, under the name of understanding, brings combination into the manifold of intuition. (B162 n.)

On this account, it is not so surprising to learn that, in the last analysis, schemata are concepts after all. But if schemata are just concepts, how can they also serve as the mediating representations that we need in order to solve a homogeneity problem? Kant's answer, apparently, is that schemata are not *just* concepts; they are *sensible* concepts. In addition to being, like all concepts, intellectual, schemata are *also* sensible. What are we to make of this?

Well, the next thing that we need to recall is that the fact that our *intuition* is sensible, and not intellectual, is specifically manifested in the *deictic* character of perceptual judgments. The individual concepts that function as the subject terms of such judgments have a demonstrative aspect. Particularity gets built into the subject term of a perceptual judgment *indexically*, by its demonstrative relation to a "presented" sensorily constituted item. The application of an indexical individual concept, functioning as the subject term of a perceptual judgment, is the intuit*ing* of that corresponding intuit*ed* item. This intuited item itself, on Kant's account, turns out to be an "image", constructed by the productive imagination from raw materials provided by the manifold of sense, but conceived under object-concepts. And as we have seen, at this point in Kant's story, the perceiving *subject* also comes into the picture, for, crucially, the intuited "appearance" is always necessarily conceived as an object *apprehended from a determinate point of view*.

That is what Kant's "triangle" example ultimately serves to remind us. The first point is that any *image* of a triangle must be an image of a determinate sort of triangle—acute, right, or obtuse; scalene, isosceles, or equilateral. That is the fundamental reason why "no image of a triangle could ever be adequate to the concept of it" (A141/B180). The triangular image constructed by a mathematician "serves to express the concept without damage to its universality" only because he takes into account nothing more than "the action of constructing" the figure in accordance with the concept of a triangle *in general*, i.e., a closed three-sided plane figure, "to which many determinations, e.g., those of the magnitude of the sides and angles, are entirely indifferent" (A714/B742). What the mathematician constructs is thus a *partially indeterminate* image, e.g., with respect to the absolute lengths of its three sides, which could be instantiated in diverse sizes in different spatial locations and orientations.[4]

The second and crucial point, however, is that any image of a triangle *given in experience* must be an image of a determinate sort of triangle *perspectivally situated thus-and-so in space*. And this implies that, in order to form the concept of an *intuited* triangular item, we need to mobilize not only the general concept of a determinate sort of triangle but also the concept of a determinate way of being related to the intuiting subject in space.

Essentially the same point is at issue in Kant's example regarding the mathematical concept of a *number*.

Thus, if I place five points in a row, ..., this is an image of the number five. On the contrary, if I only think a number in general, which could be five or a hundred, this thinking is more the representation of a method for representing a multitude in an image (e.g., a thousand) in accordance with a certain concept than the image itself, which in this case I could survey and compare with the concept only with difficulty. (A140/B179)

Recall our example of counting as keeping a tally. As in the case of "constructing a triangle", we can keep such a tally either on paper or "through mere imagination". In either case, we successively produce *images* of collections of strokes: $| \rightarrow || \rightarrow ||| \rightarrow ||||$. These images are the intuit*ed* items. But what, in this instance, are the corresponding conceptual intuit*ings*?

Here it is useful to think of each operation of adding a stroke as accompanied by a descriptive "commentary" taking the form of an explicit judgment:

---

[4] I am grateful to an anonymous commentator on an earlier draft for setting me straight on central features of Kant's philosophy of mathematics and thereby sensitizing me to an important difference between the "triangle" example in the Schematism and the one given later in the Doctrine of Method. Any confusions which remain are, of course, entirely mine.

This vertical mark directly in front of me is the *first* tally stroke.

This mark standing to the right of the one just produced is the *second* tally stroke.

This mark standing to the right of the two already produced is the *third* tally stroke...[5]

At each stage, the "commentary" includes, so to speak, a summary of the results of the total diachronic counting activity from its inception. The mark added in the *n*th step of the process is conceived as—and thereby also *seen as*—the *n*th tally stroke in the counting series. This much of the conceptualization belongs to "thinking a number in general". But, crucially, insofar as my judgments are about the individual *intuited* items, the demonstrative singular concept mobilized at each stage also includes a representation of the determinate spatial and temporal relationships of the marks and their production not only to each other but also to me, the counting subject.

Nor do these observations pertain only to geometrical diagrams and mathematical abstracta. As we have seen, I cannot, for instance, perceive just a book or a house (period). My perceptual experience of a book or a house is necessarily always of a book or house *determinately perspectivally situated in space and time*, e.g., of "this book over there now facing me slantwise". Once again, I form the demonstrative singular concept under which I intuit a specific individual item by mobilizing both the general concept of a kind of object and the particular concept of the determinate spatial and temporal relationships between the intuited object and me, the intuiting subject, the particular concept, as I shall henceforth put it, of a *determinate mode of sensible presentation*.

---

[5] If what I am up to is not just "open-ended" counting, but rather counting up to a determinate number, say 3, the intended outcome gets caught up directly in the accompanying conceptualization:

This vertical mark directly in front of me is the first *of three* tally strokes.
This mark to the right of the one just produced is the second *of three* tally strokes.
This mark to the right of the two already produced is the third (and last) *of three* tally strokes.

In counting *objects*, the generic notion of a "unit" (a "mark") is replaced by specific conceptualizations delimiting—both sortally and spatio-temporally—the determinate collection of items to be counted, e.g., "this *leftmost book on the shelf*", "this *piece of furniture closest to me in the room*", "this *object nearest to the edge on the table in front of me*", "this *shot of the 21-gun salute*". "All cognition requires a concept," Kant reminds us, "however imperfect or obscure it may be; but as far as its form is concerned the latter is always something general, and something that serves as a rule" (A106).

Transcendental schemata are precisely such concepts of determinate modes of sensible presentation. A specific schema, e.g., the concept *over there now facing me slantwise*, combines with the unschematized—i.e., generic, non-perspectival—concept of an object, e.g., *book*, to yield a schematized object-concept: *book over there now facing me slantwise*. Like any other concept, a schema belongs to the understanding. But a schema is a *sensible* concept insofar as its sole function is to particularize a general object-concept to a determinate mode of *sensible presentation*, and, since the imagination just *is* the understanding considered in its functional relationship to the sensibility, schemata can also be regarded as belonging to the imagination.

Indeed, in an important sense, schemata *constitute* the imagination, for it is schemata that make it possible for objects to be perceptually presented in sensory images.

[T]he *image* is a product of the empirical faculty of productive imagination, the *schema* of sensible concepts (such as figures in space) is a product . . . of pure *a priori* imagination through which and in accordance with which the images first become possible, but which must be connected with the concept, to which they are in themselves never fully congruent, always only by means of the schema that they designate. (A141–2/B181)

Any intuitable image of an object, in other words, must always necessarily be the image of the object *in a determinate mode of sensible presentation*, which, like the image of a triangle, will not "be adequate to the concept of it", i.e., not "fully congruent" to the *general* object-concept, but rather "connected" with it "only by means of the schema".

Consequently, a schema is the "representation of a general procedure of the imagination for providing a concept with its image" (A140/B179). Here is where Kant's insight that concepts function as *rules* comes to the fore. For, as we have seen, the concepts that come together to form the conceptual intuit*ing* that is the singular subject term of a perceptual judgment also function as rules guiding the process of "drawing" the corresponding intuit*ed* item, i.e., the image. That is what accounts for the *affinity* of the intuited sensory manifold.[6] And this brings us back to the theme of *homogeneity*.

---

[6] "There must therefore be an objective ground . . . on which rests the possibility, indeed even the necessity of a law extending through all appearances . . . for regarding them throughout as data of sense that are associable in themselves and subject to universal laws of a thoroughgoing connection in reproduction. I call this objective ground of all association of appearances their *affinity*" (A122; cf. A113).

Homogeneity: two ways to "apply a concept"

Concepts can be *applied* in two significantly different senses. The notion of "applying a concept" that is most salient in the Schematism is explicitly *predicative*. A concept C applies to an item in this sense if the item can be subsumed under the concept, i.e., if it is correct to judge that the item is C (or: is a C). Call this 'applies$_1$". Thus

(A1)   a concept C *applies$_1$* to X if X falls under C as an instance.

It is in this sense, for example, that the concept of roundness (circularity) applies to a round plate. (A137/B176). But there is also a looser notion of "applying a concept" that is, we might say, broadly *functional*. In this sense, we apply a concept to an item whenever the item is implicated in *any* actual use of the concept, not only in predicative applications of the concept in the first sense, but crucially also in its role as guiding the "drawing" or constructing of sensory images. Call this 'applies$_2$'. In particular,

(A2)   a concept C *applies$_2$* to X if the way in which X is used is
determined in accordance with C functioning as a rule.

A Kantian transcendental schema can consequently be "applied to intuitions" in two different senses, and it is in this way that it will be able to "stand in homogeneity with the category [concept] on the one hand and the appearance [intuited object] on the other" and to be both *"intellectual* on the one hand and *sensible* on the other" (A138/B177). In the first instance, a schema is applied$_2$ to the *manifold of sense* by being mobilized or activated in response to it and thereby determining, as a rule, the manner in which that manifold is taken up into a unitary figurative synthesis (B151) to form "the appearance", i.e., the image of an object determinately perspectivally situated in space and time. This image, however, is also "an intuition", i.e., something intuit*ed*, and, in the second instance, the schema is applied$_1$ to *it* by contributing to the indexical perspectival individual concept under which the intuited item is thought, i.e., by being incorporated into the intuit*ing* of the appearance under an object-concept, the locus of "the category" (see Fig. 6.1).

Thus Kant is not arguing, fallaciously, that "the appearance", the intuit*ed* item, and "the category", the intuit*ing* concept, have something in common simply because each has something in common with the schema. That would be a blatant *non sequitur*. In order to be valid, such

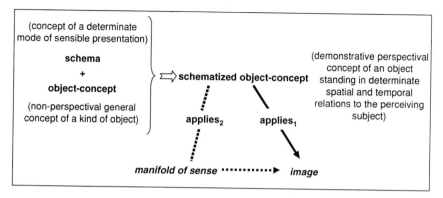

FIG. 6.1. Two senses of "applying a concept to intuitions"

reasoning requires a stronger premise to the effect that there is some *one* thing that *both* "the appearance" and "the category" have in common with the schema. Kant's picture secures this stronger premise precisely by properly respecting the ambiguities in both the notion of "an intuition" and that of "applying a concept".

What "the appearance" (the intuited image) and "the category" (the individual concept) both have in common with the schema, and so with each other, thus turns out to be *determinate perspectivality*. The intuited image presents an object as determinately disposed in space and encountered from a particular spatio-temporal point of view. Correlatively, the intuiting individual concept represents that intuited image precisely *as* an object so disposed in space and encountered from that point of view. It is because the specific characters of both the sensory presentation and its singular conceptual representation are determined by one and the same schema, i.e., one and the same concept of a determinate mode of sensory presentation, that they necessarily track together in this way. That is what constitutes the unity of a perceptual act; i.e., that is why and how intuited objects are homogeneous with the concepts under which they are judgmentally subsumed.

Schematizing the categories

So far we have explored and elucidated Kant's notion of schematism only in connection with formal mathematical concepts and empirical object-concepts. But Kant's fundamental concern in the Schematism chapter is with the pure concepts of the understanding, that is, the categories. A schema turned out to be the concept of a determinate mode of sensory presentation, and a schematized *object-concept* was consequently the concept of an intuited object standing in determinate perspectival spatial and temporal relations to the intuiting subject. As we saw earlier, however, the pure concepts of the understanding do not directly sort or classify intuitable items in the natural world, but rather, in the first instance, other *conceptual* items according to their most general logical and epistemic roles. *Concepts*, of course, are not intuit*ed*, and so, trivially, they also stand in neither spatial nor temporal relationships to a subject who mobilizes them in cognition. How, then, are we to understand the notion of a schematized *category*?

The pure concepts of the understanding are the forms of judgment specialized to cognitions of *sensibly intuited* items. The *pure* categories concern the intelligible synthetic unity of an intuited manifold *in general*, its unity according to a rule under object-concepts. They tell us what it is for a concept to *be* an object-concept—the concept of an object of representations—and so specify only the *generic* form of such an intelligible unity. By themselves, however, the categories yield no determinate cognitions of the world. They first become *applicable* only by way of determinate concepts mobilized in the context of some determinate form of sensible intuition. The *schematized* categories will consequently be *specifications* of the pure concepts of the understanding to a particular determinate form of sensible intuition. If we think of the pure categories as meta-conceptual genera, their schemata will be the corresponding specific differences that "limit" or "restrict" them.

> Without schemata ... the categories are only functions of the understanding for concepts, but do not represent any object. This significance comes to them from sensibility, which realizes the understanding at the same time as it restricts it. (A147/B187)

At the most general level, Kant thinks of the pure categories as being the same for all beings who, like us, are sensorily passive discursive apperceptive intelligences. But notice that I have left something out. *We* are *temporally* discursive beings. *Our* most fundamental form of sensibility is *time*. That is what both outer and inner experience, both perception and introspection, have in common (see Fig. 6.2).

In theory, then, the pure categories could be schematized by being restricted to *various* determinate forms of sensibility, only one of which is *our* (basic, temporal) form of sensibility, i.e., could provide principles of

152

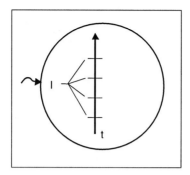

FIG. 6.2. Temporal discursiveness

intelligible unity for *various* kinds of passively given sensory manifolds, only one of which is *our* kind. In practice, however, as Kant himself continually stresses, we can have no knowledge of any forms of sensibility other than our own. The pure concepts of the understanding are thus schematized *for us* by being restricted to their role as principles of intelligible unity for *temporal* manifolds. Transcendental schemata, Kant tells us, are "transcendental time-determinations", i.e., "*a priori* time-determinations in accordance with rules" (A145/B184).

> The concept of the understanding contains pure synthetic unity of the manifold in general. Time, as the formal condition of the manifold of inner sense, thus of the connection of all representations, contains an *a priori* manifold in pure intuition. . . . Hence an application of the category to appearances becomes possible by means of the transcendental time-determination which, as the schema of the concept of the understanding, mediates the subsumption of the latter under the former. (A138–9/B177–8)

Kant orders these "*a priori* time-determinations in accordance with rules" under four headings, which correspond to the four main divisions of the Table of Categories. Schemata pertaining to

> the *time-series* correspond to the categories of Quantity;
> the *content of time*, to the categories of Quality;
> the *order of time*, to the categories of Relation; and
> the *sum total of time*, to the categories of Modality. (A145/B184–5)

Let us see how this is supposed to work.

As we have observed, Kant thinks of *number* procedurally, in terms of *counting*, understood on the model of keeping a tally by means of the temporally successive accumulation of intuited "units". Number, "which is a representation that summarizes the successive addition of one (homogeneous) unit to another" (A142/B182), is therefore also the schema of the categories of Quantity—or, as Kant here puts it, the pure schema of *magnitude*. Intuited units are "homogeneous" just in case they can all be subsumed under a single concept, and any (sortal) concept will do. Thus we can count *objects*—e.g., books, trees, stones, cabbages, kings, shoes, and ships[7]—but also such non-objects as twinges of pain, flashes of lightning, claps of thunder, interruptions, and performances of *Die Zauberflöte*. In any event, we *apply* the categories of Quantity, in the first instance, by counting under concepts.

A stretch of time might be filled or empty, but if it is filled, then, in the last analysis, *what* it is filled with is sensations.

Reality is in the pure concept of the understanding that to which a sensation in general corresponds, that, therefore, the concept of which in itself indicates a being (in time). Negation is that the concept of which represents a non-being (in time). The opposition of the two thus takes place in the distinction of one and the same time as either a filled or an empty time. (A143/B182)

A particular sensation that fills a stretch of time might, so to speak, be affiliated with an object—e.g., the green color of a thick green book, the warmth of a glowing coal, or the sweetness of a ripe apple—but, again, it needn't be, for a given stretch of time could also be filled with, for instance, a shrill sound or a dull ache. In any case, Kant proceeds to point out, "every sensation has a degree or magnitude, through which it can more or less fill the same time" (A143/B182). What Kant has in mind here is that temporally congruent instances of what is *qualitatively* the same sensation can still vary in *intensity*. An instance of, say, Kelly green can be bright or dim (think of the same green book viewed in sunlight and in shadow); a shrill sound can be loud or soft. And, for any sensation, there is a continuous spectrum of such intensities, grading off, as Kant puts it, "from reality to negation, that makes every reality representable as a quantum".

[The] schema of a reality, as the quantity of something insofar as it fills time, is just this continuous and uniform generation of that quantity in time, as one descends in time from the sensation that has a certain degree to its disappearance or gradually ascends from negation to its [actual] magnitude. (A143/B183)

---

[7] But not sealing wax. Its concept is not that of a kind of thing, but that of a kind of *stuff.*

In short, we *apply* the categories of Quality, in the first instance, by bringing the sensory contents of a stretch of time under a concept that admits of degrees.

At this point in the First Critique, the connection between the categories of Relation and the *order* of time is not particularly clear. Kant offers us, in essence, only a terse enumeration: The schema of *substance* is "the persistence of the real in time, i.e., the representation of the real as a substratum of empirical time-determinations in general, which . . . endures while everything else changes"; the schema of *causality* is "the real upon which, whenever it is posited, something else always follows. It therefore consists in the succession of the manifold insofar as it is subject to a rule"; and the schema of *community* is "the simultaneity of the determinations of one [accident of a substance] with those of [another], in accordance with a general rule" (A144/B183–4). Kant's fundamental idea is that our ability to represent time as a *determinately ordered linear continuum of instants*, stretching from the distant past through the present into the far future, is correlative to our representing a world of causally interactive substances, but this thesis and Kant's reasons for holding it do not really come into proper focus until the Analogies of Experience. At this point, we will just have to treat Kant's claim as a promissory note: We *apply* the categories of Relation by thinking intuited items under *object-concepts*.

Finally, Kant tells us, the schema of *possibility* is "the agreement of the synthesis of various representations with the conditions of time in general, [and so] the determination of the representation of a thing to some time"; of *actuality*, "existence at a determinate time"; and of *necessity*, "the existence of an object at all times" (A144–5/B184). In the latter two cases, the relation between the schemata and "the sum total of time" is relatively straightforward. What is actual is what in fact exists during some part of that temporal totality; what is necessary is what exists throughout the whole of it.[8] What is possible then fits into this picture by being what *could be* consistently assigned to some *one* determinate part of the temporal whole, "since opposites cannot exist in one thing at the same time". In any event, in the first instance, we *apply* the categories of Modality by making *objective judgments* (about what could be, is, or is always the case).[9]

---

[8] Here the attentive reader may recall Kant's claim that "Necessity and strict universality are . . . secure indications of an *a priori*, and also belong together inseparably" (B4).

[9] The fact that schemata for the first three groups of categories basically concern particular modes of application of *concepts*, while the schema for the categories of Modality explicitly

A priori principles

The Schematism chapter thus establishes that, and how, it is possible to apply the pure concepts of the understanding in judgments, and, in particular, in *synthetic* judgments, to objects of possible experience. Indeed, Kant concludes, that is the *only* way in which *we* can legitimately apply the categories.

Thus the schemata of the pure concepts of understanding are the true and sole conditions for providing them with a relation to objects, thus with *significance*; and hence the categories are in the end of none but a possible empirical use, since they merely serve to subject appearances to general rules of synthesis through grounds of an *a priori* necessary unity (on account of the necessary unification of all consciousness in an original apperception), and thereby to make them fit for a thoroughgoing connection in one experience. (A146/B185)

It is now time to remember that the pure concepts of the understanding are precisely the *a priori* concepts (C_{AP}) that occurred essentially in the synthetic *a priori* every–must judgments (J_{SAP}) whose problematic epistemic legitimacy exercised us early on. In demonstrating the legitimate applicability of the categories to objects of possible experience, then, we have in effect secured the first group of judgments promised by Strategy K, i.e., judgments of the form

    (K1)   The *a priori* concept 'C_{AP}' applies in the world.

At this point, then, it should also be possible to secure the second group of judgments promised by Strategy K, i.e., judgments of the form

    (K2)   The synthetic *a priori* judgment 'J_{SAP}' is true of the world,

and that is precisely Kant's next project in the First Critique.

Now our task is to exhibit in systematic combination the judgments that the understanding actually brings about *a priori* . . . for which our table of the categories must doubtless give us natural and secure guidance. (A148/B187)

invokes the notion of complete *judgments* reflects a distinction that Kant first noted in connection with the Table of Forms of Judgment during the course of the Metaphysical Deduction:

The modality of judgments is a quite special function of them, which is distinctive in that it contributes nothing to the content of the judgment (for besides quantity, quality, and relation there is nothing more that constitutes the content of a judgment), but rather concerns only the value of the copula in relation to thinking in general. (A74/B99–100)

What Kant here calls to our attention is nowadays reflected in the fact that we represent possibility and necessity, not in the way that we represent concepts, i.e., by predicates, but by *sentential operators* (and actuality by the absence of any such qualifying operator).

The "judgments that the understanding actually brings about *a priori*", however, in fact include more than just the synthetic *a priori* judgments characteristic of traditional rationalist metaphysics. They also include principles belonging to mathematics, e.g., "The sum of the interior angles of a triangle must be equal to two right angles", and to mathematical physics, e.g., "For every action there must be an equal and opposite reaction", and, of course, all *analytic* judgments are *a priori* as well. In the Analytic of Principles, Kant tells us, "we will limit ourselves merely to those principles that are related to the categories" (A149/B188), and so not consider the sorts of *a priori* judgments regarding space and time that were treated in the Aesthetic or *a priori* mathematical propositions *per se*. However, he adds,

we must also speak of the principle of analytic judgments, in contrast, to be sure, to that of synthetic judgments, with which we are properly concerned, since precisely this contrast will free the theory of the latter from all misunderstanding and lay their particular nature clearly before our eyes. (A149–50/B189)

Kant's first step in his systematic exposition of *a priori* principles is consequently to elucidate "the supreme principle of all analytic judgments", namely, the "principle of contradiction": "No predicate pertains to a thing that contradicts it" (A151/B190). The principle applies to all cognitions as such, independent of considerations regarding their specific content, and so properly belongs to general (formal) logic. Since freedom from contradiction is a necessary, but clearly *not* sufficient, condition for the truth of a judgment, the principle of contradiction serves primarily negatively, as a ground for rejecting particular claims. But it has, Kant points out, a limited positive use as well, for, in the case of an *analytic* judgment,

whether it be negative or affirmative, its truth must always be able to be cognized sufficiently in accordance with the principle of contradiction. For the contrary of that which as a concept already lies and is thought in the cognition of the object is always correctly denied, while the concept itself must necessarily be affirmed of it.... (A151/B190)

This, of course, is just the account of analyticity with which Kant began long ago in the Introduction to the First Critique (A6/B10).

Kant carefully formulates the principle of contradiction as a principle of pure formal logic. Most of the more familiar, received formulations, he complains, are less careful. The formulation "It is impossible for something to be and not to be *at the same time*", for instance, is contaminated both by a superfluous element—the word 'impossible', which adverts to an apodictic certainty which must "be understood from the proposition itself" (A152/B191)—and by a material restriction—the condition of time, for a purely logical principle "must not limit its claims to temporal relations" (A153/B192). Thus, Kant points out, the principle of contradiction by itself suffices to establish the analyticity of the judgment "No unlearned person is learned", since the contradictory of the predicate-concept, *learned*, is contained in the subject-concept, *unlearned person*. On the other hand, he argues, "A person who is unlearned is not learned" is *not* analytic. Here, Kant tells us, the concept *unlearned* has been "abstracted" from the concept *unlearned person* and is being considered as combined with the subject only synthetically. The truth of the judgment is consequently subject to a further condition—viz., *at the same time*—"for one who is unlearned at one time can very well be learned at another time" (A153/B192).

When we turn from analytic to synthetic judgments, then, we leave pure general logic behind. Establishing the possibility of synthetic *a priori* judgments and the conditions of their validity is rather the job of *transcendental* logic. In synthetic judgments, we always

go beyond the given concept in order to consider something entirely different from what is thought in it as in a relation to it, a relation which is therefore never one of either identity or contradiction, and one where neither the truth nor the error of the judgment can be seen in the judgment itself. (A154–5/B193–4)

We must therefore concede, Kant concludes, that the synthesis of a subject-concept and a predicate-concept not contained in it requires "a third thing . . . in which alone the synthesis of two concepts can originate". This "third thing", the "medium of all synthetic judgments", is just the "one totality in which all of our representations are contained, namely inner sense and its *a priori* form time" (A155/B194).

This is just the moral of the Transcendental Deduction. Our most fundamental synthetic judgments are precisely those constitutive of the "*one* experience, in which all perceptions are represented as in thoroughgoing and lawlike connection" (A110). Such judgments represent concepts as combined in an *object*, and specifically, in the first instance, in an *intuited* object.[10]

---

[10] Indeed, Kant adds, echoing a thesis that we first encountered at B146–8, in §22 of the B Deduction, "even space and time . . . would still be without objective validity and without sense and significance if their necessary use on the objects of experience were not shown" (A156/

Without that the concepts are empty and through them one has, to be sure, thought, but not in fact cognized anything through this thinking, but rather merely played with representations. (A155/B194–5)

Intuited objects are presented through the figurative synthesis of a sensory manifold, and, as we have seen, this synthetic unity of representations is in turn correlative to the synthetic unity of apperception, the "one totality in which all of our representations are contained". "The *possibility of experience* is therefore that which gives all of our cognitions *a priori* objective reality" (A156/B195).

The supreme principle of all synthetic judgments is, therefore: Every object stands under the necessary conditions of the synthetic unity of the manifold of intuition in a possible experience. (A158/B197)

The synthetic *a priori* principles that Kant will proceed to enumerate and elucidate will thus be expressions of such necessary conditions, "namely general rules of unity in the synthesis of appearances" (A157/B196).

The conditions of the *possibility of experience* in general are at the same time conditions of the *possibility of the objects of experience*, and on this account have objective validity in synthetic judgments *a priori*. (A158/B197)

Kant has already argued that these conditions of the possibility of experience, i.e., the "general rules of unity in the synthesis of appearances", are precisely the pure concepts of the understanding enumerated in the Table of Categories. The (synthetic *a priori*) *principles* of pure understanding can consequently also be enumerated in a table, and, like the categories, they will fall under four basic headings (see Fig. 6.3).

As our diagram indicates, Kant divides the four basic sets of synthetic *a priori* principles into two groups. This is a division that we have encountered before, in Kant's parenthetical remarks in B on the structure of the Table of Categories (B109 ff.), but here he is finally in a position to begin to justify and explain it. The Axioms and Anticipations, he tells us, are *mathematical* principles, not in the sense of belonging to mathematics, but in the sense of being principles which ground "the possibility and *a priori*

B195). Cf. "Thus although in synthetic judgments we cognize *a priori* so much about space in general or about the shapes that the productive imagination draws in it that we really do not need any experience for this, still this cognition would be nothing at all, but an occupation with a mere figment of the brain, if space were not to be regarded as the condition of the appearances which constitute the matter of outer experience . . . " (A157/B196).

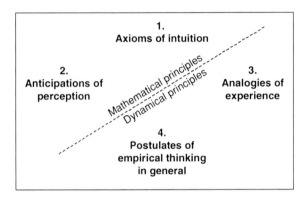

FIG. 6.3. The Table of Principles (A161/B200)

objective validity" (A160/B199) of general mathematical truths, i.e., by being, so to speak, meta-mathematical principles. They express the necessary conditions of a mode of synthesis or combination (*conjunctio*) that Kant in B calls composition (*compositio*), "the synthesis of a manifold of what *does not necessarily* belong *to each other*" (B201). Although the notion ultimately gets extended to encompass various forms of measurement, his basic paradigm is precisely the sort of synthesis of disparate "homogeneous units" that we saw in action in the earlier examples of counting.

The Analogies and Postulates, in contrast, are *dynamical* principles, not because they belong to "dynamics", the physics of matter in motion, but because, as we shall see, they are concerned with the synthesis of *diachronic* manifolds. Unlike the mathematical principles, which pertain "merely to intuition"—since the "marks" with which one keeps a tally or the "figures" constructed by a geometer can be pure *formal* intuitions, "drawn" by the productive imagination only in thought—the dynamical principles pertain to "the *existence* of an appearance in general", that is, they concern the temporal synthesis of manifolds of *real* contents, given in sensation (A160/B199). They express conditions of a mode of combination that Kant in B calls connection (*nexus*), "the synthesis of that which is manifold insofar as they *necessarily* belong *to one another*, as e.g., an accident belongs to some substance, or the effect to the cause" (B201).[11]

Kant's specification and demonstration of the synthetic *a priori* principles actually falling under these four headings is the consummation of the project of epistemic legitimization begun in the Transcendental De-

---

[11] That is why, as Kant earlier observed, the categories of Relation and Modality come in pairs of "correlates" (B110).

duction. The Transcendental Analytic carries on for a bit afterwards, but the System of Principles essentially rounds off the *constructive* moment of the First Critique. Kant's reflections and arguments are complicated, and our exploration of them will consequently occupy us for quite a while. In the next chapter, in particular, I will explicitly engage the text only of the mathematical principles, the Axioms and Anticipations. Then, using an ingenious thought experiment originally suggested by P. F. Strawson, I will try to provide a general orientation to some of the more difficult themes of the Analogies. These will turn out to need two chapters—roughly, one for substance and one for causation—and only then will we be in a position to examine the Postulates, which will propel us into other important Kantian themes. That, then, is our immediate agenda, and it is surely high time that we began to carry it out. I turn, therefore, to the Axioms and Anticipations.

Synchronic Manifolds:
The Axioms and
Anticipations

A concept is essentially the sort of thing that can have instances, a one over against a (potential) many. A concept thus serves as a principle of unity for a manifold insofar as it collects the items that are subsumed under it. Correlatively, however, concepts serve as rules for counting the items that are subsumed under them. That is, with respect to a particular concept, C, and a manifold of presented items, we can normally ask *how many* Cs (or: C items) are or were present in the given manifold. Although, as Kant stresses, the *process* of counting occurs only over a stretch of time, the question can be framed either synchronically—How many Cs are present *at t?*—or diachronically—How many Cs were present *during the interval t_i–t_j?* We can think of the mathematical principles of pure understanding, the Axioms of Intuition and Anticipations of Perception, as addressed to the first of these questions.

Insofar as they bracket diachronic considerations, then, both the Axioms and the Anticipations are "anticipatory" of experiences of full-fledged spatio-temporal *objects*, i.e., items in the world that can be encountered and re-encountered at various times. The principle of the Axioms tells us something about all "intuitions" (i.e., intuited*s*), and the principle of the Anticipations about all "appearances", but an intuition or an appearance need not be an object. Pains, sounds, afterimages, and even feelings can qualify.[1] The Axioms and Anticipations, we might say, unpack the generic concept:

[1] In a handwritten note inserted in his personal copy of A, Kant explicitly observes that "the concept of an extensive magnitude does not pertain merely to that wherein there is extension, i.e.,

(appearance of) an *item* in an *environment*;

the Analogies of Experience will then unpack the richer, but more specific concept:

(perception of) an *object* in the *world*.

An item in an environment

In order to be aware of any item, we must be able to distinguish what belongs to the item from what is distinct from it. Thus, whenever we have an item in an environment, there must be a *boundary* between them. Now any boundary is *where something differs* (see Fig. 7.1). What falls on one side of a boundary must be different, at least in *some* respect, from what falls on the other side of it. Thus we are led to distinguish what *constitutes* an item from what constitutes its environment. What the item consists of is its *matter*; how it is bounded in its environment is its *form*. In Figure 7.1, for example, the item is a particular figure, a dark gray cross; the environment, the light gray background against which it appears. 'Dark gray' indicates the matter; 'cross', the form.

To have an item in an environment, then, we need both "matter" and "form". In Kant's terminology, the "matter" is "the real, which is an object of the sensation" (B207; cf. A166); the "form", an "intuition in space and time" (B202). An item is so much so-and-so configured such-and-such stuff. This is plainly an Aristotelian conception, and directly

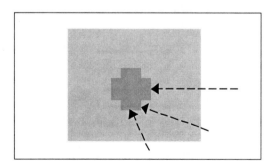

FIG. 7.1. A boundary (in space)

merely to our intuition. Satisfaction has extensive magnitude in accordance with the length of the time that is agreeably spent, although it also has magnitude *intensive* according to the degree of this agreeableness."

contrary to Descartes' conclusions regarding the bit of wax that figures in his thought experiment in the Second Meditation:

> The truth of the matter... is that this wax was... only a body which a little while ago appeared to my senses under these forms and which now makes itself felt under others. But what is it, to speak precisely, that I imagine when I conceive it in this fashion? Let us consider it attentively and, rejecting everything that does not belong to the wax, see what remains. Certainly nothing is left but something extended, flexible, and moveable. (AT 31 = CS 20)

Extension, flexibility, and moveability encompass the geometrical properties of size, shape, and (changing) position; but when we ask *what it is* to which these formal properties pertain, Descartes' account, which deliberately excludes all sensory *contents*, supplies no answer. "Attentively considered", the wax turns out to be all "form" and no "matter".

Locke's representative realism delivers the corresponding "empiricist" picture: The *occurrent* properties of "matter" are all "primary qualities"; "secondary qualities" exist only in the mode of potentiality, as dispositions or "powers". But already Berkeley saw that this will not do. Although "it is an easy matter to *consider* extension and motion by themselves, abstracted from all other sensible qualities" as mathematicians do, we cannot "separate the ideas of extension and motion from the ideas of all those qualities which they who make the distinction term 'secondary' ".[2] Like Cartesian "extended substance", Lockean "matter" is ultimately form without content, an incoherent conception.

Descartes' and Locke's accounts are both explicitly concerned with *objects*, but, as Kant recognized, the principles that they fail to respect obtain more generally. The distinction between the "form" and "matter" of an "appearance"—and the correlative distinction between "extensive magnitude" and "intensive magnitude"—is more fundamental than the distinction between a (persisting) substance and its (changing) attributes. The Axioms and Anticipations, we might say, formulate synthetic *a priori* truths that hold for all *empirical consciousness*.

Although Kant's section headings speak in the plural of "axioms" of intuition and "anticipations" of perception, in each case he offers us only one *principle*. For the Axioms, it reads (in B):

All intuitions are extensive magnitudes. (B202)

---

[2] George Berkeley, *Three Dialogues between Hylas and Philonous*, ed. Jonathan Dancy (Oxford and New York: Oxford University Press, 1998), 79–80.

for the Anticipations:

In all appearances the real, which is an object of the sensation, has intensive magnitude,
i.e., a degree. (B207)

Taken together with the opening remarks of Kant's "proof" of the principle of the Anticipations in B, the formulation of the principle of the Axioms in A—"All appearances are, as regards their intuition, *extensive magnitudes*" (A162)—makes it clear that these principles are in fact intended to have the same *scope*, namely, all "empirical consciousness, i.e., one in which there is at the same time sensation". As instances of such empirical consciousness, appearances

are more than pure (merely formal) intuitions, like space and time (for these cannot be perceived in themselves). They therefore also contain in addition to the intuition the materials for some object in general (through which something existing in space or time is represented), i.e., the real of the sensation, as merely subjective representation, by which one can only be conscious that the subject is affected . . . . (B207)

In short, while the principle of the Axioms, and so extensive magnitude, pertains to "the intuition", i.e., the "form" of a presented item (how it is configured and bounded in space or time), the principle of the Anticipations, and so intensive magnitude, pertains to "the real of sensation", i.e., its "matter" (the sensory content that is thus configured and bounded). Each principle, Kant will argue, guarantees the possibility of a fundamental form of *applied mathematics*.

The axioms of intuition and anticipations of perception *themselves* are the synthetic *a priori* principles of *mathematics* whose objective validity is to be secured by those arguments. The former paradigmatically include the axioms of geometry; the latter, the fundamental principles of the mathematics of infinitesimals.[3] What Kant articulates and defends at this point in the First Critique, in other words, are philosophical meta-principles, i.e., not the synthetic *a priori* principles that properly belong to mathematics but

---

[3] e.g., the lemmas regarding "the method of first and last ratios of quantities" formulated by Newton in Book I, Section 1, of *Principia Mathematica*. (An example: "Quantities and the ratios of quantities which in any finite time converge continually to equality, and before the end of that time approach nearer the one to the other than by any given difference, become ultimately equal.") The principle of the Axioms of Intuition also subsumes and validates the synthetic *a priori* truths of basic arithmetic, e.g., '7 + 5 = 12', but there are, Kant tells us, too many of these to count them all as *axioms* (A165/B205). The Peano Postulates might have served, but, of course, they hadn't yet been formulated.

those on which the possibility and objective *a priori* validity of the latter are grounded, and which are thus to be regarded as the principle of these principles .... (A160/B199)[4]

At the conclusion of these sections, Kant consequently remarks that the principles of the Axioms and the Anticipations were called "mathematical" (in contrast to the "dynamical" principles which will follow) precisely

in consideration of the fact that they justified applying mathematics to appearances ... and taught how both their intuition [i.e., their form] and the real in their perception could be generated in accordance with rules of a mathematical synthesis, hence how in both cases numerical magnitudes and, with them, the determination of the appearance as a magnitude, could be used. (A178/B221)

It is here, in other words, that we finally find the essentials of Kant's explicit solution to the Pythagorean puzzle—and that is surely worth a closer look.

Extensive magnitude

A *magnitude*, in essence, is a *determinate quantity*, i.e., a quantity that is susceptible to being *measured*. The Axioms concern magnitudes pertaining in the first instance to the *forms* of appearances, that is, to determinate regions of *space* or stretches of *time* insofar as they are susceptible to measurement. Now think of how we go about measuring a determinate length or interval. One thing that we need to do is to select some *units*, e.g., centimeters or seconds. The representation of any determinate length or interval is always the representation of an aggregate of such units—e.g., fifteen centimeters, twelve seconds—and, in that sense, we always implicitly represent the spatial or temporal region itself as if it had been produced, centimeter by centimeter or second by second, by a *successive synthesis* of such "homogeneous" units. Kant calls such a magnitude—"in which the representation of the parts makes possible the representation of the whole (and therefore necessarily precedes the latter)" (A162/B203)—*extensive*.

---

[4] Cf. A733/B761: "To be sure, in the Analytic, in the table of the principles of pure understanding, I have also thought of certain axioms of intuition; but the principle that was introduced there was not itself an axiom, but only served to provide the principle of the possibility of axioms in general, and was itself only a principle from concepts. ... Philosophy thus has no axioms and can never simply offer its *a priori* principles as such, but must content itself with justifying their authority through a thorough deduction."

Since, however, space and time *per se* cannot be perceived—the forms of intuition cannot themselves be intuit*ed*—in order to assign a determinate measurement to a length or interval, we also need to make both what we are measuring and the units with which we propose to measure it *sensible*. Thus we might in particular measure, for example, *the distance between a bed and a desk* (to see whether there is enough room for a bookcase) using the successive centimeter marks on a meter stick as our units. Similarly, we might measure *the time between a flash of lightning and a clap of thunder*, using the ticks of a clock or oscillations of a pendulum as our units. In any event, our ability to assign a determinate measure to a spatial region or temporal interval depends upon our ability to assign such a measure to the *contents* of such a region or interval. Insofar as regions of space and intervals of time are susceptible to measurement, in other words, they need to be "generated" or "constructed" through the successive synthesis of a "homogeneous manifold".

I cannot represent to myself any line, no matter how small it may be, without drawing it in thought, i.e., successively generating all its parts from one point, and thereby first sketching this intuition. It is exactly the same with even the smallest time. I think therein only the successive progress from one moment to another, where through all parts of time and their addition a determinate magnitude of time is finally generated. (A162–3/B203)

As we recall, however, Kant has earlier argued that the representation of anything *in* space or time presupposes just such a synthesizing activity on the part of the productive imagination.

Thus even the perception of an object, as appearance, is possible only through the same synthetic unity of the manifold of the given sensible intuition through which the unity of the composition of the homogeneous manifold is thought in the concept of a *magnitude*, i.e., the appearances are all magnitudes, and indeed *extensive magnitudes*, since as intuitions in space or time they must be represented through the same synthesis as that through which space and time in general are determined. (B203)

And that is the principle of the Axioms of Intuition.

The axioms of geometry, Kant argues, are grounded on "this successive synthesis of the productive imagination, in the generation of shapes" (A163/B204). That

between two points only one straight line is possible; two straight lines do not enclose a space, etc.... are the axioms that properly concern only magnitudes (*quanta*) as such. (A163/B204)

Kant takes very seriously the idea that geometrical demonstrations rest on the possibility of *constructing* figures in space. That is why the axioms and theorems of geometry are *synthetic* propositions. The first chapter of the "Transcendental Doctrine of Method", near the end of the Dialectic, contains a revealing discussion of the difference between analytical philosophical reasoning from concepts and synthetic geometrical reasoning from constructions.

Give a philosopher the concept of a triangle, and let him try to find out in his way how the sum of its angles might be related to a right angle. He has nothing but the concept of a figure enclosed by three straight lines, and in it the concept of equally many angles. Now he may reflect on this concept as long as he wants, yet he will never get anything new. He can analyze and make distinct the concept of a straight line, or of an angle, or of the number three, but he will not come upon any other properties that do not already lie in these concepts. (A716/B744)

A geometer, in contrast, begins by *constructing* a triangle (either in imagination or on paper).

Since he knows that two right angles together are exactly equal to all of the adjacent angles that can be drawn at one point on a straight line, he extends one side of his triangle [AD], and obtains two adjacent angles [<ACB, <BCD] that together *are* equal to two right ones. [See Fig. 7.2.]
Now he divides the external one of these angles by drawing a line [EF] parallel to the opposite side of the triangle, and sees that here there arises an external adjacent angle [<BCE] which is equal to an internal one [<ABC], etc.

That is, by the same principle, <BAC is equal to <ACF, which in turn is equal to <ECD (See Fig. 7.3).

In such a way, through a chain of inferences that is always guided by intuition, he arrives at a fully illuminating and at the same time general solution of the question. (A716/B744)

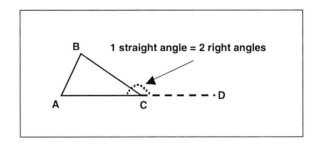

FIG. 7.2.   A proof by construction: step 1

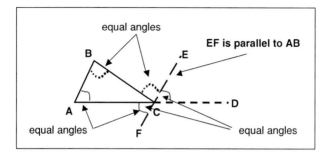

FIG. 7.3. A proof by construction: step 2

On Kant's view, as we have seen, our most fundamental *number concepts* also rest on the possibility of constructions, in particular, on the possibility of the sort of successive synthesis of homogeneous units that takes place in *counting*. In principle, every positive integer is the schema of a particular manifold generated by the successive addition of such units (A142/B182).[5] Any such number can consequently be *constructed* in only one way, "even though the subsequent *use* of these numbers is general" (A164/B205).

The most important use of such numbers, of course, is their use in measurement. That is how the principle of the Axioms ultimately bears on the Pythagorean puzzle.

This transcendental principle of the mathematics of appearances yields a great expansion of our *a priori* cognition. For it is this alone that makes pure mathematics in its complete precision applicable to objects of experience .... (A165/B106)

It is ultimately because whatever can be measured must first be made sensible and so presented in space and time that the figures and numbers constructed by a successive synthesis in *pure* intuition apply to characteristics of whatever objects are presented in *empirical* intuition.

The synthesis of spaces and times, as the essential form of all intuition, is that which at the same time makes possible the apprehension of the appearance, thus every outer experience, consequently also all cognition of its objects, and what

---

[5] Although Kant doesn't mention it, the successive synthesis of homogeneous units in counting is only the first of an indefinite number of possible mathematical constructions. Starting from the positive integers, we can construct other useful sorts of numbers—negative integers, rational numbers, real numbers, complex numbers, etc. The construction of the numerical subject matter of pure basic arithmetic, however, remains fundamental, for all such further possibilities ultimately rest upon the operations of basic arithmetic, and so presuppose it.

mathematics in its pure use proves about the former[6] is also necessarily valid for the latter. (A165–6/B206)

What we find in the Axioms, in other words, is in essence an argument from the subjective conditions of intuition to an objectively valid conclusion regarding intuit*ed* items, a conclusion that finds expression in, and thereby secures the epistemic legitimacy of, a synthetic *a priori* judgment about those items. Because regions of space and stretches of time must be "constructed" by a successive synthesis of "homogeneous units" and so necessarily have an extensive magnitude, the items intuited *in* space and time must also have an extensive magnitude. Since space and time are *our* forms of intuition, it follows that *all* intuitions (i.e., all intuit*eds*) necessarily have an extensive magnitude.

Intensive magnitude

Extensive magnitude pertains in the first instance to the spatial and temporal form of intuited items; intensive magnitude, to their sensory content. In empirical consciousness, we are affected by something, and the immediate result of being so affected is *sensation*. The principle of the Anticipations of Perception is fundamentally concerned, however, not with sensation but with "the real which corresponds to it in the object" (A166). As in the case of the Axioms, in other words, Kant is here arguing from the subjective conditions of intuition to an objectively valid conclusion regarding intuit*ed* items. To put it in a nutshell, because every sensation necessarily has an intensive magnitude, "the real, which is an object of the sensation" (B207) must also have an intensive magnitude. Since *our* intuition is passive, and we are consequently aware of items only insofar as we are affected by them, it follows that in *all* appearance what corresponds to its sensory content necessarily has an intensive magnitude.

Like extensive magnitude, intensive magnitude concerns an aspect of empirical consciousness that is susceptible to measurement. Now, while we cannot anticipate *a priori* the particular sensory contents of our aware-

[6] Another one of those lovely Kantian ambiguities: Does 'the former' refer back to the synthesis, the apprehension of the appearance, the appearance [itself], or outer experience? (The grammar of the original German text allows all of these readings.) I take Kant's meaning to be that what pure mathematics tells us about the *synthesis of spaces and times* (the pure forms of intuition) that is a condition of our apprehending objects in space and time will necessarily also apply to those apprehended objects.

ness, Kant observes that "there is something which can be cognized *a priori* in every sensation, as sensation in general (without a particular one being given)" (A167/B209). In particular,

every sensation is capable of a diminution, so that it can decrease and thus gradually disappear. (A168/B209–10)

It is important to understand what sort of "diminution" Kant has in mind here, for there are two ways in which an intuited *item* might "decrease" and "gradually disappear". This is clearest in the case of items intuited in space. One way that such an item might "gradually disappear" is by *shrinking*. Instant by instant, the region of space filled with sensory content becomes smaller. The item "disappears" *part by part*. From moment to moment, there is less sensory "matter". This mode of "diminution" is a loss of *extensive* magnitude.

The sort of "diminution" that Kant has in mind in the Anticipations, however, is not shrinking but rather *fading*. When an item intuited in space, so to speak, "fades out", the *same* region of space remains *entirely* filled with a determinate sensation at every instant, although from moment to moment there is clearly *something* different about the contents of that region.

[Between] reality in appearance and negation there is a continuous nexus of many possible intermediate sensations, whose difference from one another is always smaller than the difference between the given one and zero, or complete negation. (A168/B210)

Kant is thus concerned here with an aspect of empirical consciousness that is not "constructed" by the successive synthesis of "homogeneous units", but which, so to speak, can be apprehended "all at once" in *each* instant.

Apprehension, merely by means of sensation fills only an instant (if I do not take into consideration the succession of many sensations). As something in the appearance the apprehension of which is not a successive synthesis, proceeding from the parts to the whole representation, it [i.e., sensation] therefore has no extensive magnitude; the absence of sensation in the same moment would represent this as empty, thus $= 0$. (A167/B209)

Now just as one can assign a measure to the spatial and temporal form of an intuited item, so one can in principle also assign a measure to that aspect of the item's content which in every instant "can only be apprehended as a unity" and whose apprehension thus "does not proceed from parts to the whole" (A168/B210), i.e., the aspect which would vary if the item were to "fade out". Such a measure is what Kant calls an *intensive magnitude* or a *degree*.

In inner sense ... empirical consciousness can be raised from 0 up to any greater degree, so that the very same extensive magnitude of intuition (e.g., an illuminated surface) can excite as great a sensation as an aggregate of many other (less illuminated) surfaces taken together. One can therefore abstract entirely from the extensive magnitude of appearance and yet represent in the mere sensation in one moment a synthesis of uniform increase from 0 up to the given empirical consciousness. (A176/B217–18)

Since any appearance is an object of empirical consciousness, "every sensation, thus also every reality in appearance, however small it may be, has a degree, i.e., an intensive magnitude" (A169/B211). And that is the principle of the Anticipations of Perception.

Continuity and its consequences

Continuity, Kant tells us, is "the property of magnitudes on account of which no part of them is the smallest (no part is simple)" (A169/B211). Magnitudes of this sort, he adds, can also be called *flowing* (A170/B212). Since this property does not correspond to the formal mathematical (epsilon/delta) understanding of continuity subsequently worked out by Weierstrass and Cauchy in the nineteenth century, it would perhaps be better to call it 'kantinuity', but apart from this one cautionary note and bad pun, I shall stick to Kant's own terminology.[7] And the first point that Kant wants to make about continuity (in his sense) is that it is also a property of *extensive* magnitudes, and so of space and time.

Space and time are *quanta continua*, because no part of them can be given except as enclosed between boundaries (points and instants), thus only in such a way that this part is again a space or time. Space therefore consists only of spaces, time of times. (A169/B211)

---

[7] "Kantinuity" corresponds roughly to the property of ordered sets that contemporary mathematicians call *density*: viz., that between every two members there is always another. "Between two instants there is always a time, and between two states in those instances there is always a difference that has a magnitude ...." (A208/B253). The real numbers form a continuum. The rational numbers (represented by integer fractions), in contrast, are "gappy"—notoriously, e.g., none of them is a solution to the equation $x^2 = 2$—but the set is dense, and there is no smallest positive rational number.

If space and time did consist of actual smallest parts, then those parts would either have some minimum extension and duration or be unextended points and durationless instants, and both options are arguably incoherent. On the one hand, we can always consistently conceive of further subdividing any extended spatial region or stretch of time, however small, and, on the other, it is impossible to understand how an extended region of space or temporal duration could be built up by accumulating unextended points or durationless instants.[8] On Kant's view, however, points and instants are nothing actual.

Points and instants are only boundaries, i.e., mere places of... limitation [of "spaces" (regions) and "times" (intervals)], but places always presuppose those intuitions that limit or determine them, and from mere places, [considered] as components that could be given prior to space or time, neither space nor time can be composed. (A169–70/B211)

On this account, points and instants are *virtual* parts of space and time. A virtual part is a part in concept only—e.g., the left half of a square centimeter of red, the first second of a three-second burst of $C^\#$—distinguishable in thought without any corresponding sensory demarcation. More precisely, Kant regards points and instants as *ideal* virtual parts. The concept of a point or an instant is the concept of the *limit* of a process of successive "bracketing" of ever smaller parts of something given in space or time by the sorts of extended regions or intervals that can be determined in intuition. What corresponds to the concept of the point at which two lines given in intuition intersect, for example, is the *possibility* of sensibly demarcating successively smaller regions, each of which always includes an extended part of each line (see Fig. 7.4).

Space and time can thus be treated *as if* they were composed of points and instants, and so fall within the scope of the mathematics of infinitesimals, i.e., the calculus. But they couldn't actually *be* composed of points and instants, for those are merely "virtual" items and always presuppose the differences of *sensory content* that demarcate ("limit or determine") spatial regions or temporal intervals, the only sorts of "spaces" and "times" of which space and time can literally *consist*. This is just a consequence of a point already established in the Aesthetic. Space and time are *forms* of intuition, and so essentially correlative to intuitable

---

[8] This is precisely the reasoning that lies at the center of the second Antinomy of Pure Reason (A434/B462 ff.) in the Dialectic, about which more later.

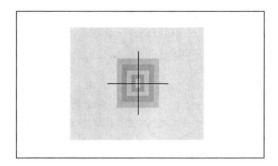

FIG. 7.4. A point as the limit of successively smaller regions

contents. Both can be *thought* of as empty of sensory "matter", but neither could actually *be* empty.

Kant consequently concludes that

all appearances whatsoever are accordingly continuous magnitudes, either in their intuition, as extensive magnitudes, or in their mere perception (sensation and thus reality), as intensive ones. (A170/B212)[9]

One might then suppose, he next suggests, that one could straightaway infer that all *changes of state*—e.g., a leaf's turning from green to yellow or a moving body's accelerating from one uniform velocity to another—must also be continuous, but that would be a mistake. As it turns out, Kant will later (A206/B252 ff.) defend essentially that thesis, but here, we need to recall, we are still dealing fundamentally with synchronic manifolds. We've not yet secured even the *possibility* of persisting items (substances) and a mode of causality "which alters the state of [such] things, i.e., determines them to the opposite of a certain given state", much less that such alterations actually occur, which, in the end, "experience alone can teach us" (A171/B213).

Nevertheless, Kant insists, we are now in a position to draw other useful conclusions from the continuity of all extensive and intensive magnitudes. For example, since

---

[9] This must not be read as an exclusive disjunction. Indeed, Kant's original text doesn't present such a straightforward case of disjunction as the Guyer–Wood translation here offers us. The German version contains neither "entweder...oder" (i.e., "either...or") nor "sowohl...als auch" (i.e., "not only...but also"), but rather the curiously mixed construction "sowohl... oder"—in full: "sowohl ihrer Anschauung nach, als extensive, oder der bloßen Wahrnehmung ...nach, als intensive Größen". Other translators correspondingly offer a conjunction at this point. Pluhar has "both in terms of their intuition, viz., as extensive magnitudes, and in terms of their mere perception...viz., as intensive magnitudes"; Kemp-Smith, "alike in their intuition, as extensive, and in their mere perception...as intensive".

every sense must have a determinate degree of receptivity . . . , no perception, hence also no experience, is possible that, whether immediately or mediately (through whatever detour in inference one might want), would prove an entire absence of anything real in appearance; i.e., a proof of empty space or of empty time can never be drawn from experience. (A172/B214)

Now it's clear enough that, since no degree of intensive magnitude is the smallest, there can in principle be indefinitely many situations in which a region of space or time is entirely filled with something real whose intensity is nevertheless too small to affect our receptivity. Since "the entire absence of the real in sensible intuition cannot be perceived" (A172/B214), i.e., empty space or time also does not affect our receptivity, it plainly follows that we cannot establish that a region of space or time is *in fact* empty by, so to speak, simply inspecting our experience of it.

It is not immediately as obvious, however, that we cannot establish by *inference* that at least some parts of a region of space or time must actually be empty, and some cogent instances of *empirical* reasoning do in fact have essentially that form. Consider, for example, the striking contrast between *balsa* and *teak*. Balsa is a "light" wood; teak, a "heavy" one. More precisely, the average density of balsa wood is about 0.16 g/cm^3, while teak is on average more than four times as dense, about 0.67 g/cm^3. One way in which we might account for the fourfold difference in weight between, say, a cubic centimeter of balsa and a cubic centimeter of teak is by supposing that there is actually less "*stuff*" (less matter) in a cube of balsa than in a same-sized cube of teak, i.e., that some not directly perceptible parts of the cube of balsa are in fact *empty*. And experience evidently teaches us that this hypothesis is correct, for balsa, but not teak, turns out to be readily *compressible*. If all the "stuff" in a cubic centimeter that was apparently entirely filled with balsa also fits into a smaller region of space, then some (imperceptible) parts of the original region must not have been filled with (balsa) matter after all.

Sometimes, however, experience is not so accommodating. A cubic centimeter of aluminum is no more compressible than a cubic centimeter of iron, but the iron (with a density of 7.87 g/cm^3) is still almost three times as heavy as the aluminum (2.70 g/cm^3). Nevertheless, Kant observes, "nearly all natural philosophers" (in his day) tend to reason in such cases as we did in the case of balsa and teak.

[Since] they perceive a great difference in the quantity of matter of different sorts in the same volumes, . . . [they] unanimously infer from this that this volume (extensive magnitude of the appearance) must be [partly] empty in all matter, although to be sure in different amounts. (A173/B215)

But that inference, however plausible, is simply invalid. More precisely, it rests on a presupposition,

for they assume that the *real* in space ... is *everywhere one and the same*, and can be differentiated only according to its extensive magnitude, i.e., amount. (A173/B215)

And, since every reality in appearance also has an *intensive* magnitude, that presupposition is "merely metaphysical" and at best gratuitous. For it follows that,

although equal spaces can be completely filled with different matters in such a way that in neither of them is there a point in which the presence of matter is not to be encountered, nevertheless everything real has for the same quality its degree (of resistance or of weight) which, without diminution of the extensive magnitude or amount, can become infinitely small until it is transformed into emptiness and disappears. (A174/B216)

What manifests itself in experience as the difference in weight between two same-sized cubical regions that are, respectively, *entirely* filled with iron and aluminum, in other words, could be a difference in the *intensive* magnitude of those two "different matters". Kant himself carefully does not *endorse* this alternative explanation. His aim is

only to establish ... that the nature of our perception makes an explanation of this sort possible, and that it is false to assume that the real in appearance is always equal in degree and differs only in aggregation and its extensive magnitude .... (A174–5/B216)

But for this limited aim, his argument clearly suffices—and, as we shall see when we come to the Paralogisms, this has important consequences for traditional metaphysical questions of a very different kind.

Before we examine the Paralogisms, however, we still have quite a long road to travel with Kant. We have now established our first synthetic *a priori* principles—the "mathematical" principles of the Axioms and the Analogies—and that is a considerable accomplishment, but objective validity still needs to be secured for the synthetic *a priori* judgments characteristic of the traditional metaphysics of experience. The next topic, both in the First Critique and on our agenda, is consequently the Analogies of Experience—both in general (the theme of the next chapter), and with regard to what they specifically imply about *substance* and *causation* (each of which will subsequently have a chapter of its own).

Diachronic Manifolds: 8
The Analogies of
Experience

In the last chapter, we secured the objective validity of two synthetic *a priori* meta-principles that apply to all appearances, i.e., to all intuit*eds*. The principles of the Axioms and Anticipations

> pertained to appearances with regard to their mere possibility, and taught how both their intuition [i.e., spatio-temporal form] and the real in their perception could be generated in accordance with the rules of a mathematical synthesis, hence how in both cases numerical magnitudes and, with them, the determination of the appearance as magnitude, could be used. (A178/B221)

Kant calls such principles 'constitutive', since they tell us how any item is constituted in its environment.

The synthetic *a priori* principles whose objective validity is to be secured in the Analogies, in contrast, are not constitutive but rather *regulative*. They concern appearances, Kant tells us, with regard not to "the synthesis of their empirical intuition" but "merely their *existence* and their *relation* to one another" (A178/B221). What the principles of the Analogies specifically regulate is the way in which temporally distinct appearances, however constituted, must be thought as related in order to be grouped together as multiple perceptual encounters with one object and, ultimately, as elements of *one experience* determinately related to each other in time.

In both the Axioms and the Anticipations, we found Kant arguing from the subjective conditions of *intuition* to an objectively valid conclusion regarding all *intuited* items, a conclusion that found its expression in a synthetic *a priori* judgment about such items. The same pattern of reasoning also informs the Analogies. Here, however, Kant will be arguing from the subjective conditions of *experience* to objectively valid conclusions regarding all *experienced* items, i.e., all *objects*, which will also find expression in, and thus secure the epistemic legitimacy of, synthetic *a priori* judgments about them.

As we discovered earlier, the axioms of intuition and anticipations of perception themselves did not belong to philosophy but rather to mathematics, and so Kant there articulated and defended only a pair of philosophical meta-principles which implied "the possibility and objective *a priori* validity" (A160/B199) of the corresponding mathematical principles. In the present case, in contrast, the three analogies of experience themselves properly belong to philosophy, and so Kant will explicitly formulate and argue for the three synthetic *a priori* judgments that express them. But, like the Axioms and Anticipations, the "possibility and objective *a priori* validity" of the Analogies is also grounded in a philosophical meta-principle, and it is with this *general* principle of the Analogies that Kant begins. Here is how Kant formulates it in A:

As regards their existence, all appearances stand *a priori* under rules of the determination of their relation to each other in *one* time. (A176)

Philosophical analogies

Kant's term 'analogy' itself comes from mathematics, where it refers to *ratios* or *proportions*. The mathematical paradigms, Kant tells us,

are formulas that assert the identity of two relations of magnitude, and are always *constitutive*, so that if two members of the proportion are given, the third is also thereby given, i.e., can be constructed. (A179/B222)

Thus, given two equal ratios, $a:x = x:b$, we can calculate the *geometrical mean*, $x = \sqrt{ab}$. The case of a *philosophical* analogy, however, is different. It concerns the equality of

two *qualitative* relations, where from three given members, I can cognize and give *a priori* only the *relation* to a fourth member, but not *this* fourth *member* itself, although I have a rule for seeking it in experience and a mark for discovering it there. (A179–80/B222)[1]

---

[1] To secure parallelism with what Kant here says about *philosophical* analogies, the Academy edition of the German text reformulates the earlier claim about *mathematical* analogies to say that

It is not entirely obvious what Kant has in mind here, but one way we might understand it is by reflecting on causal relations. The experiential "mark" of a causal relationship is surely *regular succession*. The rule for seeking the cause of some recurrent phenomenon, E, in experience is consequently to search for a type of phenomenon, C, whose occurrences are related to occurrences of E in the same regular way that, for example, flashes of lightning are related to claps of thunder. On this reading, the "two qualitative relations" are two causal relations—between lightning and thunder and between C and E—and the "three given members" are lightning, thunder, and occurrences of E.[2]

Kant's reformulation of the general principle of the Analogies in B sheds some additional light on the matter. Where the principle in A is framed as a condition that applies to all appearances "as regards their existence", in B it explicitly becomes a condition of the possibility of experience:

Experience is possible only through the representation of a necessary connection of percep-tions. (B218)

What connects the two formulations is the unperceivability of time.

---

the *fourth* member of a proportion, *three* of whose members are given, can be constructed, e.g., that given $a:b = c:x$, we can calculate $x = bc/a$. My own inclination, rather, is to modify the present text to secure parallelism with the claim regarding mathematical analogies as originally formulated, since that facilitates what strikes me as a more straightforward interpretation of Kant's *point*; but this inclination evidently finds no resonance among properly Apollonian scholars.

[2] Or perhaps the "three given members" are, say, a flash of lighting, the thunderclap that results from it, and a further clap of thunder. The "two qualitative relations" are, again, two causal relations—one between the given lightning flash and the first thunderclap, and the other between the second clap of thunder and *its* cause, whatever it might be. The rule for seeking the fourth member in experience is then, roughly, "search for something of the same kind as the cause of the first thunderclap (i.e., a flash of lightning) that stands in the same (temporal) relationship to the second one".

Both interpretations strike me as a bit far-fetched, but I'm hard pressed to come up with a better one. I can do a bit better, I think, if the text is first modified to secure parallelism with the corresponding claim about mathematical analogies, i.e., to speak of "two qualitative relations where from *two* given members I can cognize and give *a priori* only the relation to a *third* member but not this *third* member itself" (A179–80/B222; see the preceding note). In this case it is more useful to reflect on persisting substances. Here the "two given members" would be, e.g., two temporally separated perceptual encounters with a leaf, in the spring when it is green and in the autumn after it has turned red. The cognized "relation to a third member" is *substantial identity*; i.e., I represent my two perceptions *as* two encounters with one and the same item, and this "third member itself" is the object, the leaf, which I thereby represent as a substance that persists uninterrupted through a duration of time while undergoing a change of *accidents*.

In experience, appearances are cognized as "*objects* of the senses", "not merely of the intuition or sensation of the senses" (B218). Now the concept of such an object is the concept of something that exists independently of our perceptions of it, and so of something that can be perceptually encountered on many different occasions. As we have already observed, we represent such encounters as episodes in two histories—the history of the encountered object as an item in nature and our own history as a subject of thoughts and experiences—and all the episodes of both of these histories belong to *one* unitary objective time. The concept of an object, we recall, is the concept of something that explains the intelligibility and coherence of the apprehended manifold in the perceiving subject, and this one unitary *objective* time always plays an indispensable role in such explanations.

[Since] experience is a cognition of objects through perception, consequently the relation in the existence of the manifold is to be represented in it not as it is juxtaposed in time but as it is objectively in time .... (B219)

We cannot, however, place occurrences in objective time by, so to speak, simply *noticing* their temporal determinations. Time itself is not perceived, neither as an attribute of things in time nor as an independent existence that can be coordinated with them. Consequently,

the determination of the existence of objects in time can come about only through [the] combination [of perceptions] in time in general, hence only through *a priori* connecting concepts. Now since these always carry necessity along with them, experience is thus possible only through a representation of the necessary connection of the perceptions. (B219)

And that is the general principle of the Analogies in B.

The three individual Analogies of Experience will consequently correspond to what Kant calls the three *modes* of time—*persistence*, *succession*, and *simultaneity* (A177/B219). As Kant repeatedly stresses, time is *our* most fundamental form of sensibility.

For the original apperception is related to inner sense (the sum of all representations), and indeed related *a priori* to its form, i.e., the relation of the manifold empirical consciousness in time. (A177/B220)

Time is what both inner and outer experience have in common, and, considered merely as modifications of mind, both sorts of experience have the *same* temporal form.

The apprehension of the manifold of appearance is always successive. The representations of the parts succeed one another. (A189/B234)

When we turn to the empirical consciousness of objects, however, the three temporal modes come into play. Two successive perceptions, that is, can be *represented* as two encounters with one persisting item, or as encounters with distinct successively existing items, or as encounters with distinct simultaneously existing items. And each of these objective time-determinations of the items perceived implies that our perceptions of them cannot be "determined at pleasure or arbitrarily" but "insofar as they are to relate to an object our cognitions must also necessarily agree with each other in relation to it" (A104–5), i.e., must themselves be represented as necessarily connected.[3]

The Auditory Model

Now it is surely not immediately obvious that representing our perceptions as cognitions of objects implies that we must represent those perceptions themselves as necessarily connected to one another, much less how such an implication might be established. In this connection, it has proved a useful exercise to actually carry through the relevant reasoning with respect to the contents of a simplified "world". The example derives from an ingenious thought experiment conducted by P. F. Strawson in his superb book *Individuals*.[4] He calls it the "No-Space world", but, for reasons that will become clear as we proceed, I shall simply call it "the Auditory Model".

Although the sensory content of all appearances in the Auditory Model consists only of *sounds*, the model nevertheless contains two fundamentally different sorts of intuited items. One sort consists of pure musical tones of constant pitch. There are many of these; they are heard at different times; and they vary in loudness. I will represent these by

---

[3] The remainder of this chapter consists of the detailed working through of a rather complex illustrative model, the "Auditory Model", that is intended to elucidate and illuminate what Kant is up to in the Analogies. For many readers, however, the very complexity and detail of this illustration may well make it more of an impediment than an aid to understanding. Such readers should feel free simply to ignore and skip over the entire discussion of the Auditory Model. The model is at best helpful and at worst confusing, but in either case, it is *not essential* for understanding the explicit discussions of the several individual Analogies in the next two chapters and so may comfortably be omitted without any serious expository loss.

[4] (London: Methuen, 1959); cited in this chapter as *Ind.*

expressions of the form 'S_i^j', where a given subscript indicates a particular constant pitch, and different superscripts, various degrees of loudness, i.e., '$S_{pitch}^{loudness}$'. The other sort has exactly one member, but it is, so to speak, omnipresent, i.e., it is heard at all times. Like Strawson, I shall call it the "master sound". He describes it as "a sound of a certain distinctive timbre ... at a constant loudness though with varying pitch", and compares it to "the persistent whistle" which sometimes accompanies all the programs heard over a defective radio (*Ind.* 68). I will represent it by expressions of the form 'M_i', where the (potentially varying) subscripts will again indicate the (potentially varying) pitch. Since the loudness of the master sound is constant, no superscripts are necessary.

What we want to explore are the conditions that need to be satisfied in order to be able to represent our intuitings of S-tones not as a mere "rhapsody of perceptions" (A156/B195), but rather as encounters with *sound-objects*. It will be possible to do this only if we can arrive at a principled answer to the question "How many objects were perceived during a given temporal interval?", i.e., if we can introduce into our model a determinate distinction between multiple encounters with *one* object and encounters with each of *many* objects. We will need, that is, principles for sorting appearances into the conceptual pigeonholes "the same sound-object again" (although perhaps from another point of view) and "another sound-object" (although perhaps exactly similar). What we require, in other words, are determinate, non-arbitrary rules for *grouping perceptions* that will be sufficient to allow us, in Strawson's terminology, to *reidentify* sound-objects across time.

It is worth noting here, in an anticipatory way, that this would also suffice to secure at least one kind of *realism*. If the *esse* of intuited items were *percipi* (*sentiri, concipi*), then the count of items perceived would necessarily have to agree with the count of acts of perceiving. There could consequently be no principled distinction between two encounters with one item and encounters with two (perhaps exactly similar) items. Just this is what we find in the case of items whose existence we *do* regard as consisting in our awareness of them, for instance, *pains*. Precisely here there is *no* determinate, non-arbitrary distinction to be drawn between feeling one and the same pain on several occasions ("Doctor, *that pain* is back again") and feeling several exactly similar pains from occasion to occasion ("Doctor, *those pains* keep coming back").[5] We shall return

---

[5] We could, of course, make the reidentification of pains parasitic on the identity of their *causes*, e.g., posit that two occasions of feeling pain are encounters with one and the same pain if

to this observation in connection with Kant's own Refutation of Idealism.

One strategy for discovering the necessary conditions for our being able to represent our intuitings of S-tones as encounters with *sound-objects*, then, is to suppose that we *do* have a determinate, non-arbitrary way of distinguishing between one item twice encountered and two (perhaps exactly similar) items each once encountered. That is, we stipulate for our Auditory Model the following

Postulate P: Given two perceptions, e.g., of a S_i^j at t_1 and of a S_i^k at t_2, there is a determinate, non-arbitrary answer to the "identification question" of whether they are perceptions of one and the same item ("sound-object") or of two different items, e.g., whether the S_i^j heard at t_1 is numerically identical to or distinct from the S_i^k heard at t_2.

Postulate P will constrain all our subsequent stipulations regarding the Auditory Model. Any assumption which would imply the falsity of P will be inadmissible, and its falsehood will consequently be one of the necessary conditions that we are seeking.

The answer to the identification question, of course, will clearly depend on more than the two intuited items themselves. Whatever else is heard at t_1 and t_2, for instance, will presumably be relevant—given its omnipresence, this will always include at least the master sound, **M**—and it is plausible to suppose that what was heard during the interval *between* t_1 and t_2 will prove to be as well. In short, we will need to consider our Auditory Model *diachronically*, and that brings us directly to the topic of *change*.

Change in the Auditory Model

The master sound, for example, varies in pitch, but not in loudness. We will need a notation for such changes. I will use the arrow '$\Rightarrow$' (read: "changes to"). The expression '$M_i \Rightarrow M_j$' thus represents the pitch of the master sound changing from **i** to **j**. Heard S-tones, in contrast, can vary in loudness, but not in pitch. The expression '$S_n^i \Rightarrow S_n^j$' represents one such tone, of given pitch **n**, changing in loudness from **i** to **j**.

Since the master sound is omnipresent, we can treat it as an auditory *environment* within which the changing S-tones are heard. From this

and only if they result from the *same nerves* being stimulated, but the decision to do so would remain entirely arbitrary.

perspective, heard changes of S-tones can be regarded as falling into two distinct classes according to whether or not they are accompanied by a change in the pitch of the master sound. We'll call changes of S-tones that occur in a *changing* environment "A-changes"; those that occur in a *constant* environment, "B-changes".

(A-change) $S_n^i \Rightarrow S_n^j$ *while* $M_a \Rightarrow M_b$.
(B-change) $S_n^i \Rightarrow S_n^j$ *while* $M = M_c$ (i.e., while the pitch of M remains c).[6]

The next thing that we need to observe is that we will be able successfully to organize our S-tone perceptions into encounters with sound-objects in a non-arbitrary, determinate way only if the world of our Auditory Model is, so to speak, suitably cooperative. Kant makes essentially this point in the A Deduction regarding the necessary conditions of the possibility of the "threefold synthesis".

If cinnabar were now red, now black, now light, now heavy, [or] if a human being were now changed into this animal shape, now into that one, [or] if on the longest day the land were covered now with fruits, now with ice and snow, then my empirical imagination would never even get the opportunity to think [for instance] of heavy cinnabar on the occasion of the representation of the color red ... [and] no empirical synthesis of reproduction could take place. (A100–1; cf. A653–4/B681–2)

Analogously, we can conclude that

(X) If *any* S-tone (of whatever pitch and/or loudness) could occur in *any* (M-) environment (i.e., be heard simultaneously with any pitch of the master sound), then we could never arrive at a determinate principle for organizing S-tone perceptions into encounters with sound-objects.

Postulate P, in other words, implies that S-tones of a particular pitch and/or loudness will need to be "affiliated" with certain pitches of the master sound, M, and not others. It follows that our experience in the world of the Auditory Model will need to exhibit some *regularities*. The first of these that we will stipulate is that all S-tones have a fixed *maximum* loudness,

---

[6] Considerations of symmetry clearly allow for another pattern: (C) $S_n = S_n^v$ *while* $M_a \Rightarrow M_b$, i.e., the heard S-tone of fixed pitch **n** remains at a constant loudness **v** while the pitch of the master sound changes from **a** to **b**. This, of course, doesn't exemplify a third class of changes for S-tones, for it doesn't represent a *change* in an S-tone at all. What it might represent, and whether such occurrences are admissible stipulations in our Auditory Model, remains to be seen.

S_i^{max}. (The maximum loudness could be different for different S-pitches or the same for all S_is. Either choice would work in what follows; but, for the sake of simplicity, I will adopt the second option, i.e., one maximum degree of loudness for S-tones of all pitches.[7]) Given such a maximum, two sorts of regularities immediately suggest themselves:

(co) S_i^{max} *whenever* $M = M_p$,

i.e., we hear an S_i of maximum loudness whenever the pitch of the master sound is p, and

(su) $S_i^j \Rightarrow S_i^{max}$ *whenever* $M_x \Rightarrow M_p$, and correlatively,
$S_i^{max} \Rightarrow S_i^0$ *whenever* $M_p \Rightarrow M_{p \pm \epsilon}$,

i.e., an S_i approaches maximum loudness as the pitch of the master sound approaches p and diminishes from its maximum loudness to complete inaudibility (loudness $= 0$) as the difference between the pitch of the master sound and p increases within a fixed range. (co) is a regularity of *co-occurrence*; (su), a regularity of *succession*. When both regularities obtain, I shall say that an S_i is *stationed* at M_p. If we represent the varying pitch of the master sound along the horizontal axis and the degree of loudness of the heard S-tone along the vertical axis, we can capture such a situation in a picture (Fig. 8.1).

To help us think about the Auditory Model, we can also, so to speak, construct a model of the model. Let us avail ourselves of Strawson's comparison between the master sound and the whistling of a defective radio, systematically changing in pitch as we turn the dial. I will call this the Radio Model. Different **M**-pitches will then correspond to different radio frequencies within a given range. Correlatively, we can think of

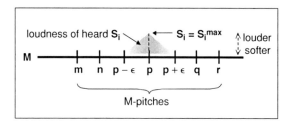

FIG. 8.1.   An S_1 stationed at M_p

<hr />

[7] We could also begin by positing an entirely different regularity. What recommends this one is that it turns out to be particularly useful for making the relevant points; i.e., the inferential route from it to the various illustrative conclusions is manageable and surveyable.

S-tones as being broadcast continuously by individual transmitters at specific frequencies within that range. An S-tone S_i will be stationed at an M-pitch, p, if the frequency of the transmitter broadcasting at pitch i corresponds to the frequency at which we hear a whistling of pitch p. The regularity of co-occurrence (co) is a manifestation of this coincidence of frequencies. It represents what we hear whenever our radio is tuned to that frequency. The transmitted S_i comes through with maximum clarity and loudness. The regularities of succession (su), correlatively, represent what we hear as we gradually tune our radio to that frequency or tune from it to another frequency.

Some of the usual idioms for describing this sort of situation are revealing. We tune to a radio station by "traversing" a range of frequencies or, even better, "moving up and down the dial". In the Radio Model, in other words, we sometimes think of *ourselves* as traveling through an environment of frequencies by moving from one to another, and this suggests a corresponding interpretation for the Auditory Model: Heard changes in the pitch of the master sound reflect the movements of the *perceiver* within the environment. The explanation of A-changes will appeal *inter alia* to such movements.

We have so far dealt only with A-changes, specifically, the A-changes characteristic for the regularities of succession (su). But now we need to consider what to say about B-changes, e.g.,

(b1) $S_m^0 \Rightarrow S_m^{max}$ *while* $M = M_c$ (say, during the interval t_i–t_j), and

(b2) $S_n^{max} \Rightarrow S_n^0$ *while* $M = M_d$ (during the interval t_g–t_h)

As the perceptual scenario abbreviated by (b1) begins, at t_i, we hear no tone with pitch m (loudness = 0). Then we begin to hear an S_m-tone, at first very faintly but gradually increasing in loudness until it reaches its maximum, S_m^{max}, at t_j. The pitch of the master sound remains constant at c during the whole interval t_i–t_j. In the perceptual scenario abbreviated by (b2), conversely, the loudness of an S_n-tone is at its maximum, S_n^{max}, at t_g, and gradually decreases until, at t_h, we hear no tone at all with pitch n. The pitch of the master sound again remains constant, this time at d, during the whole interval.

Inspired by the Radio Model, we interpreted A-changes in terms of motion, in particular, as indicating movements of the perceiver within the M-environment. One natural option, then, is to extend this mode of interpretation to B-changes, i.e., to interpret *all* heard changes in terms of motion. The constant pitch of the master sound definitive for B-changes, however, implies that the *perceiver* in such cases does *not* move within the environment during the relevant interval, but remains at rest. If we are nevertheless to interpret B-changes in terms of movements, then they will need to be movements of what we hear as *S-tones*. On this reading,

(m1) (b1) represents a moving S_m *approaching* a stationary perceiver at M_c,

(m2) (b2) represents a moving S_n *receding from* a stationary perceiver at M_d.

On the face of it, however, there is another, equally natural, interpretation for such B-changes. In scenario (b1), the location M_c is empty at the beginning (at t_i), but there is something there at the end (at t_j). Analogously, when scenario (b2) begins (at t_g) something occupies the location M_d, but there is nothing there when it ends (at t_h). Why not, then, straightforwardly interpret such B-changes in terms of *generation* and *corruption*?

(g1) (b1) represents an S_m *coming into existence (arising)* at M_c,

(g2) (b2) represents an S_n *passing out of existence (perishing)* at M_d.

The answer, of course, is straightforward. If the generation and corruption of S-tones were possible, then an S-tone of any arbitrarily selected pitch might come into existence *wherever* the perceiver happened to be "located", i.e., at any M_i. That is, any S-tone could occur in any (M-) environment, and principle (X) reminds us that we could then never arrive at a determinate principle for organizing our S-tone perceptions into encounters with sound-objects. The supposition that S-tones can come into and pass out of existence, in other words, is incompatible with our fundamental postulate P. And that is just what Kant says!

[The unity of experience] would never be possible if we were to allow new things (as far as their substance is concerned) to arise. (A186/B229)[8]

To begin with, then, our working hypothesis, that we can consistently treat an episode of hearing an S-tone as an encounter with a sound-object, implies that we must regard B-changes as we did A-changes, i.e., as manifestations of the relative motion of the perceiver and the item perceived.

---

[8] Cf. A206/B251: "[Creation] cannot be admitted as an occurrence among the appearances, for its possibility alone would already undermine the unity of experience."

Substance in the Auditory Model

At this juncture, it is important to appreciate the way in which the Auditory Model maps onto Kant's conceptual apparatus. How, for instance, do the pitch and loudness of an S-tone relate to the notions of extensive and intensive magnitude? It lies near at hand, of course, simply to import the corresponding distinctions from our *customary* way of thinking about sounds—the duration of a sound is its extensive magnitude; its loudness, its intensive magnitude—but to do this would be to fail to appreciate the peculiarities of the Auditory Model. Given our interpretation of heard changes in S-pitch as manifestations of relative motion, the length of time for which an S-tone is heard will obviously depend upon, so to speak, the locations and "relative velocities" of the perceived item and the perceiver within the (M-) environment. In other words, if, as we are supposing, we can treat S-tones as sound-objects, then although an episode of *hearing* an S-tone will have a determinate duration, the item that is thereby *heard* will not. That is precisely the moral of our most recent reflections on B-changes. S-tone *objects* do not come into existence. They are, as it were, continuously "available" to be heard by any suitably located perceiver.

Nor will the extensive magnitude of such a sound-object consist in a range of M-pitches, i.e., the "region" of the M-environment within which it is heard. On the interpretation that we have so far endorsed, at any given time, an S-tone is *stationed at* a particular M-pitch, but not "spread out" over a range of such pitches. *What* we are hearing throughout the whole interval when we experience, for example, the regularities (su) is always the sound-object S_i stationed at M_p. Considered in relation to their environment, in other words, the sound-objects that we have so far been considering are all "punctiform".[9] Differences in loudness are explained in terms of the relative locations of the object and the perceiver.

Reflecting on the notions of *form* and *content* sheds useful light on the question of the extensive and intensive magnitudes of sound-objects. As we have seen, in Kant's story, an intuited individual is basically an Aristotelian complex of "enformed matter", a "this-such". Intensive magnitude pertains to the "this", i.e., to the *content* of an appearance, the "real" of which it consists. In light of our earlier discussion of change and motion, if we now ask what a sound-object consists of, the answer must surely be something like "$C^{\#}$" ("E^{b}", etc.). More precisely, any

---

[9] In this connection, see n. 10 below.

sound-object will presumably be a determinate quantity of some S-tone. Here 'quantity' adverts to an extensive magnitude, and so pertains to the "such", i.e., to the way in which an item is configured in the environment. But if the extensive magnitude of a sound-object is neither its duration nor the range of M-pitches at which it can be heard, what could it be? Only one possibility remains. In the Auditory Model, the extensive magnitude of a sound-object is its *loudness*. The quantity of "sound stuff" in the Auditory World, in other words, is measured in, say, *decibels*, and the stipulations that we have so far adopted imply that the individual S-tone objects are not only all "punctiform" but also all "the same size". Each S_i consists of **max** decibels of the fixed pitch **i**.[10] (See Fig. 8.2.)

An increase or decrease in the heard loudness of an S_i encountered in the Auditory World is thus analogous to, for instance, the *growing* or *shrinking* of a patch of color intuited in space. Such a change in extensive magnitude would be what I will call a *change of ontological consequence*, since from moment to moment it results in the existence of either *more* or *less* constitutive content.[11] What our recent reflections on the interpretation of B-changes have shown, however, is that changes of ontological

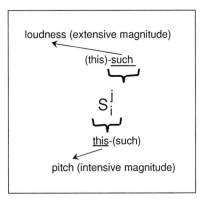

FIG. 8.2.   The structure of a sound-object

[10] These observations also yield a natural interpretation for the pattern of constancy and change mentioned in n. 6 above: **(C)** $S_n = S_n^v$ *while* $M_a \Rightarrow M_b$, at least for the case in which v = **max**. Where a sound-object S_n consists of **max** decibels of the fixed pitch **n**, then, where **v = max**, **(C)** represents such an object "spread out" over the range of M-pitches from **a** to **b**. To simplify our story as much as possible, I will continue to suppose that all sound-objects are "punctiform", i.e., that the experience described by **(C)** never occurs.

[11] Given our stipulations so far, the Auditory Model contains no changes of *intensive* magnitude. But it might. Such a change could sound like this: **(D)** $S_m^v \Rightarrow S_n^v$ *while* $M = M_c$, i.e., a heard sound of constant loudness **v** changes from one *pitch*, **m**, to another, **n**, while the pitch of the master sound remains constant at **c** (and the perceiver consequently "at rest" within the M-environment). Again for simplicity's sake, however, I will also assume that no such experiences occur.

consequence must be *merely ostensible*, or more precisely, that our perceptual experience can consistently be interpreted as encounters with sound-*objects* only if we stipulate that the constitutive content of those objects can neither arise nor perish, i.e., that content is actually conserved through such ostensible changes. Such a constitutive content that persists unchanged through variations in the way it appears to us is *substance*.

Our fundamental postulate P thus carries with it a train of consequences that have so far brought us to Kant's First Analogy. Here's what it looks like in A:

All appearances contain that which persists (*substance*) as the object itself, and that which can change as its mere determination, i.e., a way in which the object exists. (A182)[12]

In our example, it is the amount of "sound-stuff" in the Auditory World that is constant. Correlatively,

> (1.1) Ostensible changes of ontological consequence (perceived increases or decreases in extensive magnitude) must be merely apparent.[13]

In our model, this implies a distinction between actual and apparent loudness. The *apparent* loudness of a sound-object, S_n, i.e., the loudness heard at a given time t_i, will be "veridical", i.e., correspond to the *actual* loudness of the object (namely, **max**) just in case the M-pitch location of the perceiver at t_i is identical to M-pitch location of the S_n at t_i. So we can also observe that

> (1.2) The perceiver always has a location in the *same* (M-) environment as the objects that are perceived.

This is what makes it possible for ostensible changes of ontological consequence to be explained in terms of the locations and relative motions

---

Parenthetically, it is interesting to observe that *all* the sorts of changes that we have been considering in connection with the Auditory Model are sometimes (but not always) explained with respect to sounds as *ordinarily* conceived, i.e., as adverbial on the behavior of sounding *objects* (e.g., the tuning fork loudly emits $C^\#$ at t_i), in terms of the relative motion of the source and the perceiver. A train whistle grows fainter as the train recedes into the distance, its changing pitch simultaneously manifesting a Doppler shift.

[12] In B: "In all change of appearances substance persists, and its quantum is neither increased nor diminished in nature" (B224).

[13] As we shall see, this corresponds to Kant's terminological distinction between *change* (an actual generation or corruption, e.g., of accidents) and *alteration* (an apparent generation or corruption, e.g., of an actually persisting substance). "[I]n all alterations in the world the *substance* remains and only the *accidents* change" (A184/B227).

of the perceiver and the perceived sound-objects. An apparent *ceasing to exist*, for example, is explained as an "auditory threshold effect", i.e., an actual *ceasing to be perceived*. So our model is also, as we earlier remarked, *realist* in the sense that

> (1.3)   The existence of perceived (sound-) objects does not consist in their being perceived.

Encountered S-tone objects that cease to be perceived at a given time *ex hypothesi* remain available to be *re*-encountered at some later time.

Causality in the Auditory Model

The general principle of the Analogies (as formulated in B) is that the possibility of experience depends on "the representation of a necessary connection of perceptions" (B218). Now the "perceptions" of our Auditory Model are the diverse episodes of hearing this or that S-tone, but, although our endeavor consistently to *conceive* such episodes as dateable encounters with persisting "sound-objects" existing in a shared (M-) environment has yielded a number of inferentially interrelated (conditionally) necessary truths *about* those perceptions, we have not yet had to posit any necessary connections *among* them. We have, of course, had to stipulate that our experience in the Auditory World necessarily exhibits various *regularities*, but for all we have said so far, we remain free to think of those regularities themselves as merely *de facto* and contingent.

The idea of a necessary connection among perceptions comes explicitly to the fore, however, in connection with the notion of *causality*, the specific theme of Kant's Second Analogy. In A, its principle reads

Everything that happens (begins to be) presupposes something which it follows in accordance with a rule (A189);

in B:

All alterations occur in accordance with the law of the connection of cause and effect. (B232)

We might well ask, then, whether these conclusions also pertain to our Auditory Model, and, if so, how.[14] In order to answer this question, we

---

[14] From one point of view, we can already answer in the negative. In an important sense, nothing *happens* in the Auditory World. That is, *sound-objects* undergo no alteration. Only the

need to begin by subjecting the stipulations and assumptions that we have already made to closer scrutiny.

While we have ruled out various thinkable patterns of experience along the way, our story so far has admitted two sorts of changes—A-changes (varying M-pitch), which we interpreted in terms of motions of the perceiver relative to a stationary sound-object, and B-changes (constant M-pitch), which we interpreted in terms of motions of sound-objects relative to a stationary perceiver. Now suppose that, at t_1, I encounter the S_n at M_c, i.e., I simultaneously hear S_n^{max} and M_c. I then "travel" to, say, M_k, "arriving" there at t_2. Let us suppose that I hear an increasingly fainter S_n only during the first part of the interval t_1–t_2, so that at t_2, when $M = M_k$, no S_n is heard. Finally, during the interval t_2–t_3, I reverse my journey, "returning" to M_c, where I again hear S_n^{max}. Call this bit of experiential biography "Scenario Σ". Figure 8.3 is a picture of the scenario in the form of a "time-line", highlighting its two A-changes.

Now, according to postulate P, there must be a determinate, non-arbitrary answer to the "identification question" regarding qualitatively identical S-tones heard at different times, and so, in particular, with respect to the two S_n that, in Scenario Σ, I hear at t_1 and t_3. And, given our stipulations so far, it is certainly natural to conclude that my perceptions at t_1 and t_3 are distinct encounters with one and the same sound-object, i.e., that the S_n that I hear at t_i is *identical* to the S_n that I hear at t_3.

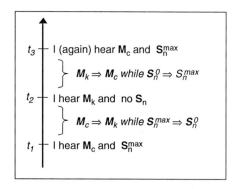

FIG. 8.3.   Scenario Σ

perceiver alters, viz., undergoes changes of place, but he moves through an unchanging landscape. The considerations which follow will consequently be a looser fit with Kant's own reflections on causality than were our earlier considerations with his reflections on substance.

But let us now assume that the Auditory World originally contained *two* S_ns—one stationed at M_c and another one stationed at M_a, so that at t_1 $S_n = S_n^{max}$ both when $M = M_c$ and when $M = M_a$. In Scenario Σ, I was *in fact* at M_c at t_1 and encountered the S_n stationed there, i.e., I heard S_n^{max}. But if I *had been* at M_a at t_1, then I *would have* encountered the S_n stationed there, i.e., I would *also* have heard S_n^{max}. This assumption, of course, immediately suggests another possibility. Perhaps while I was "away", so to speak, "visiting" M_k, the two S_ns *changed places*. Perhaps the S_n that I hear at M_c at t_3 is not identical to the one I heard there at t_1, but is instead the S_n that was *originally* stationed at M_a. Postulate P specifies that there should be a determinate, non-arbitrary answer to the question of which hypothesis is correct; but it is hard to see how there could be, since my *experience* would clearly be the same in both cases. Both hypotheses are plainly compatible with Scenario Σ, and they at least appear to be compatible as well with all our stipulations to date.

But let us take a more careful look. While the two hypotheses indeed imply no *actual* experiential differences, it turns out that they imply a great number of *counterfactual* experiential differences. Consider, for example, what I *would have* heard during the interval t_1–t_3 if, instead of "traveling" to M_k, I had remained "at rest" at M_c. First, say, during the interval t_1–t_2, I would have experienced an S_n "departing", i.e., heard $S_n^{max} \Rightarrow S_n^0$ while $M = M_c$. Then I would have experienced an S_n (the other one) "arriving", i.e., heard $S_n^0 \Rightarrow S_n^{max}$ while $M = M_c$. That is, I would have experienced two *B-changes*.

But now consider what a perceiver would have experienced during the interval t_1–t_3 if he had been located (and remained at rest) at an M_b that was, so to speak, "between" M_a and M_c. Letting 'π' represent the *actual* perceiver in Scenario Σ, and 'φ' his counterfactual counterpart, the picture is as in Figure 8.4.

Not to put too fine a point on it, what perceiver φ would have experienced is also two B-changes, namely, a *very unusual* S_n, first "approaching" *very fast* and then "departing" *very slowly*. For observe, to begin with, that for a perceiver at rest in the Auditory World at M_b, there is no experiential distinction between an S-tone object's approaching from one (M-) "direction", e.g., through a range of M-pitches *higher* than M_b, and its approaching from the other (M-) "direction", e.g., through a range of M-pitches *lower* than M_b. In either case, all that the stationary perceiver *hears* is an S-tone gradually increasing in loudness while the pitch of

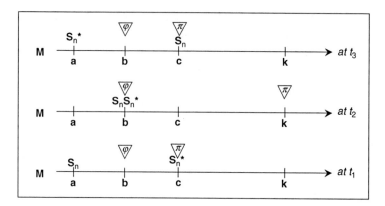

FIG. 8.4. Two perceivers in Scenario Σ with duplicate S_n objects

the master sound remains constant.[15] It follows that, if two S_ns simultaneously approach a perceiver at rest from *both* M-directions, what he will *hear* is an S_n-tone that increases in loudness twice as rapidly as it would were only one such sound-object approaching.[16] Correlatively, when the two S_ns depart from a given location, the S_n heard by a perceiver at that location will decrease in loudness twice as slowly as in the case of a single departing sound-object.

But not only would the experienced B-changes have a different *tempo*. They would also have a different *outcome*. For, since one of the S_ns moves from M_a to M_c and the other from M_c to M_a during the interval t_1–t_3, there will be a time and a location—we might as well suppose these to be t_2 and M_b—when, as it were, their paths cross. We have assumed that all S-tone objects are the "same size", i.e., have the same maximum loudness, **max**, but what a perceiver located at M_b at t_2 would *hear* is an S_n of loudness $2 \times$ **max** (i.e., S_n^{2max})—and that, it turns out, implies that our collection of stipulations is in fact internally incoherent. More precisely, our subsequent assumptions are collectively incompatible with postulate P. There *cannot* be an answer to the identification question that is both determinate and non-arbitrary.

The incoherence that we have just uncovered in fact lies very deep, for once we admit the possibility that numerically distinct S-tone objects might be experientially *superimposed*, i.e., simultaneously located at the same M-pitch, then even our *synchronic* counts of sound-objects cease to be

---

[15] There are, of course, many *counterfactual* differences between the two possibilities.

[16] To simplify matters as much as possible, I assume that all the relevant "velocities" are the same and that the corresponding "auditory thresholds" are also fixed and identical.

determinate. What we have been treating as a single object, e.g., *one* S_i^{max} stationed at M_g could then in principle also be interpreted the "superposition" at M_g of 2, 3, 4, ... S_is, each of loudness $1/2, 1/3, 1/4$ ... max. Each of these interpretive options will imply different particular counterfactual experiential possibilities. If, for instance, the *apparent* S_i^{max} stationed at M_g were *actually* a "superposition" of *two* S_is, each of loudness $1/2$ max, it would in principle be possible to experience the B-change, $S_i^{max} \Rightarrow S_i^{1/2max}$ while $M = M_g$, as one of the two superimposed S_is "departed".

But what is ultimately responsible for this incoherence? The clear culprit is *B-changes*. For any given B-change, e.g., $S_b^j \Rightarrow S_b^k$ while $M = M_h$, can in principle be interpreted as the experience of an *indeterminate number* of S_bs of loudness totaling $|j-k|$ arriving at (or departing from) M_h. And this indeterminacy is radical and contagious, for any given *A-change* could then in principle be interpreted as a kind of experiential "vector sum", resulting from any of an indefinite number of *combinations* of simultaneous separate motions of the perceiver and the perceived "sound objects".[17]

The upshot is that, once we admit *any B-changes at all* into the Auditory Model, we lose all hope of a determinate, non-arbitrary answer to any identification question, diachronic or synchronic. In short, if B-changes are *possible*, then postulate P must be false. Postulate P thus implies a crucial *modal* consequence: *B-changes must be represented as impossible.* But representing B-changes as impossible is equivalent to denying that the M-pitch location of a "sound-object" can change, and that, in turn, is precisely equivalent representing certain regularities as necessary. Specifically, if S-tone objects *cannot* "wander", then we must regard the regularities of co-occurrence, e.g.,

(co) S_i^{max} *whenever* $M = M_p$,

and succession, e.g.,

(su) $S_i^j \Rightarrow S_i^{max}$ *whenever* $M_x \Rightarrow M_p$, and correlatively
$S_i^{max} \Rightarrow S_i^0$ *whenever* $M_p \Rightarrow M_{p \pm \epsilon}$,

---

[17] The experienced A-change, $S_c^{2q} \Rightarrow S_c^{5q}$ while $M_d \Rightarrow M_e$, for example, could be the outcome of a the perceiver's moving "further away" from an S_c of, say, loudness $4q$ stationed at $M_{d-\delta}$ while *another* S_c of, say, loudness $9q$ simultaneously "approached" "from the other direction", i.e., from $M_{e+\eta}$. A hypothetical perceiver who had remained "stationary" at M_d, e.g., might then have experienced the B-change $S_c^{2q} \Rightarrow S_c^{3q}$ while $M = M_d$, whereas one who had remained "stationary" at M_e might have experienced the B-change $S_c^0 \Rightarrow S_c^{7q}$ while $M = M_e$. But the specific numbers are, of course, completely arbitrary.

which correspond to the "stationing" of a sound-object, an S_i, at a particular M-pitch, M_p, as necessary. The perception of an S_i^{max} is thereby necessarily connected with the perception of M_p. "Experience is possible only through the representation of a necessary connection of perceptions" (B218). Such necessary regularities of co-occurrence and succession are the experiential expressions of the Auditory World's *natural laws*.

Space in the Auditory Model

Reference to the master sound, M, occurs in a number of fundamental *explanations* of perceptual experiences in the Auditory World. A perceiver's hearing or not hearing a particular sound-object, S_i, for example, is explained in terms of their relative M-locations. A perceiver hears an S_i stationed at M_x just in case he himself is located between $M_{x - \epsilon}$ and $M_{x + \epsilon}$, i.e., just in case the M-pitch that he hears falls between those two values. The pitch of the master sound thus functions as a parameter in a rudimentary "science of auditory thresholds". In addition, as we have seen, an ostensible change of ontological consequence—an experienced change of S-tone loudness—is also explained by appealing to the master sound, i.e., as a mere appearance, resulting from an actual change in the perceiver's location relative to the M-station of the heard tone.

The basic job of the master sound in the Auditory World, in other words, is to supply a family of relations, defined over both the objects of that world (the S-tones) and perceivers of those objects, which can enter into explanations of the "modes of sensible appearing" of those objects to such perceivers. In each instance, the explanatory load is carried by a suitable acknowledgment of their *relative M-pitch locations*. This explanatory role is the characteristic and definitive mark of the *form of outer sense*. We explain in just the same way, for example, why a particular object cannot be seen (e.g., because it is occluded by another object located between it and the perceiver) or why a nearby object which is *actually* smaller than a distant one nevertheless *appears* to be larger than it. Strawson characterized his Auditory Model as a "No-Space world", but if, with Kant, we understand by 'space' the form of outer sense, then the Auditory World is "spatial" after all.

The point perhaps stands out more sharply if we imagine recasting the explanations of modes of sensible appearing of objects in the Auditory World in a more familiar form. Instead of thinking of the master sound itself as *constituting* the environment within which both S-tones and perceivers are "located", we might instead think of the "space" of the Auditory World as a (posited) one-dimensional continuum of *positions*, p_i, within which not only S-tones and perceivers but also the M-pitches themselves can be located.[18] We could then coordinatize this posited continuum by selecting an arbitrary M-pitch, e.g., M_o, as an *origin*, $p = 0$, and an arbitrary M-pitch *interval*, δ, as a spatial *unit*.

The movements of a perceiver, α, could then be described by a *location function*, P, relating position and time, $P(\alpha, t_i) = p_j$. Individual S_ys, in contrast, would have fixed positions within the spatial continuum. This fact would be reflected in *laws*, expressing the necessity of regularities of co-occurrence, of the form:

$$(t)[P(S_y, t) = c],$$

where S_y^{max} whenever $M = M_x$ and $c = \delta(x-o)$; i.e., S_y is located at the position p_c which is $(x-o)$ δ units from the (stipulated) origin. Finally, explanations of the apparent loudness of an S-tone could be expressed by another function, L, relating the apparent loudness, Λ, of an S_j heard by a perceiver α at a given time t_i to their relative positions at that time:

$$\Lambda(\alpha, S_j, t_i) = L[P(\alpha, t_i), P(S_j, t_i)],$$

where $0 \leq \Lambda(\alpha, S_j, t_i) \leq max$. The existence of "auditory thresholds", for instance, would then be reflected in laws, expressing the necessity of regularities of succession, of the form:

$$(t)(\chi) [|P(\chi, t) - P(S_j, t)| > \delta\in \rightarrow \Lambda(\chi, S_j, t_i) = 0],$$

and the "permanent presence" of an S_i at a given position c, in a law of the form

$$(t)(\chi) [P(\chi, t) = c \rightarrow \Lambda(\chi, S_j, t_i) = max],$$

where the substituends for 'χ' designate perceivers, e.g., α.

In this mode of representation, once the spatial continuum has been coordinatized, explicit reference to the master sound would drop out of our explanatory accounts. But the whole *content* of the resulting functionally expressed Auditory World laws of nature ultimately derives from the fact that we must represent specific regularities of co-occurrence and succession among perceptions of S-tones and M-pitches as necessary.

---

[18] One might think of these as analogous to the *frequencies* in our Radio Model.

Reference to the posited continuum of positions serves only to mediate inferences of possible perceptual encounters from actual perceptual encounters and of apparent form (i.e., experienced loudness) from actual form. Taken at face value, this sort of spatial "container" would be, as Kant put it in the Aesthetic, a "self-subsisting non-entity (*Unding*)" (A39/B56). But now we can better understand that this appearance is only a by-product of an adventitious mode of representation. What is primary in the order of understanding is the explanatory role of the master sound as the form of outer sense. Perhaps surprisingly, then, our reflections on the Auditory World both confirm and further clarify Kant's thesis of the transcendental ideality of space.

The Auditory Model has, I hope, proved a useful tool for understanding in general what Kant is up to in the Analogies of Experience. It has helped us to see why and how an experience of *objects* is correlative to a representation of necessary connections among *perceptions*, and it has shed some first light on the corresponding notions of substance and causality. The time has come, however, to leave the Auditory World and return to the text of the Critique. Our next order of business is to see what Kant himself has to say about substance—and that is precisely what we find in the *first* Analogy of Experience.

Duration and Persistence: 9
Substance in the Analogies

From the Schemata chapter, we know that the Analogies are fundamentally concerned with *time-order*, that is, our ability to represent time as a single determinately ordered linear continuum of instants encompassing all particular times—past, present, and future. The three categories of Relation—substance, causality, and community—correspond to three ways in which we can represent two temporally successive perceptions: as two encounters with a single persisting item, as encounters with numerically distinct, successively existing items; or as encounters with numerically distinct, simultaneously existing items. Our present concern is with the first of these temporal modes.

Hume on identity and duration

Consider, then, what we normally think of as two temporally separated perceptions of a single object, say, a thick green book encountered on Monday and again on Tuesday. As Hume observed, considered simply in themselves, such perceptual experiences are numerically distinct occurrences "in the mind", separated from each other by an incredibly diverse stream of innumerable items of the same sort ("impressions"). Consequently, he found our unreflective idea of a further item of a radically different sort, an object to which we attribute "a *continued* existence . . . *distinct* from the mind and perception" (*THN* I. iv. 2; 188), thoroughly problematic.

Duration and Persistence

Earlier we explored some of the philosophical commitments that underlie and give rise to Hume's puzzlement here, and outlined his general strategy for dealing with such worries by attributing to us the tendency habitually to mistake purely subjective "impressions of reflection" for objective features of perceived items and objective relations among them. His diagnosis of "the source of the error and deception with regard to identity, when we attribute it to [the object of][1] our resembling perceptions, notwithstanding their interruption" (*THN* I. iv. 2; 202), has precisely this characteristic form.

We find by experience, that there is such a *constancy* in almost all the impressions of the senses, that their interruption produces no alteration on them .... I survey the furniture of my chamber; I shut my eyes, and afterwards open them; and find the new perceptions to resemble perfectly those which formerly struck my senses. This resemblance ... naturally connects together our ideas of these interrupted perceptions by the strongest relation, and conveys the mind with an easy transition from one to another. An easy transition or passage of the imagination, along the ideas of these different and interrupted perceptions, is almost the same disposition of mind with that in which we consider one constant and uninterrupted perception. It is therefore very natural for us to mistake one for the other. (*THN* I. iv. 2; 204)

The "mistake" that Hume here diagnoses consists in our *identifying* [the object of] our earlier and later perceptions, i.e., our judging that [the object of] the earlier perception = [the object of] the later perception. What will prove more directly relevant to our present concerns, however, is the fact that Hume's worries extend to the very *idea* of such a relation of identity. What troubles Hume is essentially the same as the question that troubled Frege: How can '$a = b$' be both true and informative, since, if it is true, what it says can only be that $a = a$, while it can be informative only if a and b are *somehow* different? Hume frames the issue as a tension between *unity* and *number*. The relation of identity must be "an idea which is a medium betwixt unity and number" (*THN* I. iv. 2; 201), but since

both number and unity are incompatible with the relation of identity, it must lie in something that is neither of them. [But] betwixt unity and number there can be no medium .... After one object is supposed to exist, we must either suppose another

---

[1] On Hume's view, we are *first* unreflectively inclined to identify our earlier and later *impressions*, i.e., thinking of our interrupted perceptions themselves as continuously existing. Later, however, we begin "feigning a double existence", "by ascribing these contrary qualities to different existences; the *interruption* to perceptions, and the *continuance* to objects" (*THN* I. iv. 2; 215). The parenthetical insertion here is intended to gloss over such exegetical nuances.

one also to exist; in which case we have the idea of number: Or we must suppose it not to exist; in which case the first object remains a unity. (*THN* I. iv. 2; 200)

What Hume wants is an account of the way in which the idea of a relation of identity can be derived from original impressions, but his Separability Principle evidently implies that no such account can be forthcoming. Since an impression of a relation must be a relation of impressions, no *single* impression could give rise to the idea of *any* relation, and no *multiplicity* of distinct relata could give rise to the idea of one single item's self-identity. The idea of a relation of identity, in short, seems to be yet another that Hume's principles imply we simply cannot have.

The notion that Hume in fact invokes in response to these puzzles about identity is that of a *duration of time*. His idea is roughly that the notion of a *mere passage of time* can provide for something functionally analogous to Frege's "modes of presentation"—namely, an *informative* difference in an aspect of experience—without introducing any real, separable difference in *content*. By a "fiction of the imagination",

a single object placed before us and surveyed for any time without our discovering in it any interruption or variation is able to give us a notion of identity. For when we consider any two points of this time, we may place them in different lights: We may either survey them in the very same instant, in which case they give us the idea of number, both by themselves and by the object .... Or, on the other hand, we may trace the succession of time by a like succession of ideas and ... imagine afterwards a change in the time without any *variation* or *interruption* in the object, in which case it gives us the idea of unity. Here then is an idea which is a medium betwixt unity and number, or, more properly speaking, is either of them according to the view in which we take it: And this idea we call that of identity. (*THN* I. iv. 2; 201)

Given Hume's principles, however, a *mere* "change in the time", without change or alteration, is not so easy to imagine. Like Kant, Hume is clear that time itself cannot be perceived.

... [T]ime cannot make its appearance to the mind, either alone, or attended with a steady unchangeable object, but is always discovered by some *perceivable* succession of changeable objects. (*THN* I. ii. 3; 35)

Time, concludes Hume, "can plainly be nothing but different ideas, or impressions, or objects disposed in a certain manner, that is, succeeding each other" (*THN* I. ii. 3; 37). Strictly speaking, then, any consciousness or awareness of time requires a consciousness or awareness of change. The source of the idea of time is an *impression of a succession* (= a succession of impressions), and the only coherent temporal *idea* is consequently the idea of a succession. In particular,

the idea of duration is always derived from a succession of changeable objects, and can never be conveyed to the mind by any thing steadfast and unchangeable. (*THN* I. ii. 3; 37)

Thus, although we apparently dispute about "the idea of time without any changeable existence", Hume concludes "that we really have no such idea, is certain". Nevertheless, he adds, here too "we can easily point out those appearances which make us fancy we have the idea":

For ... there is a continual succession of perceptions in our mind, so that, the idea of time being forever present with us, when we consider a steadfast object at five o'clock and regard the same at six, we are apt to apply to it that idea in the same manner as if every moment were distinguished by a different position or an alteration of the object. The first and second appearances of the object, being compared with the succession of our perceptions, seem equally removed as if the object had really changed. To which we may add, what experience shows us, that the object was susceptible of such a number of changes betwixt these appearances .... [In this way we come to] imagine we can form the idea of a time and duration without any change or succession. (*THN* I. ii. 5; 65)

This is not an easy passage to interpret. Two different scenarios seem to be tangled together:

> (s1)   contemplating a "steadfast object" *while* having a series of (contemporaneous) changing perceptions,

and

> (s2)   encountering a "steadfast object", *then* having a series of changing perceptions, and *then* encountering the "steadfast object" *again*.

In either case, however, the idea of a (mere) duration of time is evidently a "fiction of the imagination" which depends on the idea of a "steadfast object"—and that is surely just the idea of a *persisting* object, i.e., one which remains *self-identical across time*.

We have just seen, however, that, according to Hume, the idea of such a "steadfast object" is itself a "fiction of the imagination" which, since it includes the idea of reidentifiability across time, depends on the idea of a (mere) duration of time. Hume's principles thus apparently leave us with the unsatisfactory picture of *mutually supporting fictions*, a pair of illegitimate ideas—the ostensible idea of a persisting ("steadfast") object and the ostensible idea of a (mere) duration of time—neither of which we could have unless we already had the other.

Now we have long since taken leave of Hume's austere version of empiricism according to which all legitimate ideas must be derivable from original impressions. Hume's considerations, however, perceptively illustrate the *correlativity* of the concept of a persisting object and the concept of a duration of time, and on this point Kant is in complete agreement.

Only through that which persists does *existence* in different parts of the temporal series acquire a *magnitude*, which one calls *duration*. For in mere sequence alone existence is always disappearing and beginning, and never has the least magnitude. Without that which persists there is therefore no temporal relation. (A183/B226)

Where Kant and Hume part company is on the issue of epistemic legitimacy. The arguments of the Transcendental Deduction and Schematism have already secured the epistemic legitimacy of applying the pure concepts of the understanding in synthetic judgments, i.e., to objects of possible experience. What is at issue in the Analytic of Principles is thus not *whether* the experiential application of the schematized categories is legitimate, but only *how* such applications are reflected in determinate synthetic *a priori* judgments about the experienced world.

Persistence, alteration, and change

The Transcendental Deduction highlighted the relationship between the unity of the experiencing subject and the unity of the experienced world. Each of these is fundamentally a unity *in time*. The unity of the subject is "the necessary unity of apperception with regard to all possible empirical consciousness (of perception) *at every time*", and the unity of the world is consequently a "synthetic unity of all appearances according to their relations in time" (A177/B220). Since time itself is not an intuitable experiential content, the totality of appearances can be temporally unified "only through *a priori* connecting concepts" (B219), i.e., only by thinking them under object-concepts and hence as necessarily related to each other.

This *synthetic unity* in the temporal relation of all perceptions . . . is thus the law that all empirical time-determinations must stand under rules of general time-determination . . . . (A177–8/B220)

The several Analogies of Experience, Kant tells us, are precisely such rules.

The most fundamental sort of persistence that animates the First Analogy, however, is not the persistence of things *in* time but rather the persistence *of* time.

All appearances are in time, in which, as substratum ([namely,] as persistent form of inner intuition), both *simultaneity* as well as *succession* can alone be represented. The time, therefore, in which all change of appearances is to be thought, lasts and does not change; since it is that in which succession or simultaneity can be represented only as determinations of it. (B224–5)[2]

As Kant repeatedly stresses, however, this lasting temporal form "cannot be perceived by itself" (B225, A183/B226).

Consequently, it is in the objects of perception, i.e., the appearances, that the substratum must be encountered that represents time in general and in which all change or simultaneity can be perceived in apprehension through the relation of the appearances to it. (B225)

But how can the representation of a unitary unchanging time be encountered in the appearances, when "our *apprehension* of the manifold of appearance is always successive, and is therefore always changing"? (A182/B225).

Here it is important to remember the fundamental ambiguity in the notion of "apprehension". Our apprehend*ings* are always successive and always changing, but such successiveness can be *conceptualized* as experiential encounters with apprehend*eds* that are themselves either successive or simultaneous—different states of a single persisting object, e.g., colors of a leaf; or different relationships among multiple persisting objects, e.g., a ship sailing downstream past rocks and trees; or different parts of a single persisting object, e.g., the foundation and roof of a house. Kant's basic point is that, as such examples illustrate, *both* modes of conceptualization, as successive *and* as simultaneous, presuppose the notion of a *continuant*, an object that persists while its states or relationships (to other objects or to the perceiver) change.

---

[2] Cf. A182–3/B226: "Only in that which persists... are temporal relations possible (for simultaneity and succession are the only relations in time), i.e., that which persists is the *substratum* of the empirical representation of time itself, by which alone all time-determination is possible.... For change does not affect time itself, but only the appearances in time ....".

Without what persists there is therefore no temporal relation. . . . [Thus] this persisting thing in the appearances is the substratum of all time-determination, consequently also the condition of the possibility of all synthetic unity of perceptions, i.e., of experience . . . . Therefore in all appearances that which persists is the object itself, i.e., the substance (*phaenomenon*), but everything that changes or that can change belongs only to the way in which this substance or substances exists, thus to their determinations. (A183–4/B226–7)[3]

And that is precisely the principle of the First Analogy as it occurs in A (A181).

The "determinations" of a substance "that are nothing other than particular ways for it to exist" are called *accidents* (A186/B229). Although we speak of accidents as "inhering" in substances, which themselves "subsist", Kant is clear that the inherence of an accident in a subsisting substance is not literally a relation between two distinct items. Although "the conditions of the logical use of our understanding", i.e., the fact that we operate with concepts, inevitably lead us to abstract what is changeable from "what is really persistent and fundamental",

it is more precise and correct if one characterizes the accident only through the way in which the existence of a substance is positively determined. (A187/B230)

Hence, although substance belongs to the categories of Relation, Kant remarks, it is "more as their condition than as itself containing a relation" (A187/B230).

In Kant's terminology, *change (Wechsel)* consists in something's arising or perishing, coming into existence or passing out of existence. In contrast, *alteration (Veränderung)* "is a way of existing that succeeds another way of existing of the very same object" (A187/B230). Consequently, what undergoes alteration persists; its states and relationships change. Thus while we say informally that leaves change color in autumn, as Kant sees it, the leaves undergo alteration, and their color is what changes, e.g., from green (which ceases to exist as a determination of the persisting leaf) to brown (which begins to exist as a determination of the same leaf).[4]

---

[3] The grammatical infelicity of the last sentence echoes that in the original text: . . . *gehört nur zu der Art, wie diese Substanz oder Substanzen existieren, mithin zu ihren Bestimmungen.* I have preserved it here to emphasize that, at this stage of Kant's reasoning, the possibility of *multiple* substances is evidently still open.

[4] This is one of the places where the differences between current translations can lead to serious confusion. While Guyer–Wood follows Kemp-Smith in translating *Wechsel* by 'change' and *Veränderung* by 'alteration', Pluhar elects to translate *Wechsel* by 'variation' and *Veränderung* (alas) by 'change'. The translations offered here conform to the Guyer–Wood conventions.

Substance as object and substance as matter

Considered as the persisting subjects of changing color-predicables, then, leaves apparently satisfy Kant's description of substances. On the face of it, however, leaves themselves not only undergo alteration but also *change*, i.e., arise and perish. In winter, the trees are bare. New leaves come into existence in the spring, and, after they have fallen from the trees in autumn, they ultimately pass out of existence as well—either slowly, as they decay and decompose, or more quickly, e.g., by being burned. This last possibility echoes one of Kant's own illustrative examples:

A philosopher was asked: How much does the smoke weigh? He replied: If you take away from the weight of the wood that was burnt the weight of the ashes that are left over, you will have the weight of the smoke. (A185/B228)

This hypothetical philosopher plainly assumed that there is something, call it *matter*, that manifests itself in our experience as weight and is conserved through even the dramatic transformation of dry wood into smoke and ashes, i.e., something of which wood, smoke, and ashes all *consist*. Kant's point, of course, is that there is a sense of 'substance' which is roughly equivalent to 'matter', and that it belongs to our concept of *such* a substance that it can neither arise nor perish, but only undergo alterations in its form. This sense of 'substance' is clearly what is at issue in the principle of the First Analogy as it is formulated in B:

In all change of appearances substance persists, and its quantum is neither increased nor diminished in nature. (B224)

The A formulation, in contrast, according to which substance is "the object itself", apparently harmonizes better with the Aristotelian notion of a "first substance", i.e., the individual subject of multiple (possibly incompatible) predicables. In fact, however, Kant seems from the beginning to have in mind the sense of 'substance' in which "we can grant an appearance the name of substance only if we presuppose its existence at all time" (A185/B228). For he tells us both that "the proposition that substance persists is tautological" (A184/B227) and that, although the word 'persistence' "pertains more to future time", nevertheless "the inner necessity of persisting is inseparably connected with the necessity of always having existed" (A185/B228–9).

When Kant argues that the temporal relations of succession and simultaneity are possible, and hence that *experience* is possible, only on the condition that something lasts and persists, he intends his conclusion to be that there is something that *always* exists (A182/B225), such that

all existence and all change in time can only be regarded as a *modus* of the existence of that which lasts and persists. (A183/B226–7, my emphases)

We can better understand Kant's reasoning here when we recall (from the Aesthetic) that the representation of time is not discursive or general, but rather *singular*, and that temporal concepts are systematic in a way that presupposes the concept of the *unitary individual*, time. We consequently need to find something in the field of appearances that can represent not only the necessary comprehensiveness of time but also its necessary *unity*. This, however, would

never be possible if we were to allow new things (as far as their substance is concerned) to arise. For then everything would disappear that alone can represent the unity of time, namely the identity of the substratum in which alone all change has its thoroughgoing unity. (A186/B229)

Kant consequently concludes that we must represent every change of appearances as the alteration of a persisting substance. This includes all *ostensible* instances of coming to be (e.g., maggots appearing in rotting meat or clouds forming in the sky) and of ceasing to exist (e.g., finding only loam where leaves have fallen or the evaporation of a pool of water). A genuine *substantial change*, i.e., the arising or perishing of a substance

cannot be a possible perception unless it concerns merely a determination of that which persists, for it is this very thing that persists that makes possible the representation of the transition from one state into another, and from non-being into being, which can therefore be empirically cognized only as changing determinations of that which lasts. (A188/B231)

The most straightforward interpretation of Kant's claim here is that the experience of an ostensible transition "from non-being into being" cannot be an experience of a transition from *nothing* to *something*, for "an empty time that would precede is not an object of perception" (A188/B231). Such an ostensible instance of coming-to-be would necessarily occur at some determinate point of time, and that presupposes something, a temporal *content*, which already exists. The item that putatively comes into existence would thereby be connected "to things that existed antecedently and which endure until that which arises". But then, Kant continues, "the latter [i.e., that which ostensibly arises] would be only a determination of the former [i.e., things that existed antecedently], as that which persists" (A188/B231).

Now this conclusion may well strike the reader as too quick. For hasn't Kant overlooked a possibility here? He is surely correct in observing that any ostensible coming-to-be must occur at some determinate point of time, and that we can "attach" such an event to a particular time only if something already exists with the help of which we can, so to speak, *mark* time. Time itself cannot be perceived, and so we can fix the time of one occurrence only relative to another: dinner will be served *when* the clock strikes seven; Nero fiddled *while* Rome burned. But that, it might be objected, requires only that we *relate* the ostensibly wholly new item "to things that existed antecedently and which endure until [it] arises", not, as Kant has it, that we *connect* (*anknüpfen*) it to those things in such a way that it is "only a determination" of them.

Evidently, therefore, we could consistently suppose that all items were only *relatively* "persistent", i.e., that *each* of them, at some time, "absolutely" comes into existence, endures for a finite stretch of time, and then "absolutely" passes out of existence. Call these 'quasi-substances'. The most that Kant's argument shows, the objection continues, is that there couldn't be a time at which *no* such "transient" things exist, i.e., a time subsequent to which *everything* comes into existence. In other words, although Kant is entitled to conclude that, necessarily,

(α) there is no time *t* such that, for all items *x*, *x* does not exist
      at *t*,

it does not follow that there must be anything that exists at *all* times, i.e., that

(β) there is some item *x* such that, for all times *t*, *x* exists at *t*.

That, for every item, there is some time at which it does not exist— "$(x)(\exists t)\sim(x$ exists at $t)$"—does *not* imply that there is some time at which nothing exists—"$(\exists t)(x)\sim(x$ exists at $t)$". To suppose that we can deny the latter only if we deny the former is to commit an elementary logical error. For the former, and so (α), would be true, for instance, if every individual item were a quasi-substance that existed for exactly six years, but, like US senators, the items had, so to speak, *overlapping terms*.

As Figure 9.1 plainly shows, such a world would contain no completely empty time. That is the possibility, the objection concludes, that Kant seems simply to have overlooked.

The objection is both perceptive and ingenious, but it is nevertheless, I think, not ultimately telling. Not only has Kant not overlooked the

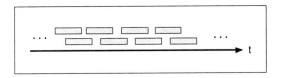

FIG. 9.1.   Items with overlapping terms

possibility of transient quasi-substances with "overlapping terms", but the First Analogy concludes with a suggestive argument that is plausibly intended precisely to address and reject it:

Substances (in appearance) are the substrata of all time-determinations. The arising of some of them and the perishing of others would itself remove the sole condition of the empirical unity of time, and the appearances would then be related to two different times, in which existence flowed side by side, which is absurd. For there is *only one* time, in which all different times must not be placed simultaneously but only one after another. (A188–9/B231–2)

Now it is admittedly not immediately obvious what Kant has in mind here, but a careful look at Figure 9.1 will at least help us along the way to an interpretation. For when we ask how the necessary unity of time is represented in our diagram, i.e., the fact that there is only *one time*, the answer can only be: by means of the *one time-arrow*—but that arrow, of course, precisely does not represent any *appearance*, i.e., any intuitable content. The (one) time-arrow represents only the (one) time that "cannot be perceived by itself". When Kant speaks of removing the condition of the *empirical* unity of time, then, he is calling to our attention the fact that there is nothing in the experiential contents depicted in Figure 9.1 that represents the *necessary* unity of time. And his idea seems to be that, absent some genuinely persistent substance to which *all* the items could be related, each quasi-substance could be thought of as determining its own "local" time.

Here we might take as a model the "internal" time of an episodic dream. Suppose, for example, that I dream one night, say Tuesday, that I am a pearl-fisher, Pete, on a tropical island, and another night, say Friday, that I am an astronaut, Abe, visiting a research station in orbit around the earth. In each dream, I experience events as determinately ordered in time. In the pearl-fishing dream, for instance, Pete dives (at t_{1p}), finds a promising oyster (t_{2p}), brings it to the surface (t_{3p}), opens it (t_{4p}), and discovers a lovely pearl (t_{5p}). In the astronaut dream, Abe dons his space suit (at t_{1a}), enters the airlock (t_{2a}); exits the station (t_{3a}); floats to a bank of solar cells (t_{4a}); and replaces a defective element (t_{5a}). But there is no determinate answer to the question of whether, for instance, Pete finds the oyster before or after Abe enters the airlock, i.e., whether t_{2p} is earlier or later than t_{2a}. I have no way of coordinating the "internal" times of the two dreams. That would require a single unitary "external" time within which I can think *all* of the events as determinately located.

Now in fact we do not think of the "internal" times of our episodic dreams as necessarily commensurable. What we in fact coordinate are the times of the *dreamings*. My experience (Tuesday) of dreaming of Pete's finding the oyster *objectively* precedes my experience (Friday) of dreaming of Abe's entering the airlock, i.e., precedes it in the *one* time within which all *actual* occurrences can be determinately located. We regard the dreamed events—Pete's finding the oyster; Abe's entering the airlock—in contrast, as *mere* appearances. They are not actual but "illusory", and, to anticipate, our eschewing the demand for a determinate answer to the question of *their* temporal relationships is an essential aspect of their being so. That is one of the characteristic constitutive differences between dreaming and perceiving.

Now, in our hypothetical world of overlapping transient quasi-substances, we could perhaps imagine *coordinating* an event within the "local" time of one item with an event within the "local" time of another (as we might decide to coordinate Pete's finding the oyster with Abe's exiting the station). It might then appear to make sense to think of the "local" *times* of those events, i.e., the times at which they occur, as themselves simultaneous, but, as Kant points out, that is simply absurd. *Events* can be simultaneous if they occur at the *same time*, i.e., at the same moment of the *one* "global" time within which we can think of *all* events as determinately located. But *times* cannot be simultaneous. Different times (different moments) are always necessarily related as earlier and later. However, if instead we think of the events *themselves* as simultaneous, then, as we have seen, we already presuppose a unitary comprehensive "global" time, and thereby something that *genuinely* persists, i.e., a substance that exists at all times. In either case, then, the picture of an experiencable world containing *only* transient quasi-substances ultimately proves to be incoherent.

Our hypothetical objector is unlikely to be satisfied. Kant, he will point out, claims more than that there must be *some* genuinely persisting substance. The principle of the First Analogy asserts that substance persists in *all* change of appearances, and Kant correlatively claims that a coming into existence or ceasing to exist of something that is not "merely a determination of that which persists" *cannot* be a possible perception. To demonstrate this, however, what he needs to show is that there cannot be *any* "transient quasi-substances", i.e., that *nothing* can "absolutely" arise or perish, and this argument is not yet forthcoming.

But perhaps we have actually made more progress toward establishing Kant's thesis than our objector realizes. It is important to remember that what we are exploring is the possibility of experiencing the arising or perishing of an *object*, i.e., something "corresponding to and therefore also distinct from the cognition" (A104). As Kant will shortly remind us (in the Second Analogy), we are concerned with *appearances* "not insofar as they are (as representations) objects, but rather only insofar as they designate an object" (A190/B235). An "absolute" coming-to-be, for instance, is therefore to be conceptualized as an event *in nature*, and our experience of it as a (veridical) perception, in contrast to a dream or an hallucination.

When Kant speaks of the necessity of our "attaching" the point of time of such an "origination" to that which already exists, then, he means more than that we need to be able to locate our *experiencing* of it in time— as I can determinately locate my dreaming of Pete's finding the oyster or Abe's exiting the station. We need to be able to locate the ostensible origination *itself* as an objective event that occurs at some determinate time *rather than another*—and this arguably indeed requires us to "connect" the content of that event, i.e., the *object* that ostensibly comes into existence, to things that existed antecedently.

For that is what it takes to make it an *object in nature* and not just, for instance, the content of an hallucination or a dream. Pete's oyster and Abe's space suit, for example, are, in a sense, experienced as "transient quasi-substances". They "exist" only insofar and only for so long as I dream of them, and they are precisely not "connected" to anything that existed in nature antecedently to my dreaming. But *for just that reason* I conceive of such items not as actual objects but only as *mere* appearances.

In contrast, as we saw earlier, insofar as I conceive of what I experience as an *object*, I necessarily represent it as something with a history of its own, independent of my experience of it. This point was already clear to Descartes, and he explicitly invoked it in the Sixth Meditation in response to his puzzle about how to distinguish waking life from sleep.

[If] someone, while I was awake, quite suddenly appeared to me and disappeared as fast as do the images which I see in sleep, so that I could not know from whence the form came nor whither it went, it would not be without reason that I should

211

deem it a specter or a phantom formed by my brain [and similar to those which I form in sleep], rather than a real man. (AT 89–90 = CS 61–2)

In other words, my conviction that the history of an ostensibly generated item does not *in any way* precede the point of my experiencing its putative arising is a sufficient ground for me to conclude that the apparent item is "illusory", i.e., that there is no such *object*, but only a change in the determinations of my inner state, i.e., a hallucination or a dream. But insofar as I conceive my experience as the veridical perception of an object whose history *in some way* precedes my encounter with it, I necessarily also conceive of what appears, not as an item generated *ex nihilo*, but as a new determination of something that existed antecedently. In short, to put it aphoristically, any ostensible coming-to-be is an actual becoming. And if this is right, then Kant can in fact plausibly secure the principle of the First Analogy in its strongest form, as the global "conservation principle" formulated in B,

In all change of appearances substance persists, and its quantum is neither increased nor diminished in nature. (B224)

Substance in action

We find a bit more about substance in the Second Analogy, once the principle of causality has been established, since "causality leads to the concept of action, this to the concept of force, and thereby to the concept of substance". Action, Kant tells us, is the *empirical criterion* of substance,[5] i.e., substance "seems to manifest itself better and more readily through action than through the persistence of the appearance" (A204/B249).

The notion of *action* to which Kant here appeals comes from physics. It signifies, he explains, "the relation of the subject of causality to the effect" (A205/B250). In the Newtonian paradigm, one thing acts on another by exerting a force on it. Think of the Third Law of Motion: "For every action there is an equal and opposite reaction." Since, according to the principle of the Second Analogy (which will occupy us in the next chapter), "all alterations occur in accordance with the law of the connection of cause and effect" (B232), and, as the First Analogy has established, "all

---

[5] Kant thereby makes good a promissory note issued at the end of the First Analogy: "As to the empirical criterion of this necessary persistence and with it of the substantiality of appearances, ... what follows will give us the opportunity to note what is necessary" (A189/B232).

change (succession) of appearances is only alteration" (B233), we can conclude that

> actions are always the primary ground of all change of appearances, and therefore cannot lie in a subject that itself changes, since otherwise further actions and another subject, which determines this change, would be required. (A205/B250)

The intended conclusion is evidently that the "subject" in which causally efficacious actions "lie" must be a persisting substance. The unacceptable alternative is apparently supposed to be an infinite regress, but it is not immediately obvious what regress he has in mind. Let us see if we can get clearer about it.

Any effect, Kant reminds us, "consists in that which happens, consequently in the changeable" (A205/B250), and, from the First Analogy, we know that *changes* are always determinations of something that persists, a substance which is successively the subject of incompatible predicables. (The substance itself, as we saw, undergoes only an *alteration*.) What is caused is thus always a determination of some persisting substance, and what causes it is always the action of some "subject". Now if we think of such a "subject" as itself another *event*, i.e., something that happens, then the Second Analogy tells us that this event itself must also be an *effect*, that is, a determination of some persisting substance caused by the action of another "subject", and we indeed stand on the threshold of an infinite regress. What Kant thus concludes is that we must ultimately think of the "subject" of such causally determinative actions as the persisting substance itself:

> For that the *primary* subject[6] of the causality of all arising and perishing cannot itself arise and perish (in the field of appearances) is a certain inference, which leads to empirical necessity and persistence in existence, consequently to the concept of a substance as appearance. (A205/B251, my emphasis)

Shortly, we will have occasion to explore the Second Analogy and Kant's account of causation in considerable detail, but at the moment we are concerned only with what he takes to be the connection between our conceptions of causation and substance. What the line of reasoning that we have just surveyed is intended to establish is that any imputation of a causal relationship already presupposes a genuinely persisting substantial subject of changing determinations. Whatever empirically entitles me to posit an action consequently "proves substantiality without it being ne-

---

[6] The German is *erste Subjekt*. 'First subject' would be a more straightforward translation.

cessary for me first to seek out its persistence through compared perceptions", which, in any case, could never yield "the completeness that is requisite for the quantity and strict universality of the concept" (A205/B250–1), i.e., could never, as it were, inductively establish a necessary existence at all times.

The upshot is that our conceptual commitment to the existence of genuinely persisting substances is only nominally separable from our commitment to the principle that all events in nature are caused. Since our ability to represent a unitary determinately ordered temporal continuum is reflected in all three Analogies of Experience, this should not come as a surprise. Just as the general philosophical meta-principles of the Axioms and Anticipations each secured the objective validity of a *family* of inferentially interrelated (mathematical) synthetic *a priori* judgments, too numerous to be usefully itemized, so too the general philosophical meta-principle of the Analogies secures the objective validity of a *family* of inferentially interrelated (metaphysical) synthetic *a priori* judgments, three of which are then explicitly enumerated in the principles of persistence, successiveness, and simultaneity. In this chapter we have seen what Kant makes of persistence. It is time to move on to successiveness and simultaneity.

Succession and Simultaneity: Causation in the Analogies

In the last chapter, we discovered that the three modes of time are not quite on an equal footing. Persistence is a condition of the representation of a unitary time *per se* within which items can then be experienced as successive or simultaneous. The Second and Third Analogies are concerned with the conditions of such temporally structured experiences. As it turns out, both sorts of experiences depend upon items in nature standing in *causal relationships*. The Second Analogy secures the objective validity of causation in general as a condition of the experience of items as successive:

All alterations occur in accordance with the law of the connection of cause and effect. (B232)[1]

The Third Analogy then argues that *reciprocal* causality is a condition of the experience of items as simultaneous:

All substances, insofar as they can be perceived in space as simultaneous, are in thoroughgoing interaction. (B256)[2]

The Third Analogy thus presupposes the outcome of the Second.

In an important sense, the Second Analogy is the centerpiece of the Analytic of Principles. It occupies almost twice as many pages as the other

[1] In A: "Everything that happens (begins to be) presupposes something which it follows in accordance with a rule" (A189).
[2] In A: "All substances, insofar as they are *simultaneous*, stand in thoroughgoing community (i.e., interaction with one another)" (A211).

two Analogies combined, and Kant there formulates his argument no fewer than three times, gaining a little more clarity each time.[3] It is also one of the few places in the First Critique where Kant offers us *examples*, and it will in fact prove useful to begin by reviewing what he has to say about one of them.

Successive apprehendings: the problem

The problem of the Second Analogy rests on the observation that our experience is temporally discursive; that is, as Kant repeatedly stresses:

The apprehension of the manifold of appearance is always successive. The representations of the parts succeed one another. (A189/B234; cf. A192/B237, A198/B243, A201/B246)

Kant refers to this as the *subjective succession* of apprehension (A193/B238). The crucial observation is that such a subjective succession can be the manifestation of *objective* states of affairs having quite different temporal structures.

Figure 10.1, for instance, schematically exhibits one possible subjective succession: an apprehending of a small red balloon, followed by an apprehending of a middle-sized red balloon, followed by an apprehending of a large red balloon. One way in which I could come to have such a sequence of apprehendings, of course, is by watching a balloon expand, for instance, as it is heated by the sun, that is, by observing an objective alteration in the intrinsic determinations of a single object (see Fig. 10.2). But such a sequence of apprehendings could also result from my watching a balloon of constant diameter that is approaching me from a distance, that is, my observing an objective alteration in the *relational* determinations of a single object (see Fig. 10.3).

Or the same sequence of apprehendings might be the result of my successively *noticing* each of three different-sized balloons in my vicinity. Here nothing alters but my perceptual attention. The items that

---

[3] At B232–4, new material, not found in A; at A191–5/B236–40, from "Now let us proceed to our problem" through "[And] only under this presupposition alone is the experience of something that happens possible"; and at A201–2/B246–7, from "The ground of proof of this proposition, however, rests solely on the following moments" through "Hence, the principle of the causal relation in the sequence of appearances is valid for all objects of experience".

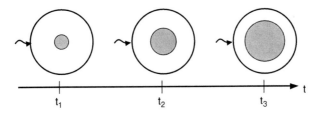

FIG. 10.1. A subjective succession

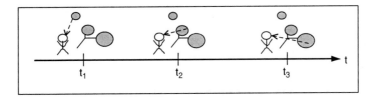

FIG. 10.2. An objective succession: watching a ballon expand

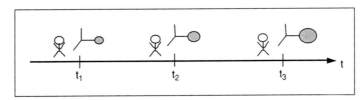

FIG. 10.3. An objective succession: watching a ballon approach

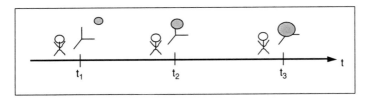

FIG. 10.4. An objective succession: noticing each of three balloons

I successively apprehend all *exist* simultaneously (see Fig. 10.4). An inventive reader will likely be able to think of still other possibilities.

Kant himself invites us to consider both "the apprehension of the manifold in the appearance of a house" (A190/B235) and the experience of seeing a ship drifting downstream (A192/B237). In the first case, the represented "parts" of the manifold might be, for instance, first the foundation, then the walls, and then the roof; in the second case, the ship adjacent first to a pier, then to a boulder, and then to a tree. In the first case, we have

217

> (H) successive apprehendings of parts of an *objectively simultaneous* manifold;

in the second,

> (S) successive apprehendings of *objectively successive* states of affairs.

Our ability to distinguish between these two sorts of cases is clearly a condition of our experiencing a temporally determinate natural world. Otherwise, as Kant points out,

we would have only a play of representations that would not be related to any object at all, i.e., by means of our perception no appearance would be distinguished from any other as far as the temporal relation is concerned . . . . (A194/B239)

The best we could do is to say that one *apprehending* follows another "which is something merely *subjective*, and . . . cannot count as the cognition of any object (not even in the appearance)" (A195/B240). In other words, just as in the First Analogy, we are here concerned with the conditions of the possibility of experiencing the items *apprehended* as themselves determinately located in time. (The contrast between *dreaming* that something happens and *perceiving* that something happens is again apposite; cf. A202/B247.) We need to be able to show

what sort of combination in time pertains to the manifold in the appearance itself even though the representation of it in apprehension is always successive. (A190/B235)

The difficulty is that, considered only subjectively, as sequences of apprehendings, the cases (H) and (S) are evidently indistinguishable.

I am . . . only conscious that my imagination places one state before and the other after, not that the one state precedes the other in the object, or, in other words, through the mere perception the *objective relation* of the appearances that are succeeding one another remains undetermined. (B233–4)

Successive apprehendeds: Kant's solution

The general principle of the Analogies, we recall, is that "experience is possible only through the representation of a necessary connection of perceptions" (B218). The concept of an apprehended object is precisely the concept of something that determines the way in which our perceptions, i.e., our apprehend*ings* are necessarily connected.

218

If we investigate what new characteristic is given to our representations by the *relation to an object*, ... we find that it does nothing beyond making the combination of the representations necessary in a certain way, and subjecting them to a rule .... (A197/B242)

Now when we apprehend "the manifold in the appearance of a house", i.e., experience an objectively simultaneous manifold, the fact that we think the successively apprehended items as *parts of a house* does not by itself determine the order of our apprehendings. Rather, in thinking of the apprehended items as parts of a house, we think of them, so to speak, as having been perceptually available throughout the whole time that we are experiencing the house. Considered only insofar as they are parts of a house, what we apprehend in a particular order—e.g., first the foundation, then the walls, and finally the roof—we *could have* apprehended in a different order—e.g., first the roof, then the walls, and finally the foundation. (Cf. A192/B237-8)[4]

In contrast, when we watch a ship drifting downstream, i.e., experience an objectively successive manifold, the fact that we think of the successively apprehended relationships between the ship and items on the shore as *occurrences* or *events*, i.e., as alterations in the position of the ship, implies that we think of them as, one after another, first *becoming* and then *ceasing to be* perceptually available. That is, insofar as we think of what we apprehend as events, we think of the apprehended relationships—e.g., the ship adjacent first to the pier, then to the boulder, and finally to the tree—as items that we could have apprehended *only* in that determinate order. Thinking of the order of our perceptions as, in this way, necessary and irreversible, Kant proposes, is the characteristic mark of experiencing an objective succession:

[I]f in the case of an appearance that contains a happening I call the preceding state of perception *A* and the following one *B*, then *B* can only follow *A* in apprehension, but the perception *A* cannot follow but only precede *B*. E.g., I see a ship driven downstream. My perception of its position downstream follows the perception of its position upstream, and it is impossible that in the apprehension of this appearance the ship should first be perceived downstream and afterwards upstream. (A192/B237)

---

[4] The restricting condition here is crucial. When I factor in my own objective history—as a perceiver with eyes in space—I then think of my apprehendings of the parts of a house as themselves *objectively* successive events (happenings) in nature, and, correlatively, of the order of my (subjective) awarenesses of them as necessary and irreversible. Kant himself picks up this thought in the Third Analogy, at A213/B260.

This passage has led some philosophers to invent fanciful scenarios, peculiar physical and physiological conditions of perception, in which the ship is in fact apprehended in its downstream position *before* it is apprehended in its upstream position. This misses Kant's point. The case in question is one in which "the appearance contains a happening", i.e., the ship is perceived as *moving downstream,* and his claim is that "it is impossible that in the apprehension *of this appearance* the ship should first be perceived downstream and afterwards upstream". Insofar as I *conceptualize* what I experience as a determinate alteration in the position of the ship—the ship's being *first* upstream and *then* downstream—that is, I cannot also think of such hypothetical differently ordered apprehensions as straightforwardly veridical perceptions. Just as I can see something *to be* red by observing that it *looks* black in green light, a subjective succession in which a ship *seems* to move upstream can—in suitably abnormal circumstances—be an instance of perceiving the ship *to be* moving downstream. But the possibility of such deviant roundabout cases clearly presupposes that there is a normal case in which the subjective temporal order is determined *directly* by the objective temporal order.

In order to experience an event, then, I must think the (subjective) order of my apprehendings as determined by the (objective) order of the apprehendeds. As Kant puts it, I must "derive the *subjective sequence* of apprehension from the *objective sequence* of appearances" (A193/B238). But if I think the order of my perceptions as necessary and determined by an objective order of determinations of persisting items in nature, I cannot then think of the order of those objective determinations as itself arbitrary.

Therefore I always make my subjective synthesis (of apprehensions) objective with respect to a rule in accordance with which the appearances in their sequence, i.e., as they occur, are determined through the preceding state, and only under this presupposition alone is the experience of something that happens even possible. (A195/B240)

It is important to remember that, when Kant speaks of "the appearances", what he has in mind are apprehended *objects,* i.e., items in nature. There are consequently two relations of necessitation implicated in his account of an experience of objective successiveness. On the one hand, we represent a necessary connection among our *perceptions,* i.e., our apprehend*ings.* In the ship case, Kant writes, "the order in the sequence of the perceptions in apprehension is . . . determined, and the apprehension is bound to it" (A192/B237). The subjective succession is *thought* as necessary and irreversible, but such irreversibility, of course, is not a *datum*, something of which we are somehow directly aware, that could be used as *evidence* that what we are experiencing is a happening, occurrence, or event. Rather, we think the order of our apprehendings as *dependently* necessary precisely *by* thinking them as determined by an *objective* succession, i.e., a determinate temporal ordering of the apprehended items, which we *also* think as necessary and irreversible.

But how do we "confer temporal order on the appearances and their existence" and assign each of them "a place in time"? For, as Kant stresses, "this determination of position cannot be borrowed from the relation of the appearances to absolute time (for that is not an object of perception)" (A200/B245). We have already seen that our successive apprehendings alone cannot yield such an objective determination, and Kant also notes that the objective temporal significance of a represented succession

cannot consist in the relation to another representation . . . for that would simply raise anew the question: How does this representation in turn go beyond itself and acquire objective significance in addition to the subjective significance that is proper to it as a determination of the state of mind? (A197/B242)

Only one possibility remains: We must think the relation of necessitation as *internal* to the apprehended items themselves.

[T]he appearances themselves must determine their positions in time for each other, and make this determination in the temporal order necessary, i.e., what follows or happens must succeed that which was contained in the previous state in accordance with a general rule . . . .

That something happens, therefore, is a perception . . . which becomes actual if I regard the position of the appearance as determined in time, thus if I regard it as an object that can always be found in the connection of perceptions in accordance with a rule. This rule for determining something with respect to its temporal sequence, however, is that in what precedes, the condition is to be encountered under which the occurrence always (i.e., necessarily) follows. (A200/B245–6)

The "rule" of which Kant here speaks is the sort of general principle that licenses counterfactual inferences. In this connection it is useful to recall the results of our investigation of the Auditory World.[5] What we discovered was that the substantiality (persistence) of a sound-object, S_i, stationed at a particular master sound pitch, M_p, corresponded to the

---

[5] A reader who has skipped over the discussion of the Auditory Model in Ch. 8 should simply ignore the next sentence.

necessity of particular regularities of co-occurrence and succession and our correlative entitlement to draw determinate conclusions regarding what a perceiver *would* hear in various circumstances from premises specifying what he *does* hear in various situations.

Kant's conclusion in the Second Analogy has the same form. An experience of objective successiveness is correlative to a general entitlement to draw conclusions about something *preceding* and *necessitating* whatever is perceived as happening or occurring—i.e., a general commitment to the *causal lawfulness* of nature.

If...my perception is to contain the cognition of an occurrence,...then it must be an empirical judgment in which one thinks that the sequence is determined, i.e., that it presupposes another appearance in time which it follows necessarily or in accordance with a rule....Thus the relation of appearances (as possible perceptions) in accordance with which the existence of that which succeeds (what happens) is determined in time necessarily and in accordance with a rule by something that precedes it, consequently the relation of cause to effect, is the condition of the objective validity of our empirical judgments with regard to the series of perceptions, thus of their empirical truth, and therefore of experience. (A201–2/B246–7)

Since every occurrence in time is an alteration, i.e., "a successive being and not-being of the determinations of [a] substance that persists" (B232), that is precisely the principle of the Second Analogy as Kant formulates it in B.

This is a radically innovative account of causation. As Kant himself observes,

it seems as if this contradicts everything that has always been said about the course of the use of our understanding, according to which it is only through the perception and comparison of sequences of many occurrences on preceding appearances that we are led to discover a rule, in accordance with which certain occurrences always follow certain appearances, and are thereby first prompted to form the concept of cause. (A195/B240–1)

What Kant has in mind, of course, is Hume's account of our "mistaking" feelings of compulsion ("impressions of reflection") that accompany expectations arising from repeated experience of a regular succession ("constant conjunction") among events for a relation of causal necessitation in nature. On this account, the experience of objective succession is a precondition of our possessing *any* concept of causation, even one which is thus "confused" or "mistaken". "On such a footing", Kant points out, this concept would be merely empirical, and the rule, . . . that everything that happens has a cause, would be just as contingent as the experience itself: its universality and necessity would then be merely feigned, and would have no true universal validity. . . . (A196/B241)

Kant's own account precisely inverts the Humean order of dependency. A commitment to the universal validity of the principle of causation is a condition of possible experience, including the experiences of objective temporal successiveness, the happenings and occurrences, that Hume's account simply takes for granted. We do not "extract" the concept of cause from experience. It is "the condition of the synthetic unity of the appearances in time", and thereby "the ground of experience itself" (A196/B241). The principle of causation—or, equivalently, the principle of sufficient reason (A201/B246)—is thus grounded and its objective validity guaranteed *a priori*.

Hume's concept of causation is "forward-looking". He begins with a regular succession, repeated instances of apprehension of one sort of event, B, following apprehension of another, A, and his *question* is then: Can we find anything in an occurrence of A which necessitates the subsequent occurrence of B? Since, however, "the contrary of any matter of fact is always possible", and hence there is no contradiction in the idea of an apprehension of A that is *not* followed by an apprehension of B, he concludes that there is never any such thing to be found. And since, on his view, we could acquire a legitimate concept of such a thing only by first finding it, Hume's official position is that we don't even *have* such a concept.

Kant's concept of causation, in contrast, is "backward-looking". Since he sees clearly that an apprehension of A followed by an apprehension of B is not yet an experience of A followed by B, his question is: How is the latter experience, i.e., the experience of B as something that *happens*, possible? His answer is that it is possible only on the condition that I can appropriately place A and B determinately in time.

Thus if I perceive that something happens, then the first thing contained in this representation is that something precedes, for it is just in relation to this that the appearance acquires its temporal relation, that, namely, of existing after a preceding time in which it did not. But it can only acquire its determinate temporal position in this relation through something being presupposed in the preceding state on which it always follows, i.e., follows in accordance with a rule . . . . (A198/B243)

We must consequently posit that there is something *antecedent* to B from which "this determinate occurrence inevitably and necessarily follows" (A198/B243–4), i.e., a necessitating cause.

Notice that Kant's reasoning does not yet tell us what the necessitating cause of B *is*, only that there must be one. Insofar as it has come to be, a particular state, e.g., B,

points to some preceding state as a correlate, to be sure still undetermined, of this event that is given, which [given event] is, however, determinately related to the latter [i.e., to the correlate], as its consequence, and necessarily connected with it in the temporal series. (A199/B244)

This is a reflection of the *regulative* character of the Second Analogy. It does not give us the cause of a given event *a priori* but only its *relation to* a cause and "a rule for seeking it in experience and a mark for discovering it there" (A180/B222). Nevertheless, we can plausibly identify at least one sort of case where we can suppose Kant to be confident that both the specific cause and the general rule are known.

Think of one billiard ball (say, the cue ball) hitting another (say, the red one) and causing it to move. This traditional Humean archetype can also serve as a paradigm of the kind of event causation that Kant has in mind. We experience that something *happens*. The red ball alters its state from being at rest to being in motion, and this alteration is (thought as) caused by the impact of the cue ball. Here we have a *dateable event* and a causal story which appeals to something "in" the preceding state of affairs (the impact of the moving cue ball on the stationary red ball) upon which the subsequent state of affairs (the target ball's new state of motion) follows "according to a rule". The "rule" in question is, of course, Newton's Second Law, $F = ma$. Since what properly falls within the scope of a causal account is an alteration, i.e., a change of state of some substance, for a good Newtonian like Kant, it will be the red ball's *acceleration*, i.e., the change of state of its motion, which receives a causal explanation.[6] Newton's mechanics gives us the general form of such an explanation: Object O (of mass m) accelerates from velocity v at t to velocity v' $(= v + \Delta v)$ at t' $(= t + \Delta t)$ *because O is subjected to a force of magnitude F at t.*

---

[6] From this perspective, as Kant himself recognizes, the earlier example of the moving ship was ill-chosen: "Note well that I am not talking about the alteration of certain relations in general, but rather of the alteration of the state. Hence, if a body is moved uniformly, then it does not alter its state (of motion) at all, although it does if its motion increases or diminishes" (A207/B252 n.).

Simultaneous causation

Kant's argument for the principle of the Second Analogy irredeemably links the fundamental conception of causation to *successions*. Kant is quite explicit about this.

If...my perception is to contain the cognition of an occurrence, namely that something actually happens, then it must be an empirical judgment in which one thinks that the sequence is determined, i.e., that it presupposes another appearance in time which it follows necessarily or in accordance with a rule. (A201/B246–7)

A causal relationship requires that there must "lie in that which in general precedes an occurrence the condition for a rule, in accordance with which this occurrence always and necessarily follows" (A193/B239).[7] Thus, as he recognizes, the very notion of *simultaneous* causation immediately presents Kant with a prima facie problem.

Here, however, there is a reservation that must be raised. The principle of causal connection among appearances is, in our formula, limited to the succession of them, although in the use of this principle it turns out that it also applies to their accompaniment [i.e., co-occurrence], and cause and effect can be simultaneous. (A202/B247)

Kant proceeds to offer several examples of what he has in mind:

E.g., there is warmth in a room that is not to be encountered in the outside air. I look around for the cause, and find a heated stove. Now this, as the cause, is simultaneous with its effect, the warmth of the chamber; thus here there is no succession in time between cause and effect, rather they are simultaneous, yet the law still holds. (A202/B247–8)

If I consider a ball that lies on a stuffed pillow and makes a dent in it as a cause, it is simultaneous with its effect. (A203/B248)

The glass [filled with water] is the cause of the rising of the water above its horizontal plane [at the rim], though both appearances are simultaneous. (A204/B249)

The first thing we need to notice is how different these examples are from the paradigmatic Humean-Newtonian billiard ball. These new examples do not direct our attention to any alteration at all, to any event or happening, but rather to the (mere) *existence* of a state of some substance

---

[7] Cf. A195/B240: "If, therefore, we experience that something happens, then we always presuppose that something else precedes it, which it follows in accordance with a rule."

(broadly construed)—warmth in a room, a dent in a cushion, the convexity of the surface of a quantity of water—and what is identified and characterized as the cause of that state, in turn, is neither an occurrence nor a state of affairs, but rather an *object*—a stove, a lead ball, a glass. What we evidently have here, in other words, is a *second causal idiom*, and one way of formulating Kant's problem, to begin with, is as the question of how to accommodate this notion of causality in terms of the sort of *event* causation that he has argued is a necessary condition of the possibility of temporally determinate experience.

One issue here concerns what we might call *continuous* or *sustaining causes*. The heavy ball is the cause of the dent in the pillow. If the pillow is suitably resilient, the indentation exists only so long as its cause is in place. Similarly, the room remains warm only so long as the stove continues to heat it. When the stove goes out, the room cools down. One way in which an object can be a cause that is simultaneous with its effect, then, is by being implicated in a *persisting* state of affairs which continuously sustains that effect.

What makes these more than just odd special cases is the fact that, as Kant puts it, "the majority of efficient causes in nature are simultaneous with their effects, and the temporal sequence of the latter is occasioned only by the fact that the cause cannot achieve its entire effect in one instant" (A203/B238). What Kant has in mind here, I think, are again some typical Newtonian causal-explanatory scenarios, somewhat more elaborate than our billiard ball impact example, as when, for instance, an object accelerates from v_1 to v_2 during the interval t_1-t_2 because a force of (constant) magnitude F is applied to it throughout the interval t_1-t_2. This sort of case occurs far more frequently than the occasional instantaneous impact. Indeed, many of Newton's most triumphant explanations—the accelerations of falling objects, planets orbiting the sun, moons orbiting a planet—have this form, a *continuous* change of state (acceleration) resulting from the workings of a *continuously concurrent* cause (gravitational force).

Kant's account of these cases refers such persisting (object) causes back to the paradigm of event causation: The *onset* of the *operation* of such a cause is an event which has the *coming-to-be* of the relevant state or condition as its effect. *Placing* the ball on the pillow causes the *change* of shape from smooth to indented. It is such a consideration of the onset of the state which is subsequently "sustained" by the (object) cause that Kant has in mind when he speaks of distinguishing the two "by means of the temporal relation of the dynamical connection" (A203/B238).

We can consequently think of Kant as offering an analysis of one, derivative, causal idiom—object–causes–state (e.g., stove causes warmth)—in terms of another, fundamental, one—event–causes–event (e.g., impact causes motion). To say that the lead ball caused the dent in the pillow is to say that the *change of state* of the pillow from smooth at t to indented at $t + \Delta t$ occurred *because* the ball was placed on the pillow at t. Thought of in this way, the effect indeed follows "in accordance with a rule", i.e., that the pillow thus alters its state can legitimately *be inferred* from the (factual *or* counterfactual) hypothesis that a lead ball is placed upon it, but not conversely, as Kant himself observes: "[If] I lay the ball on the pillow, the dent follows its previously smooth shape; but if (for whatever reason) the pillow has a dent, a leaden ball does not follow it" (A203/B248–9); i.e., the hypothesis that the pillow's shape changed from smooth to indented does not imply that a lead ball was placed upon it. There's more than one way to dent a pillow.

One problem that Kant is considering under the rubric "simultaneous causation", then, is how to identify the cause of a state—either continuously sustained or continuously changing—that persists over an interval, where that cause is operative over the same interval. The gist of his solution is to point out that, when such states are "dynamically" referred back to their onsets or origins, the causal principle of the Second Analogy imposes a *counterfactual asymmetry* which suffices to distinguish the continuous cause from the sustained effect despite the absence of any literal successiveness. But that is not the only problem that is troubling Kant at this point. For, as he realizes, he also needs an account of *instantaneous* simultaneous causality.

This problem comes into view in Kant's observation that "the time between the causality of the cause and its immediate effect can be *vanishing* (they can therefore be simultaneous), but the temporal relation of the one to the other still remains determinable" (A203/B248). It is important to appreciate that Kant is here no longer thinking only about continuous or sustaining causes. Rather, he is explicitly addressing a *second*, deeper and more challenging, problem that also falls under the rubric "simultaneous causation", the fact that, as he puts it, "in the instant in which the effect first arises, it is *always* simultaneous with the causality of its cause" (A203/B248; my emphasis). What Kant is here saying is that *every* instance of causation—even instances of paradigmatic successive event causation (which are arguably, so to speak, prior in the order of knowing)—in fact presupposes and depends upon an instance of *simultaneous*

227

causation which is consequently, in a certain sense, prior in the order of being. Let us see if we can figure out what he has in mind.

Consider our original example of billiard ball causation: the impact of the cue ball on the stationary red ball causes the target ball to move. Can there be a *temporal interval* between the cue ball's impact and the target ball's motion, a sort of "action at a temporal distance"? Kant thinks not. The causality of the cause, he says, is always simultaneous with the *onset* of its effect. But just what does Kant mean by "the causality of the cause"? What, for instance, is the causality of the impact of the cue ball on the red ball?

Recall what our billiard ball example looks like when it is "subjected to a rule", i.e., from the point of view of Newtonian mechanics. The (initially stationary) red ball, an object O of mass m, accelerates from rest (velocity $v = 0$) at t to some specific velocity v' ($= v + \Delta v$) at t' ($= t + \Delta t$) *because O is subjected to a force of determinate magnitude F at t*. What *causally explains* the target ball's acceleration (the change in its state of motion), in other words, is the applied force, F. The velocity *increment v* is a function only of the magnitude of the force F and the mass, m, of O, but is independent of the initial velocity v. The impact of the cue ball, in short, is the cause of the (change of state of) motion of the red ball only insofar as that impact is identical to the application of that force to that target. Otherwise put, the cause is the impact *qua* application of force. What Kant means by "the causality of the cause" is that aspect or feature of the antecedent state of affairs which figures in this way in the appropriate causal-explanatory "rule", i.e., in the causal law. Here, then, where the impact is the cause, it is the application of force that is the causality of that cause.

We can now better appreciate what is involved in Kant's remark that "the time between the causality of the cause and its immediate effect can be *vanishing*". His point is not, for instance, epistemic or psychological. He does not have in mind only purely psychological or psycho-physical thresholds of discrimination. His point is that there is *no temporal interval* between the moment of impact—when the moving cue ball applies the force F to the target ball and thereby exerts its causality—and the instant at which the target begins to accelerate, i.e., the onset of the effect. In other words, there is no time at which the force F *has been applied* to the target (the impact has occurred) but the state of motion of the target *has not yet begun to change* (the target has not yet begun to accelerate). Despite the fact that the application of force and the onset of acceleration are conceptually distinguishable events, and, indeed, distinguishable as cause and effect, there is not only no *discernible* lapse of time between them; there is no lapse of time between them at all. What is at issue is, as it were, the metaphysics of the situation, and the disturbing fact seems to be that the *instantaneous* event that Kant calls "the causality of the cause" is distinguishable *only* conceptually from the instantaneous event which is the onset of "its" effect. The ostensible difference between a cause and its effect seems to collapse into what Hume would call a mere "distinction of reason". But how can such a "distinction of reason" express an actual causal relationship?

Kant proposes to address *this* simultaneity worry by stressing the distinction between time-*lapse* and time-*order*. The latter, he suggests, is correlative to the truth of various *counterfactuals*: "[I]f the cause had ceased to be an instant before, then the effect would never have arisen.... [The] relation remains even if no time has elapsed" (A203/B248).

Here it is important to remember that, for Kant, the notion of an instantaneous event is already an idealization. The essential elements of Kant's solution have consequently already been adumbrated in our discussion of the Axioms and the Anticipations. Here, again, is the key passage:

Points and instants are only boundaries, i.e., mere places of...limitation [of "spaces" (regions) and "times" (intervals)], but places always presuppose those intuitions that limit or determine them, and from mere places, [considered] as components that could be given prior to space or time, neither space nor time can be composed. (A169–70/B211)

On Kant's official view, in other words, the *instantaneous* impact of the cue ball on the target is only nominally, even broadly speaking, an object. Properly understood, the concept of the instant at which such an impact occurs is the concept of an *ideal virtual part* of a stretch of time containing (subjectively prior) intervals during which the cue ball is in motion and the target at rest, the distance between them continuously decreasing, and (subjectively subsequent) intervals during which the cue ball is (let us suppose) at rest and the target ball in motion, the distance between them continuously increasing. We *experience* this diachronic manifold as containing an instantaneous causal event by thinking it under idealizing limit-concepts of instantaneous changes in the state of motion of each of two objects and positing (Newtonian) causal interactions between them.

Thus the experiential cash-value of the instantaneous change in the state of motion of our exemplary billiard ball and the simultaneity of that change with "the causality of its cause" is roughly an open-ended family of indefinitely contractible (nested) intervals, spanning the nominal moment of impact, where *every* such interval is thought as including a subinterval (*prior* to the impact) during which the cue ball is still in motion and the target at rest and a subinterval (*subsequent* to the impact) during which the cue ball is at rest and the target is in motion—while, even in thought, we exclude the possibility of any subinterval which is both subsequent to the cue ball's being at rest and prior to the target ball's motion.

That we think the successive apprehensions of pairs of subintervals as *irreversible* is what, on Kant's analysis, corresponds to the impact's being the *cause* of the motion. In no spanning interval can any subinterval within which the target is in motion and the cue ball at rest precede any subinterval within which the cue ball is in motion and the target ball at rest. That is Kant's point about the *order* of time. The nesting is necessarily *order-invariant* "all the way down".

The posited *absence* of any subinterval that is both subsequent to the cue ball's being at rest and prior to the target's being in motion, in turn, is what grounds our talk of an "instantaneous event" and the correlative simultaneity of the impact with the *onset* of the motion. Such an "instantaneous impact" is a sort of boundary-marker erected *in thought* between times during which the cue ball is in motion and the target at rest and times during which the target is in motion and the cue ball at rest. That is Kant's point about the (absence of) a *lapse* of time, the "vanishing" of the time between the causality of the cause and its immediate effect. The "moment of impact" is a "mere place of limitation" that "presupposes those intuitions" that it is intended to limit, i.e., perceptions of the two billiard balls as variously in motion or at rest.

Kant's "law of the continuity of all alteration" (A209/B254) extrapolates this conceptual structure to temporally extended changes of state conceived of as resulting from the operation of a continuous or sustaining cause.

The question . . . arises, how a thing passes from one state $= a$ into another one $= b$. . . . [Every] transition from one state into another happens in a time that is contained between two instants, of which the former determines the state from which the thing proceeds, and the second the state at which it arrives. Both are therefore boundaries of the time of an alteration, consequently of the intermediate state between two states, and as such they belong to the whole alteration. Now every alteration has a cause which manifests its causality in the entire time during which the alteration proceeds. Thus this cause does not produce its alteration suddenly (all at once or in an instant) but rather in time, so that as the time increases from the initial instant a to its completion in b, the magnitude of the reality $(b - a)$ is also generated through all the smaller degrees that are contained between the first and the last. All alteration is therefore possible only through a continuous action of causality. . . . (A208/B253–4)

When we apply this description to the pattern of Newton's triumphant causal-explanatory successes—an object O of mass m accelerating from v_1 to v_2 during the interval t_1–t_2 because a force of (constant) magnitude F is applied to it throughout the interval—we see that Kant's story is in fact a quite reasonable approximation to what subsequent mathematical physicists made precise, the representation of motion by an everywhere differentiable continuous function whose first derivative at each point yields a corresponding "instantaneous velocity".

Reciprocal causation

Notice that, considered as an instantaneous event, the collision of the cue ball and the red ball is the cause of *two* alterations: a change in the state of motion of the red ball and a change in the state of motion of the cue ball. The impact of the cue ball *on* the red ball causes the latter to accelerate from rest to v'; the cue ball's impact *with* the red ball causes the former to decelerate from, say, v_c to rest. This, of course, is simply an instance of Newton's *Third* Law, and it also brings us explicitly into contact with the principle of Kant's Third Analogy. In fact, both of these principles have tacitly been accompanying our discussion for quite a while, at least since we placed the lead ball on a suitably resilient pillow. The principle of the Third Analogy is that

All substances, insofar as they are *simultaneous*, stand in thoroughgoing community (i.e., interaction with one another). (A211)[8]

According to the Third Law, the interaction between the ball and the pillow is precisely an instance of such *reciprocal* causation. Under the influence of gravity, the ball exerts a force on the pillow, producing an indentation, and the compressed resilient pillow simultaneously exerts an equal and opposite force on the ball.[9]

---

[8] In B: "All substances, insofar as they can be perceived in space as simultaneous, are in thoroughgoing interaction" (B256).

[9] In this particular instance, we have a sort of *dynamic* equilibrium, as evidenced by the pillow's return to its original form when the ball is removed. A full Newtonian account of the matter would involve such technical arcana as the distinction between potential and kinetic energy. For present purposes, however, apart from this note, I will continue simply to ignore such complications.

231

Kant's argument for the principle of the Third Analogy is a straightforward extension of his argument for the principle of causation in the Second. As the house example already illustrates, the characteristic mark of the simultaneous existence of apprehended items in space is the *reversibility* of our successive apprehendings of them.

But one cannot perceive time itself and thereby derive from the fact that things are positioned at the same time that their perceptions can follow each other reciprocally. (B257)

Nor can we "read off" the reversibility of our apprehendings directly from our awareness of them, for

the synthesis of the imagination in apprehension would . . . only present each of these perceptions as one that is present in the subject when the other is not, and conversely, but not that the objects are simultaneous, i.e., that if one is then the other also is in the same time, and that this is necessary in order for the perceptions to be able to succeed each other reciprocally. (B257)

Here again, therefore, we need to think the reversibility of the sequence of perceptions as grounded in the apprehended items, and this again requires that we think those items as determinately located in time. As in the case of objective successiveness, we do this by thinking the temporal determinations of simultaneous items, A and B, as internal to those items themselves.

In addition to their mere existence, there must therefore be something through which A determines the position of B in time, and conversely also something by which B does the same for A, since only under this condition can those substances be empirically represented as *existing simultaneously*. Now only that determines the position of another [thing] in time which is the cause of it or its determinations. Thus each substance . . . must simultaneously contain the causality of certain determinations in the other and the effects of the causality of the other i.e., they must stand in dynamical community (immediately or mediately) if their simultaneity is to be cognized in any possible experience. (A212/B259)

A *dynamical* community among items (Kant cites the Latin word *commercium*) consists in their mutual interaction. Distinct items in mutual interaction constitute a composite (*compositum reale*), as opposed, for instance, to a mere collection. Kant himself contrasts such "commerce" with what we might call *minimal* community (*communio*), i.e., membership in a common whole, and argues that it is a presupposition of the empirical cognition even of the mere coexistence of items in space.

[Only] continuous influence in all places in space can lead our sense from one object to another... [The] light that plays between our eyes and the heavenly bodies effects a mediate community between us and the latter and thereby proves the simultaneity of the latter .... (A213/B260)

Perhaps it does not take too wild an imagination to see in these remarks a suggestive anticipation of Einstein's later relativistic rethinking of the classical notion of simultaneity.

This concludes our discussion of Kant's Analogies of Experience, which, he observes, "really exhibit the unity of nature in the combination of all appearances" (A216/B263). Considered individually, they elucidate

the three dynamical relations, from which all others arise, ... those of inherence, of consequence, and of composition. (A215/B262)

Taken together with the Axioms and Anticipations, the principles of the Analogies also complete Kant's solution to the Pythagorean puzzle, for the world of reciprocally causally interacting persisting substances whose experience they make possible is precisely the natural world whose mathematical intelligibility already amazed and challenged the very first philosophers. Guided by the Table of Categories, however, we see that there is still some unfinished business in this part of the Analytic of Principles. Kant's "systematic representation of all synthetic principles of pure understanding" will not be complete until he has also identified and elucidated the synthetic *a priori* judgments corresponding to the categories of modality. These are the "postulates of empirical thinking in general", and it is to them, and their most significant implications, that we next turn.

The World as Actual: 11
The Postulates and the
Refutation of Idealism

The "postulates of empirical thinking in general" are concerned with the categories of modality: possibility, actuality, and necessity. Kant clearly understands that, as we might nowadays put it, there are different *species* of modality, e.g., alethic and epistemic. In the first instance, we have the *logical* modalities. Their applicability can be established entirely through considerations regarding formal consistency and the relations of entailment among concepts, but these are not what is at issue here. The Postulates are rather principles regarding the modalities in their *empirical* use. They are to concern what we might call *real* possibilities and *material* necessities, i.e.,

things and their possibility, actuality, and necessity, [and so] must pertain to possible experience and its synthetic unity, in which alone objects of cognition are given. (A219/B267)

Real possibility and material necessity

As in the case of the Axioms, Anticipations, and Analogies, the considerations adduced in the Postulates are intended to establish the objective validity of a group of synthetic *a priori* judgments. The principles of the Postulates, however, have the peculiarity, Kant tells us, that

as a determination of the object they do not augment the concept to which they are ascribed in the least, but rather express only the relation to the faculty of cognition. (A219/B266)

They are consequently not "objective-synthetic"; i.e., they don't add anything to the representation of the object, but they are nevertheless synthetic, although

only subjectively, i.e., they add to the concept of a thing (the real), about which they do not otherwise say anything, the cognitive power whence it arises and has its seat .... The principles of modality therefore do not assert of a concept anything other than the action of the cognitive faculty through which it is generated. (A234/B286–7)

That, Kant explains, is ultimately why he calls them "postulates", for, in mathematics, a postulate, properly understood, is "the practical proposition that contains nothing except the synthesis through which we first give ourselves an object and generate its concept" (A234/B287). The traditional postulates of Euclidean geometry, for example, basically express *rules of construction*: "a straight line can be drawn between any two points"; "a straight line can be indefinitely extended"; "a circle of any given radius can be described about any given point".

Alternatively, we can think of the postulates of geometry as formulating implicit definitions of the corresponding *concepts*—'point', 'straight line', 'circle', 'right angle', and so on. Analogously,

the principles of modality are also nothing further than definitions of the concepts of possibility, actuality, and necessity in their empirical use .... (A219/B266)

That is how we should read the three principles of the Postulates:

1. Whatever agrees with the formal conditions of experience (in accordance with intuition and concepts) is *possible*.
2. That which is connected with the material conditions of experience (of sensation) is *actual*.
3. That whose connection with the actual is determined in accordance with general conditions of experience is (exists) *necessarily*. (A218/B265–6)

The principle of the first Postulate elucidates what we might call the concept of a *real* (empirical) possibility. As Kant explains, more is required for a concept to express such a possibility than that it be free from formal logical contradiction. The concept of a closed figure formed by two straight lines, for example, contains no contradiction.

[Rather] the impossibility rests not on the concept in itself, but on its construction in space, i.e., on the conditions of space and its determinations; but these in turn have their objective reality ... because they contain in themselves *a priori* the form of experience in general. (A220–1/B268)

The concepts of substance, causation, and community elucidated in the Analogies, Kant observes, can be shown to express real possibilities only in this way, in relation to "the form of an experience in general and the synthetic unity in which alone objects can be empirically cognized" (A222/B269). He contrasts these with three "invented" concepts: the ether ("a substance that was persistently present in space yet without filling it", A222/B270), prescience (the power to *intuit* the future), and telepathy (a "community of thoughts" over arbitrary distances). Such concepts also contain no contradictions, but

these are concepts the possibility of which is entirely groundless, because it cannot be grounded in experience and its known laws. (A223/B270)

One can, indeed, always play with such notions "in fictions", but they will express real possibilities only if they can be shown to be compatible with the "formal and objective conditions of an experience in general" (A223/B271).

Similarly, the principle of the third Postulate, Kant tells us,

pertains to material necessity in existence, not the merely formal and logical necessity in the connection of concepts. (A226/B279)

Such material or natural necessity is always *conditional*. The existence of things cannot be cognized *a priori*, and the existence of states of things only as consequences of prior states, i.e., as the outcomes of alterations. In short, no existence can be cognized as necessary

except the existence of effects from given causes in accordance with laws of causality. . . . Hence we cognize only the necessity of *effects* in nature, the causes of which are given to us, and the mark of necessity in existence does not reach beyond the field of possible experience . . . . (A227/B279–80)

Consequently, material necessity is reflected in principles for inferring *a priori*, i.e., factually or counterfactually, from one existence (the cause) to another (the effect), that is, in laws of nature.

Since, as the Second Analogy has taught us, every event has a cause, it follows that, as Kant puts it, "everything that happens is hypothetically necessary", or equivalently, "Nothing happens through a mere accident" (A228/B280). This conclusion echoes the classical proposition that *in mundo non datur casus*, i.e., "In the world there is no chance", which, Kant remarks, consequently formulates an *a priori* law of nature. '*Non datur casus*' belongs to a family of traditional expressions of the lawful intelligibility of the natural world. Kant cites three more:

in mundo non datur fatum; "In the world there is no fate";
in mundo non datur saltus; "In the world there is no leap";
in mundo non datur hiatus; "In the world there is no hiatus".

'Non datur fatum' reflects the conditionality of natural necessity. Something that is "fated" to happen is something that will happen *no matter what*, i.e., something whose occurrence would be *unconditionally* necessary. Appeals to chance and fate have no explanatory force, but 'non datur fatum' tells us that, as Kant puts it, "no necessity in nature is blind" (A228/B280). That is, whatever happens in nature is both explicable and comprehensible in terms of its necessitating conditions.

Like 'non datur casus', 'non datur fatum' is a consequence of the principle of causality, although the latter "adds to the causal determination the concept of necessity". 'Non datur saltus' and 'non datur hiatus', in contrast, are basically consequences of the principle of community, which forbids "any leap in the series of appearances (alterations)...but also any gap or cleft between two appearances in the sum of all empirical intuitions in space" (A228/B281). These four classical principles, Kant adds, can easily be aligned with the Table of Categories—he leaves this as an exercise for the reader—but they all convey fundamentally the same idea. Each of them prohibits us from ascribing to the empirical synthesis anything

that could violate or infringe the understanding and the continuous connection of all appearances, i.e., the unity of its concepts. For it is in this alone that the unity of experience, in which all perceptions must have their place, is possible. (A229–30/B282)

The many faces of idealism

The most important of the three Postulates, however, is the second, for it is the notion of *actuality* that Kant mobilizes in his critique of material or empirical idealism. What the Second Postulate—"That which is connected with the material conditions of experience (of sensation) is *actual*" (A218/B266; cf. A376)—tells us, Kant explains, is that

cognizing the actuality of things requires *perception*... —not immediate perception of the object itself the existence of which is to be cognized, but still its connection with some actual perception in accordance with the analogies of experience, (A225/B272) that is, in accordance with laws of nature. His conception of empirical existence thus allows for the actuality of *theoretical* entities whose "immediate perception... is impossible given the constitution of our [sense] organs". Kant is no "fictionalist" about such unobservable items, but rather one sort of what we would nowadays call a "scientific realist". His own example is our cognition of the existence of "a magnetic matter penetrating all bodies from the perception of attracted iron filings" (A226/ B273), i.e., the *explanatory inference* to the cause of an observed effect.

Thus wherever perception and whatever is appended to it in accordance with empirical laws reaches, there too reaches our cognition of the existence of things. (A226/B274)

It is at this point in B that Kant proceeds to offer his notorious "Refutation of Idealism". This section both rewrites and relocates a discussion which occurs much later in A, at A366–80, in connection with the fourth Paralogism of Pure Reason in the Dialectic. The relocation is appropriate, since the sort of idealism that Kant wants to invalidate rests on considerations related precisely to the sort of explanatory inference that he has just been discussing. Thus the fourth Paralogism in A begins with the premise that "that whose existence can be inferred only as a cause of given perceptions has only a *doubtful existence*" (A366).

That what is at issue is the *doubtfulness* of the existence of inferred entities, i.e., an epistemological thesis, signals that what Kant is concerned to refute is what he calls (in A) *skeptical* or (in B) *problematic* idealism. The contrast is with what (in both editions) he calls *dogmatic* idealism. A problematic or skeptical idealist holds that the existence of entities of a particular sort is "merely doubtful and indemonstrable"; a dogmatic idealist holds the existence of entities of a particular sort to be "false and impossible" (B274; cf. A377). In the case of the idealism to be refuted, the particular sort of entities in question are "objects in space outside of us" (B274), or, as Kant variously formulates it in A, "outer appearance", "empirically external objects", or, in a phrase later adopted by G. E. Moore, "things that are to be encountered in space" (A373). That makes it a species of *empirical* idealism.

The reason for all this terminological fussiness, of course, is that, as we have seen, Kant himself notoriously advocates a form of idealism, namely, *transcendental* idealism,

the doctrine that [all appearances] are all together to be regarded as mere representations and not as things [as they are] in themselves, and accordingly that space and time are only sensible forms of our intuition, but not determinations given for themselves or conditions of objects as things in themselves. (A369)

The contrary thesis is *transcendental realism*, which regards space and time as independent of our sensibility and consequently

represents outer appearances (if their actuality[1] is conceded) as things in themselves, which would exist independently of us and our sensibility.... (A369)

The parenthetical remark here reflects the fact that both transcendental idealism and transcendental realism are complex and sophisticated philosophical theses regarding what is traditionally called the *mode of being* of items in space, items which *both* views can concede to be *actual*.

It is important to see that Kant is working with more distinctions than his philosophical predecessors. In particular, Kant distinguishes an item's *being actual* from its *existing [as it is] in itself.* The existence of a thing "in itself" is its existence considered in abstraction from the conditions of possible experience. The contrary notion is existence "for us", i.e., the existence of a thing considered *as* an object of possible experience. 'Actual', in contrast, is the empirical reality predicate. Its contraries include, for instance, 'illusory', 'dreamed', 'imaginary', and 'fictional'. To deny the *actuality* of items in space is to be a *dogmatic* empirical idealist. It follows that, for such an idealist, the question of whether items in space are *transcendentally* real or ideal cannot arise. Kant's paradigm is Berkeley, "who declares space ... to be something that is impossible in itself, and who therefore also declares things in space to be merely imaginary" (B274).

The ascription is arguably legitimate. Recall that two interpretations of the notion of an "idea" or a "mental state" were operative during the modern era, viz., thoughts and sensations, and that one prevailing paradigm of a sensation, in turn, was the example of *pain*. A feeling of pain is a case or instance of pain. Its existence consists in its being felt. On this model, an impression of red would be a case or instance of redness, and its existence would consist in its being sensed. But any sensed instance of redness necessarily has a *shape*, and that would seem to imply that a modification of the mind could have a shape, which looks absurd. Nevertheless,

---

[1] The German text has *Wirklichkeit*, which Guyer–Wood here translate as 'reality'. I have altered the translation to emphasize the relationship of the Fourth Paralogism in A to the Refutation of Idealism in B, which Kant sets in the context of his discussion of the Second Postulate: "That which is connected with the material conditions of experience (of sensation) is *actual [wirklich]*." Pluhar has 'actuality'; Kemp-Smith, 'reality'.

Berkeley's official view is that all "ideas", including both sensed colors and sensed shapes, cannot exist "without the mind", *in the same way* that pains cannot exist "without the mind", and this is essentially to hold that the concept of shaped items which are not mental states is incoherent in the same way that the concept of a pain which is not a mental state is incoherent.

Kant, in contrast, is quite clearly committed to the view that space and items in space cannot be "mental states" in the sense that pains are conceived to be. Items in space are *transcendentally* ideal because space is a form of our sensibility, but there is nothing problematic about the concept of an *actual* spatial item that is not a modification of mind but rather an object of possible experience.

The idealism that Kant sets out to refute, then, is neither transcendental idealism nor dogmatic empirical idealism, but rather *problematic empirical idealism*. As we have seen, this is essentially an epistemological thesis. It is, in fact, a form of skepticism. Kant's paradigm here is Descartes, "who declares only one empirical assertion, namely *I am*, to be indubitable" (B274). More precisely, Descartes is committed to *two* relevant theses:

(I1)   The existence of inferred entities is always doubtful and uncertain. Certainty attaches only to our knowledge of what we immediately experience.[2]

(I2)   Objects in space outside us are inferred entities. All immediate experience is *inner* experience, i.e., experience of objects of inner sense.

A skeptical or problematic idealist, Kant tells us, is

not someone who denies the existence of external objects of sense, but rather someone who only does not admit that it is cognized through immediate perception and infers from this that we can never be fully certain of their actuality[3] from any possible experience. (A368–9)

Taken together, (I1) and (I2) clearly commit Descartes to this form of empirical idealism, and it is this form of idealism that Kant proposes to refute. As we will see, he does so by rejecting (I2), i.e., by arguing that at least some of our "outer experience is really immediate" (B276), a deter-

---

[2] Certainty, of course, also attaches to whatever we "clearly and distinctly perceive", e.g., mathematical truths, but what we can thus know "by the light of reason", i.e., independently of experience, is not here at issue.

[3] See n. 1 above.

mination of the self by *empirically actual* items, the veridical perception of things in space.

Idealism refuted

Kant's argument ingeniously turns the tables on Descartes. Descartes takes it for granted that we command a clear and distinct idea of our own *inner* experience, i.e., of our "thoughts" (*cogitationes*). We know what we think, and we know that we think it. Kant's strategy is to argue that such a determinate awareness of our inner experience presupposes *outer* experience, i.e., an immediate perceptual awareness of items in space.

The mere, but empirically determined, consciousness of my own existence proves the existence of objects in space outside me. (B275)

As Kant's "proof" of this "theorem" proceeds to make clear, what is at issue is the "mere, but empirically determined, consciousness of my own existence" *in time*. I conceive of my inner life as determinately spread out and ordered in time. *Inter alia*, I *recollect*—perhaps mostly correctly, but perhaps also sometimes mistakenly—having been in various perceptual states. My consciousness of my inner experience, that is, includes, not only an awareness of my *now having* (ostensible) outer perceptions, but also (ostensible) memories of my *having had* such experiences. It is a consciousness of a *temporally determinate* experiential biography.

But if that is so, then the proof of Kant's theorem can already straightforwardly be read off the results of the Analogies:

- The actuality of a genuinely persisting substance is a condition of the possibility of representing a unitary time within which occurrences can be experienced as successive or simultaneous. (First Analogy)
- The actuality of causal relationships among predecessor and successor states of objects is a condition of the possibility of the experience of events as determinately located and ordered within such a unitary time. (Second and Third Analogies)
- Hence, the possibility of a temporally determinate inner experience requires the actuality of a world of causally interactive substances, i.e., "objects in space outside me". QED

To put it briskly, the only way that I can temporally order my *representations* of things outside me is by relating them to alterations in *actual* things outside me. To locate changes in my inner determinations in time, I must refer them to events in the outer world, i.e., in space.

As Kant readily concedes, his argument does not show that *all* outer experience is a veridical perception of objects in space. A given "intuitive representation of outer things...may well be the mere effect of the imagination (in dreams as well as in delusions)" (B278). But such "deceptive" outer experiences only counterfeit veridical perceptual experiences whose possibility presupposes the actuality of objects in space, and all that needs to be demonstrated in order to refute problematic empirical idealism is that

inner experience in general is possible only through outer experience in general. Whether this or that putative experience is not mere imagination must be ascertained according to its particular determinations and through its coherence with the criteria of all actual experience. (B278–9)

For *particular* determinations of actual existence, that is, we can only rely on the principle of the Second Postulate.

Idealism from within

Empirical idealism in general is the thesis that the being of things consists in their being represented.[4] On the face of it, one implication of this view is that the *count* of items represented cannot be different from the *count* of representings of items. A resolute idealist, that is, cannot properly entertain the hypothesis that qualitatively indistinguishable but numerically distinct representings are multiple encounters with one numerically identical represented item. Similarly, a resolute idealist cannot properly entertain the hypothesis that some item is *merely represented as* being Φ, although no Φ item *actually exists*. An "internally idealist" *conceptual scheme* would consequently *lack* a number of distinctions that are characteristic of our own empirical realism:

---

[4] This section offers a model of idealism and its problems intended to illustrate and support the fundamental idea of Kant's Refutation. It can, however, be omitted without significant expository loss.

the distinction between *being* and *being represented*,

the distinction between *numerical identity* and *exact qualitative similarity*,

the distinction between *being* and (merely) *seeming to be*, in several variants:

existing *vs* (merely) seeming to exist,

being *vs* (merely) seeming to be Φ,

being *vs* (merely) seeming to be identical to a previously encountered item α.[5]

These distinctions, and the distinctions among them, are represented in our own conceptual framework, *inter alia*, by the multiple senses attaching to the copula, 'to be'. One way to begin formally to articulate an internally idealist conceptual scheme is consequently to hypothesize a representational system containing (only) a *univocal* copula. Let us try the experiment.

We begin by positing a sensorily passive intelligence—I shall call him 'George'[6]—whose copula, 'be*', is relevantly univocal. To bring the idealist character of George's conceptual framework into sharp relief, let us suppose that what he experiences are various sorts of *pains*—aches, twinges, pangs, etc.—of various intensities, which we will suppose he measures in "ouches". And let us make our job as easy as possible by simply *giving* George two families of concepts which he arguably cannot be entitled to have: concepts of various *places* within the (sensible) body, p_i, and of various *times* (represented by temporal coordinates), t_i, at which his assorted pains occur, including the indexical of temporal presence '*now*'.

George then has the conceptual resources to formulate a variety of generalizations describing *regularities* in his pain-experience, e.g.,

---

[5] But couldn't Berkeley, who was unquestionably and paradigmatically an idealist, distinguish between reality and appearance, being and seeming? Yes and no. The distinction makes sense for *us* precisely because, on Berkeley's account, the veridicality of one of *our* representations consists in its correspondence to an "external permanence", i.e., to something whose existence is independent of *our* representing it, viz., an idea in the mind of God. *Our* conceptual scheme is not *internally* idealist. In that sense, Berkeley is an empirical *realist*. He differs from Locke only in his account of the nature of the relevant "external permanence". For Locke, it is something that has, as Berkeley put it, an "*absolute* existence without the mind", viz., matter. Berkeley's "external permanence" is *another idea*, and so exists only "in" a mind, specifically, in God's mind. *God's* conceptual scheme, we may suppose, *is* internally idealist. For him, there is no distinction between being and being represented. (God said, "Let there be light", and there *was* light.) But then, for God, there can also be no distinction between being and seeming. For an omniscient being, how things seem is necessarily always how things are.

[6] In honor of two historically prominent idealists, George Berkeley and Georg Wilhelm Friedrich Hegel.

(CI) $(t)_{<now}$ (n ouches of A be* at p_1 at t $\leftrightarrow$ m ouches of B be* at p_2 at t),

(SI) $(t)_{<now}$ (j ouches of F be* at p_3 at t $\rightarrow$ k ouches of G be* at p_4 at t $+ \Delta$t).

(CI) expresses a regularity of co-occurrence; (SI) a regularity of succession. '$(t)_{<now}$'—which we read: "so far whenever"—is a *bounded* quantifier. It expresses the *defeasibility* of such generalizations, i.e., the fact that no necessity attaches to them. That is, they summarize and make explicit experienced regularities, but do not have for George the status of natural laws.

Finally, we shall suppose that George is an *apperceptive* intelligence, i.e., that he can represent his own representations *as* representations. The simplest way to do this is to equip him with a species of *quotation marks*. I will use Continental quotes. With this addition, George becomes able to represent his commitment to idealism in the form of an explicit judgment:

(I) $(t)(x)(p)$ (x be* at p at t $\leftrightarrow$ $\gg x$ be* at p *now* $\ll$ be* at t),

TO BE   is   TO BE REPRESENTED,

and we will suppose that he does so. Notice that all the quantifiers in (I) are *unbounded*. Within George's conceptual scheme, that is, (I) has the status of an *indefeasible* or *necessary* principle.

That, then, is George's idealism—and, like Kant, we shall now proceed to refute it. The thesis that we will establish is this:

(T) If he remains a resolute idealist, George cannot, in any principled way, set his "experiential autobiography" determinately in order.

In particular, George does not have, and cannot develop, appropriate conceptual resources for dealing with *divergent ostensible memories*.

George has two sorts of ostensible memories. There are, so to speak, "factual" memories, regarding what *occurred* at an earlier time, say, t_e, e.g.,

(m1) (Only) 3 ouches of ache be* at p_a at t_e.[7]

And there are "apperceptive" or "biographical" memories, regarding what was *experienced* at an earlier time, e.g.,

---

[7] The parenthetical 'Only' is intended to indicate that George's factual memory regarding the contents of a given place at a given time always, so to speak, carries a commitment to give a *complete* picture of the actual state of affairs then and there.

(m2) $\gg$5 ouches of twinge be* at p$_a$ *now* $\ll$ be* at t$_e$.

These two sorts of memories are obviously inferentially linked by the idealist principle (I), and we shall suppose that George draws all the relevant conclusions, i.e.,

(c2) 5 ouches of twinge be* at p$_a$ at t$_e$,

(c1) $\gg$3 ouches of ache be* at p$_a$ *now* $\ll$ be* at t$_e$.

The ostensible memory (m1) and its consequence (c1) inform George that at t$_e$ he was experiencing three ouches of ache; the ostensible memory (m2) and its consequence (c2), that at t$_e$ he was experiencing five ouches of twinge. What, if anything, should George conclude about what, as *we* could put it, he was *actually* experiencing at t$_e$?

Couldn't George himself also put it that way? At first blush, it may well seem so. While I have argued that his commitment to the principle of idealism (I) is incompatible with his having a being–seeming distinction that applies to the contents of ostensible *perceptions*, i.e., to what he represents as occurring *now*, it is not immediately obvious that George couldn't command a being–seeming distinction with respect to the contents of ostensible *memories*, i.e., to what he represents as having occurred *in the past*, for instance, at t$_e$. Although, arguably, he can make no distinction between veridical and non-veridical *perceptual* experiences, it might seem reasonable to suppose that he could still draw a distinction between veridical and non-veridical *memorial* experiences. If so, then he could sensibly ask to *which* of his ostensible memories and their consequences regarding t$_e$, (m1) + (c1) or (m2) + (c2), he should give credence. How might George go about answering that question?

Well, perhaps he also accepts some pertinent *generalizations*, for instance,

(S1) (t)$_{<now}$(p)[6 ouches of pang be* at p at t $\rightarrow$ (t')(t<t'<t + 5
$\rightarrow$ 3 ouches of ache be* at p at t')];

that is, so far whenever there have been six ouches of pang at some place at some time, there have subsequently been three ouches of ache in that place during the next five time units, and when he consults his factual memory regarding the time-period immediately before t$_e$, it obligingly delivers an instance of (S1)'s antecedent, e.g.,

(m3) (Only) 6 ouches of pang be* at p$_a$ at t$_e$ − 3.

On the face of it, (S1) and (m3) together imply (c3), "3 ouches of ache be* at p_a at t_e", which plainly confirms (m1) but not (m2). Thus George could apparently now have a good reason for regarding (m1), and hence (c1), as veridical and (m2), and hence (c2), as mistaken. But this appearance is misleading.

First, of course, in the context of (S1), (m3) confirms (m1) only if (m3) is *itself* veridical, and, if George is in a position to inquire into the veridicality of (m1) and (m2), he is also in a position to raise the same question regarding the veridicality of (m3). In this way, the question of veridicality can certainly be transferred from one ostensible memory to another, but that is not yet to give it a determinate, non-arbitrary answer. But, more significantly, even if George had good independent grounds for supposing (m3) to be veridical, he would still be confronted with the choice either to continue to accept (S1)—and so to conclude that (m1) is confirmed—or to regard (m2) but *not* (m1) as veridical—and so to *reject* (S1) as disconfirmed by the occurrences before and at t_e. For (S1) contains only the *bounded* temporal quantifier "so far whenever", and it is therefore itself contingent and defeasible. And George has other options open to him, for there is nothing available to George *now* that logically rules out the conclusion that *neither* (m1) *nor* (m2) is veridical, i.e., that what *actually* happened at t_e was something else entirely. Not to put too fine a point on it, we have not yet encountered anything that shows that it is reasonable for George to accept *any* of his ostensible memories.

There is, in short, no *logical* obstacle to George's accepting any of *various* sets of his ostensible memories as veridical. As long as he accepts (I) as a necessary truth, and regards all his generalizations regarding past regularities as contingent and defeasible, he will be able consistently and coherently to ascribe to himself at t_e either or neither of the perceptual experiences expressed by (c1) and (m2).[8] Furthermore, what holds for George's experiential self-ascriptions regarding t_e at times later than t_e holds for *all* his experiential self-ascriptions regarding *any* past time at *every* later time. It follows that George *cannot* be in a position to draw any principled distinction between what *actually* occurred at an earlier time and what *he's now inclined to believe* occurred, between what he actually experienced and what

---

[8] Or, for that matter, *both* of them, i.e., to accept as veridical both (m1) and (m2), as well as (S1) and (m3). For, come to think of it, we have also not encountered any consideration that shows that it would be *un*reasonable for him to do so. We have, indeed, supposed that George's factual memories carry an implicit claim to completeness, but that does not imply that he himself is epistemically justified in accepting that claim.

he's now inclined to believe he experienced. As Wittgenstein put it, "One would like to say here that whatever will seem right [to George] is right. And that only means that we can't here speak about being 'right'."[9]

This establishes our thesis (T)—and it is also precisely Kant's point. A skeptical idealist presupposes, so to speak, the availability of a truth-predicate applying to his "inner" life, i.e., that it is possible for him to know what he *actually* experienced, which then delivers the premises from which any "outer" actuality can be inferred only problematically. Descartes, for instance, takes it for granted that he is in command of a conceptual distinction between, e.g., *merely ostensible* memories and *veridical actual* memories. But what Kant demonstrated, and what the example of George has confirmed, is that any such "inner" truth-predicate presupposes an "outer" truth-predicate. The concept of "what one actually *experienced*" is parasitic on the concept of "what actually *happened*".

For consider what it would take for George to be able in principle to eliminate the arbitrariness and indeterminacy from his experiential autobiography. One thing that would do the trick, of course, is for him simply to introduce a distinction between veridical and non-veridical *perceptual* representations, i.e., to directly abandon his idealism. But it would also suffice for him to treat some of the generalizations expressing experiential regularities of co-occurrence and succession as *necessary*, i.e., to accept them with *unbounded* temporal quantifiers, as holding at *all* times. Doing that, however, also amounts to abandoning idealism, for it is equivalent to treating (I) as itself contingent and capable of being defeated by appeal to *natural laws*.

A would-be problematic idealist needs a conception of *the past* that is strong enough to support the possibility of an intelligible contrast between how he *was then* and how he *now recollects having been*. He can arrive at a determinate conception of his actual earlier states, however, only by using such evidence as is available to him *here and now*, and so, in the first instance, by relying on his memory. One way for him to show that it is *reasonable* to do so is by checking his ostensible memories against actual states of affairs and discovering them to be generally reliable; but, of course, the requisite actual *past* states of affairs are precisely not available to him *here and now* to serve as evidential terms of comparison. He must consequently rely on *conclusions* regarding such past states of affairs from

---

[9] "Man möchte hier sagen: richtig ist, was immer mir als richtig erscheinen wird. Und das heiße nur, daß hier von 'richtig' nicht geredet werden kann" (*PI* §258).

presently available data and, as we have seen, this requires the inferential mediation of appropriate *generalizations*. His present ostensible recollection of having experienced X will be *relevant* to his present ostensible recollection of having experienced Y, however, only if there is a *necessary* connection between X's occurring and Y's occurring, i.e., an objective lawful order of things in nature that he acknowledges to be independent of his present representational propensities. But if he does so, then he can no longer be a problematic idealist.

Phenomena and noumena

The Analytic of Principles, and thereby the Transcendental Analytic as a whole, concludes with a third chapter "On the ground of the distinction of all objects in general into *phenomena* and *noumena*" (A235/B294 ff.), and an Appendix "On the amphiboly of the concepts of reflection through the confusion of the empirical use of the understanding with the transcendental" (A260/B316ff.). The chief aim of the final chapter of the Analytic is precisely to elucidate and emphasize the distinction between legitimate empirical and illegitimate transcendental uses of the understanding. The fundamental theme of the Appendix, to put it briskly, is that Leibniz was confused about just that distinction. Although Kant's interpretation and critique of Leibniz's philosophy are indeed worth exploring, I won't here undertake to say anything more about the Amphiboly. Kant's discussion of phenomena and noumena, in contrast, not only continues the elucidation of his own transcendental idealism but also prepares the way for the transition into the Dialectic, and it is consequently appropriate to say a few words about it before proceeding to the Paralogisms.

As the chapter opens, we find Kant waxing uncharacteristically eloquent. The "land of pure understanding" through which we have been traveling, he tells us, is an island,

the land of truth (a charming name), surrounded by a broad and stormy ocean, the true seat of illusion, where many a fog bank and rapidly melting iceberg pretend to be new lands and, ceaselessly deceiving with empty hopes the voyager looking around for new discoveries, entwine him in adventures from which he can never escape and yet also never bring to an end. (A235–6/B294–5)

The Dialectic to follow will be devoted to "searching all the latitudes" of that ocean for additional truths; but, before setting sail, Kant wants first to look back over the ground that he has covered with two questions in mind: Can we, and must we, be satisfied with the *a priori* concepts and synthetic *a priori* principles that we have discovered? With what right can we claim and defend our entitlement to employ those concepts and apply those judgments to the world?

The answers, of course, have been given in the preceding sections of the Analytic, their essential conclusion being that both the scope and authority of all synthetic *a priori* cognition are determined by the conditions of possible experience.

[T]he understanding can therefore make only empirical use of all its *a priori* principles, indeed of all its concepts, but never transcendental use .... (A238/ B297)

where the transcendental use of a concept, Kant explains, "consists in its being related to things *in general* and *in themselves*; its empirical use, however, in its being related merely to *appearances*,[10] i.e., objects of a possible *experience*" (A238–9/B298).

The fundamental constraint on experience, in turn, is embodied in the "doctrine of two sources".

For every concept there is requisite, first, the logical form of a concept (of thinking) in general, and then, second, the possibility of giving it an object to which it is to be related. Without this latter it has no sense, and is entirely empty of content .... Now the object cannot be given to a concept otherwise than in intuition.... Thus all concepts and with them all principles, however *a priori* they may be, are nevertheless related to empirical intuitions, i.e., to *data* for possible experience. (A239/B298)

Kant proceeds to review the Axioms, Anticipations, Analogies, and Postulates from this perspective, i.e., emphasizing the role of sensible intuition in providing *conditions of application* for the corresponding concepts and principles. The summing-up occurs several pages later:

The Transcendental Analytic accordingly has this important result: That the understanding can never accomplish *a priori* anything more than to anticipate the form of a possible experience in general, and, since that which is not appearance cannot be an object of experience, it can never overstep the limits of sensibility, within which alone objects are given to us. (A246–7/B303)

---

[10] *Not*, it is important to stress: "to mere appearances"! "Appearances" are the objects of possible experience, but "*mere* appearances" are the contents of *non-veridical* experiences.

Notice that we have to do here with *humanly possible* experiences. This harks back to Kant's distinction between pure and transcendental logic at the beginning of the Analytic (A50/B74 ff.). Insofar as *we* are temporally discursive and sensorily passive apperceptive intelligences, the remark that it is through sensibility alone that objects are given to *us* is, in effect, analytic. The constraints on the legitimate use of our understanding, that is, are determined by what sort of being we are.

We should notice, too, that the distinction between form and content that Kant here invokes is a different one from the distinction between "scheme" and "content" that exercises such influential contemporary critics of the possibility of *a priori* cognition as Davidson and Rorty.[11] In the picture that they (rightly) criticize, *content* is something that does not vary from scheme to scheme. *The world* supplies this invariant content in the guise of the entities that our theories are intended to characterize or the phenomena that they are supposed to "save", while *we* supply various "schemes" in the form of alternative theoretical conceptualizations or systematizations. On Kant's account, in contrast, what *we* provide is a *general* form—space, time, and the categories—for which sensible intuition supplies the only content that this invariant humanly possible "scheme" can possibly have.

At this point in A, Kant introduces a first distinction between *phenomena*, namely, appearances insofar as they are thought "in accordance with the unity of the categories", and *noumena*, or "things that are merely objects of the understanding and that, nevertheless, can be given to an intuition, although not to sensible intuition" (A248–9). The idea of an intuition that is not a *sensible* intuition is the idea of an *intellectual* intuition, one form of which we have already encountered in the view, shared by Descartes, Spinoza, and Leibniz, that sensing is an *indistinct* or *confused* mode of conceptual thinking.

As Kant points out, however, one might here have in mind a significantly different notion of an intellectual intuition, suggested by the contrast between appearances and things in themselves—"which would not concern merely the logical form of the indistinct or distinct cognition of one and the same thing" (A249)—but rather would be a cognition

---

[11] Cf., e.g., Donald Davidson, "On the Very Idea of a Conceptual Scheme", *Proceedings of the American Philosophical Association*, 17 (1973–4), 5–20, and Richard Rorty, "The World Well Lost", *Journal of Philosophy*, 69 (1972), 649–66.

in which no sensibility is encountered, and which alone has absolutely objective reality, through which, namely, objects are represented to us *as they are*, in contrast to the empirical use of our understanding, in which things are only cognized *as they appear*. (A249–50)

If we had, in *this* sense, a non-sensible intuition, then, in addition to their empirical use, the categories could have for us also a "pure and yet objectively valid" transcendental use.

That, however, is precisely what the arguments of the Analytic have ruled out. Our understanding indeed relates all appearances to an *object* of empirical intuition, and so to a *something*, "but this something is to that extent only the transcendental object", something

that can serve only as a correlate of the unity of apperception for the unity of the manifold in sensible intuition, by means of which the understanding unifies that in the concept of an object. (A250)

There is no way for us to pry loose from sensible data the notion of an object of experience as something that we, "in accordance with the current constitution of our understanding" (A250), might nevertheless think under the categories. Properly understood, then, this conception of a noumenon is

not at all positive and does not signify a determinate cognition of any sort of thing, but only the thinking of something in general, in which I abstract from all form of sensible intuition. (A252)

Kant significantly revised this chapter of the Analytic for the second edition, and, in particular, the ambiguity in the notion of a noumenon to which he wants to call our attention comes into clearer focus in B. The initial phenomena–noumena contrast there is between "beings of sense" and "beings of understanding" (B306), but Kant immediately points out that it would be a serious mistake to take "the entirely *undetermined* concept of a being of the understanding" for a *determinate* concept of a being that we could somehow cognize entirely through the understanding. We must consequently distinguish the legitimate notion of a noumenon "in the *negative* sense", namely, the idea of "a thing *insofar as it is not an object of our sensible intuition*", from the problematic notion of a noumenon "in the *positive* sense", namely, the idea of "an *object of a non-sensible intuition*" (B307).[12]

---

[12] In contrast, although, as we have seen, Kant in effect adverts to the notion of a noumenon "in the negative sense" at A252, he never introduces an explicit "positive *vs* negative" distinction into his discussion in A.

Judgments making use of the negative notion of a noumenon are *exclusionary*. We reach this conception of noumena by beginning with a conception of phenomena and then removing the condition of sensibility. The notion of a noumenon in its negative sense, that is, results directly from spelling out the implications of the "doctrine of two sources", i.e., the fact that *our* intuition is not intellectual but sensible, and that cognition consequently requires the cooperation of spontaneous and receptive faculties. Judgments making use of the positive notion, in contrast, are ostensibly *predicational*.[13] They purport to tell us something about what noumena *are*, and thereby "assume a special kind of intuition, namely intellectual intuition" (B307).

> If...we wanted to apply the categories to objects that are not considered as appearances, then we would have to ground them on an intuition other than the sensible one, and then the object would be a noumenon in a *positive sense*. (B308)

As Kant quickly adds, however, *such* an intellectual intuition "lies absolutely outside our faculty of cognition". To be sure, the concept of a noumenon as "a thing that is not to be thought of as an object of the senses but rather as a thing in itself (solely through the understanding)" is not *contradictory*, since we cannot justifiably claim that our passive sensibility is the only possible form of intuition. But the concept is nevertheless, as Kant puts it, *problematic* insofar as the objective reality of a noumenon "can in no way be cognized" (A254/B310). A noumenon is not a "special *intelligible object* for our understanding" (A256/B311) on which we could ground a legitimate transcendental use of the pure concepts of the understanding, distinct from their objectively valid empirical use in relation to objects of possible sensory experience.

> With us *understanding* and *sensibility* can determine an object *only in combination*. If we separate them, then we have intuitions without concepts, or concepts without intuitions, but in either case representations that we cannot relate to any determinate object. (A258/B314)

Kant's "doctrine of two sources" consequently implies the possibility of forming two different "limit notions", both of which we have now encountered in the text. As we have just seen, the notion of a noumenon in the negative sense—of "a thing insofar as it is not an object of our

---

[13] The distinction between exclusionary and predicational judgments should remind the reader of the distinction between "negative" and "infinite" judgments under the heading of Quality in the Table of Judgments. Here we begin to see that Kant's nominal distinction is not purely architectonic, but does in fact mark a significant conceptual difference.

sensible intuition" (B307)—is formed by abstracting from the particular spatio-temporal conditions of sensibility through which an object can be given. On the other hand, the notion of "the transcendental object $= x$"— which "concerns nothing but that unity which must be encountered in a manifold of cognition insofar as it stands in relation to an object" (A109; cf. A250)—in effect posits a unifying object for sensible intuition but considers it in abstraction from the particular categorial conditions of understanding whereby the object can be thought. Both of these notions are intelligible, however, only by contrast with the full-fledged concept of an object of possible experience. They are, in this sense, radically "incomplete" and hence, strictly speaking, not proper concepts at all. For, as you surely recall, intuitions without concepts are blind, and concepts without intuitions, empty (A51/B75), a Kantian thesis whose full implications we can now much better appreciate.

As we will see, the contrast between exclusionary and predicational judgments which figured in Kant's discussion of phenomena and noumena also has a significant role to play in the interpretation and critique of Descartes' arguments for the ontological independence of mind and body. Those arguments belong to what Kant calls 'rational psychology', the traditional project of giving an *a priori* categorial account of the transcendental ego, "this I, or He, or It (the thing), which thinks" (A346/B404)—a project that, by his lights, is destined to fail. That the conclusions at which it ostensibly arrives are all "transcendental illusions" is, in fact, the theme of the Paralogisms of Pure Reason, and, conveniently, they are the topic of our next chapter.

The Thinking Self as an Idea of Reason: The Paralogisms

12

The leading question of Kant's Transcendental Dialectic can be formulated quite briskly: "Does reason in itself, i.e., pure reason, contain *a priori* synthetic principles and rules, and in what might such principles consist?" (A306/B363). Kant's ultimate answer is equally compact: No. It unavoidably and persistently *seems* to do so, but that is a "transcendental illusion". When all the chips are down, reason is

> only a merely subordinate faculty that gives to given cognitions a certain form, called "logical" form, through which cognitions of the understanding are subordinated to one another, and lower rules are subordinated to higher ones .... (A305/B362)

We will, of course, not be able to survey all of Kant's arguments for this conclusion—they stretch over hundreds of pages—but by the time we are finished, we will at least have gained a better idea of what is actually at stake in the Dialectic and explored two important examples of Kant's critical reasoning.

The very idea of an idea of reason

In the Introduction to the Dialectic, Kant seems at a bit of a loss to explain just what reason *is*. Echoing his characterization of the understanding as the faculty of rules, he calls it the *faculty of principles* (A299/B356), but, as he goes on to confess, in a certain sense, the understanding and reason are basically in the same line of work, namely, making *ones* out of *manys*. Most broadly construed, a "cognition from principles" is any cognition "in which I cognize the particular in the universal through concepts" (A300/B357). Since any bit of deductive reasoning which departs from a general premise answers to this description, we can, in this broad sense, call any universal generalization a "principle", including the principles of the pure understanding whose objective validity was established in the Analytic.

But when we consider the synthetic *a priori* generalizations secured in the Analytic of Principles "as to their origin", Kant continues, we see that they are not "principles absolutely", but only "principles comparatively" (A301/B358). That is, they are not, strictly speaking, cognitions *from concepts*, for their validity depends upon our sensible intuition as a condition of possible experience. An *absolute* principle would be a *synthetic* cognition from concepts alone—and it is the possibility of principles in this narrow and restricted sense that is at issue in the Dialectic. As Kant earlier "isolated" sensibility in the Aesthetic and understanding in the Analytic, he will "isolate" reason in the Dialectic (A305/B362), in essence, as a faculty for unifying general judgments under *more* general judgments.

If the understanding may be a faculty of unity of appearances by means of rules, then reason is the faculty of unity of the rules of understanding under principles. Thus [reason] never applies directly to experience or to any object, but instead applies to the understanding, in order to give unity *a priori* through concepts to the [its] manifold cognitions, which may be called "the unity of reason", and is of an altogether different kind than any unity that can be achieved by the understanding. (A302/B359)

The *formal* use of pure reason, argues Kant, is governed by a "logical maxim": "to find the unconditioned for conditioned cognitions of the understanding, with which its unity will be completed" (A307/B364). His paradigm is the Aristotelian syllogism. The major premise, functioning as a "universal rule", e.g., "All humans are mortal", formulates a *condition* for applying a given predicate, 'mortal'. In the minor premise, a cognition is *subsumed* under that condition, e.g., "All scholars are human", and finally, in the conclusion, the given cognition is subsumed under the given predicate, e.g., "All scholars are mortal" (A303–4/B360).

To understand Kant's conception of reason, we need to think of such a correct syllogism as, so to speak, discharging a *task*. We begin with the judgment formulated in the *conclusion* and seek *its* "condition", i.e., a warrant or justification for it, placing it in what Wilfrid Sellars called "the logical space of having and giving reasons" by finding an appropriate, more general, major premise from which it may be (syllogistically) derived. This task is repeatable, i.e., the major premise "is once again exposed to this same attempt of reason, and the condition of its condition thereby has to be sought" (A307/B364)—for instance, although Kant himself does not give this example, "All animals are mortal". Kant calls this process *prosyllogistic* reasoning (A331/B387). It issues in an "ascending series" of syllogisms "on the side of the conditions" (*per prosyllogismus*), and Kant's "logical maxim" formulates in essence the *motivation* for constructing it. In constantly seeking the condition of any given condition, reason is, so to speak, guided by the vision of a *final* condition, i.e., an *unconditioned* condition, from which the whole series of conditions could be derived by a "descending series" of (epi-) syllogisms "on the side of the conditioned" (*per episyllogismus*) (A331/B338).

The logical maxim tells pure reason what to seek. The corresponding *principle* of pure reason says, in essence, that it is there to be found:

[When] the conditioned is given, then so is the whole series of conditions subordinated one to the other, which is itself unconditioned, also given . . . . (A307–8/B364)

As Kant points out, this is a *synthetic* principle—"for the conditioned is analytically related to some condition, but not to the unconditioned" (A308/B364). Like the "supreme principle of all synthetic judgments" in the Analytic—"Every object stands under the necessary conditions of the synthetic unity of the manifold of intuition in a possible experience" (A158/B197)—it is a *meta*-principle, i.e., a principle for validating a further family of synthetic *a priori* judgments.

Different synthetic propositions must arise from it, of which the pure understanding knows nothing, since it has to do only with objects of a possible experience, whose cognition and synthesis are always conditioned. [The] unconditioned, if it actually occurs, . . . must thereby give us material for many [additional] synthetic propositions *a priori*. (A308/B364–5)

The particular conditions of possible experience which ground the objective validity of the specific synthetic *a priori* judgments established in the Analytic of Principles are the pure concepts of the understanding, i.e., the categories. Analogously, if the (meta-) principle of pure reason also validates a family of synthetic *a priori* propositions, these will be severally grounded by particular "pure concepts of reason". Kant proposes to call them "transcendental ideas" (A310/B368; cf. A321/B378).[1]

A transcendental idea is basically the concept of something absolutely unconditioned. There will consequently be as many different kinds of transcendental ideas as there are kinds of conditions or, equivalently, kinds of syllogisms. Kant recognizes three:

(a) *categorical* syllogisms, yielding the idea of an absolutely unconditioned categorical synthesis of determinations in a subject;
(b) *hypothetical* syllogisms, yielding the idea of an absolutely unconditioned hypothetical synthesis of the members of a series;
(c) *disjunctive* syllogisms, yielding the idea of an absolutely unconditioned disjunctive synthesis of the parts of a system. (A323/B379)

None of these, Kant stresses, is a concept that is useable in experience, because no experience is unconditioned.

Hence the objective use of the pure concepts of reason is always *transcendent*, while that of the pure concepts of understanding must by its nature always be *immanent*, since it is limited solely to possible experience. (A327/B383)

Since the transcendental ideas exceed the boundaries of experience, no object adequate to them can ever be concretely given. They are consequently, Kant says, *only* ideas (A328–9/B384–5), and, in contrast to the categories, no objective deduction of them is possible (A336/B393). Nevertheless, Kant argues, they have a certain sort of *subjective inevitability* in that reason, "exclusively through the synthetic use of the same function it employs in [syllogisms]", must necessarily arrive at concepts of three corresponding sorts of absolutely unconditioned, absolutely unified *beings*:

(a) the thinking subject,
(b) the natural world, and
(c) "the being of all beings", i.e., God,

giving rise to the ideas of three *a priori* disciplines:

---

[1] And he immediately takes several pages (A312–20/B368–77) to explain and justify his choice of terminology. He is clearly rather annoyed by the way that his immediate philosophical predecessors have corrupted Plato's original notion of an "idea".

a transcendental doctrine of the soul (*psychologia rationalis*),
a transcendental science of the world (*cosmologia rationalis*), and finally also,
a transcendental cognition of God (*theologia transcendentalis*). (A334–5/
   B391–2)

Despite the naturalness, inevitability, and persistence of these ideas, Kant argues, they are all ultimately transcendental *illusions*.[2] The reasonings on which they are based are *dialectical* syllogisms, i.e., "*sophistical* rather than rational inferences".

They are sophistries not of human beings but of pure reason itself, and even the wisest of all human beings cannot get free of them; perhaps after much effort he may guard himself from error, but he can never be wholly rid of the illusion, which ceaselessly teases and mocks him. (A339/B397)[3]

Nevertheless, Kant will devote the rest of the Dialectic to uncovering and demonstrating the sophistical character of the inferences which theoretically ground the ostensible disciplines of rational psychology, rational cosmology, and transcendental theology. For, as he says at the end of his critique of transcendental illusion,

there will never be an end to discussion unless one gets to the bottom of the illusion that can fool even the most rational, and . . . [it is therefore] necessary to carry out an exhaustive examination of the vain elaborations of speculative reason in their entirety down to its primary sources . . . and store it in the archives of human reason, so as to prevent future errors of similar kind. (A703–4/B731–2)

The "I" who thinks

As we noted long ago, both Descartes and Hume believed that we can know something *a priori* about the "I" who thinks, i.e., the thinking *subject* or, briefly, the *self*[4]—Descartes, that the self is a substance; Hume, that it

---

[2] Kant compares them to certain natural, inevitable, and persistent *perceptual* illusions: The oar in the water still looks bent, even when we know that it's not, and the rising full moon seems just as huge to the knowledgeable astronomer as it does to the uninformed layman (A297/B354).

[3] One can hardly fail to hear a bit of autobiography in these remarks. They have the same ring as Wittgenstein's famous comment, "The real discovery is the one that makes me capable of stopping doing philosophy when I want to" ("Die eigentliche Entdeckung ist die, die mich fähig macht, das Philosophieren abzubrechen, wann ich will") (*PI* §133).

[4] All of these nominal expressions are contentious in one way or another, but they are nevertheless all preferable, I think, to a further expression that we repeatedly find in Kant's own text, viz., 'the *soul*', at least in lacking its overtly religious overtones. I shall consequently often take the liberty of replacing Kant's term 'soul' by 'self' or occasionally, when it is appropriate, by 'mind'.

is *not* a substance. If either of these views were correct, it would pose a significant problem for Kant, for the application of such *a priori* concepts is constrained by the conditions of possible experience, and the "I" who thinks is *not* an object of possible experience. It is not *intuitable*. "[The] I is, to be sure, in all thoughts, but not the least intuition is bound up with this representation" (A350; cf. B412–13).[5]

That is a point, indeed, on which both Hume and Descartes concur. It is clearly the moral of Hume's famous introspective thought experiment, which, we recall, yielded the result that, as he put it, "I never can catch *myself* at any time without a perception, and never can observe anything but the perception" (*THN*, I. iv. 6; 252). But it is also the motor that drives Descartes' *cogito* reasoning. We cannot be deceived about the formal reality of the thinking subject precisely because, in contrast to an object of possible experience, it is not something that we can ostensibly *encounter*, i.e., it does not exist objectively *in* any thought.

Now Kant can deal with Hume's views fairly quickly. As we recall, Hume officially espoused a "bundle theory" according to which the self *consists* of suitably related "ideas and impressions", but he was never entirely happy with it and ultimately expressed his continued worries and reservations in an appendix to his *Treatise on Human Nature*. The problem, as we saw earlier, is that there is no way to pick out the "ideas and impressions" that are to constitute the "bundle" that is supposed to be *me* except as *my* ideas and impressions. As Kant clearly realized, that is, the terms in which Hume tells his reductive story *presuppose* the idea of a subject who senses and thinks, and so cannot constitute an analysis of it. In contrast, however, as Kant sees it, Descartes' views need to be taken very seriously.

It would be a great, or indeed, the only stumbling block to our entire critique, if it were possible to prove *a priori* that all thinking beings are in themselves simple substances . . . . For in this way we would have taken a step beyond the sensible world, entering into the field of *noumena* . . . . For the proposition "Every thinking being as such is a simple substance" is a synthetic proposition *a priori*. . . . Thus synthetic propositions *a priori* would not, as we have asserted, be feasible and admissible merely in relation to objects of possible experience . . . . (B409–10)

We have already observed Descartes, in the Second Meditation, beginning to develop his conception of the self as *res cogitans*, a "thing that

---

[5] Parts of the treatment of the Paralogisms in this section are derived from the more detailed interpretation presented in ch. 3 of *The Thinking Self*: "The Thing Which Thinks *vs. Res Cogitans*".

thinks", i.e., a "thing that doubts, understands, affirms denies, wills, refuses, and that also imagines and senses". When we unpack this conception what we find is the idea of a *single simple subject* of many "thoughts":

(1) a *subject* = a basic substance, i.e., something not itself predicable of anything else, an "unhad haver"; thus a *first* subject, not an aspect, feature, or characteristic of anything ontologically more basic;

(2) *simple* = an indissoluble unity, i.e., neither a composite of independent parts or elements nor a system of other ontologically more basic items;

(3) *single* = a persisting continuant, i.e., strictly identical across time, not a series or sequence of other ontologically more basic items.

The traditional discipline of "rational psychology"—Kant also sometimes calls it "pure" or "transcendental" psychology—purports to derive these characteristics of the self from the mere concept *I* "insofar as it occurs in all thinking". It is "a putative science, which is built on the single proposition *I think*" (A342/B400), and, in this capacity, offers itself as a rational basis for received religious conceptions of the self as the *soul*, the immaterial, imperishable, and immortal spiritual essence of a person (A345/B403).

This threefold Cartesian characterization of the self corresponds (in A) to the first three Paralogisms.[6] As Kant sees it, rational psychology undertakes to demonstrate the three ostensibly synthetic *a priori* judgments which give expression to it by appeal to three prima facie compelling arguments. His clearest formulation of such an argument occurs in B:

What cannot be thought otherwise than as subject does not exist otherwise than as subject, and is therefore substance.

Now a thinking being, considered merely as such, cannot be thought otherwise than as subject.

Therefore it also exists only as [subject], i.e., as substance. (B410–11; cf. A348)

Although he does not explicitly produce them in B, the corresponding text in A clearly implies the availability of strictly parallel arguments for the absolute simplicity and diachronic persistence of the self:

[6] The Fourth Paralogism in A is what becomes the Refutation of Idealism in B, and we have already examined much of the relevant text in that connection. Kant's discussion of the Paralogisms is considerably shorter in B than in A, and the architectonic structure somewhat different, but the critical content remains the same.

What cannot be thought otherwise than unitary (identical across time) does not exist otherwise than as unitary (identical across time), and is therefore simple (persisting).

Now a thinking being, considered merely as such, cannot be thought otherwise than as unitary (identical across time).

Therefore it also exists only as unitary (identical across time), i.e., as simple (persisting). (Cf. A352, A361)

Kant's official line on these arguments is expressed most directly at B411: They are fallacious *"per Sophisma figurae dictionis*, hence by means of a deceptive inference"*, specifically, by reason of equivocation. It is hardly immediately obvious, however, what equivocation he has in mind, and the corresponding footnote, in which he explains that " 'Thinking' is taken in an entirely different signification in the two premises", does not bring much in the way of immediate illumination. Consequently, to understand Kant's criticism, we need to look carefully at some of its details, in particular at what he has to say about the minor premises. This, in contrast, is most clearly spelled out in A, where his exposition stays closer to the first person.

The minor premise of the First Paralogism there reads: "I, as a thinking being, am the *absolute subject* of all my possible judgments, and this representation of Myself[7] cannot be used as a predicate of any other thing" (A348). This proposition reflects a line of thought that also works to preclude the Humean identification of the self with the collection of its determinations, namely, that I always necessarily represent myself as something *other* than those determinations. "[In] every judgment I am always the *determining* subject of that relation that constitutes the judgment" (B407; cf. A349). The "I" who thinks always remains, so to speak, *outside* any judgmentally represented predicative relationship as its "determining subject" i.e., as the represent*er* of all such represent*ings*. Consequently, I cannot coherently represent *myself* as a determination of anything else. The attempt to do so is always self-defeating. It follows, Kant observes, that

everyone must necessarily regard Himself as a substance, but regard his thinking only as accidents of his existence and determinations of his state. (A349)

Kant arrives at analogous conclusions regarding the minor premises of the Second and Third Paralogisms. In A, the first of these takes the form of a judgment to the effect that

---

[7] The unusual capitalizations here and later correspond to those in Kant's text, in this instance, '*Mir selbst*'.

My action, as a thinking being, "can never be regarded as the concurrence of many acting things". (A351)

The fundamental consideration supporting this judgment is that *thoughts* have a kind of unity that precludes their being the product of collaborating causes.

[Because] representations that are distributed among different beings (e.g., the individual words of a verse) never constitute a whole thought (a verse), the thought can never inhere in a composite as such. (A352)

That I think, e.g., that S is P cannot mean that one thing thinks of S and another thing thinks that something is P. The parts of my thought that S is P cannot be distributed among different subjects any more than can the warmth and friendliness of my warm friendly smile. Hence, as Kant concludes, "the subjective *I* cannot be divided or distributed, and this *I* we presuppose in all thinking" (A354).

Finally, his fundamental point in A in connection with the Third Paralogism is that I am prima facie *conscious* of my numerical identity across time. More precisely, since I am an object of inner sense, and time is the form of inner sense, I necessarily "relate each and every one of my successive determinations to the numerically identical Self in all time" (A362). That is, I cannot help but represent the "I" who thinks X (at t_1) as strictly identical to the "I" who thinks Y (at t_2). We have met such representations before, of course—in the Transcendental Deduction under the rubric "the analytical unity of apperception"—and, as Kant here interprets the minor premise of the Third Paralogism, it simply reiterates his earlier observation that "this principle of the necessary unity of apperception is . . . itself identical, thus an analytical proposition" (B135).

Kant sums up these considerations in the remark that "mere apperception ('I')" is substance, simple, and persisting *in concept* (A400). The contrast is with something's being this or that *in appearance*, which presupposes a corresponding intuition, and the point is that these are all conclusions about how I necessarily *think of* myself. They are not conclusions about how I necessarily *experience* myself, precisely because I *don't* experience myself. All I have to work with, so to speak, is

the simple and in content for itself wholly empty representation *I*, of which one cannot even say that it is a concept, but a mere consciousness that accompanies every concept. Through this I, or He, or It (the thing), which thinks, nothing further is represented than a transcendental subject of thoughts $= x$, which is recognized only through the thoughts that are its predicates, and about which, in abstraction, we can never have even the least concept.... [The] consciousness in itself is not even a representation distinguishing a particular object, but rather a form of representation in general... (A345–6/B404)

That is the reason why the three Paralogism arguments do not establish three new and important synthetic *a priori* propositions.

The unity of consciousness... is here taken for an intuition of the subject as an object, and [for instance] the category of substance is applied to it. But this unity is only the unity of *thinking*, through which no object is given; and thus the category of substance, which always presupposes a given *intuition*, cannot be applied to it, and hence this subject cannot be cognized at all. (B421–2)

Rational psychology, in other words, mistakes a *form of representation*—the transcendental unity of apperception; the 'I think' that must be able to accompany every representing that is mine (B131)—for the *representation of an object*—the noumenal self—to which the categories could then be applied. As Kant elegantly puts it in A, "it passes off the constant logical subject of thinking as the cognition of a real subject of inherence" (A350).

The fatal fallacious equivocation that Kant finds in the arguments of the Paralogisms consequently attaches to the phrase 'cannot be thought otherwise than as X'. As we have just seen, there is a reading that makes the minor premise in each instance come out true. Indeed, interpreted as propositions about *the form of first-person thinking*, they are not only true but in fact, as Kant variously observes (cf. B407–8), *analytically* true. But so understood, they have no metaphysical consequences. To put it in contemporary terms, they tell us only something about the "logical grammar" of the first-person pronoun 'I'.[8] If, however, 'subject', 'unitary', and 'identical across time' in the major premises are to be interpreted in conformity with the categories, then the key phrase must be taken in the sense of 'cannot be *cognized* otherwise than as X', and, on that reading, the three minor premises all come out *false*, for, since it is not intuitable, the "I" who thinks cannot be cognized at all.

[T]hus if we stay merely with thinking, we also lack the necessary condition for applying the concept of substance... and the simplicity of substance that is bound up with the objective reality of this concept completely falls away.... (B413)

---

[8] Roughly, that (1) it has no predicative use; (2) it is not analyzable or definable; and (3) it is univocal within a given user's discourse.

Dissolving the transcendental illusion

The broader goals of rational psychology, Kant observes, can be expressed in the form of three "dialectical questions":

1) about the possibility of the community of the soul with an organic body, i.e., the animality and the state of the soul in the life of a human being; 2) about the beginning of this community, i.e., of the soul in and before the birth of a human being; and 3) as to the end of this community, i.e., of the soul in and after the death of a human being (the question concerning immortality). (A384)

Since, however, as he has argued, "the whole of rational psychology, as a science transcending all the powers of human reason, collapses", we have no option but "to remain within the limits of those questions that do not go beyond that whose content can be provided by possible inner experience" (A382), and, from these resources, no answers to those dialectical questions can be derived.

Kant consequently decisively parts company with Descartes by concluding that from considerations concerning the (first-person, "meditative") *representation* of the "I" who thinks we cannot derive any propositions regarding the *essence* or *ontological constitution* of the thinking self. That the self is *in concept* substance, simple, and persisting is entirely compatible with its being *in itself*, for instance,

(i)   a mode of a Spinozistic substance or an aspect of a Strawsonian "person";
(ii) a plurality of noumenal items that we also experience as an organized collection of molecules constituting a multi-cellular organism; or
(iii) a "harmony" of Sellarsian "absolute processes".

It is consequently, in particular, a mistake to conclude that the thinking self as it is in itself—the reality underlying the representations of inner sense—is distinct from material things in space as they are in themselves—the reality underlying the representations of outer sense. It could rather very well be the case that

the very same thing that is called a body in one relation would at the same time be a thinking being in another .... Thereby the expression that only [minds] (as a particular species of substances) think would be dropped; and instead it would be said, as usual, that human beings think, i.e., that the same being that as outer appearance is extended is inwardly (in itself) a subject, which is not composite, but is simple and thinks. (A359–60)

And one welcome corollary of this conclusion is that the received *Cartesian* mind–body problem—what Kant calls the problem of the "community" between mind or soul and body or matter—simply evaporates.

[The] question is no longer about the community of the [mind] with other known but different substances outside us, but merely about the conjunction of representations in inner sense with the modifications of our outer sensibility, and how these may be conjoined with one another according to constant laws, so that they are connected into one experience. (A386)

We are no longer confronted with an ostensible choice among the intellectually unattractive options of *"physical influence* ['interactionism'], of *pre-established harmony* ['parallelism'], and of *supernatural assistance* ['occasionalism']" (A390). For all three options presuppose the Cartesian thesis that thinking things and extended things are distinct and mutually independent substances.

But if one considers that the two kinds of objects are different not inwardly but only insofar as one of them *appears* outwardly to the other, hence that what grounds the appearance of matter as thing in itself might perhaps not be so different in kind, then this difficulty vanishes . . . . (B427–8)

Analogously, although I necessarily represent myself as a single persisting continuant—as *one* identical thinker of *many* thoughts—the reality underlying and corresponding to such representations could very well be that of a noumenal succession of distinct but related thinking subjects.

The identity of the consciousness of Myself in different times is . . . only a formal condition of my thoughts and their connection, but it does not prove at all the numerical identity of my subject, in which—despite the logical identity of the I—a change can go on that does not allow it to keep its [ontological numerical] identity; and this even though all the while the identical-sounding "I" is assigned to it, [a change] which in every other state, even in the replacement of the subject, still keeps in view the thought of the previous subject, and thus could also pass it along to the following one. (A363)

The self as it is in itself, in other words, could resemble, e.g., the New York Yankees. At any given time, insofar as it consists of its members at that time, such a baseball team is composite. But the team *per se* is nevertheless something distinct from its various members. Lou Gehrig and Yogi Berra both played for the Yankees, but no one who belonged to the team when Gehrig did was also a member when Berra was. Nevertheless, the cumulative record of wins and losses of the Yankees during

Gehrig's era was "passed along" to the Yankees during Berra's, and continues to be "passed along" to that same team during our own.[9]

Arguments for the *imperishability* of the mind or soul, in contrast—and thereby arguments for the postmortem survival of the person—classically rest on the thesis of its absolutely simplicity. As experience teaches us, whatever exists as an organized system of parts—e.g., a building, a plant, an animal body—normally ceases to exist as such by *coming apart*, and anything composite can in principle suffer the same fate. As traditionally conceived, however, souls literally have no parts. (Plato's "tripartite division" of the soul, for instance, is merely nominal; Platonic souls have only, so to speak, *virtual* parts.) Since an absolutely simple soul cannot come apart, it was traditionally concluded that souls cannot cease to exist at all.

The philosopher Moses Mendelssohn was not convinced by this reasoning. As Kant reports it:

This acute philosopher soon noticed that the usual argument, through which it is to be proved that the soul (if one grants that it is a simple being) cannot cease to exist through *disintegration*, is insufficient for the aim of securing the soul's necessary continuing duration, since one could still assume cessation of its existence by *vanishing*. (B413)

Mendelssohn consequently set out to fill this argumentative lacuna. His strategy had two parts. The first was to argue that nothing could possibly cease to exist by vanishing *instantaneously*, since then, again quoting Kant, "there would be no time at all between a moment in which it is and another moment in which it is not, which is impossible". The second was then to argue that something absolutely simple could also not cease to exist by vanishing *gradually*, "since it cannot be diminished and thus lose more and more of its existence . . . (since it has no parts and thus no plurality in itself)" (B413–14).

Now as we have seen, Kant argues that any change or succession in appearances is only an alteration through which substance is always conserved. Nevertheless, he clearly allows for the coming-to-be and ceasing-to-exist of something real, namely, the states or determinations of such a persisting substance, and, with regard to *their* arising or perishing, he seems to agree with the conclusion of Mendelssohn's *first* argument.

---

[9] Kant's own explanatory footnote, A363–4 n., compares such "passing along" of representations and the consciousness of them to the (complete) transfer of momentum from, e.g., one billiard ball to another in a (perfectly) elastic collision.

No difference of the real in appearance is *the smallest*, just as no difference in the magnitude of times is, and thus the new state of reality grows out of the first [one], in which it did not exist, through all the infinite degrees of reality, the differences between which are all smaller than that between 0 and [the initial state] *a*. (A209/B254)

Let us suppose that this "law of the continuity of all alteration" would also apply to the vanishing of a simple soul. If so, we would expect Kant's disagreement with Mendelssohn to be addressed to the *second* part of his strategy, and so it is.

Mendelssohn's argument against the possibility of gradual vanishing, Kant observes, simply takes it for granted that the only way in which this could occur would be by *shrinking*, i.e., by a loss of *extensive* magnitude.

Yet he did not consider that even if we allow . . . that [the soul] contains no manifold [of parts] *outside one another*, and hence no extensive magnitude, one nevertheless cannot deny to it . . . an intensive magnitude, i.e., a degree of reality in regard to all its faculties, indeed to everything in general that constitutes its existence, which might diminish through all the infinitely many smaller degrees . . . . (B414)

Even an absolutely simple substantial soul, in other words, could vanish by *fading* or, as Kant puts it, by "elanguescence", "a gradual remission of all its powers" (B414). Consciousness itself always has a degree, and "there are infinitely many degrees of consciousness down to its vanishing" (B415 n.). Despite Mendelssohn's efforts, Kant concludes, the persistence of the soul "merely as an object of inner sense" remains "unproved and even unprovable" (B415).

In light of his broader aims, however, it is crucial for Kant to emphasize that, considered as claims about the self as it is in itself (the noumenal self), the *contraries* of the theses of substantiality, immateriality, simplicity, imperishability, strict diachronic identity, and the like *also* remain "unproved and even unprovable". When it comes to "explaining my existence", that is, "materialism" is just as indefensible as "spiritualism" (B420). The possibility of *any* cognition

going beyond the bounds of possible experience yet belonging to the highest interests of humanity disappears, as far as speculative philosophy is concerned, in disappointed expectations . . . . (B423–4)

Kant explicitly restricts his conclusion here to one regarding the limits of *speculative* philosophy, and that is both deliberate and important. For reason can be practical as well as theoretical or speculative, and, as he puts it near the end of the First Critique (A805/B833), *all* the interests of reason consequently give rise to *three* questions:

1. What can I know?
2. What should I do?
3. What may I hope?

The first question, Kant writes, is purely speculative, and the second, purely practical, but the third "is simultaneously practical and theoretical, so that the practical [aspect] leads like a clue to a reply to the theoretical question and, in its highest form, the speculative question" (A805/B833). Thus, although the answer to the first question defended in the First Critique precludes the possibility of any theoretical knowledge of an imperishable soul, Kant will argue, in his *Second* Critique, that such personal immortality is a necessary postulate of pure *practical* reason, and thereby a legitimate object of hope. And because this is so, he adds,

much is still won if, through the free confession of my ignorance, I can nevertheless repel the dogmatic attacks of a speculative opponent, and show him that he can never know more in which to deny my expectations about the nature of my [self] than I can in order to hold to them. (A383–4; cf. B424–6)

Just here, in other words, we find one of those places where, as Kant promised in the Preface to B, his denial of knowledge "makes room for faith" (Bxxx).

Reason in Conflict with Itself: A Brief Look at the Antinomies

13

In search of world-concepts

The Paralogisms are fallacious *categorical* syllogisms, which purported to ground a discipline of "rational psychology", dealing with the unconditioned unity of the *subjective* conditions of all representations. Kant next turns to a series of fallacious *hypothetical* syllogisms, purporting to ground a discipline of "rational cosmology", dealing with the unconditioned unity of the *objective* conditions in appearance. The corresponding transcendental ideas—Kant calls them *world-concepts*—consequently concern "the absolute totality in the synthesis of appearances" (A408/B434), i.e., everything empirical.

What is especially devious about these world-concepts, he suggests, is that they give rise to *antinomies*, i.e., pairs of seemingly compelling arguments that support prima facie contradictory conclusions, reflecting "a wholly natural antithetic" of human reason.[1] This is perhaps a useful safeguard against "the slumber of an imagined conviction", but it also risks degenerating into dogmatic stubbornness or skeptical hopelessness ("the euthanasia of pure reason"), both of which mark "the death of a healthy philosophy" (A407/B434).

What we need first is obviously a systematic enumeration of such world-concepts. As usual, the categories will be our guide, and, since we

[1] Kant defines a 'thetic' as "any sum total of dogmatic doctrines". An 'antithetic', in contrast, is "the conflict between what seem to be dogmatic cognitions...without the ascription of a preeminent claim to approval of one side or the other" (A420/B448).

are still ostensibly seeking synthetic *a priori* principles not subject to the limitations of possible experience, the principle of pure reason once again comes into play:

(PPR) *If the conditioned is given, then the whole sum of conditions, and hence the absolutely unconditioned, is also given,* through which alone the conditioned was possible. (A409/B436)

The enumeration of world-concepts, or "system of cosmological ideas", will consequently have four main headings, corresponding to the system of categories; but, since a world-concept always presupposes relationships among a multiplicity of conditions and their consequences, the principle of pure reason in this instance will be applied only to items in a categorial synthesis that constitute a *series* of successively subordinated conditions for something conditioned.

The relationship between conditions and consequences is asymmetric. Conditions make consequences possible, but not conversely. Hence, as Kant puts it, "in regard to a given conditioned, conditions are regarded as already presupposed and given along with the conditioned" (A410/B437). Reason thus demands an "ascent" to the absolutely unconditioned, but is noncommittal regarding whether one reaches a corresponding "totality" in "descending" from conditions to consequences.

Thus one necessarily thinks of the fully elapsed time up to the present moment as also given (even if not as determinable by us). But as to the future, since it is not a condition for attaining to the present, it is a matter of complete indifference for comprehending the present what we want to hold about future time, whether it stops somewhere or runs on to infinity. (A410/B437)

Kant calls the "ascending" synthesis of a series on the side of the conditions *regressive* or proceeding *in antecedentia*. The "descending" synthesis that continues on the side of the (conditioned) consequences, in contrast, is *progressive* and proceeds *in consequentia* (A411/B438). The system of cosmological ideas is concerned with absolute totalities of conditions. We must consequently consider each of the categories in terms of a regressive synthesis, proceeding *in antecedentia*.

We begin with Quantity. Recall the Axioms of Intuition. What corresponds to the categories of Quantity in appearances, we saw there, is their *extensive magnitude*, and this is so precisely because appearances are intuitions in space or time. Kant's strategy here is thus to consider directly "the two original *quanta* of all intuition, space and time". Time is easy, since it is not only itself a series but in fact is also the formal condition of all series. Thus with regard to a given present moment, its *antecedentia*, times past, are distinguished *a priori* from its *consequentia*, times in the future, and the world-concept or cosmological idea we are seeking is simply that of *all past time*. What (PPR) tells us, in other words, is that "the whole elapsed past time is thought of as given necessarily as the condition for the given moment" (A412/B439).

Space, however, is harder, since it is not a series but only an *aggregate*. Nothing is a condition of the existence of a point of space in the way in which *all preceding times having passed* is a condition of the existence of a point in time. But, although space itself isn't a series, the synthesis of the manifold *parts* of space through which we *apprehend* space always occurs in time and so always contains a series. Since parts of space can be given only as regions bounded by differences in their contents, Kant concludes, we get a suitable conditioning relationship when we consider *boundaries*. We can think of the spatial region on either side of a boundary as a condition of the region on the other side being bounded. This is plainly a symmetric relationship, and so doesn't yet yield a regressive synthesis—"*regressus* and *progressus* in space appear to be one and the same" (A413/B440).

Nonetheless, because a part of space is not given through another part but is only bounded by it, we must to that extent regard every bounded space as also conditioned, presupposing another space as the condition of its boundary, and so forth. Thus regarding boundedness, the progression is also a regress, and the transcendental idea of the absolute totality of a synthesis in the series of conditions also applies to space, and I can also ask about the absolute totality of appearances in space as well as in past time. (A413/B440)

What Kant has in mind seems to be something along these lines: We can think of, for instance, a table as occupying a bounded region of space in a room; the room as occupying a bounded region of space in an apartment; the apartment in a building; the building in a neighborhood; the neighborhood in a city; and so on. Ultimately we arrive at the idea of something occupying a bounded region of *space*, period. This idea of space is "the transcendental idea of the absolute totality of a synthesis in the series of conditions", and when we "ask about the absolute totality of appearances in space", it is space thus conceived which is at issue, and which the principle of pure reason tells us is given as absolutely unconditioned.

What corresponds to the categories of Quality in appearances, we recall from the Anticipations of Perception, is the *intensive magnitude* of "the real, which is an object of sensation''. In the sense in which any region of space is conditioned with respect to its boundedness, Kant argues, so too is "reality in space, i.e., *matter*". Here, however, the regressive synthesis proceeds in the other direction. The "inner conditions" of a quantum of matter "are its parts, and the parts of those parts are the remote conditions, so that there occurs here a regressive synthesis whose absolute totality reason demands" (A413/B440). In other words, if a quantum of matter is given, then, in accordance with the principle of pure reason, the entire regressive series of its parts, the parts of those parts, etc., is necessarily thereby also thought as given, and so something correspondingly absolutely unconditioned, the result of such a completed division, "in which the reality of matter [as something divisible] disappears either into nothing or else into that which is no longer matter, namely the simple" (A413/B440).

Among the categories of Relation, the only one which gives rise to a series is *Causality*. Effects are conditioned consequences; their causes are their conditions. The requisite regressive synthesis of a given effect is thus the series of its causes, their causes, the causes of those causes, and so on. Finally, under the categories of Modality, only the concept of something *contingent* leads to a suitable regressive synthesis. A contingent existence is conditioned by that upon which it is contingent, and so, in accordance with the principle of pure reason, refers to "a condition...which it is necessary to refer...to a higher condition, until reason attains to unconditioned *necessity* only in the series in its totality" (A415/B442). In this way, Kant arrives at his enumeration of world-concepts. (See Fig. 13.1.)

1. The *absolute completeness* of the *composition* of a given whole of all appearances.

2. The *absolute completeness* of the *division* of a given whole in appearance.

3. The *absolute completeness* of the *arising* of an appearance in general.

4. The absolute completeness of the *dependence* of the *existence* of the alterable in appearance.

FIG. 13.1.   Table of Cosmological Ideas (A415/B443)

The necessary conflicts of cosmological ideas

It is hardly obvious what Kant has in mind under these four headings. In fact, since each cosmological idea is supposed to give rise to an antinomy, it turns out that in each case he has *two* things in mind. There are, he tells us, two ways of relating the notion of an *absolutely complete regressive synthesis of conditions* to the notion of something *absolutely unconditioned*.

[One] can think of this unconditioned either as subsisting merely in the whole series, in which thus every member without exception is conditioned, and only their whole is absolutely unconditioned, or else the absolutely unconditioned is only a part of the series, to which the remaining members of the series are subordinated but that itself stands under no other condition. (A417/B445)

Thinking of the absolutely unconditioned given by a series of conditions in the first way—let's call it "from the outside"—is incompatible with thinking of it in the second way—let's call it "from the inside". This is why the cosmological ideas give rise to antinomies.

If every member of a regressive series of conditions is itself conditioned, the whole series must itself be "given without bounds (without a beginning), i.e., it is given as infinite and at the same time whole" (A417/B445). The absolutely unconditioned, in this first, "outside", way of thinking, is an unconditioned *series*, thought of as a completed infinite whole, even though the *regress* which generates that series is only *potentially* infinite, i.e., one can always take another step and thereby ascend to a further condition. On the second, "inside", way of thinking, in contrast, the absolutely unconditioned is an unconditioned *condition*, i.e., a "first member" which is ultimately a condition of all the other members of the series, e.g., a first time ("the beginning of the world"), an indivisible first part of a bounded composite whole ("the simple"), or an uncaused cause ("absolute self-activity") (A418/B446).

As we saw in connection with the Paralogisms, Kant holds that reason naturally and inevitably seeks the absolutely unconditioned, and the principle of pure reason asserts that what reason seeks is always "given", and so can indeed be found. In the case of the cosmological ideas, however, reason finds two different candidates for the absolutely unconditioned, which give rise to distinct doctrines—a "Thesis" and an "Antithesis"—which, Kant proceeds to argue, are necessarily incompatible. Since each cosmological idea is generated by considering a regressive "synthesis according to rules", it must be "congruent with the understanding"; but, at the same time, as the idea of "the absolute unity of this synthesis", it

273

must also be "congruent with reason". The conditions of such an absolute unity, concludes Kant, will consequently be either "too small for reason" or "too large for the understanding" (A422/B450).

In other words, insofar as we restrict our attention to the *potentially* infinite regressive series of conditions that is the point of departure for reason's ascent to a world-concept, our thinking remains "congruent with the understanding". The understanding has no quarrel with such potential infinities. But the resultant idea is then "too small for reason", which proposes to think of such series as a *completed* whole. On the other hand, when we focus on the idea of something absolutely unconditioned, whether it be that of a completed infinite series of conditions or that of an absolutely unconditioned member of such a series, our thinking becomes "congruent with reason". Such an idea, that is, satisfies the demands of pure reason. But the idea then becomes "too large for the understanding". "From this", concludes Kant, "there must arise a contradiction that cannot be avoided no matter how one may try" (A422/B450).

Each of the world-concepts thus gives rise to a "conflict of transcendental ideas", a pair of incompatible doctrines corresponding to the "inside" and "outside" ways of thinking about the absolutely unconditioned, ostensibly guaranteed by the principle of pure reason. In each case, the proposition asserting what PPR implies from the "inside" perspective serves as the Thesis; the proposition asserting what PPR implies from the "outside" perspective is the corresponding Antithesis, as shown in the enumeration.

Kant supplies a "Proof" for each Thesis and each Antithesis, and each proof is followed by a supplementary "Remark". One can spend a great deal of time on these. Indeed, whole books have been written about various of the Antinomies, especially the Third, which the astute reader has doubtless recognized as a form of the perennial problem of free will *vs* determinism. In what follows, however, I shall limit myself to a brief discussion of the First Antinomy as an illustrative example. This will enable me to trace one relatively clear interpretive path through this part of the Dialectic which can then serve as a model for reading and, I hope, understanding Kant's treatment of the other three Antinomies as well.

The arguments of the First Antinomy

Kant offers four compact arguments as "Proofs" in the First Antinomy, two for the two parts of the Thesis, time and space, and two for the

Thesis	Antithesis
1. The world has a beginning in time, and in space it is also enclosed in boundaries (A426/B454).	1. The world has no beginning and no bounds in space, but is infinite with regard to both space and time (A427/B455).
2. Every composite substance in the world consists of simple parts, and nothing exists anywhere except the simple or what is composed of simples (A434/B462).	2. No composite thing in the world consists of simple parts, and nowhere in it does there exist anything simple (A435/B463).
3. Causality in accordance with laws of nature is not the only one from which all the appearances of the world can be derived. It is also necessary to assume another causality through freedom in order to explain them (A444/B472).	3. There is no freedom, but everything in the world happens solely in accordance with laws of nature (A445/B473).
4. To the world there belongs something that, either as a part of it or as its cause, is an absolutely necessary being (A452/B480).	4. There is no absolutely necessary being existing anywhere, either in the world or outside the world as its cause (A453/B481).

corresponding parts of the Antithesis. Each of the arguments has the form of a *reductio ad absurdum*. Kant, in fact, never undertakes to argue *directly* for any Thesis or Antithesis.

On the face of it, at least at first encounter, none of the arguments offered is very convincing. At this point, many commentators emphasize that Kant's work predates Cantor's pioneering studies in transfinite arithmetic and Riemann's investigations of non-Euclidean geometries. Consequently, he could hardly be expected to have a fully coherent conception of infinite series, sequences, and magnitudes, or to be aware of the distinction between a *closed* space and a *bounded* space, hence of the possibility of a space which is closed (and so finite) but unbounded. While this is of course correct, we also need to remember that, as we noted in our discussion of the Transcendental Aesthetic, the space and time of theoretical physics are arguably not the indexical and perspectival space and time of our experience. It is the latter, however, that are at issue in the First Antinomy.

Consider, for example, the Big Bang theory of the origin of the physical universe. Any serious attempt to work out the conceptual consequences of the Big Bang theory, I think, inevitably generates a certain uneasiness. It is not difficult to *repeat* crude lay versions of what sophisticated physicists tell us—e.g., that the Big Bang was the beginning of both space and time, and that the physical universe has thereafter been continuously expanding—but it is rather more difficult to *understand* what that is supposed to mean, much less to *believe* it. What it presumably does mean—and what it is not so difficult to believe—is something like this: Given particular assumptions, when the values of the s and t parameters in certain equations descriptive of the dynamic evolution of the physical universe are considered retrospectively, they converge asymptotically to 0. But it is hard to shake the feeling that what s and t represent in such equations then *cannot* be *our* space and time, i.e., the order of before and after and here and there in our experience. For it certainly *seems* to make sense to ask, in terms of *that* perspectival space and anisotropic time what was going on *before* the Big Bang, and why it "banged" just *then* and *there* and not earlier or later or somewhere else, and what was going on *here* when it was "banging" *there*, and, come to think of it, what has the physical universe been expanding *into*?

Kant's *reductio* arguments for the Antithesis trade on such intuitions. "Many series of things may begin in the world," he concedes, "but the world itself cannot have any beginning" (A427/B455). If it could, it would need to begin at some definite past time, that is, at one time rather than another. Since we are thinking of the regressive series of past times as a series of *conditions*, i.e., as generated by explanatory considerations, we would then need some explanation of why the world began at that time rather than at any other. But any time prior to the arising of the world would necessarily be *empty* (an analytic claim), and "no part of such a time has, in itself, prior to another part, any distinguishing condition of its existence rather than its nonexistence" (A427/B455).

Similarly, if the world were finite and bounded, then, since a boundary is *where something differs*, there would need to be something to *contrast* with the world at the boundary. But "besides [the world] there is encountered no object of intuition, and hence no correlate of the world to which the world could stand in relation" (A429/B457). It follows that the world cannot be bounded, and hence, Kant concludes, that it cannot be finite either.[2]

"The proofs for the infinity of the world-series and of the sum total of the world", he observes in his subsequent Remarks, "turn on the fact that in the contrary case an empty time, and likewise an empty space, would have to constitute the boundary of the world" (A431/B459). That, in essence, would be to think of space and time as Newtonian "containers", *absolute* space and time, and, as we have seen, like Leibniz, Kant rejects that conception out of hand. Space and time are *forms* of outer and inner sense, "not a correlate of appearances, but rather the form of appearances themselves".

Thus things, as appearances, do determine space, i.e., among all its possible predicates (magnitude and relation) they make it the case that this or that one belongs to reality; but space, as something subsisting in itself cannot conversely determine the reality of things in regard to magnitude and shape, because it is nothing real in itself. (A431/B459)

A space, therefore (whether it is full or empty), may well be bounded by appearances, but appearances cannot be bounded by *an empty space* outside of themselves. The same holds also for time. (A433/B461)

It is important to remember, he reminds us, that we are talking here about the phenomenal world (*mundus phaenomenon*). We consequently cannot abstract from the indispensability of sensory contents for thinking of boundaries in space or time. "The world of sense, if it is bounded, necessarily lies in an infinite emptiness. If one wants to leave this out..., then the whole world of sense is left out" (A433/B461).

So much for the Antithesis. The *reductio* arguments for the Thesis, on the other hand, are less intuitive. Each of them turns on the notion of a *completed successive synthesis*. As we noted in our discussion of the Axioms of Intuition, the paradigms of such a synthesis are *tasks* carried out by operations or procedures that we can think of as "the repeated additions of [homogeneous] units to each other"—e.g., counting from 1 to 7, timing a track and field event with a stopwatch, or measuring the length of a football field with a yardstick. Kant's line of thought here is somewhat clearer with respect to space than to time.

---

[2] This last step, we now know, is problematic, since we can consistently characterize mathematically higher-dimensional "spaces" which, like the two-dimensional surface of a sphere, are closed and finite but unbounded. But when we remember that Kant is talking about the oriented and perspectival space of our *experience* and consider such notions as the universe's *expanding*, his considerations, I think, nevertheless remain intuitively compelling.

Suppose, for *reductio*, that the world is infinite as regards space. It would then be, he writes, "an infinite given whole of simultaneously existing things" (A426/B454). Now, unlike a given *finite* spatial whole, the world thus considered couldn't be given in a single intuition. Even in principle, we cannot be presented with an infinite spatial totality in a single perceptual Gestalt. In order to think an infinite space-filling world *as a whole*, then, we would have to do what we do when we engage in a successive synthesis (e.g., "drawing a line in thought"), that is, "add units to units", but in this case for an infinite number of "units". Such an infinite successive synthesis of homogeneous units, however, plainly couldn't be completed in a finite length of time.

In the enumeration of all coexisting things, an infinite time would have to be regarded as having elapsed, which is impossible. Accordingly, an infinite aggregate of actual things [viz., the contents of space] cannot be regarded as a given whole, hence cannot be regarded as given *simultaneously*. (A428/B456)

Kant's basic claim with respect to time is identical: "The infinity of a series consists precisely in the fact that it can never be completed through a successive synthesis" (A426/B454). Although we don't find here any explicit mention of the totality of elapsed time being "given" or of an enumeration of "units", Kant's fundamental line of thought is surely the same. To think an elapsed "eternity" consisting of "an infinite series of states of things in the world" *as a whole*, we would need to "complete" it "through a successive synthesis", i.e., run through all the members of the series. But, even in principle, this is again impossible. It follows that neither space nor time can be infinite, and that is just what the Thesis asserts.

In general, whenever Kant invokes the idea of a completed infinite totality, he is thinking of it as the product of a completed infinite *task* of successive synthesis. As he puts it in his Remarks on the Thesis,

The true (transcendental) concept of infinity is that the successive synthesis of unity in the traversal of a quantum can never be completed. (A430/B458)

And he adds a footnote to the effect that the quantum "thereby contains a multiplicity (of given units) that is greater than any number, and that is the mathematical concept of the infinite" (A432/B460). He contrasts this with what he calls "a defective concept of infinity" according to which "a magnitude is *infinite* if none greater than it (i.e., greater than the multiple of a given unit contained in it) is possible" (A430/B458). This is roughly the idea of *the largest possible number of units*, and since, as Kant recognizes, there is no such largest possible number, "because one or more units can always be added to it", this concept is indeed "defective", that is, ill-defined. In fact, Kant seems well on the way to the Cantorian conception of an infinite set or series as one which can be put in one-to-one correspondence with a proper subset or subseries of itself. For he envisions constructing infinite wholes out of greater or smaller units— think of counting by ones, twos, threes, etc.—and suggests that, nevertheless, "infinity, since it consists merely in the relation to this given unit, would always remain the same" (A432/B460).

Reason's interests and reason's attitudes

Let us now leap ahead to the point where Kant has completed offering his proofs for and remarking on the Thesis and Antithesis of each of the four Antinomies.

Now we have before us the entire dialectical play of the cosmological ideas, which do not permit an object congruent to them to be given in any possible experience, which, indeed, do not even permit reason to think them in agreement with the universal laws of experience, but which have not been thought up arbitrarily; reason, rather, in continuous progression of the empirical synthesis, has been led to them necessarily when it tries to liberate from every condition and to grasp in its unconditioned totality, that which can always be determined only conditionally in accordance with rules of experience. (A462/B490)

What we would naturally expect at this point is that Kant would begin to tell us how to *deal with* these Antinomies. Instead, however, he pauses to reflect on the intellectual situation in which we now find ourselves. If philosophy could *answer* the questions at issue in the Antinomies, he observes, it would outshine all the other human sciences, "since it would promise to ground our greatest expectations and prospects concerning the ultimate ends in which all reason's efforts must finally unite" (A463/B491). Unfortunately, he concludes, reason sees itself instead "entangled in a crowd of arguments and counterarguments" (A464/B492) which preclude both indifference and neutrality. No option remains, he concludes, except for reason to adopt a diagnostic and therapeutic attitude, i.e., "to reflect on the origin of this disunity of reason with itself, on whether a mere misunderstanding might perhaps be responsible for it" (A464/B492).

Such remarks certainly *seem* to move the resolution of the Antinomies to the top of Kant's agenda, but he has other priorities. Before proceeding to that task, he proposes to consider which side of each Antinomy we would *prefer* to accept if we were compelled to take sides. Issues of truth aside, which doctrine, the Thesis or the Antithesis, would better serve our *interests*? The question is surely a curious one, and all the more so because Kant promptly recasts it in terms of a contrast between *dogmatism* and *empiricism*. Whereas the assertions of the Antitheses express "a principle of pure *empiricism*", he writes, the distinguishing mark of the assertions of Theses is that they posit "intellectualistic starting points"; they can therefore be called "the *dogmatism* of pure reason" (A466/B494).

Kant proceeds to observe that the Theses (a) answer to our *practical* interest, since what they assert "are so many cornerstones of morality and religion"; (b) answer to the *speculative* interests of reason, for they purport to enable us to "grasp the whole chain of conditions fully *a priori* and comprehend the derivation of the conditioned, starting with the unconditioned"; and (c) have the advantage of *popularity*, since "the common understanding does not find the least difficulty in the idea of an unconditioned beginning for every synthesis" (A466–7/B494–5). The Antitheses, in contrast, (a) seem to deprive morality and religion of all theoretical support, and so of all validity, although they do (b) offer the speculative interests of reason the attractive prospect of indefinitely extensible "secure and comprehensive cognitions" in which understanding remains "on its own proper ground, namely the field solely of possible experiences" (A468/B496). Nevertheless, the empiricism of the Antitheses is (c) "completely contrary to everything popular" since, "for the common understanding every speculative interest vanishes before practical interest, and it imagines itself to have insight and knowledge into whatever its apprehensions or hopes impel it to assume or believe" (A473–4/B501–2). Finally, since the dogmatism of the Theses does, while the empiricism of the Antitheses does not, offer "a first or starting point that would serve absolutely as the foundation for its building a completed edifice of cognition" (A474/B502), the former better serves (d) the *architectonic* interest of human reason. If interests and not truth are what matter, then, "comfort and vanity" would seem on balance to recommend the dogmatism of the Theses, and if what matters is indeed truth, then, confronted with the Antinomies, reason would perhaps be well counseled to "keep quiet and concede that it is ignorant" (A473/B501). But a healthy philosophy might demand something more.

When what is at issue is whether a given action is morally right or wrong, just or unjust, Kant points out, we are not allowed to plead unavoidable ignorance. We are seeking to determine our moral *duty*, and "we cannot have any obligation to do what *we cannot know*" (A476/B504). In contrast, in the natural sciences, we normally feel comfortable conceding that many questions remain, at least at present, *de facto* unanswerable for us. It thus makes sense to ask whether transcendental philosophy is in this respect more like morality or natural science, that is, whether we are allowed to respond to the questions posed by the Antinomies by holding that we are "so entirely lacking in means or faculties that we can never give the answer" (A477/B505). Perhaps surprisingly, Kant's answer is that it is more like morality:

[Among] all speculative cognition, transcendental philosophy has the special property that there is no question at all dealing with an object given by pure reason that is insoluble by this very same human reason; and that no plea of unavoidable ignorance and the unfathomable depth of the problem can release us from the obligation of answering it thoroughly and completely; for the very same concept that puts us in a position to ask the question must also make us competent to answer it, since the object is not encountered at all outside the concept .... (A477/B505)

This conclusion applies to the questions raised by "rational cosmology", the Antinomies, argues Kant, but not to those raised by "rational psychology", the Paralogisms. The crucial difference is that the object of an ostensible rational psychology, the "I" who thinks, is "transcendental and thus in itself unknown", i.e., not intuited, while the object of an ostensible rational cosmology, the world, is "given empirically" (A478/B506).

The cosmological ideas alone have the peculiarity that they can presuppose their object, and the empirical synthesis required for its concepts, as given, and the question that arises from them has to do only with the progression of this synthesis, insofar as it is to contain an absolute totality.... (A479/B507)

Such an absolute totality, of course, is *not* empirical, that is, not given in any experience. The questions about *the world* raised by the Antinomies consequently do not have to do with any *object* of experience.

[In] regard to possible experience, the question asks not about what can be given *in concreto* in experience, but rather about what lies in the idea which the empirical synthesis is merely supposed to approximate: therefore, this question must be able to be resolved from the idea alone; for this idea is merely a creature of reason, which therefore cannot refuse the responsibility and pass it on to the unknown object. (A479/B507)

Thus we cannot evade the obligation of giving at least a critical resolution of the questions of reason before us by lamenting the narrow limits of our reason and confessing, with the appearance of a modest self-knowledge, that it lies beyond our reason to settle [them]. (A481/B509)

The *object* with whose nature those questions are ostensibly concerned, the *"world-whole"*, can never be given in any experience, because "with all possible perceptions, you always remain caught up among *conditions*, ... and you never get to the unconditioned" (A483/B511). Experience can consequently never deliver a solution to the problems posed by the Antinomies, and so

you cannot say that it is uncertain what is to be ascribed to the object regarding them. For your object is merely in your brain and cannot be given at all outside it; hence all you have to worry about is agreeing with yourself.... (A484/B512)

It follows that a *dogmatic* solution to those problems, i.e., a definitive verdict in favor of the Thesis or the Antithesis, is impossible. What Kant will provide, therefore, will be a *critical* solution, which "does not consider the question objectively at all, but instead asks about the foundations of the cognition in which it is grounded" (A484/B512), that is, about the epistemic credentials and status of the "world-concepts" or cosmological ideas to which the Antinomies appeal.

Unraveling the Antinomies

Kant's "critical solution" begins with what he calls a "skeptical presentation" of the questions raised by each of the four cosmological ideas. We might be able finally to stop being plagued by such cosmological questions, he suggests, if we were convinced from the beginning that *neither* dogmatic answer could ever satisfy our epistemic desires. A "skeptical presentation" of the questions is a tool for exploring this possibility. Ignoring the *arguments* for the Thesis and Antithesis, it focuses directly on the corresponding *doctrines* and asks "what one would gain if the answer turned out on one side or on the opposite side" (A485/B513). If, as Kant expects, it should fortuitously turn out that, in *either* case, the result was "something quite empty of sense (nonsense)", then we would have a good reason to stop *asking* those questions and take a hard *critical look* at them instead. In this way, "one can with little expense exempt oneself from a great deal of dogmatic rubbish" (A485/B513).

282

It is important to interpret the question of "what one would gain" epistemologically. What Kant proposes to show is that one thing that demonstrably could *not* be gained is a satisfactory *understanding* of the world-whole, e.g., as either bounded or unbounded in space and time. To this end, he returns to his earlier observation (A422/B450), that a cosmological idea which is "congruent with reason", i.e., which satisfies the demand of pure reason for something absolutely unconditioned, cannot also be "congruent with the understanding". In particular, he now proceeds to argue, "whatever side of the unconditioned in the regressive synthesis of appearances it might come down on, it would *be* either *too big* or *too small* for every *concept of the understanding*" (A486/B514).

In the case of the First Antinomy, for example, the assumption that the world has no beginning in time (the Antithesis) is *too big* for our concept of the understanding, for that concept "consists in a successive regress [which] can never reach the whole eternity that has elapsed" (A486/B514). Similarly, the assumption that the world is infinite and unbounded in space is "*too big* for every possible empirical concept". On the other hand, the assumption that the world does have a beginning in time (the Thesis) is *too small* for our concept of the understanding,

[for] since the beginning always presupposes a preceding time, it is still not unconditioned, and the law of the empirical use of the understanding obliges you to ask for a still higher temporal condition, and the world is obviously too small for this law. (A487/B515)

Analogously, a finite, bounded world is "*too small* for your concept".

What gives these observations their bite, Kant argues, is that "for the absolute totality of the empirical synthesis it is always demanded that the unconditioned be an empirical concept" (A487/B515). Since, however, a "*world-idea* is either too big for the empirical regress, hence for every possible concept of the understanding, or else too small for it" (A489/B517), it precisely cannot be an *empirical* concept. But

it is possible experience alone that can give our concepts reality; without it every concept is only an idea, without truth and reference to an object. Hence the possible empirical concept [is] the standard by which it [has] to be judged whether the idea is a mere idea and a thought-entity or instead encounters its object within the world. (A489/B517)

We are consequently entitled to a "well-grounded suspicion that the cosmological ideas... are perhaps grounded on an empty and merely imagined concept of the way the object of these ideas is given to us"

(A490/B518). And, when we properly appreciate the implications of the *transcendental idealism* establishing in the earlier sections of the First Critique, Kant proceeds to argue, that suspicion is indeed borne out.

The leading idea of transcendental idealism, he reminds us, is that "the objects of experience are *never* given *in themselves*, but only in experience" (A402/B521). As we have already seen, this does not imply that every possible object of experience must be directly perceivable.

> That there could be inhabitants of the moon, even though no human being has ever perceived them, must of course be admitted; but this means only that in the possible progress of experience we could encounter them; for everything is actual that stands in one context with a perception in accordance with the laws of the empirical progression. Thus they are [actual] when they stand in an empirical connection with my [actual] consciousness, although they are not therefore real in themselves, i.e., outside this progress of experience. (A493/B521)[3]

This, of course, is just the Second Postulate (A218/B266), and 'actual', we recall, is Kant's *empirical* truth-predicate. The relationship that Kant here calls "standing in one context with a perception" and "standing in empirical connection with my real consciousness" we there met under the rubrics "being connected with some perceptions in accordance with the principles of their empirical connection (the Analogies)" and "being connected with our perceptions in a possible experience" (A225–6/B273). And we noted that the relationship in question is one of *explanatory* coherence that, as Kant understands it, is liberal enough to enable us to "cognize the existence of a magnetic matter" which cannot directly affect our "crude" senses.

Precisely because our faculty of sensible intuition is "only a receptivity for being affected in a certain way", Kant is willing to speak of a "non-sensible cause" of our representations, but stresses that it is "entirely unknown to us, and therefore we cannot intuit it as an object" (A494/B522).[4] In an *extended* (analogical) sense of 'object', however,

---

[3] I have again modified the Guyer–Wood translation. The two bracketed occurrences of 'actual' replace occurrences of 'real'. The first (unbracketed) occurrence of 'actual' and the occurrence of 'real' in "real in themselves", in contrast, correspond to Guyer–Wood's own translations. In all four instances, the German text has *wirklich*. The use of 'actual' to translate the first three occurrences of *wirklich* strikes me as preferable, since what is at issue there is precisely what is *empirically* real, which is then explicitly contrasted with things "real *in themselves*", i.e., with what is *transcendentally* real.

[4] Strictly speaking, Kant's use of 'cause' here can't be right. We're dealing here with (mere) thoughts, not cognitions, and the pure concepts of the understanding are consequently out of play. Fortunately, all that Kant needs here is something to which he *is* entitled, not the *categorial* relationship of cause and effect, but the *conditional* relationship of ground and consequence, which *inter alia* admits of a purely formal or logical use.

we can call the merely intelligible cause of appearances in general the transcendental object, merely so that we may have something corresponding to sensibility as a receptivity. To this transcendental object we can ascribe the whole extent and connection of our possible perceptions, and say that it is given in itself prior to all experience. But appearances are, in accordance with it, given not in themselves but only in this experience, because they are mere representations, which signify a real object only as perceptions, namely when this perception connects up with all others in accordance with the rules of the unity of experience. (A494/B522–3)

Our epistemological relationship to "the real things of past time" is consequently the same as our epistemological relationship to "magnetic matter". Although they are "given in the transcendental object of experience", they are objects and real in past time for me "only insofar as I represent to myself that, in accordance with empirical laws . . . a regressive series of possible perceptions . . . leads to a time-series that has elapsed as the condition of present time" (A495/B523). The actuality of the past, in other words, consists in its *explanatory* coherence with present and possible future experience, and our epistemic access to it is correspondingly inferential and indirect. We should not, however, over-intellectualize the matter. Such access need not appeal to anything as sophisticated as, e.g., the fossil record or carbon dating or the red shift exhibited by the light of distant galaxies. It can also be as straightforward as noting that an event's having occurred is usually the best explanation of one's ostensible memory of it.

The moral of these epistemological reminders is that our representation of "all existing objects of sense in all time and all spaces"—the "world-whole"—is fundamentally *procedural*. It is "nothing other than the thought of a possible experience in its absolute completeness" (A495/B524), i.e., the thought of objects in space and time to be encountered "in the part of experience *to which* I, starting with the [present] perception, must first of all [inferentially] progress" (A496/B524).[5]

These last observations finally put Kant in a position to consummate his "critical solution" to the Antinomies. Underlying and fundamental to all of them is a *hypothetical syllogism* having the principle of pure reason as its major premise (A497/B525):

---

[5] "To call an appearance a real thing prior to perception means either that in the continuation of experience we must encounter such a perception, or it has no meaning at all" (A493/B521). It's not an accident that this stretch of text sounds very Peircean. Kant's work here is precisely what inspired the leading ideas of C. S. Peirce's pragmatism.

> (A1) If the conditioned is given, then the whole series of all conditions for it is also given.
> (A2) Objects of the senses are given as conditioned.
> (A3) Consequently, the whole series of all conditions for them is also given.

In light of his treatment of the Paralogisms, we should not be too surprised to hear that Kant also finds this syllogism fallacious *per sophisma figurae dictionis*, i.e., by reason of equivocation.

[The] major premise of the cosmological syllogism takes the conditioned in the transcendental signification of a pure category; while the minor premise takes it in the empirical signification of a concept of the understanding applied to mere appearances. (A499/B527)

As in the case of the Paralogisms, however, it is again not immediately clear just what equivocation Kant has in mind. While the passage just cited suggests that the equivocation attaches to 'conditioned', it is probably more useful to take a careful look at Kant's various notions of *being given*.

One of them, for instance, Kant calls "being given *as a task*".

If the conditioned is given, then through it a regress in the series of all conditions for it is *given* to us *as a task*;[6] for the concept of the conditioned already entails that something is related to a condition, and if this condition is once again conditioned, to a more remote condition, and so through all members of the series. (A498/B526)

Here Kant is simply reminding us of the "logical maxim" governing the *formal* use of pure reason that we met earlier: "to find the unconditioned for conditioned cognitions of the understanding, with which its unity will be completed" (A307/B364). As we have seen, Kant holds that the task of

---

[6] I here again depart slightly from the Guyer–Wood translation, "*given* to us *as a problem*", in the direction of Kemp-Smith's "*set* us *as a task*". Pluhar, in contrast, has "*assigned* to us". None of these translations of the German *aufgegeben* is indefensible, but none is ideal. Something that is *aufgegeben* is an *Aufgabe*, and an *Aufgabe*, although it may indeed take the form of a problem (something to be solved), is generically any job or task (something to be done). In school, e.g., an *Aufgabe* is an exercise or *assignment* (e.g., a homework or written or reading assignment), which explains Pluhar's proposal. And "*given* to us *as a task*" is preferable to "*set* us *as a task*", since it preserves the relationship between *aufgegeben* and *gegeben* ("given") which plainly figures in Kant's own thought, e.g.: "Wenn das Bedingte so wohl, als seine Bedingung, Dinge an sich selbst sind, so ist, wenn das erstere gegeben worden, nicht bloß der Regressus zu dem zweiten *aufgegeben*, sondern dieses ist dadurch wirklich schon mit *gegeben*" ("If the conditioned as well as its condition are things in themselves, then when the first is given not only is the regress to the second *given as a task*, but the latter is thereby really already *given* along with it") (A498/B526).

286

reason as such is to expand our understanding by "ascending" through a serious of explanatory "prosyllogisms". Since empirical actuality just *is* "standing in empirical connection with my real consciousness" (A493/B521), the conditional proposition here, he concludes, is *analytic*, "and beyond any fear of a transcendental criticism" (A498/B526).

A different notion of *being given*, however, clearly comes into play in Kant's claim that

> if the conditioned as well as its condition are things in themselves, then when the first is given not only is the regress to the second *given as a task*, but the latter is thereby really already *given* along with it; and, because this holds for all members of the series, then the complete series of conditions, and hence the unconditioned is thereby simultaneously given . . . . (A498/B526)

This passage should strike the astute reader as peculiar, since Kant has only recently reminded us of his conclusion that things in themselves are *not* "given", i.e., that things are not given as they are in themselves; "the objects of experience are *never* given *in themselves*, but only in experience" (A402/B521). Even more recently, however, he has also introduced another extended, analogical sense of *being given* to go along with the extended, analogical notion of a transcendental object—"To this transcendental object we can ascribe the whole extent and connection of our possible perceptions, and say that it is *given in itself* prior to all experience" (A494/B522–3; my emphasis)—and that is the notion being invoked in this passage.

> Here the synthesis of the conditioned with its conditions is a synthesis of the mere understanding, which represents things *as they are* without paying attention to whether and how we might achieve acquaintance with them. (A498/B526)

We might say that what is "given" in this sense is not given *to us*, i.e., not given in experience, but, in the first instance, given only *to our receptive sensibility*, insofar as it functions as a ground of our experience, i.e., as a "condition", that is entirely unknown *to us*. This usage thus also introduces an ambiguity in the notion of a *condition* parallel to that arising from the extended and analogical senses of 'object' and 'given'. One might perhaps expect Kant to call this a "transcendental condition" (a condition in the transcendental sense), but he doesn't. It will somewhat simplify our exposition, however, if we do so.

The point of introducing a sense—admittedly transcendental and problematic—in which things are "given" as they are in themselves is to contrast it with the way in which things are given in experience. As Kant has argued at considerable length, objects are only in a nominal sense "given" in perceptual experience. From the perspective of transcendental philosophy, "the *appearances*, in their apprehension, are themselves nothing other than an empirical synthesis (in space and time) and thus are given only *in this synthesis*" (A499/B527). In *this* sense of 'being given', however,

it does not follow at all that if the conditioned (in appearance) is given, then the synthesis constituting its empirical condition is thereby also given and presupposed; on the contrary, this synthesis takes place for the first time in the regress, and never without it. (A499/B527)

When it comes to the *empirical* conditions of what is given *in appearance*, in other words, the entire series of conditions is never given as a completed totality but only as an open-ended task.

[In] such a case one can very well say that a *regress* to the conditions, i.e., a continued empirical synthesis on this side is demanded or *given as a task*, and that there could not fail to be conditions given through this regress. (A499/B527)

The *multiple* ambiguities in the hypothetical syllogism which serves as the key dialectical argument of the Antinomies should now be clear. When the major premise, (A1), is read as an instance of the principle of pure reason, the conditioned is being thought of as *given in itself*, and what is thereby "given" as a completed totality is the series of *transcendental* conditions. In the minor premise, (A2), however, the conditioned is an appearance and is consequently given *in experience*. The conclusion, (A3), thus refers only to a series of *empirical* conditions, and these, as we have just seen, are "given" only *as a task*. Here's how Kant puts it:

The synthesis of the conditioned with its condition and the whole series of the latter (in the major premise) carries with it no limitation through time and no concept of succession. The empirical synthesis, on the contrary, and the series of conditions in appearance (which are subsumed in the minor premise), is necessarily given successively and is given only in time, one member after another; consequently here I could not presuppose the absolute *totality* of synthesis and the series represented by it .... (A500/B528)

And this gives Kant what he needs in order to consummate the "critical solution" to the Antinomies that has been suggested by their "skeptical presentation", namely, that they rest on a transcendental illusion and are really "quite empty of sense".

Long ago, when we were examining the Table of Forms of Judgment (A76/B95), I claimed that Kant's distinction between negative judgments, e.g., "The soul is not mortal", corresponding to the category of Negation, and "infinite" judgments, e.g., "The soul is immortal", corresponding to the category of "Limitation" carries significant critical implications. In Chapter 11, we found one expository application of the distinction in the contrast between negative and positive notions of noumena. We are now in a position to put the distinction to a more important critical use. Recall that negative judgments are *exclusionary*, and "infinite" judgments are *predicational*. A negative judgment, that is, simply excludes its subject from the class of items to which the predicate term truly applies, while an "infinite" judgment, in contrast, itself predicates a determinate property of its subject. The key observation now is that only an *exclusionary* judgment can *contradict* a predicational one. Two predicational "infinite" judgments cannot be contradictories. But two such judgments are just what each Antinomy delivers.

Accordingly, if I say that, as regards space either the world is infinite or it is not infinite (*non est infinitus*), then if that first proposition is false, its contradictory opposite, "the world is not infinite," must be true. Through it I would rule out only an infinite world, without positing another one, namely a finite one. But if it is said that the world is either infinite or finite (not-infinite), then both propositions could be false. For then I regard the world as determined in itself regarding its magnitude, since in the opposition I not only rule out its infinitude...but I also add a determination of the world, as a thing active in itself, which might likewise be false.... (A503–4/B531–2)

The contradictory predicational and exclusionary judgments, Kant writes, are in "analytical opposition", but the two predicational judgments, i.e., the Thesis and the Antithesis, are merely in "dialectical opposition". They are, that is, merely *contraries* which "could both be false, because one does not merely contradict the other, but says something more than is required for a contradiction" (A504/B532).

The "something more" that is implicit in both the Thesis and the Antithesis is the idea that *the world*, i.e., "the whole series of appearances", is a thing in itself—for if the world were such a thing, then it would indeed necessarily be either a *finite* thing or an *infinite* thing.

But if I take away this presupposition, or rather this transcendental illusion, and deny that it is a thing in itself, then the contradictory conflict of the two assertions is transformed into a merely dialectical conflict, and because the world does not exist at all (independently of the regressive series of my representations), it exists neither as *an in itself infinite* whole nor as *an in itself finite* whole. (A504–5/B532–3)

289

In the case of the Paralogisms, it turned out that the 'I' of the apperceptive "I think" was not the representation of an object, the noumenal self, but signified only a form of representation, the formal unity of consciousness. The case of the Antinomies, we now see, manifests just the same sort of "transcendental illusion". The expression 'the world' as it occurs in the Antinomies is also not the representation of an object, the world *as it is in itself*, but merely represents the permanent possibility of an empirical regress, i.e., a continued open-ended "ascent" through explanatory pro-syllogisms from conditioned items *given in experience* to their conditions. Kant consequently finds in the Antinomies another dramatic confirmation of the leading thesis of transcendental idealism.

The proof would consist in this dilemma. If the world is a whole existing in itself, then it is either finite or infinite. Now the first as well as the second alternative is false (according to the proofs offered above for the antithesis on the one side and the thesis on the other). Thus it is also false that the world (the sum total of all appearances) is a whole existing in itself. From which it follows that appearances in general are nothing outside our representations, which is just what we mean by their transcendental ideality. (A506–7/B534–5)

We have also, Kant concludes, now arrived at a proper understanding of the principle of pure reason, PPR—"If the conditioned is given, then the whole sum of conditions, and hence the absolutely unconditioned, is also given" (A409/B436)—namely, that if the conditioned is given *in experience*, then the series of its conditions is given *as a task*.

Thus the principle of reason is only a *rule*, prescribing a regress in the series of conditions for given appearances, in which regress it is never allowed to stop with an absolutely unconditioned. (A509/B537)

The synthetic principles of pure understanding, i.e., the Axioms, Anticipations, and Analogies, characterize the most general (categorial) form of any possible object of experience, and so can be thought of as "constitutive". In contrast, the principle of pure reason, properly understood, "cannot say *what the object is*, but only *how the empirical regress is to be instituted* so as to attain to the complete concept of the object" (A510/B538).[7] It merely

---

[7] Of course, we never *do* "attain to the complete concept of the object". The explanatory "ascent" from conditioneds given in experience to their empirical conditions has no determinate stopping point. PPR is rather "a principle of the greatest possible continuation and extension of experience, in accordance with which no empirical boundary would hold as an absolute boundary" (A509/B537).

postulates what is to be done in the regress, i.e., how inquiry should proceed, and so, Kant concludes, is only a *regulative* principle of reason.

Kant's last preparatory task before returning to the individual Antinomies is to provide a philosophically enlightening characterization of the sort of series which arises through inquiry regulated by the principle of pure reason, that is, as he puts it, "to determine precisely the synthesis of a series insofar as it is never complete". To this end, he introduces two distinctions: the first, between a *regress* and a *progression*; and the second, between a "regress to infinity" (*in infinitum*) and a "regress extending indeterminately far" (*in indefinitum*). A progression proceeds from the condition to the conditioned. Kant's model is continuously extending a line—drawing all the shorter stages is a condition of drawing any longer one. Progressions in this sense are entirely open-ended, and reason has no totalizing impulse with respect to them, because the series "is not presupposed as a condition as given, but it is only added on as something conditioned, which is capable of being given, and this without end" (A512/B540). There is thus no sense to the question of how far such a progression extends. One can extend it *in indefinitum*, i.e., as far as one wishes, and *in infinitum*, i.e., without ever stopping.

A regress, in contrast, always proceeds from something conditioned to its conditions, and so one can always sensibly ask, so to speak, how far *back* it extends, i.e., "whether I can say . . . that there is a *regress to infinity* or only a regress extending *indeterminately far*" (A512/B540). In the former instance, I in effect know in advance that I can always "ascend" to a still higher condition; in the latter, only that "as far as I have gone back, there has never been an empirical ground for holding the series to be bounded anywhere" (A512/B540). The difference turns on just what is given in experience as conditioned.

If the whole was given in empirical intuition, then the regress in the series of its inner conditions goes to infinity. But if only one member of the series is given, from which the regress to an absolute totality is first of all to proceed, then only an indeterminate kind of regress (*in indefinitum*) takes place. (A512/B540)

The successive division of a material body into parts, parts of those parts, and so on illustrates a regress "to infinity". Not only "is there nowhere an empirical ground to stop the division, but the further members of the continuing division [i.e., the parts] are themselves empirically given prior to this ongoing division''. In contrast, the regress of empirical conditions for one's own existence that runs from one's parents through one's grandparents, one's great-grandparents, and so on is only a regress *in indefinitum*.

[Since] the members that might supply the conditions for it . . . do not already lie in the empirical intuition of the whole prior to the regress, . . . [it] goes to an indeterminate distance, search for more members for the given, which are once again always given only conditionally. (A513/B541)

But in neither of these cases, Kant cautions, ''is the series of conditions regarded as being given as infinite in the object. It is not things in themselves that are given, but only appearances, which, as conditions of one another, are given only in the regress itself'' (A514/B542).

The First Antinomy resolved

As we have seen, the principle of pure reason cannot be used to generate new synthetic *a priori* constitutive principles for appearances. Its empirical use is only regulative:

Thus the only thing left to us is the *validity of the principle of reason* as a rule for the *continuation* and magnitude of a possible experience . . . . (A516/B544)

The ground of this regulative use of the principle of pure reason in the case of all four cosmological questions, Kant tells us,

is the proposition that in the empirical regress there can be encountered *no experience of an absolute boundary*, and hence no experience of a condition as one that is *absolutely unconditioned empirically*. (A517/B545)

Only ''nothing'', or ''the void'', for example, could be an absolute boundary to the ''world-whole'' of all appearances, but ''nothing'', or ''the void'', is not an object of possible experiential encounter.

Thus, no matter how far we ''ascend'' through explanatory prosyllogisms in a regress of empirical conditions, we reach only conditions that we must regard as themselves empirically conditioned. Framed as a regulative principle, this conclusion amounts to the rule that ''however far I may have come in the ascending series, I must always inquire after a higher member of the series, whether or not this member may come to be known to me through experience'' (A518/B546). The only question that remains in connection with the First Antinomy is whether in the regress to the unconditioned magnitude of the world-whole (in time and in space), this never bounded ascent can be called a *regress to infinity*, or only an *indeterminately continued regress*. (A518/B546)

The key to a correct answer, Kant argues, is given by the fact that, since my representation of the "world-whole" is "nothing other than a possible empirical regress that I think, . . . I always have the world-whole only in concept, but by no means (as a whole) in intuition" (A519/B547). Any conception of "the magnitude of the world" will consequently have to be derived from a conception of the magnitude of the empirical regress, about which, however,

I never know anything more than that from any given member of the series of conditions I must always proceed empirically to a higher (more remote) member. . . . [Hence] one cannot say that this regress goes to infinity, because this would anticipate the members to which the regress has not yet attained, and would represent their multiplicity as so great that no empirical synthesis can attain to it . . . . (A519/B547)

Since the *rule* determining the empirical regress "says nothing more than that however far we may have come in the series of empirical conditions, we should never assume an absolute boundary", the series itself is an "indeterminately continued regress", or *regressus in indefinitum*, "which, because it determines no magnitude in the object, can be distinguished clearly enough from the regress *in infinitum*" (A520/B548).

It follows that we cannot correctly say that the world is *infinite* in past time or in space, for the world cannot be given as infinite *in experience*, as an infinite object of sense; nor, as we have just seen, does the empirical regress "from a given perception to everything bounding it in a series, in space and in past time", go *to infinity*. But we also cannot correctly say that the world is *finite* in past time or in space, for "an absolute boundary is likewise empirically impossible".

Thus to the cosmological question about the magnitude of the world, the first and negative answer is: The world has no first beginning in time and no outermost boundary in space. (A520/B548)

Now this looks quite a bit like the Antithesis of the First Antinomy,

The world has no beginning and no bounds in space, but is infinite with regard to both space and time. (A427/B455)

But the difference is absolutely crucial. The "negative answer" to the first cosmological question is purely *exclusionary*. The Antithesis, in contrast, treats this exclusionary conclusion as equivalent to the *predicational* claim that the world has a determinate, infinite, magnitude in both space and time, and that is precisely the step that we cannot validly take. (Cf. Kant's footnote to A521/B549.) There is indeed, Kant tells us, also an *affirmative* answer to the cosmological question about the magnitude of the world, namely,

The regress in the series of appearances in the world, as a determination of the magnitude of the world, goes on *in indefinitum*...(A521/B549)

But this answer is, so to speak, purely procedural. It concerns only the rule governing the empirical regress of conditions,

namely always to progress from each member of the series, as a conditioned, to a still more remote member (whether by means of one's own experience, or the guiding thread of history, or the chain of effects and their causes), and nowhere to exceed the extension of the possible empirical use of one's understanding, since this extension is the sole and proper business of reason in its principles. (A521–2/B549–50)

It follows that, although "appearances are *in the world* only conditionally, *the world* itself is neither conditioned nor bounded in an unconditional way" (A522/B550). The Thesis and the Antithesis are thus not contradictories, but only contraries; they can both be false. The only cash-value for the concept of "the magnitude of the world" in space or time is a rule determining an indeterminate regress *in indefinitum*, and such a rule cannot and does not validate either *predicational* claim, that of the Thesis or that of the Antithesis.

... and a quick glance at the other three

While Kant in fact holds that none of the four Thesis and Antithesis pairs presents a contradiction, it would be remiss to leave this chapter without at least briefly noting what he nevertheless takes to be a crucial difference between the first two, "mathematical" Antinomies and the last two, "dynamical" ones. Kant's resolution of the First Antinomy carries over straightforwardly to the Second. Its Thesis and its Antithesis, he concludes, are also not contradictory, but only contraries, and both can be false. In each case, he argues, this outcome is a consequence of the fact that we are dealing with a "synthesis of homogeneous things"—but this is not so in the case of the two "dynamical" Antinomies. In the first two

Antinomies, both what is conditioned and the series of its envisioned conditions "stay *within appearance*" (A529/B557).

[In] the mathematical connection of series of appearances, none other than a *sensible* condition can enter, i.e., only one that is itself a part of the series; whereas the dynamical series of sensible conditions, on the contrary, allows a further condition different in kind, one that is not a part of the series but, as merely *intelligible*, lies outside the series. (A530/B558)

In consequence of this difference, Kant concludes, the Third and Fourth Antinomies both offer us the possibility of a *reconciliation*, i.e., of *reinterpreting* both the Thesis and the Antithesis in a way that satisfies *both* the sensible constraints of understanding *and* the totalizing demands of reason.

[While] the dialectical arguments that seek unconditioned totality on the one side or the other collapse, the rational propositions, on the contrary, taken in such a corrected significance, may *both be true* .... (A532/B560)

As we have seen, Kant's "negative answer" to the first cosmological question (and *mutatis mutandis* to the second) in essence preserves the exclusionary conclusion of the Antithesis of the corresponding Antinomy while abandoning its ostensible but illusory predicational consequence. The purely procedural "affirmative answer" to each question, in contrast, preserves nothing of either Thesis. It is not an accident, however, that Kant is not prepared analogously simply to abandon the Theses of the Third and Fourth Antinomies. For each of them purports to establish something essential to his *practical* philosophy: the reality of freely willed action ("causality through freedom") in one instance and the existence of "an absolutely necessary being" in the other.

In his Second Critique, Kant will argue that there are *three* necessary postulates of pure practical reason—God, freedom, and immortality. Although speculative philosophy cannot *establish* the thesis of immortality, as we observed in connection with the Paralogisms, neither can it provide a demonstration of the soul's necessary mortality. Immortality is thus a *rationally admissible* postulate of practical reason and a legitimate object of hope. Just this, we now see, is Kant's stance with respect to the other two necessary postulates of pure practical reason as well. If, despite the inability of speculative philosophical reasoning demonstratively to *establish* them, the Theses of the Third and Fourth Antinomies, in contrast to those of the First and Second, *might be true*, then freedom and God will also be rationally admissible postulates of practical reason and legitimate objects of hope.

"I cannot even *assume God, freedom, and immortality* for the sake of the necessary practical use of my reason unless I simultaneously *deprive* speculative reason of its pretension to extravagant insights," wrote Kant in the Preface to B. Like the Paralogisms, the Antinomies precisely serve to undermine such "extravagant pretensions" of speculative reason by making manifest and helping to articulate its legitimate scope. So once again, we discover, Kant is led to "deny *knowledge* in order to make room for *faith*" (Bxxx).

Epilogue: The Rest of the First Critique

In A, the First Critique ends on page A855; in B, on page B883. If we generously credit ourselves with having discussed all four Antinomies, in terms of raw page count, we have now taken a relatively detailed look at about two-thirds of Kant's text. In terms of the book's philosophical content, on the other hand, we have come quite a bit further. We have, at least briefly, met and elucidated all of its constructive theses as well as its most fundamental critical conclusion, and in the last two chapters we have explored its implications regarding two central areas of traditional metaphysics: the ostensible *a priori* disciplines of rational psychology and rational cosmology.

In the balance of the Transcendental Dialectic, devoted to the "ideal of pure reason", Kant in effect critically engages what remains of traditional speculative metaphysics, the putative discipline of transcendental theology with its traditional ontological, cosmological, and teleological "proofs" of the existence of God. A great deal goes on in these sections—much of it both philosophically and historically important—but the ultimate outcome is the same: No satisfactory proof of the existence of God is possible. Detached from the conditions of possible experience, pure reason has at best a subsidiary organizing function. The idea that it can serve as an independent source of synthetic *a priori* propositions is and remains a "dialectical illusion".

The balance of the Transcendental Dialectic is not, however, the balance of the First Critique. The Dialectic is the second division of the Transcendental Logic—its first division was the Transcendental

Analytic—which, together with the Transcendental Aesthetic, makes up what Kant calls the "Transcendental doctrine of elements". But after all this comes the "Transcendental doctrine of method", which, so to speak, spirals down to the end of the book through a series of four increasingly shorter chapters devoted to the "discipline", the "canon", the "architectonic", and the "history" of pure reason.

The last of these is just four pages long. It offers a "cursory outline" in which Kant classifies some of his most salient predecessors in respect of their views regarding "the *object* of all our rational cognitions" ("sensual" *vs* "intellectual" philosophers) and "the *origin* of pure cognitions of reason" ("empiricists" *vs* "noologists"[1]), and, finally, in respect of their *method* ("naturalistic" *vs* "scientific") (A853–5/B881–3).

Kant has little patience with "the naturalist of pure reason", who elevates "common understanding" above science to such an extent that he asserts, for instance, "that one can determine the magnitude and breadth of the moon more securely by eye than by mathematical rigmarole". "Mere misology brought to principles" is Kant's crisp dismissal (A855/B883).[2] Followers of the scientific method, in turn, proceed either dogmatically, e.g., Christian Wolff, or skeptically, e.g., David Hume, but, as we have seen, on Kant's view, both of these philosophical approaches also fail to yield satisfactory and defensible conclusions regarding speculative metaphysics and the metaphysics of nature. Is there any alternative? Of course there is.

The *critical* path alone is still open. If the reader has had the kindness and patience to travel along this path in my company, then he can now judge ... whether or not what many centuries could not accomplish might not be attained even before the end of the present one: namely, to bring human reason to full satisfaction in that which has always occupied its craving for knowledge, but until now in vain. (A855/B883)

Well, more than two centuries have elapsed since Kant wrote those closing words, and we can hardly claim to have reached anything approaching the "full satisfaction" of our desires for philosophical understanding. But we are still reading and learning from Kant's *Critique of Pure Reason*, and, if the reader has had the kindness and patience to travel along in *my* company on this journey through a goodly part of it, then he or she may perhaps better know *why*.

---

[1] i.e., what we would call "rationalists". Locke is his paradigm empiricist; Leibniz, his paradigm noologist.

[2] *Misology*, the reader may recall, was Socrates' term for the distrust of reason characteristically induced by sophistical rhetoric.

Bibliography: Works Cited and Suggestions for Further Reading

WORKS BY KANT

Critique of Pure Reason
  trans. Paul Guyer and Allen W. Wood (Cambridge: Cambridge University Press, 1998).
  trans. Werner Pluhar (Indianapolis and Cambridge: Hackett Publishing Co., 1996).
  trans. Norman Kemp-Smith (London: Macmillan; New York: St Martin's Press, 1929, 1933, 1965).
Prolegomena to any Future Metaphysics that will be able to present itself as a Science
  trans. Günter Zöller (Oxford and New York: Oxford University Press, 2003).
  trans. J. Ellington (Indianapolis: Hackett Publishing Co., 1977).
Metaphysical Foundations of Natural Science
  ed. M. Friedman, K. Ameriks, and D. M. Clarke (Cambridge: Cambridge University Press, 2004).
Critique of Practical Reason
  ed. M. J. Gregor, K. Ameriks, and D. M. Clarke (Cambridge: Cambridge University Press, 1997).
  trans. Werner Pluhar (Indianapolis and Cambridge: Hackett Publishing Co., 2002).
Groundwork of the Metaphysics of Morals
  ed. M. J. Gregor, K. Ameriks, and D. M. Clarke (Cambridge: Cambridge University Press, 1998).
  ed. Allen W. Wood and Jerome Schneewind (New Haven: Yale University Press, 2002).
Critique of [the Power of] Judgment
  ed. Paul Guyer and Allen W. Wood, trans. Eric Matthews (Cambridge: Cambridge University Press, 2001).
  trans. Werner Pluhar (Indianapolis: Hackett Publishing Co., 1987).

Bibliography

GENERAL WORKS ABOUT THE *CRITIQUE OF PURE REASON*

Allison, Henry E., *Kant's Transcendental Idealism* (New Haven and London: Yale University Press, 1983).

Bennett, Jonathan, *Kant's Analytic* (Cambridge and London: Cambridge University Press, 1966).

—— *Kant's Dialectic* (Cambridge and London: Cambridge University Press, 1974).

Gardner, Sebastian, *Kant and the Critique of Pure Reason* (London and New York: Routledge, 1999).

Guyer, Paul, *Kant and the Claims of Knowledge* (Cambridge and New York: Cambridge University Press, 1987).

Strawson, P. F., *The Bounds of Sense* (London: Methuen, 1966).

WORKS ABOUT SPECIFIC TOPICS WITHIN THE *CRITIQUE OF PURE REASON*

Ameriks, Karl, *Kant's Theory of Mind: An Analysis of the Paralogisms of Pure Reason* (Oxford and New York: Oxford University Press, 1982).

Bird, Graham, *Kant's Theory of Knowledge* (London: Routlege & Kegan Paul; New York: Humanities Press, 1962, 1973).

Friedman, Michael, *Kant and the Exact Sciences* (Cambridge, Mass.: Harvard University Press, 1992, 1994).

Holden, Thomas, *The Architecture of Matter* (Oxford and New York: Oxford University Press, 2004).

Hollis, Martin, "Times and Spaces", *Mind*, 76 (1957), 524–36.

Kitcher, Patricia, *Kant's Transcendental Psychology* (New York: Oxford University Press, 1990).

Langton, Rae, *Kantian Humility* (Oxford: Clarendon Press, 1998).

Melnick, Arthur, *Kant's Analogies of Experience* (Chicago and London: University of Chicago Press, 1973).

Morrison, Margaret C., "Community and Coexistence: Kant's Third Analogy of Experience", *Kant Studien*, 89 (1998), 257–77.

Posy, Carl J., ed., *Kant's Philosophy of Mathematics: Modern Essays* (Dordrecht and Boston: Kluwer Academic Publishers, 1992).

Powell, C. Thomas, *Kant's Theory of Self-Consciousness* (Oxford and New York: Oxford University Press, 1990).

Quinton, Anthony, "Spaces and Times", *Philosophy*, 37 (1962), 130–47.

Smart, J. J. C., "The Unity of Space-Time", *Australasian Journal of Philosophy*, 45 (1967), 214–17.

Walsh, William Henry, *Kant's Criticism of Metaphysics* (Chicago: University of Chicago Press, 1976).

Watkins, Eric, "Kant's Third Analogy of Experience", *Kant Studien*, 88 (1997), 406–41.

Westphal, Kenneth, *Kant's Transcendental Proof of Realism* (Cambridge: Cambridge University Press, 2004).

Wolff, Robert Paul, *Kant's Theory of Mental Activity* (Cambridge, Mass.: Harvard University Press, 1963).

OTHER WORKS ABOUT KANT AND HIS PHILOSOPHY

Allison, Henry E., *Kant's Theory of Freedom* (Cambridge and New York: Cambridge University Press, 1990).

Guyer, Paul, ed., *The Cambridge Companion to Kant* (Cambridge and New York: Cambridge University Press, 1992).

—— *Kant and the Experience of Freedom* (Cambridge and New York: Cambridge University Press, 1993).

Körner, Stephen, *Kant* (New York: Penguin Books, 1955, 1990).

Scruton, Roger, *Kant* (Oxford and New York: Oxford University Press, 1982).

Sellars, Wilfrid, *Kant and Pre-Kantian Themes: Lectures by Wilfrid Sellars*, ed. Pedro Amaral (Atascadero, Calif.: Ridgeview Publishing Co., 2002).

—— *Kant's Transcendental Metaphysics: Sellars' Cassirer Lectures and Other Essays*, ed. Jeffrey F. Sicha (Atascadero, Calif.: Ridgeview Publishing Co., 2002).

—— *Science and Metaphysics: Variations on Kantian Themes* (London and New York: Routledge & Kegan Paul, 1968).

Walker, Ralph C. S., *Kant* (London and Boston: Routledge & Kegan Paul, 1978, 1989).

Wolff, Robert Paul, ed., *Kant: A Collection of Critical Essays* (Garden City, NY: Anchor Books; Notre Dame, Ind.: University of Notre Dame Press, 1967).

Wood, Allen W., *Kant's Moral Religion* (Ithaca, NY, and London: Cornell University Press, 1969).

—— *Kant's Rational Theology* (Ithaca, NY, and London: Cornell University Press, 1978).

OTHER WORKS CITED IN THIS BOOK

Berkeley, George, *Three Dialogues between Hylas and Philonous*, ed. Jonathan Dancy (Oxford and New York: Oxford University Press, 1998).

Bibliography

Davidson, Donald, "On the Very Idea of a Conceptual Scheme", *Proceedings of the American Philosophical Association*, 17 (1973–4), 5–20.

Descartes, René, *Meditations on First Philosophy*, trans. John Cottingham, Robert Stoothoff, and Dugald Murdoch, in *The Philosophical Writings of Descartes*, ii (Cambridge and New York: Cambridge University Press, 1984).

Hume, David, *Treatise on Human Nature* (*THN*), ed. L. A. Selby-Bigge (Oxford: Clarendon Press, 1888, 1896).

—— *Enquiry Concerning Human Understanding* (*Enq.*), ed. L. A. Selby-Bigge (Oxford: Clarendon Press, 1894).

Koch, Anton Friedrich, *Subjektivität in Raum und Zeit* (Frankfurt am Main: V. Klostermann, 1990).

Pinkard, Terry, *Hegel: A Biography* (Cambridge and New York: Cambridge University Press, 2000).

Rorty, Richard, *Philosophy and the Mirror of Nature* (Princeton: Princeton University Press, 1979).

—— "The World Well Lost", *Journal of Philosophy*, 69 (1972), 649–66.

Rosenberg, Jay F., "On a Certain Antinomy: Properties, Concepts and Items in Space", in J. Tomberlin, ed., *Philosophical Perspectives*, x: *Metaphysics* (Cambridge, Mass., and Oxford: Blackwell Publishers, 1996), 357–83.

—— *One World and Our Knowledge of It* (Dordrecht: D. Reidel Publishing Co., 1980).

—— *The Thinking Self* (Philadelphia: Temple University Press, 1986).

—— *Thinking about Knowing* (Oxford and New York: Oxford University Press, 2002).

Strawson, P. F., *Individuals* (*Ind.*) (London: Methuen, 1959).

Wittgenstein, Ludwig, *Philosophical Investigations* (*PI*), trans. G. E. M. Anscombe, (Malden, Mass., and Oxford: Blackwell, 1953, repr. 1958, 1997).

Wolff, Michael, *Abhandlung über die Prinzipien der Logik* (Frankfurt am Main: V. Klostermann, 2004).

—— *Die Vollständigkeit der Kantischen Urteilstafel* (Frankfurt am Main: V. Klostermann, 1995).

Index

Index

Index

Index

Index

Transcendental Deduction, 34–6, 47–53, 58–9, 97, 136
  objective *vs.* subjective, 108–9, 118, 257
Transcendental Dialectic, 5–6, 50, 61, 64, 91, 101, 144, 168, 173, 238, 248, 254–5, 258, 274, 297, 300
transcendental idealism, 2, 69, 72, 77–8, 86–7, 135, 198, 290, 237–8, 240, 300
transcendental illusions, 253, 258
translations, 3–4, 205, 284, 286
Tree of Porphyry, 14, 20, 27

unconditioned conditions, 255–7, 269–74, 279–80, 282–3, 286–7, 290, 292–3, 295
understanding, 22, 61–2, 64, 87–91, 93, 95–6, 102–5, 108–9, 112–13, 119–21, 126–7, 130, 137–41, 145–6, 149, 152–4, 157, 203, 237, 248, 250–2, 254–5, 273–4, 283, 286
  as a faculty of concepts, 96, 120, 140, 145
  as a faculty of judgments, 96, 120
  as a faculty of rules, 121, 140, 145, 254–5
units, 114, 116, 154, 160, 166–7, 169–71, 197, 245, 277–9
unity, 11, 13, 51–3, 55–60, 66, 84, 91–6, 98–9, 102–3, 105, 108–9, 115–19, 122–7, 130–5, 137, 139–42, 151–3, 156, 159, 162,

167, 171, 187, 200–1, 203, 205, 207, 209, 223, 233–4, 236–7, 250–1, 253, 255–6, 260, 262–3, 269, 273–4, 278, 285–6, 290
universality, 29, 67–8, 144, 147, 155, 214, 223
universals, 11, 13–14, 18, 21
unum, 102

Vahinger, Hans, 5, 142
verum, 102
virtual parts, 173, 266

Walsh, W. H., 143, 301
warrant, logical *vs.* evidential, 37–41, 43–8, 52, 256
Westphal, Kenneth, 130, 301
Wittgenstein, Ludwig, 118, 141, 145, 247, 258, 302
Wolff, Christian, 298
Wolff, Michael, 90
Wolff, Robert Paul, 143
Wood, Allen W., 4, 74, 77, 111, 115, 118, 174, 205, 239, 284, 286, 299, 301
world, 6, 9, 11–13, 29, 50–3, 58–60, 65, 67, 73, 78–81, 84–6, 88–9, 101–2, 122, 129, 134, 152, 155–6, 162–3, 181, 184, 190, 196, 203, 208, 210, 218, 233, 236–7, 241–2, 249–50, 257–9, 269–78, 281–3, 285, 289–90, 292–4
world-concepts (*see* concepts: world-concepts)

312

CPSIA information can be obtained at www.ICGtesting.com
Printed in the USA
LVOW071957011212

309680LV00002B/83/P